Digital Flows

Digital Flows

Online Hip Hop Music and Culture

Steven Gamble

OXFORD
UNIVERSITY PRESS

Oxford University Press is a department of the University of Oxford. It furthers
the University's objective of excellence in research, scholarship, and education
by publishing worldwide. Oxford is a registered trade mark of Oxford University
Press in the UK and certain other countries.

Published in the United States of America by Oxford University Press
198 Madison Avenue, New York, NY 10016, United States of America.

© Oxford University Press 2024

This is an open access publication, available online and distributed under the terms of a Creative
Commons Attribution-Non Commercial-No Derivatives 4.0 International license (CC BY-NC-ND
4.0), a copy of which is available at https://creativecommons.org/licenses/by-nc-nd/4.0/.
Subject to this license, all rights are reserved.

Inquiries concerning reproduction outside the scope of the above should be sent
to the Rights Department, Oxford University Press, at the address above.

You must not circulate this work in any other form
and you must impose this same condition on any acquirer.

Library of Congress Cataloging-in-Publication Data
Names: Gamble, Steven, author.
Title: Digital flows : online hip hop music and culture / Steven Gamble.
Description: [1.] | New York : Oxford University Press, 2024. | Includes index.
Identifiers: LCCN 2024037336 (print) | LCCN 2024037337 (ebook) |
ISBN 9780197656396 (paperback) | ISBN 9780197656389 (hardback) | ISBN 9780197656419 (epub)
Subjects: LCSH: Rap (Music)—Social aspects. | Music and the Internet. | Social media.
Classification: LCC ML3918.R37 G36 2024 (print) | LCC ML3918.R37 (ebook) |
DDC 306.4/84249—dc23/eng/20240813
LC record available at https://lccn.loc.gov/2024037336
LC ebook record available at https://lccn.loc.gov/2024037337

DOI: 10.1093/oso/9780197656389.001.0001

Contents

Acknowledgements	*vii*
1. Introduction: Hip Hop and the Internet	1
2. How Hip Hop Became the Leading Music Genre in the Digital Streaming Era: Sharing Culture	18
3. Internet Rap and Generational Tensions in Hip Hop's SoundCloud Era: 'Famous on the Internet'	49
4. Lofi Hip Hop and Community in YouTube Comments During the COVID-19 Pandemic: Chill Beats to Quarantine to	78
5. Online Hip Hop Feminism, Rap Music Videos, and Gender in YouTube Comments: Responses to Black Women Rappers on Their Hot Girl Shit	108
6. Hip Hop and Online Cultural Appropriation Discourse: Trap, Pop, and Race	130
7. Virtual Hip Hop Concerts in Video Games: One *Fortnite* only	156
8. Conclusion: It's Where You're @	181
References	*189*
Index	*221*

Acknowledgements

I owe a great deal of thanks to many people who supported the writing of this book.

Let's put all my interviewees first: a massive thank you to folks in the culture for taking time to talk and for having faith in my voice to represent for them. It can't be easy to trust a white autistic Brit to speak on behalf of the culture, but because you did, this book exists, and tries to carry your voice forward.

Next comes Jason Ng, my main collaborator on the research that this book evolved into. You were gracious enough to introduce me to online hip hop communities in your part of the world, and your enthusiasm spurred me on throughout the research stages. I have to mention, too, that bro's beats slap like nobody's business. Thanks for our collaborative writing and beatmaking. Big ups to all the other members of the online producer communities who participated with us and gave their time for interviews.

My gratitude goes also to Raquel Campos Valverde, who gave a lot of time and energy to a couple of exciting collaborations with me during the research period. I learned a lot from our cooperation and I especially appreciate the forthright conscience you bring to your work. Here's a good place to shout out the authors of our *Global Hip Hop Studies* special issue on hip hop and the internet—Alexandria Arrieta, Elloit Cardozo, Jabari Evans, Jasmine A. Henry, Alette Schoon, and Polly Withers—and the journal team, for granting us the autonomy to reflect on hip hop's online manifestations.

The ideas in the book flowed through a number of conferences to find the form they now take. Thanks to colleagues who organized events such as IASPM, RMA, and EHHSN, at which I gained feedback on this material, and to the networks that unfurled. Meetings for research on music and online cultures have been especially valuable. In December 2018, I first workshopped some ideas about online hip hop at the study day *Music and the Internet*, organized by Edward Katrak Spencer and Pablo Infante-Amate. There, I met Raquel, who co-organized *Internet Musicking* with Jason and me in 2022, and Paula Harper, who co-organized another conference called *Music and the Internet* with Kate Galloway and me in 2023. I had another opportunity to speak thanks to Ed as part of the 'Information Overload? Music Studies in the Age of Abundance' conference he co-organized with Christopher Haworth and Daniele Shlomit Sofer. At *Music and the Internet* (2) I had the surprise

viii Acknowledgements

pleasure of meeting Steve Jones, co-founder of the Association of Internet Researchers, who published a foundational article that shared its name with the conference in 2000 (in *Popular Music*, which was at that time edited by my PhD supervisor Allan Moore). Only in writing this have I properly connected the dots. Thanks to my partners in crime for all these conference opportunities, where I keep meeting cool people doing cool research.

On that note, a big thanks to the Music and Online Cultures Research Network steering committee—Joana Freitas, Maria Perevedentseva, Ed, and Jenessa Williams—and Holly Rogers for enthusiasm and literature suggestions and general camaraderie. Your support in cultivating a community for this kind of work is rewarding both professionally and personally. The same sentiments go to members of the International Society for Metal Music Studies board (especially Owen Coggins and Lewis Kennedy), for helping me see beyond hip hop, and for all sorts of resonances that informed my thinking on contemporary music cultures.

I'm touched by the generosity of my friends and colleagues for reading and providing feedback on drafts, namely: Karen-Marie Gamble, Alie Garbutt, and Justin Williams, who read the whole thing; Kai Arne Hansen, who read Chapter 3; Genevieve Arkle, who read Chapter 5; Lily Holland, who read Chapter 6; and Lindsay Carter, who read Chapter 7. I mention the chapters specifically so that if you take issue with any of them, it is this named reader's fault, he wrote sarcastically. No, in actuality, I got a bunch of really helpful comments and take full responsibility for any parts where I ignored their better judgement! Thank you also to the writing group in the Department of Music at the University of Bristol, and Dave Gamble, who offered interesting comments on some parts.

More folks deserve shout outs! Folks like Griff Rollefson, who showed support for this project from its earliest days, and Justin Williams, for being a sounding board throughout the later stages of its development. Warrick Moses, Emily Gale, Clare Geraghty, and 0phelia were there for me in Cork and helped me get things off the ground. Thanks to Allan Moore, for staying in touch and continuing to gently guide my thinking. Thanks to Jabari Evans, who I finally got to meet in-person a month before finishing the book: your work inspires me and your support means a lot. Many more people took time to talk to me about parts of the book. Thanks to Katherine Bassett for an interesting back-and-forth, and Adam Harper for entertaining my partially formed thoughts on lo(-)fi hip hop. Steve Juon reflected helpfully on the Usenet hip hop days.

Several people provided specific sources of information: Michael Robb at Common Sense Media and Orla Meehan at Newzoo for sharing survey data on Fortnite's player base; Stephen Ackroyd at The Bunker for providing the citation credit for an *Upset Magazine* article; Roger Press for awarding me year-long access to MusicID as part of a data-driven fellowship. Repo of *Ageing B-Boys Unite!* not only provided scans of some early UK hip hop magazines but also reached out to an old friend, Cool C, who kindly scanned another issue so I could double-check citing a specific quote. Legends!

This book is the product of two major research fellowships. The first is a two-year Marie Skłodowska-Curie Actions Individual Fellowship awarded by the European Commission, where I started this work at University College Cork. The second is a three-year Leverhulme Trust Early Career Fellowship, which enabled me to bring it to fruition at the University of Bristol. My thanks to the funding bodies for recognizing the value of this work and its importance to contemporary society.

I'm grateful to the editorial team at OUP (especially Lane Berger for her heroic work helping get the open access payment cleared) and the anonymous reviewers of the book, who offered a lot of helpful feedback I have taken on board.

Thank you to both the artists, tweeters, or YouTube uploaders who granted permissions to reprint their creative work and the many deidentified users whose online contributions form part of the research. You *are* online hip hop music and culture!

Thanks to friends who provided emotional support, especially in stressful times. Big love to my family, especially the lil homie Max. Fank u Pixel for all-round angel-ness. Finally, Alie: thank you always for your love and support, which imbues everything I do and ever will do.

1
Introduction

Hip Hop and the Internet

Introduction

Whenever I told people I was writing a book about the relationship between hip hop and the internet, they often went quiet and thought to themselves for a few seconds. Then they recalled from memory a unique intersection between the two. 'Is that the kind of thing you mean?'. Sometimes they suggested something pretty well-known in pop culture: Drake dancing memes; SoundCloud rap; lofi beats on YouTube; 'WAP'; or Travis Scott's *Fortnite* concert. Other times, people named more obscure hip hop happenings: artists beefing on Twitter; a WorldStar viral comedy video; a particular TikTok dance challenge; an AI-powered virtual rapper; or beatmakers livestreaming on Twitch. The list goes on. It is not always immediately apparent but, after a moment of reflection, it becomes clear that hip hop culture intersects with the internet in all sorts of interesting and important ways. However, the effects of these intersections have rarely been considered in detail. This book resolves to change that.

Hip hop is one of the most significant cultural forms of the internet age. This is not merely a coincidence. As hip hop and the World Wide Web grew up together, the culture influenced many conventions of online interaction, and vice versa. When we talk about 'the internet', we typically refer to a social, technological, and cultural entity which has become enmeshed with almost all of our daily activities.[1] In the 2000s, when the distinction between spending time online and off was clearer, people used to say they were 'on the internet' (meaning using a web browser).[2] In 2023, it would be rarer to *not* be online (now predominantly using a smartphone).[3] Both the internet and hip

---

[1] José van Dijck, Thomas Poell, and Martijn de Waal, *The Platform Society: Public Values in a Collective World* (New York: Oxford University Press, 2018), 2.

[2] André Brock, 'Beyond the Pale: The Blackbird Web Browser's Critical Reception', *New Media & Society* 13, no. 7 (2011): 1085.

[3] Trine Syvertsen, *Digital Detox: The Politics of Disconnecting* (Bingley: Emerald Group Publishing, 2020), 2.

Digital Flows. Steven Gamble, Oxford University Press. © Oxford University Press 2024.
DOI: 10.1093/oso/9780197656389.003.0001

2 Digital Flows

hop now bear a striking presence in the everyday lives of well over half the world's population.[4]

This book's title, *Digital Flows*, playfully evokes ideas of networked communication, media circulation, and self-expression using technology. Internet connectivity is often understood via the conceptual metaphor of the flow of digital information.[5] In creative contexts, a rapper's performance style—their rhythmic delivery, popularly called 'flow'[6]—is captured as digital audio in the act of recording. For at least the last two decades, hip hop audio recordings (alongside other media) have themselves been shared across online social ecosystems, sending digital flows digitally flowing across the internet.

By 'internet'—the computer-based network that powers online interaction—I am referring specifically to the World Wide Web. I am interested in hip hop's presence on websites, social networking services, community servers, audio and video and streaming platforms, video and image sharing platforms, and gaming platforms. This range of fora has been bundled under terms like 'web 2.0' and 'social web', phrases which highlight how social networking features have moved to the forefront of online activity.[7] I share André Brock's viewpoint that 'the internet today is easily understood as a technologically constructed and mediated web of communication and sociality'.[8] In this study of hip hop and the internet, I include all these digital media platforms but draw the line at private instant messaging and group chats.[9] Since 'manifestations of hip hop music and other cultural practices on online publicly accessible media platforms with "social" features' doesn't have much of a ring to it, I've gone for the condensed subtitle 'online hip hop music and culture'.

Hip hop is now inescapably online. This claim may be heresy to an older generation of hip hop heads. However, there will be some readers who

---

[4] This is far from an exaggeration. Hip hop is one of the most popular cultural forms worldwide, as scholars have repeatedly made clear, whereas over two-thirds of the world's population use the internet. See H. S. Alim, A. Ibrahim, and A. Pennycook, eds., *Global Linguistic Flows: Hip Hop Cultures, Youth Identities, and the Politics of Language* (New York and London: Routledge, 2009), 4–5; Miniwatts Marketing Group, 'World Internet Users Statistics and 2023 World Population Stats', *Internet World Stats*, 21 March 2023, https://www.internetworldstats.com/stats.htm.

[5] Maria Lindh, 'As a Utility: Metaphors of Information Technologies', *Human IT: Journal for Information Technology Studies as a Human Science* 13, no. 2 (May 2016): 67–69.

[6] Mitchell Ohriner, *Flow: The Rhythmic Voice in Rap Music* (New York: Oxford University Press, 2019).

[7] Trebor Scholz, 'Infrastructure: Its Transformations and Effect on Digital Activism', in *Digital Activism Decoded: The New Mechanics of Change*, ed. Mary Joyce (New York: International Debate Education Association, 2010), 24.

[8] André Brock, *Distributed Blackness: African American Cybercultures* (New York: New York University Press, 2020), 26.

[9] Private messages between friends are still *online* and *cultural* artifacts—and enormously influential on users' everyday consumption of online media—but are too varied in scope and use to draw broader conclusions about online hip hop culture.

consider themselves hip hop fans without ever really having interacted with it totally *offline*: even at concerts, cyphers, and breaking spots (and even in countries that the Western imagination does not consider well-connected), people are messaging, recording, sharing.[10] These habits chime with the conventional communicative practices of social media platforms and typical uses of web-connected smartphones.[11] The *onlining* of hip hop represents an important change in how we think about the culture, what with its conventional imagery of street corners, house parties, cars, and clubs.[12] Historians of hip hop have rightly emphasized the significance of space and place, its cultural connections to geographical locality and authentic urban experience.[13] Yet this culture, which was born on the streets, now thrives on transformative technologies of global reach.

In this book, I do not argue for the superiority of online hip hop over that of other spaces or eras. However, I am concerned with a nuanced analysis of what hip hop's onlining means for the culture. Subsequent chapters will address how its cultural conventions work online (Chapter 2), how new internet-infused musical forms emerge (Chapters 3 and 4), how online communities function on media platforms (Chapters 4 and 7), how mainstream feminist rappers represent and are received (Chapter 5), how fans understand white popstars' appropriations of Black culture (Chapter 6), and how video game platforms are used to host hip hop concerts (Chapter 7). For more detailed descriptions, I provide an outline at the end of this chapter.

Scope and Method

Let me elaborate on what this book addresses and how it addresses it. There is a US slant to this study, a constraint I apply for four contextual and methodological reasons. First and foremost, hip hop is Black American music, and it is US-produced hip hop that leads global music markets to this day.[14] Second,

---

[10] Ethiraj Gabriel Dattatreyan, *The Globally Familiar: Digital Hip Hop, Masculinity, and Urban Space in Delhi* (Durham, NC: Duke University Press, 2020), 3; Alette Schoon, '"Makhanda Forever?": Pirate Internet Infrastructure and the Ephemeral Hip Hop Archive in South Africa', in 'It's Where You're @: Hip Hop and the Internet', special issue, *Global Hip Hop Studies* 2 (November 2021): 199–218.

[11] Stine Lomborg, 'The Internet in My Pocket', in *The Ubiquitous Internet: User and Industry Perspectives*, ed. Anja Bechmann and Stine Lomborg (New York and London: Routledge, 2015), 35–53.

[12] Richard Bramwell and James Butterworth argue that hip hop 'derives its legitimacy, authenticity and power through its relation to "the street"'. Richard Bramwell and James Butterworth, 'Beyond the Street: The Institutional Life of Rap', *Popular Music* 39, no. 2 (May 2020): 169.

[13] Or, in some cases, authentic rural experience, where geography remains vital. See Adam de Paor-Evans, *Provincial Headz: British Hip Hop and Critical Regionalism* (South Yorkshire: Equinox, 2020).

[14] Loren Kajikawa, 'Hip Hop History in the Age of Colorblindness', *Journal of Music History Pedagogy* 5, no. 1 (2014): 117–123; IFPI, *Global Music Report 2023: State of the Industry* (IFPI, 2023), 46.

4 Digital Flows

hip hop's hold over online popular culture is primarily English-speaking. Part of this is because many of the largest global media platforms—YouTube, Facebook, Instagram, Twitter (or X),[15] Reddit, and Tumblr among them—are American-owned and operated. English is far and away the predominant language of the uncensored internet.[16] The restricted internet in China has led to different forms of mediation and state relationships to hip hop culture,[17] whereas in India, hip hop on digital platforms is 'distinctly video-centric'.[18] International variations deserve and are thankfully getting increased scholarly attention. Third, due to US music and social media predominance, hip hop in the Anglosphere is the most publicly visible intersection of the culture with the internet. As I will soon explain, the networking of societies has pushed users towards the notion of a centralized mainstream online culture. This book focuses on hip hop in this context, its most visible, popular and pervasive form, rather than spotlighting smaller sites of global practice (a concern I have taken up elsewhere).[19] Fourth and finally, as I use semantic analysis to study text derived from the internet, I am working in my first language, so I can be most confident in my interpretations.

To be clear, Anglophone hip hop is far from the only interesting or valuable form of hip hop's onlining. The field of global hip hop studies is founded on the recognition that significant sites of hip hop practice exist worldwide. Hip hop as an international form intersects with issues of locality, ethnicity and race, class, religion, gender roles, and more dynamics of global participation that warrant in-depth study. If we approach issues of space and place with curiosity, then hip hop's significant online presence also deserves in-depth

---

[15] I finished writing this book just as Twitter rebranded to X. While it would be an easy find-and-replace task to update this, there are distinct social and cultural characteristics of Twitter that appear to be changing in its X era. Online cultural mainstays, like 'Black Twitter', also refer to particular activities and conventions now marked in time by the former name. I therefore refer quite specifically to Twitter rather than X. Moreover, a consistent rendering like Twitter/X would not be easily searchable. See Summer Harlow and Anna Benbrook, 'How #Blacklivesmatter: Exploring the Role of Hip-Hop Celebrities in Constructing Racial Identity on Black Twitter', *Information, Communication & Society* 22, no. 3 (October 2017): 352–368; Jean Burgess and Nancy K. Baym, *Twitter: A Biography* (New York: New York University Press, 2022).

[16] Miniwatts Marketing Group, 'Internet World Users by Language: Top 10 Languages', Internet World Stats, 31 March 2020, https://www.internetworldstats.com/stats7.htm; W3Techs, 'Usage Statistics of Content Languages for Websites', *Web Technology Surveys*, 26 June 2023, https://w3techs.com/technolog ies/overview/content_language.

[17] Jingsi Christina Wu, 'Can China Have Its Hip Hop?: Negotiating the Boundaries between Mainstream and Underground Youth Cultural Spaces on the Internet Talent Show Rap of China', in *China's Youth Cultures and Collective Spaces: Creativity, Sociality, Identity and Resistance*, ed. Vanessa Frangville and Gwennaël Gaffric (London and New: Routledge, 2019), 55–71.

[18] Debarun Sarkar, '"Azadi's Political until You're Pressing Play": Capitalist Realism, Hip-Hop, and Platform Affordances', *Convergence* 29, no. 6 (2023): 11.

[19] Jason Ng and Steven Gamble, 'Hip-Hop Producer-Hosts, Beat Battles, and Online Music Production Communities on Twitch', *First Monday* 27, no. 6 (June 2022).

consideration. I aim to further Paul Gilroy's foundational line of questioning about the globalization of Black diasporic expressive culture:

> How are we to think critically about artistic products and aesthetic codes that, although they may be traced back to one distant location, have been somehow changed either by the passage of time or by their displacement, relocation, or dissemination through wider networks of communication and cultural exchange?[20]

The final issue Gilroy raises—of networks of cultural communication—is a primary concern of my study. In spotlighting hip hop and the Anglophone internet, I therefore hope that this book will provide a useful starting point that aids future studies of the unarguably global phenomenon hip hop is today.

Hip hop and the internet boast incredibly interdisciplinary fields of study,[21] and their combination encourages researchers to consider a breadth of theoretical and practical perspectives. In this book, I draw generously from a range of interdisciplinary and overlapping fields including hip hop studies, internet studies, popular music studies, (new) media studies, communication studies, cultural studies, Black studies, intersectional feminism, human-computer interaction, and science and technology studies. Some may feel that such an interdisciplinary scope requires explicit justification, whereas others, especially in the digital humanities, may suggest that such breadth is normative.[22] I lean towards the latter camp. I would simply suggest that being open to a diversity of approaches, assumptions, and conventions does not mean sacrificing rigour, and in most cases it helps to round out a researcher's toolkit.

My method is similarly radically integrative. The research project was conceived to combine ethnography, music and cultural analysis, and data analysis. I compare and contrast information roughly separated into three different forms:

- personal accounts of folks in the culture, from years of co-participation and fifteen semi-structured interviews;
- texts—music, videos, journalism, platform interfaces, and other media—using critical discourse analysis and (accessible) music-theoretical and audiovisual analysis;

---

[20] Paul Gilroy, 'Sounds Authentic: Black Music, Ethnicity, and the Challenge of a "Changing" Same', *Black Music Research Journal* 11, no. 2 (1991): 111.

[21] Justin A. Williams, 'Introduction: The Interdisciplinary World of Hip-Hop Studies', in *The Cambridge Companion to Hip-Hop*, ed. Justin A. Williams (Cambridge: Cambridge University Press, 2015), 2; William H. Dutton, ed., *The Oxford Handbook of Internet Studies* (Oxford: Oxford University Press, 2013), v.

[22] Eileen Scanlon, 'Digital Scholarship: Identity, Interdisciplinarity, and Openness', *Frontiers in Digital Humanities* 5 (2018), https://www.frontiersin.org/articles/10.3389/fdigh.2018.00003.

6 Digital Flows

- web texts—comments, posts, and tweets—using term frequency analysis, significance tests, and thematic coding to discover word associations in data sets.

The aim is to have a range of analytical depths—from detailed insights to broader-strokes findings—to pull out variations at different levels for further critical reflection. Edward Katrak Spencer has recently argued that this methodological orientation demonstrates an extension of musical literacies and that, 'by reframing discourse analysis as a kind of listening . . . such work identifies different groups of voices that possess contrasting beliefs, priorities, and motivations' about music and music culture.[23] In using this approach, my goal is to shed light on the developing intersections between hip hop and online cultures at scales both big and small.

A note on the ethics of web data analysis, a topic I have tackled elsewhere:[24] research using text drawn from online sources raises complex ethical issues yet it is thoroughly normalized.[25] Many of the fundamental issues with such methods concern privacy, security, and rights. I build on feminist approaches to data and indigenous data scholarship to implement principles that include:

- emphasizing relationality and an ethics of care in data management practices;[26]
- collecting only required data and avoiding data speculation;[27]
- keeping personally identifying datasets closed and text data itself open, balancing user privacy with 'FAIR' access to information;[28]
- providing freely available findings, hence this book's open-access format;
- aligning with principles of affective data visualization;[29]

---

[23] Edward Katrak Spencer, 'When Donald Trump Dropped the Bass: The Weaponization of Dubstep in Internet Trolling Strategies, 2011–2016', *Twentieth-Century Music*, forthcoming.

[24] Steven Gamble, 'Towards an Ethical Model of Data Analysis for Research on Online Music Cultures', in *Music and the Internet: Methodological, Epistemological, and Ethical Orientations*, ed. Christopher Haworth, Danielle S. Sofer, and Edward Katrak Spencer (Abingdon: Routledge, forthcoming).

[25] Helen Kennedy captures this perfectly with the title of her book on the subject. See Helen Kennedy, *Post, Mine, Repeat: Social Media Data Mining Becomes Ordinary* (London: Palgrave Macmillan, 2016).

[26] Katrin Tiidenberg, 'Research Ethics, Vulnerability, and Trust on the Internet', in *Second International Handbook of Internet Research*, ed. Jeremy Hunsinger, Matthew M. Allen, and Lisbeth Klastrup (Dordrecht: Springer Netherlands, 2020), 569–583.

[27] Rita Raley, 'Dataveillance and Countervailance', in *'Raw Data' Is an Oxymoron*, ed. Lisa Gitelman (Cambridge, MA: MIT Press, 2013), 123.

[28] Mark D. Wilkinson et al., 'The FAIR Guiding Principles for Scientific Data Management and Stewardship', *Scientific Data* 3, no. 1 (March 2016); Maggie Walter et al., eds., *Indigenous Data Sovereignty and Policy* (Abingdon: Taylor & Francis, 2021), 5.

[29] Catherine D'Ignazio and Lauren F. Klein, *Data Feminism*, Strong Ideas (Cambridge, MA: MIT Press, 2020), 77–96.

- omitting explicit citations of individual users and scrambling text to avoid reidentification.[30]

These principles fall under what Christian Fuchs calls 'critical-realist social media research ethics'.[31]

Whose voices do we hear in these data? I use internet data because they should represent diverse perspectives about online hip hop in their native context. However, anonymized big data do not contain much information about user demographics. Looking at the web in general, in the US there is more internet use by white people than Black people,[32] and in the UK there is more internet use by men than women.[33] In brief, internet use may align with other kinds of social privilege (maleness and whiteness) and my data could reflect such an imbalance.[34] Yet research by the Pew Research Center in 2010 suggested that white, Black, and Latinx people had similar levels of laptop ownership, and that people of colour frequented social networking sites far more than white people.[35] Though representation is therefore difficult to determine, my data analysis provides insights into the values, ideologies, and expressions of people posting about hip hop online regardless of

[30] Providing verbatim quotations would allow the reader to search for comments and reidentify their author, so quotations are lightly rearranged to provide a 'general feeling' of the original text while protecting their writers. It is also advisable to avoid signal-boosting hateful comments and their authors, though I recognize that unexpurgated examples can allow for a clearer examination of evidence (and that writers of hateful language online may not warrant such protections). See Kennedy, *Post, Mine, Repeat*, 118; Emma Jane, *Misogyny Online: A Short (and Brutish) History* (London: SAGE, 2017), 103–106; Latanya Sweeney, 'Only You, Your Doctor, and Many Others May Know', *Technology Science*, 28 September 2015, https://technology science.org/a/2015092903/.

[31] Christian Fuchs, *Media, Communication and Society* (London and New York: Routledge, 2022), iii:187–189.

[32] On capitalizing Black and white: recently, the politics of capitalization has been developing rapidly. Generally, the consensus is that Black should be rendered in upper case, extending the stylistic recommendation to capitalize 'adjectives and nouns denoting place, language, or indigenous people'. Anne Waddingham, ed., *New Hart's Rules: The Oxford Style Guide*, 2nd ed. (Oxford: Oxford University Press, 2014), 104. Capitalizing white similarly helps make whiteness visible as a racial and cultural designation. However, this publisher prefers lower case, and I recognize that capitalizing white risks association with the language politics of white supremacist groups. See, for example, Kwame Anthony Appiah, 'The Case for Capitalizing the "B" in Black', *The Atlantic*, 18 June 2020, https://www.theatlantic.com/ideas/archive/2020/06/time-to-capitalize-blackand-white/613159/; Kristen Mack and John Palfrey, 'Capitalizing Black and White: Grammatical Justice and Equity', *MacArthur Foundation*, 26 August 2020, https://www.macfound. org/press/perspectives/capitalizing-black-and-white-grammatical-justice-and-equity; Nell Irvin Painter, 'Why "White" Should Be Capitalized, Too', *Washington Post*, 22 July 2020, https://www.washingtonpost. com/opinions/2020/07/22/why-white-should-be-capitalized/.

[33] Pew Research Center, 'Internet/Broadband Fact Sheet', *Pew Research Center: Internet, Science & Tech* (blog), 31 January 2024, https://www.pewresearch.org/internet/fact-sheet/internet-broadband/; Office for National Statistics, *Internet Users, UK: 2020*, 6 April 2021, https://www.ons.gov.uk/businessindustryandtr ade/itandinternetindustry/bulletins/internetusers/2020.

[34] Gamble, 'Towards an Ethical Model of Data Analysis for Research on Online Music Cultures'.

[35] Aaron Smith, 'Technology Trends Among People of Color', *Pew Research Center: Internet, Science & Tech* (blog), 17 September 2010, https://www.pewresearch.org/internet/2010/09/17/technology-trends-among-people-of-color/.

8 Digital Flows

their personal identities. Still, because it is important to consider how identity impacts understandings of hip hop, I supplement my anonymized data insights with my ethnographic and discursive findings, in addition to homing in on net-native listener communities (Chapter 4), gendered commentary (Chapter 5), and social media debates (Chapter 6).

Positionality and Stance

On the topic of identity: who am I to weigh in on what online hip hop is or isn't? I am a white British man who grew up in suburban Essex, England in the 1990s. On the one hand, I appear far removed from the culture's origins, but on the other, I closely resemble the target audience of hip hop—white, male, Anglophone—in its contemporary form as a commercial media product. My horizons were formerly limited to metal, rock, and punk music, then opened to hip hop at university. Only in my adult life have I engaged closely with the culture, as an avid listener, fan, and beatmaker as well as a researcher. Scholars combining their academic training and personal investment in their area of study has given rise to the concept of the aca-fan, with which I identify.[36] Given my positionality and the terms of my engagement, I am not always the ideal person to speak for hip hop, a cultural form with Afrodiasporic ancestry and born from uniquely Black and Latinx experiences of the American inner-city.[37] My work therefore refers rigorously to the diversity of voices and breadth of scholarship that have been dedicated to hip hop. There will inevitably be things that I miss, and I accept that I cannot cover what hip hop means to everyone. What I do have to offer is because of the time generously given to me by those in the culture: I have listened, aiming to ensure that my voice *does better*, and that my actions and allyship are effective rather than extractive, or merely superficial. I aim to make a valuable contribution to give back to the culture with over a decade's experience of both communal participation in hip hop and research on popular music and the internet.

While I approach the culture with a lot of love and respect, *Digital Flows* is not a clear-cut celebration of hip hop in its internet era. Complexity and contradiction have always been defining features of hip hop,[38] and we must

---

[36] Cécile Cristofari and Matthieu J. Guitton, 'Aca-Fans and Fan Communities: An Operative Framework', *Journal of Consumer Culture* 17, no. 3 (November 2017): 713–731.

[37] I do not equate hip hop with essentialized Blackness, nor ignore its ever-present multiculturalism, but I emphasize that hip hop is defined by a self-expressive mode of Black orality. In other words, not everyone in hip hop is Black, but they are participating in a Black cultural form.

[38] H. Samy Alim, *Roc the Mic Right: The Language of Hip Hop Culture* (New York and London: Routledge, 2006), 3; Bettina L. Love, 'Complex Personhood of Hip Hop & the Sensibilities of the Culture That

take a grounded approach to its purported risks and harms while also being willing to call out toxicity. There have been many worthy critiques of hip hop's derogatory, discriminatory, and exclusory tendencies,[39] which researchers motivated by social justice should take seriously. This need is magnified by the omnipresence of prejudice in online cultures, which have been characterized as misogynistic, transphobic, and white supremacist from users' behaviour down to the very code.[40] Moreover, the political ecology of music suggests that hip hop is responsible for a considerable amount of damage to both the planet and societies burdened with the production demands of the recording industry. Kyle Devine's study of the hidden costs of vinyl, CD, and digital music distribution directly implicates hip hop, since it is one of the most widely consumed genres.[41]

Hip hop is sometimes stereotyped in the popular imagination in a few different ways:[42] as an articulation of suffering by poor, working-class, urban-dwelling people of colour; as political resistance against systemic oppression, especially white supremacy in the US context; or as extravagant performances of Black resilience, wealth, and success despite the odds. These generalizations of its political urgency should not be ignored, but they tend to overlook how hip hop provides a vessel for the expression and sharing of joy in distinctly Black traditional forms: as an attitude or ethos; a creative approach; a self-reflective mode of learning; a party soundtrack; a competition; and a community. I have written before in detail about how rap music can psychologically, bodily, and emotionally empower its listeners.[43] Hip hop, more broadly, carries the same potential. This may be especially significant in the internet age.

Fosters Knowledge of Self & Self-Determination', *Equity & Excellence in Education* 49, no. 4 (October 2016): 415–416.

[39] Tricia Rose, *The Hip-Hop Wars: What We Talk about When We Talk about Hip-Hop and Why It Matters* (New York: Basic Books, 2008), 4–8; Brittney C. Cooper, Susana M. Morris, and Robin M. Boylorn, 'Hip Hop Generation Feminism: A Manifesto', in *The Crunk Feminist Collection*, ed. Brittney C. Cooper, Susana M. Morris, and Robin M. Boylorn, xix–xxii (New York: The Feminist Press at CUNY, 2016), xix–xxii; Shanté Paradigm Smalls, *Hip Hop Heresies: Queer Aesthetics in New York City* (New York: New York University Press, 2022), 3.

[40] Safiya Umoja Noble, *Algorithms of Oppression: How Search Engines Reinforce Racism* (New York: New York University Press, 2018); Moya Bailey, *Misogynoir Transformed: Black Women's Digital Resistance* (New York: New York University Press, 2021); Shakuntala Banaji and Ramnath Bhat, *Social Media and Hate* (Abingdon: Routledge, 2021), 15–24.

[41] Kyle Devine, *Decomposed: The Political Ecology of Music* (Cambridge, MA: MIT Press, 2019).

[42] William Cheng, ed., *Loving Music Till It Hurts* (New York: Oxford University Press, 2019), 186–193.

[43] Steven Gamble, *How Music Empowers: Listening to Modern Rap and Metal* (London: Routledge, 2021). See also Raphael Travis, *The Healing Power of Hip Hop* (Santa Barbara, CA: Praeger, 2016).

The Culture in the Internet Age

Online, hip hop reaches a larger audience than ever before. Historically, heads discovered the culture in parks, clubs and record stores. Now, since 'shared content, discussion, and advice are available online 24/7',[44] hip hop is more immediately available for those with an internet connection. It is also easier to participate as a consumer and producer, with platforms like SoundCloud, Twitch, and TikTok streamlining access to hip hop media. Debates around the democratization of music and media production have proliferated[45] as social platforms have 'evolved from being an esoteric jumble of technologies to a set of sites and services that are at the heart of contemporary culture'.[46] In addition, the costs of entry to hip hop have reduced, at least for people who already spend their leisure time immersed in digital cultural activities.[47] Nowadays, hip hop is widespread to the point of unavoidable online,[48] seeming to prove André Brock's point that 'Black folk have a natural affinity for the internet and digital media'.[49]

The internet is a diverse and varied range of fora. Yet, from the late 2000s to today, the internet has increasingly been thought of in terms of a limited number of online media platforms (as articulated concisely by systems engineer Tom Eastman in Figure 1.1).

Users—and their activities, and the products of their activities—are increasingly brought together by the centralizing, even oligopolistic, processes of platforms. A few examples will demonstrate the point. Blogs, formerly posted and read on distinct subdomains, became the preserve of social media profiles or 'walls', with other users' content accrued into scrollable 'feeds'.[50] Videos were once independently hosted by website authors, and now principally exist in one vast video archive.[51] Music was perhaps the first form of

---

[44] Janice L. Waldron, 'Online Music Communities and Social Media', in *The Oxford Handbook of Community Music*, ed. Brydie-Leigh Bartleet and Lee Higgins (Oxford: Oxford University Press, 2018), 110.

[45] Patryk Galuszka, 'Music Aggregators and Intermediation of the Digital Music Market', *International Journal of Communication* 9 (January 2015): 20; David Hesmondhalgh, 'Have Digital Communication Technologies Democratized the Media Industries?', in *Media and Society*, ed. James Curran and David Hesmondhalgh, 6th ed. (New York: Bloomsbury Academic, 2019), 101–120; Johannes Brusila, Martin Cloonan, and Kim Ramstedt, 'Music, Digitalization, and Democracy', *Popular Music and Society* 45, no. 1 (October 2021): 1–12; Paul Harkins and Nick Prior, '(Dis)Locating Democratization: Music Technologies in Practice', *Popular Music and Society* 45, no. 1 (January 2022): 84–103.

[46] danah boyd, *It's Complicated: The Social Lives of Networked Teens* (New Haven, CT: Yale University Press, 2014), 6.

[47] Karl Spracklen, *Digital Leisure, the Internet and Popular Culture* (London: Palgrave Macmillan, 2015).

[48] Natalia Cherjovsky, 'Virtual Hood: Exploring The Hip-Hop Culture Experience In A British Online Community' (PhD diss., University of Central Florida, 2010), 1–2, https://stars.library.ucf.edu/etd/4199.

[49] Brock, *Distributed Blackness*, 5.

[50] Jill Walker Rettberg, *Blogging*, 2nd ed. (Cambridge: Polity, 2014), 169–170.

[51] Joana Freitas and João Francisco Porfírio, 'Foreword', in *YouTube and Music: Online Culture and Everyday Life*, ed. Holly Rogers, Joana Freitas, and João Francisco Porfírio (London: Bloomsbury Academic, 2023), xiii–xx.

Tom Eastman
@tveastman

I'm old enough to remember when the Internet wasn't a group of five websites, each consisting of screenshots of text from the other four.

7:28 pm · 3 Dec 2018

11.1K Retweets   435 Quotes   67K Likes   486 Bookmarks

Figure 1.1 A popular tweet commenting on the centralization of internet media content, courtesy of user

media to be transformed by the internet into a streamed resource that users pay a subscription to access, by and large replacing the traditional purchase and ownership of media products.[52] Though this last example includes other developments in media consumption practices, technologically speaking, music listening became centralized by streaming platforms.

Centralization is a core principle of how platforms function. They assemble users, cheaply facilitate specific actions, and collate content or services within one system. In return, platforms profit from attention,[53] advertising,[54] and the extraction of user data,[55] sometimes in addition to paid subscriptions. Platforms mediate cultural interactions on social media, leading to notions, for example, that Twitter is the 'global digital town square'[56] or that Facebook will 'bring the world closer together'.[57] The rhetoric that platform CEOs deploy implies democratizing access to online interaction and a form of public voice for all users.[58] As Nanjala Nyabola puts it, 'the internet should ideally be more

---

[52] Jeremy Wade Morris and Devon Powers, 'Control, Curation and Musical Experience in Streaming Music Services', *Creative Industries Journal* 8, no. 2 (July 2015): 106–122. Still, it is worth keeping in mind that almost every new dominant technology coexists with older technological practices.
[53] Tim Wu, *The Attention Merchants: The Epic Scramble to Get Inside Our Heads* (New York: Knopf, 2016).
[54] Nick Srnicek, *Platform Capitalism* (Cambridge: Polity Press, 2017), 50–60.
[55] Shoshana Zuboff, *The Age of Surveillance Capitalism: The Fight for a Human Future at the New Frontier of Power* (London: Profile, 2019).
[56] Catherine Powell, 'Can You Hear Me? Speech and Power in the Global Digital Town Square', *Proceedings of the ASIL Annual Meeting* 116 (January 2022): 117–119.
[57] Josh Constine, 'Facebook Changes Mission Statement to "Bring the World Closer Together"', *TechCrunch* (blog), 22 June 2017, https://techcrunch.com/2017/06/22/bring-the-world-closer-together/.
[58] This rhetoric aligns with the founding characterizations of the World Wide Web, which was designed as a public good: open and free and decentralized. See James Ball, *The System: Who Owns the Internet, and*

12 Digital Flows

egalitarian; giving more voice to individuals that don't have it'.[59] The rhetoric of free and open expression reinforces the popular idea that these platforms generate a kind of virtual or networked public sphere,[60] and conceals how corporate, privately owned platforms control and constrain user behaviour. Christian Fuchs insightfully observes that at the heart of digital platforms lies 'a colonized and feudalized public sphere dominated and shaped by the logic of accumulation and acceleration'.[61]

Keeping this framing in critical tension with the free and democratized 'Internet imaginary',[62] I use the term mainstream online culture to encapsulate the virtual spaces afforded, regulated, and mediated by social media platforms. The mainstream resembles the beating heart of popular cultures on the internet, playing out in between algorithmically 'personalized' filter bubbles and viral hashtags that centralize swathes of trending, often controversial, content. I am referring to something broader than 'internet culture': a set of common aesthetics, participatory practices, and patterns of rapid spread within an ambivalent environment.[63] Mainstream online culture covers media artefacts and discourses that both register with Extremely Online people[64]—that is, those invested in internet culture—and spill out among broader audiences, that is, everyday social media users. It is worth emphasizing that people have unequal access to, and unequal influence within, this mainstream. Indeed, it represents 'tropes and ideologies born of capitalism and supported by the entertainment industries . . . which asserts itself as natural, necessary, and monolithic despite the diversity and fragmentation of concomitant culture(s)'.[65] To 'break the internet' is to significantly impact mainstream online culture.[66]

Digital Flows argues that hip hop has increasingly shaped mainstream online culture through its key values of sharing, conspicuous creativity, nuanced—and sometimes not so nuanced—style of commentary, and viral

---

How It Owns Us (London: Bloomsbury, 2020); Christian Fuchs, *Internet and Society: Social Theory in the Information Age* (New York: Routledge, 2008), 121–125.

[59] Nanjala Nyabola, *Digital Democracy, Analogue Politics: How the Internet Era Is Transforming Politics in Kenya* (London: Bloomsbury, 2018), 45.

[60] Yochai Benkler, *The Wealth of Networks* (New Haven, CT: Yale University Press, 2006), 10–13.

[61] Christian Fuchs, *Media, Communication and Society* (London and New York: Routledge, 2023), vi:247.

[62] Paolo Bory, *The Internet Myth: From the Internet Imaginary to Network Ideologies* (London: University of Westminster Press, 2020), 33.

[63] Geert Lovink, *Social Media Abyss: Critical Internet Cultures and the Force of Negation* (Cambridge and Malden, MA: Polity Press, 2016); Whitney Phillips and Ryan M. Milner, *The Ambivalent Internet: Mischief, Oddity, and Antagonism Online* (Cambridge and Malden, MA: Polity Press, 2017); Crystal Abidin and Megan Lindsay Brown, eds., *Microcelebrity Around the Globe* (Bingley: Emerald Publishing Limited, 2019).

[64] Taylor Lorenz, *Extremely Online: The Untold Story of Fame, Influence, and Power on the Internet* (New York: Simon & Schuster, 2023).

[65] Whitney Phillips, *This Is Why We Can't Have Nice Things: Mapping the Relationship Between Online Trolling and Mainstream Culture* (Cambridge, MA: MIT Press, 2015), 21.

[66] Olivia Yallop, *Break the Internet: In Pursuit of Influence* (Melbourne and London: Scribe, 2021).

charm. The core elements of hip hop style and practice are unprecedently visible, relevant, and significant in the internet age. The term 'internet age' may already be passé. Yet it brings into sharp focus the prevalence of internet technologies in everyday life, and the attendant changes to interpersonal communication, media circulation, and cultural economies. Hip hop is an ideal example of such changes since it is now intricately entwined with the web as a significant site of communality, creativity, and commerce.

Consider, as a case study of hip hop's online impact, web-based beatmaking communities. For years—and accelerated by COVID-19 lockdowns—hip hop producers have met, competed, and collaborated in beat battle events sustained by the livestreaming platform Twitch and individual Discord servers. As Jason Ng and I previously identified, this online form of hip hop participation has a range of cultural and technological affordances: event hosts are discovering new income streams and growing their followings; producers are gaining skills, supporting peers, and advancing their careers; and participants are finding experiences of communal belonging.[67] Engaging in online cultural practices can be personally gratifying and professionally advantageous for hip hop heads, but it often means navigating online media platforms' terms, capacities, and commercial incentives. Moreover, such practices often take place on strange stages, where context collapse is rife,[68] culture wars rage on,[69] and activities we might think of as countercultural or subcultural are freely and publicly visible.[70]

With these complexities in mind, this book emphasizes an important resonance between hip hop and online cultures: the principle of sharing. Hip hop is undoubtedly a culture founded on ideas of sharing: consider the ethos of 'show and prove'[71] or the cypher—a circle formed for performance—as the basic unit of hip hop interaction.[72] Breaking, graffiti, rapping, and DJing all revolve around processes of asserting oneself creatively and feeding back on others' practices to build with each

---

[67] Ng and Gamble, 'Hip-Hop Producer-Hosts, Beat Battles, and Online Music Production Communities on Twitch'.

[68] Alice E. Marwick and danah boyd, 'I Tweet Honestly, I Tweet Passionately: Twitter Users, Context Collapse, and the Imagined Audience', *New Media & Society* 13, no. 1 (February 2011): 114–133.

[69] Angela Nagle, *Kill All Normies: Online Culture Wars from 4Chan and Tumblr to Trump and the Alt-Right* (Winchester: Zero Books, 2017).

[70] Jessa Lingel, *Digital Countercultures and the Struggle for Community* (Cambridge, MA: MIT Press, 2017).

[71] Imani Kai Johnson, 'Critical Hiphopography in Streetdance Communities (Hard Love Part 2)', in *The Oxford Handbook of Hip Hop Dance Studies*, ed. Mary Fogarty and Imani Kai Johnson (New York: Oxford University Press, 2022), 221.

[72] *The Cipher, the Circle & Its Wisdom: Toni Blackman at TEDxUMassAmherst*, YouTube video, 14 May 2013, https://www.youtube.com/watch?v=WYdb5snA1Jc; J. Griffith Rollefson, '"Yo Nací Caminando": Community-Engaged Scholarship, Hip Hop as Postcolonial Studies, and Rico Pabón's Knowledge of Self', *Journal of World Popular Music* 5, no. 2 (2018): 169–192.

other.[73] That's one definition of sharing, in terms of self-expression. Hip hop is also about sharing in terms of conspicuous reuse, remixing, and borrowing.[74] Sampling, for example, lies at the heart of hip hop music.[75] Furthermore, the peer-to-peer file-sharing that major record labels slandered as 'music piracy' at the dawn of the digital music economy merely updated pre-existing practices of hip hop propagation.[76]

Social media platforms have ingrained similar technocultural conventions, with share buttons, signal-boosting, and emoji reactions becoming the common currency of online communication. Memes are remixes of audiovisual media with added critical commentary,[77] which go hand in hand with hip hop's signifyin(g) tendencies.[78] Lee Rainie and Barry Wellman coined the phrase 'networked individualism' to describe how technocultural developments towards social network use, personalization, and pervasive mobile internet access have afforded the prevailing ideology of online interaction.[79] The internet's emphasis on individual expressivity and 'persistent personal identity'[80] chimes with hip hop's insistence on authentic individual expressivity. The social media profile, accruing updates about the user's life, achievements, and thoughts, tends to reflect commercial rap music's spotlighting of individual performers, their clout, and celebrity,[81] providing evidence of hip hop's neoliberal turn.[82] Clearly, hip hop has adapted along the flows of digitalization, but so too has it influenced the shape and style of mainstream online culture. In this book, I examine six different snapshots of these mutually transformative effects.

---

[73] Mark Katz, *Build: The Power of Hip Hop Diplomacy in a Divided World* (Oxford and New York: Oxford University Press, 2019), 17.

[74] Quentin Williams, *Remix Multilingualism: Hip Hop, Ethnography and Performing Marginalized Voice* (London and New York: Bloomsbury, 2017).

[75] Justin A. Williams, *Rhymin' and Stealin': Musical Borrowing in Hip-Hop* (Ann Arbor: University of Michigan Press, 2013).

[76] Adam Haupt, *Stealing Empire: P2P, Intellectual Property and Hip-Hop Subversion* (Cape Town: HSRC Press, 2008); Philippe Aigrain, *Sharing: Culture and the Economy in the Internet Age* (Amsterdam University Press, 2012).

[77] Anastasia Denisova, *Internet Memes and Society: Social, Cultural, and Political Contexts* (New York: Routledge, 2019), 10; Bradley E. Wiggins, *The Discursive Power of Memes in Digital Culture: Ideology, Semiotics, and Intertextuality* (New York: Routledge, 2019), 11.

[78] Henry L. Gates, Jr., *The Signifying Monkey: A Theory of African-American Literary Criticism* (New York: Oxford University Press, 1988); Sarah Florini, 'Tweets, Tweeps, and Signifyin': Communication and Cultural Performance on "Black Twitter"', *Television & New Media* 15, no. 3 (March 2014): 223–237.

[79] Lee Rainie and Barry Wellman, *Networked: The New Social Operating System* (Cambridge, MA: MIT Press, 2012).

[80] Daniël De Zeeuw, 'Impersonal Identity: Enacting the Online Self Beyond Networked Individualism', in *The Aesthetics and Politics of the Online Self*, ed. Donatella Della Ratta et al. (Cham: Springer International Publishing, 2021), 309.

[81] Jabari M. Evans and Nancy K. Baym, 'The Audacity of Clout (Chasing): Digital Strategies of Black Youth in Chicago DIY Hip-Hop', *International Journal of Communication* 16 (May 2022): 2681.

[82] Travis L. Gosa, 'The Fifth Element: Knowledge', in *The Cambridge Companion to Hip-Hop*, ed. Justin A. Williams (Cambridge: Cambridge University Press, 2015), 56.

Chapter Outline

In Chapter 2, I offer an overview of hip hop's onlining. I am concerned with fleshing out hip hop in its contemporary online form and how it got here. This means viewing hip hop music in terms of genre, an industry category which dominates the music consumption landscape despite indifference among young listeners.[83] I trace the development of hip hop and the internet from the 1960s to the present day, remixing now-familiar hip hop histories with fresh samples to emphasize how the culture has been mediated, digitalized, and platformized. Building on the brief introduction here, I elaborate on how hip hop thrives in the internet era, suggesting that the fundamental importance of public sharing has been a complementary logic to the platformization of culture.[84] As a few examples of hip hop's online prevalence, I discursively analyse hip hop memes and rap music on streaming platforms.

Chapter 3 is concerned with the fissures generated by hip hop's online flows, particularly generational tensions in the reception of contemporary rap. To provide some context for what hip hop culture typically thinks about the web, I analyse a body of rap lyrics about the internet. Then I introduce a born-online form of hip hop, commonly called 'SoundCloud rap' (I opt for the more general 'internet rap'). This immensely popular, controversial, and influential yet short-lived—essentially, viral—wave of rap music intensifies generational tensions in the culture. I analyse music, videos, and new media to investigate why this internet-native form of rap has been seen as selling the culture short. With reference to the conventions of online cultural production—especially theorizations of the attention economy and virality—I see this music representing net-native hip hop youth at their most creative, provocative, and web-savvy.

Following this look at one distinctly internet-infused hip hop genre, in Chapter 4 I analyse another—lofi hip hop music on YouTube—examining comments that reveal distinct identity formations and expressions of communality. This study catches lofi hip hop in flux, as the audience swelled due to an uptake in listening during the first year of the COVID-19 pandemic. I look at the aesthetics, conventions, and values of the YouTube lofi community predominantly through analysis of comments before and after the onset

---

[83] Jeremy Orosz, ' "Straight Outta Nashville": Allusions to Hip Hop in Contemporary Country Music', *Popular Music and Society* 44, no. 1 (January 2021): 49–59; Pamela Burnard et al., 'Pursuing Diversity and Inclusivity through Hip-Hop Music Genres: Insights for Mainstream Music Curricula', in *The Routledge Companion to Creativities in Music Education*, ed. Clint Randles and Pamela Burnard (New York: Routledge, 2022), 241.

[84] David B Nieborg and Thomas Poell, 'The Platformization of Cultural Production: Theorizing the Contingent Cultural Commodity', *New Media & Society* 20, no. 11 (November 2018): 4275–4292.

16 Digital Flows

of the pandemic. The chapter closes with some reflections on commercial and political appropriations of lofi as more generalized conventions of internet culture, especially memes, take hold. This instance of online hip hop provides important insights into how people interact with music cultures online and how platforms like YouTube (at their best) provide a space for users to express sentiments of communal belonging, personal identities, and social connectivity, within the broader context of networked publics.

I further examine how hip hop operates within these contexts in Chapter 5, which is concerned with representations of, and responses to, women at the vanguard of contemporary mainstream rap. This chapter demonstrates how hip hop feminism has been a powerful force in the culture and, crucially, how it has been received in online spaces. I detail how Black women rappers since the mid-2010s (Megan Thee Stallion, Cardi B, and more) have flipped the script on the traditional sexualization of women in hip hop music videos, providing more diverse and authentic representations of Black womanhood. I analyse a big data set of YouTube comments divided by user gender, discovering gendered themes in the online reception of rap music videos. The main thrust of the chapter is to better understand how patriarchy and misogynoir are sustained online—especially in the context of hip hop—and therefore how they can be challenged.

Having established how contemporary rap is shared among mass audiences, in Chapter 6 I examine how hip hop is appropriated by white performers in mainstream popular music. With reference to audiovisual examples, cultural criticism, and social media comments, I shed light on what pop takes from hip hop and the racial dynamics of such borrowing in the internet era. The chapter focuses on accusations of cultural appropriation levelled at Ariana Grande, combining an in-depth reading of Black musical and cultural aesthetics in her '7 rings' music video with social media discourse about her public image. Hip hop sure is shareworthy, but its adoption by white pop performers adds fuel to incendiary online debates, especially polarizing issues like cultural appropriation and callout/cancel culture.

The final full chapter, Chapter 7, focuses on a new frontier for online hip hop: video game concerts. The 'live and direct' quality of performance that hip hop holds dear[85] sits in tension with interactive media production. With reference to the concepts of virtuality and liveness, I disentangle the complex mediation of concerts such as Travis Scott's *Fortnite* concert, Lil Nas X in *Roblox*, and more DIY-inspired charity events in *Minecraft*. The first two

---

[85] David Diallo, *Collective Participation and Audience Engagement in Rap Music* (Cham: Springer International Publishing, 2019), 66.

of these are significantly commercial, corporate efforts deeply aligned with platform logics, but the latter concerts suggest that the ethos of hip hop communality can thrive on the internet. I end Chapter 7 by considering how hip hop is transformed as an art form by the commercial logics of video game platforms.

The conclusion summarizes the strands flowing throughout the book and situates hip hop's online mediation as a major development following its globalization and digitalization. Online hip hop is, in other words, the most contemporary form the culture takes, having encountered challenges and opportunities and transformations in the process of its onlining. I reflect on the scope of the overall study and suggest some pathways for future research. With new online creative technologies quickly developing, and 2023 dubbed 'the year of AI transformation',[86] the book closes by gesturing to potential futures of hip hop and the internet.

---

[86] Clint Boulton, 'Is 2023 the Year of AI Transformation?', *Forbes*, 8 February 2023, https://www.forbes.com/sites/delltechnologies/2023/02/08/is-2023-the-year-of-ai-transformation/.

2

How Hip Hop Became the Leading Music Genre in the Digital Streaming Era

Sharing Culture

Introduction

In recorded form, hip hop has always been a popular genre of music. It first broke into the top 100 bestselling albums in 1984, making two appearances that succinctly show the variety of hip hop's commercial force. The first was the soundtrack for the feel-good hip hop musical film *Beat Street*, which had a significant impact outside the United States despite tepid reviews from film critics.[1] The second was Run-DMC's self-titled debut record, which marked a shift towards what is sometimes called hardcore rap music.[2] By the turn of the millennium—the end of the much-disputed golden age[3]—hip hop was widely considered one of the most commercially successful and popular kinds of music worldwide.[4] Fast forward to 2020, and the genre makes up more than half of the top 100 bestselling albums (Figure 2.1).[5]

[1] April K. Henderson, 'Dancing Between Islands: Hip Hop and the Samoan Diaspora', in *The Vinyl Ain't Final: Hip Hop and the Globalization of Black Popular Culture*, ed. Dipannita Basu and Sidney J. Lemelle (Pluto Press, 2006), 184; Kimberly Monteyne, *Hip Hop on Film: Performance Culture, Urban Space, and Genre Transformation in the 1980s* (Jackson: University Press of Mississippi, 2013), 4–5; Leonard Schmieding, 'Taking Beat Street to the Streets in Socialist East Germany', in *Participating Audiences, Imagined Public Spheres: The Cultural Work of Contemporary American(Ized) Narratives*, ed. Sebastian M. Herrmann et al. (Leipziger Universitätsverlag, 2012), 43.

[2] Miles White, *From Jim Crow to Jay-Z: Race, Rap, and the Performance of Masculinity* (Urbana: University of Illinois Press, 2011), 42–49.

[3] Ben Duinker and Denis Martin, 'In Search of the Golden Age Hip-Hop Sound (1986–1996)', *Empirical Musicology Review* 12, nos. 1–2 (September 2017): 80–100.

[4] Todd Boyd, *The New H.N.I.C.: The Death of Civil Rights and the Reign of Hip Hop* (New York and London: New York University Press, 2002), 14–19; M. A. Neal, *What the Music Said: Black Popular Music and Black Public Culture* (New York and London: Routledge, 1999), 305–308; Jonas Polfuß, 'Hip-Hop: A Marketplace Icon', *Consumption Markets & Culture* 25, no. 3 (May 2022): 272–286.

[5] I based this visualization on the statistical analysis developed by Steve Hawtin using data sources from MusicID, a music industry data aggregation platform. His study collates album charts in eight countries and revenue estimates across thirty countries. For genre classification, I used crowd-sourced labels from the website *Rate Your Music*. Steve Hawtin, 'MusicID Revenue: Music Charts 2000 - 2021, Data Version 0.3.0063', *MusicID*, July 2021, http://revenue.musicid.academicrightspress.com/about.htm. Throughout this book, I follow graph design and colour principles laid out by Claus Wilke, *Fundamentals of Data Visualization: A Primer on Making Informative and Compelling Figures* (Sebastopol, CA: O'Reilly, 2019), 27–29.

Digital Flows. Steven Gamble, Oxford University Press. © Oxford University Press 2024.
DOI: 10.1093/oso/9780197656389.003.0002

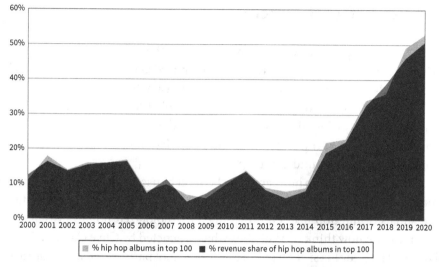

Figure 2.1 Hip hop's presence and revenue share among top 100 albums, 2000–2020

Hip hop and the commercial record industry have a storied relationship: fraught but extremely productive. Indeed, concerns over the commercialization of hip hop have characterized major debates in hip hop studies.[6] However, as the mainstream charts show, the genre has undeniably found significant audiences by playing on the industry's terms.[7] Many still encounter hip hop only as a market category, in the form of a genre-coded Spotify playlist or a YouTube video. Before platform-curated categories and recommendation systems were the dominant form of mediating music, however, the genre still had a major presence in record stores and on radio.[8] The story of hip hop's ascent to top dog among all pop genres does not begin in the digital era, but that is where we find it now. How did it get here?

---

[6] Tricia Rose, *The Hip-Hop Wars: What We Talk about When We Talk about Hip-Hop and Why It Matters* (New York: Basic Books, 2008). https://academic.oup.com/edited-volume/34741; Amy Coddington, '"Check Out the Hook While My DJ Revolves It": How the Music Industry Made Rap into Pop in the Late 1980s', in *The Oxford Handbook of Hip Hop Music*, ed. Justin D. Burton and Jason Lee Oakes (Oxford: Oxford University Press, 2018).

[7] I am defining 'genre' quite simply for now, simply akin to 'recorded music industry category', and theorize this more substantially in Chapter 6.

[8] Amy Coddington, *How Hip Hop Became Hit Pop: Radio, Rap, and Race* (Berkeley and Los Angeles: University of California Press, 2023).

Hip Hop Before the Internet

Strictly speaking, there was no hip hop before the internet. The origins of what we now think of as the internet came into existence a few years earlier.[9] However, hip hop prospered in the music industry before the internet was an aspect of daily life for most people in the Global North and the West, before the majority of wealthy households owned a web-connected computer, and well before two-thirds of the world's population could get online from computers carried around in their pockets.[10]

In the early 1970s, hip hop came into being at house and block parties across marginalized neighbourhoods in New York. One particular urban legend fills the annals of hip hop history, providing a mythologized point of origin for the music we now think of as hip hop: that concocted by Clive Campbell, aka DJ Kool Herc, for his sister Cindy's back-to-school party in the Bronx at 1520 Sedgwick Avenue. DJs looped instrumental sections of disco and funk music, known as drum breaks, to keep the beat flowing.[11] Playing off the energy of the crowd, vocal performers—often the DJs themselves, or a friend playing party host—embellished the music. Using microphones, MCs improvised short rhythmic phrases, told jokes, and recited rhymes which drew upon Afrodiasporic oral traditions such as toasting and chatting at Jamaican sound system parties (a connection Kool Herc contests).[12] Inspired by the Black Arts Movement,[13] these vocals took an increasingly poetic turn as MCs became a crucial part of the musical performance, and rapping developed into extensive verses and call-and-response refrains. Meanwhile, dancers dubbed b-boys and b-girls developed technical, impressive moves collectively known as breaking. Street artists took to tagging the urban sprawl with visually striking graffiti.

[9] This claim refers to the ARPANET, the US military network developed from the late 1960s, which is widely thought of as the progenitor of the modern World Wide Web. There were also earlier instances of cybernetic technology that laid the foundation for the internet, mostly erased or eclipsed by American imperialism. See Eden Medina, *Cybernetic Revolutionaries: Technology and Politics in Allende's Chile* (Cambridge, MA: MIT Press, 2011); Jack Linchuan Qiu and Hongzhe Wang, 'Radical Praxis of Computing in the PRC: Forgotten Stories from the Maoist to Post-Mao Era', *Internet Histories* 5, nos. 3–4 (October 2021): 214–229; Benjamin Peters, *How Not to Network a Nation: The Uneasy History of the Soviet Internet* (Cambridge, MA: MIT Press, 2016).

[10] These claims are drawn from statistics and sources assembled at Internet World Stats, https://www.internetworldstats.com/, by the Miniwatts Marketing Group.

[11] C. L. Keyes, *Rap Music and Street Consciousness* (Urbana and Chicago: University of Illinois Press, 2002), 54–59.

[12] Tricia Rose, *Black Noise: Rap Music and Black Culture in Contemporary America* (Middletown, CT: Wesleyan University Press, 1994), 85–88; David Diallo, *Collective Participation and Audience Engagement in Rap Music* (Cham: Springer International Publishing, 2019), 25–45.

[13] Reiland Rabaka, *Hip Hop's Inheritance: From the Harlem Renaissance to the Hip Hop Feminist Movement* (Lanham, MD: Lexington Books, 2011); Keyes, *Rap Music and Street Consciousness*, 32–38.

As hip hop spread across neighbourhoods, music industry personnel quickly took note. This music, invented around principles of reuse, repetition, and rapping came into contact with studio recording in the late 1970s. The first hit record was The Sugarhill Gang's 'Rapper's Delight', assembled and produced by R&B label manager Sylvia Robinson.[14] The track was an unprecedented and near-immediate hit.[15] Once Robinson convinced radio programmers to spin 'Rapper's Delight', stations and local distributors could hardly keep up with audience demand. Methods of hip hop's proliferation quickly expanded. Word of mouth soon coexisted with the potent mediating force of radio.[16] Hip hop groups across the city increasingly took to the studio, wrote lyrical bars down on paper, and inscribed beats in the fabric of vinyl records. DJs further developed their creative practices combining samples—soul horns, funk basslines, and other instruments (especially vocals) from a plethora of Black music styles—with original drum patterns made on sequencers and synthesizers.[17] Those experimenting further with vinyl developed the art of turntablism based around mixing, punch phrasing, back spinning, scratching, beat juggling and more.[18] MCs still wrote to perform live at parties and motivate audience interaction but also portrayed their environments and detailed their daily experiences as racially marginalized and often poor people in the post-industrial city.

That city was New York until around 1980. In the coming years, Los Angeles would develop its own, equally prominent version of rap. Record shops in cities across America became vital sites of the music's circulation.[19] DJs with families out of state began raiding their older relatives' record collections for breaks and sample-worthy hits.[20] Back in New York, shows became increasingly sophisticated and popular events, having evolved from house parties to

---

[14] S. Craig Watkins, *Hip Hop Matters: Politics, Pop Culture, and the Struggle for the Soul of a Movement* (Boston, MA: Beacon Press, 2005), 10–21. See also William Jelani Cobb, *To the Break of Dawn: A Freestyle on the Hip Hop Aesthetic* (New York: New York University Press, 2007), 44.

[15] See Loren Kajikawa, *Sounding Race in Rap Songs* (Berkeley and Los Angeles: University of California Press, 2015), 19–48.

[16] For more on how hip hop became a mainstream music via commercial radio programming, see Coddington, *How Hip Hop Became Hit Pop*.

[17] W. E. Perkins, 'The Rap Attack: An Introduction', in *Droppin' Science: Critical Essays on Rap Music and Hip Hop Culture*, ed. W. E. Perkins (Philadelphia, PA: Temple University Press, 1996), 12–13.

[18] S. Smith, *Hip-Hop Turntablism, Creativity and Collaboration* (Surrey: Ashgate, 2013); Mark Katz, *Groove Music: The Art and Culture of the Hip-Hop DJ* (New York: Oxford University Press, 2012).

[19] J. G. Schloss, *Making Beats: The Art of Sample-Based Hip-Hop* (Middletown, CT: Wesleyan University Press, 2004), 79–91.

[20] Jennifer Lynn Stoever, 'Crate Digging Begins at Home: Black and Latinx Women Collecting and Selecting Records in the 1960s and 1970s Bronx', in *The Oxford Handbook of Hip Hop Music*, ed. Justin D. Burton and Jason Lee Oakes (Oxford: Oxford University Press, 2018). As Stoever emphasizes, this is not only a part of hip hop's wider expansion but also how it began: without Kool Herc's mother sharing her record collection with her son (and without the music selected and played in the childhood homes of hip hop's other 'first men') there would be no hip hop.

22   Digital Flows

engage more formally with live music performance institutions like venues and promotion companies. Casual gatherings flourished while, elsewhere in the city, 'official' concerts took form with now-recognizable performers on the bill. Filmmakers took notice and captured many early hip hop moments on video, with movie studios realizing hip hop's potential for telling engaging stories of urban life.[21] Increasingly commercial efforts, like *Beat Street*, *Wild Style*, and *Breakin'*, gained particularly large international audiences, presenting fictionalized versions of the Bronx-born culture yet encouraging viewers to delve deeper.[22]

Records also travelled globally from the US as commercial exports. While the US was developing its own nascent hip hop industry, 'Rapper's Delight' was making waves abroad: the record was a chart-topping hit in Canada and several European countries.[23] Hip hop, fast becoming a major American media product, activated an expressive awareness in marginalized and migrant cultures the world over. Scenes in nearly every major city developed their own take on hip hop with local inflections.[24] The genre and the culture multiplied and diversified so rapidly that the term hip hop soon struggled to cover the variety of musical practices which took inspiration from the original New York neighbourhood parties.

Artists in other genres—mostly white performers—drew musical inspiration from the new musical style, particularly the vocals. Blondie's 'Rapture', released as a single in 1981, was the first US chart-topping song featuring a rap verse. Later that year, the music video for the track, featuring Fab 5 Freddy and Jean-Michel Basquiat, made waves on the brand-new music video channel MTV. The Beastie Boys, a group of white, mostly Jewish, New Yorkers, transitioned from hardcore punk to hip hop. By the mid-1980s, they landed rap's first number-one album on the Billboard charts with *Licensed to Ill*. Run-DMC's cover and collaboration with Aerosmith on 'Walk This Way' shortly showed hip hop's crossover potential, gaining significant airplay on both urban—that is, segregated Black music programming[25]—and pop radio

---

[21] S. Craig Watkins, *Representing: Hip-Hop Culture and the Production of Black Cinema* (Chicago and London: The University of Chicago Press, 1998), 68–76; James McNally, 'Hip-Hop into the Video Age: New York Teenhood, Malcolm McLaren and the British Eye', *Visual Culture in Britain* 20, no. 1 (January 2019): 40–63.

[22] Thomas DeFrantz refers to these Hollywood productions as "breaksploitation" films. See Thomas F. DeFrantz, 'Hip-Hop in Hollywood: Encounter, Community, Resistance', in *The Oxford Handbook of Dance and the Popular Screen*, ed. Melissa Blanco Borelli (New York: Oxford University Press, 2014), 113–131.

[23] Watkins, *Hip Hop Matters*, 18.

[24] Murray Forman, *The 'hood Comes First: Race, Space, and Place in Rap and Hip-Hop* (Middletown, CT: Wesleyan University Press, 2002), xvii–xviii.

[25] Neal, *What the Music Said*, 248–249.

stations from 1986.[26] The popularity of television, the mainstay of middle-class American homes since the 1960s,[27] provided an important stage for mediating hip hop as a visually expressive art form.[28]

From its early manifestations as an inner-city celebration of Black joy despite structural racism and communal displacement, the music was always political. However, tracks grew increasingly explicit, confrontational, and performatively aggressive. Label executives recognized the market force of energetic music with masculinist lyrics, resulting in a particularly ugly trend of white industry personnel encouraging Black artists to play up stereotypical images of gangsterism and hypersexuality.[29] Aggressively stylized visuals of Black masculinity, street fashion, and shocking lyrics—some trying to speak truth to power, but others exploring violently misogynistic fantasies—quickly fuelled moral panic around the perceived 'threat' of Black cultural difference encroaching on a mythical nice, white, middle America.[30]

Artists signed record deals that were both lucrative and exploitative, gained commercial sponsorships, and explored career opportunities in advertising, television, and film. Rappers became celebrities in the popular music industry, many starting their own fashion lines and other business enterprises, which gave rise to the figure of the hip hop mogul.[31] Hip hop became the music of choice for major sports industries, especially basketball, where the prevalence of young Black sportsmen from major cities ensured close cultural connections that quickly became part of the genre's own mythos.[32] For many poor young men of colour in the US, it has been observed that their only legal opportunities for social mobility are by leveraging skills either on the court or on the mic.[33]

---

[26] Alan Light, 'About a Salary or Reality? Rap's Recurrent Conflict', in *That's The Joint!: The Hip-Hop Studies Reader*, ed. Murray Forman and Mark Anthony Neal (New York and London: Routledge, 2004), 140.

[27] Lynn Spigel, *Make Room for TV: Television and the Family Ideal in Postwar America* (Chicago and London: University of Chicago Press, 1992), 32–35.

[28] Forman, *The 'hood Comes First*, 239–251.

[29] David Samuels, 'The Rap on Rap: The "Black Music" That Isn't Either', in *That's the Joint!*, ed. Murray Forman and Mark Anthony Neal (New York and London: Routledge, 2004), 184–192; T. D. Sharpley-Whiting, *Pimps Up, Ho's Down: Hip Hop's Hold On Young Black Women* (New York and London: New York University Press, 2007), 91; Guillermo Rebollo-Gil and Amanda Moras, 'Black Women and Black Men in Hip Hop Music: Misogyny, Violence and the Negotiation of (White-Owned) Space', *The Journal of Popular Culture* 45, no. 1 (February 2012): 118–132. On Black record executives' role in the same exploitative process, see B. Kitwana, *Why White Kids Love Hip Hop: Wankstas, Wiggers, Wannabes, and the New Reality of Race in America* (New York: Basic Civitas Books, 2005), 149.

[30] Rose, *Black Noise*, 130. See also Kitwana, *Why White Kids Love Hip Hop*.

[31] Mark Anthony Neal, 'Up From Hustling: Power, Plantations, and the Hip-hop Mogul', *Socialism and Democracy* 18, no. 2 (July 2004): 157–182.

[32] Todd Boyd, *Young, Black, Rich, and Famous: The Rise of the NBA, the Hip Hop Invasion, and the Transformation of American Culture* (Lincoln, NE and London: University of Nebraska Press, 2008).

[33] This framing was even referenced by then-President Barack Obama in a NAACP address, although his position meant churning out respectability politics to parents of Black children: 'they might think they've got a pretty good jump shot or a pretty good flow, but our kids can't all aspire to be LeBron or Lil Wayne. I want them aspiring to be scientists and engineers, doctors and teachers, not just ballers and rappers'.

24 Digital Flows

As hip hop music became codified as a recorded genre, rappers frequently featured on each other's tracks, which was an important form of gatekeeping (called co-signing) as well as an opportunity for cross-promotion.[34] Ever since the house parties, collaboration remained an important part of hip hop. A unique—albeit not entirely original—structuring of artistic creativity in hip hop took the form of the collective: a loose network of frequent collaborators, like the Native Tongues and later Wu-Tang Clan. These typically formed in and around local scenes, at least up until the millennium, when advances in communication technologies made cross-country and even cross-continental collaboration more viable.[35] Before the World Wide Web, networked communication outside of the government or military was mostly limited to US university campuses. Usenet—text boards that are in many ways a predecessor to web forums—hosted the popular newsgroups alt.rap and rec.music.funky, where the unmanageable volume of posts on hip hop led to the establishment of the dedicated discussion group rec.music.hip-hop. A broader public could soon create and access similar informational resources at scale due to the launch of internet protocols and browsers in the early 1990s. Hip hop news and lyrics websites such as Steve Juon's Original Hip-Hop Lyrics Archive set a precedent for more commercialized portals like *HipHopDX*, DatPiff, and most notably Genius.[36]

As households invested in home computers and internet connection became increasingly affordable—and fast enough to download images, even audio files, in reasonable time periods—the internet became a major site for cultural practices and social activities.[37] From the earliest days of the culture, individuals were keen to discuss hip hop music, contributing to a rich media ecosystem that had for years comprised: journalism in the form of magazines such as *The Source*, *XXL*, and *Hip Hop Connection*; radio shows including

Naturally, Lil Wayne sampled the shout-out on 2018 track 'Dedicate', albeit leaving out the belittling '*just ballers and rappers*'.

[34] Daniel Carter and Tyler Welsh, '"Everybody Wants to Work with Me": Collaborative Labor in Hip Hop', *Popular Music and Society* 42, no. 3 (2019): 267–283.

[35] See, for example, Kai Arne Hansen and Steven Gamble, 'Saturation Season: Inclusivity, Queerness, and Aesthetics in the New Media Practices of Brockhampton', *Popular Music and Society* 45, no. 1 (2021).

[36] In online hip hop circles, it is a poorly kept secret that Genius (then RapGenius) ripped all the content hosted on the Original Hip-Hop Lyrics Archive to get started. It has since developed into a platform crowdsourcing lyrics and annotations, expanding in 2014 to encompass a variety of music genres and other text-based forms. It also functions as a media producer, featuring interviews and lyric discussions with artists. See L. Kehrer, 'Genius (Formerly Rap Genius). Genius Media Group, Inc. Genius.Com', *Journal of the Society for American Music* 10, no. 4 (November 2016): 518–520. This continues a pattern of platforms stealing digital content to later develop legal business practices, as in Spotify's initial use of Pirate Bay mp3s. See Kyle Devine, *Decomposed: The Political Ecology of Music* (Cambridge, MA: MIT Press, 2019), 151.

[37] Manuel Castells, 'The Internet and the Network Society', in *The Internet in Everyday Life*, ed. Barry Wellman and Caroline Haythornthwaite (Malden, MA: Blackwell, 2002), xxix–xxxi.

Mr Magic's *Rap Attack*, *The Breakfast Club*, *Sway In The Morning*, and Tim Westwood's *BBC Radio 1 Rap Show*; television like *Yo! MTV Raps*, *Rap City*, and *Def Poetry Jam*; and cinema, from the early breaking films through Spike Lee's 'ghettocentric'[38] works to various Roc-A-Fella efforts. Hip hop moved fluidly along the flows of media globalization,[39] to radios and cinema screens and televisions, and, later, home computers the world over.

There is much more to say about the development of hip hop before the internet,[40] but this condensed telling alludes to a number of key themes: the fundamental role of technology, creativity and expressivity, urban environments, communal interaction, commercialization, and corporatization. These same themes are important to understanding the development of sociality on the internet: from the relative free-for-all of Usenet groups to the assemblage of individual and community sites on GeoCities;[41] through the dot-com bubble which birthed Web 2.0 and saw significant corporate investment in commercializing networked participation;[42] and culminating in the multimillion-user social media platforms that centralize online activities today.[43] How did hip hop navigate these changes?

Hip Hop in the Digital Music Economy

The first hip hop websites mostly attempted to create digital alternatives or extensions of previously offline business or media ventures. Magazines published articles to be read in-browser; artists developed websites to

---

[38] Watkins, *Representing*, 197–198.

[39] I. Condry, *Hip Hop Japan: Rap and the Paths of Cultural Globalization* (Durham, NC: Duke University Press, 2006), 17–20; H. Samy Alim, 'Straight Outta Compton, Straight Aus München: Global Linguistic Flows, Identities, and the Politics of Language in a Global Hip Hop Nation', in *Global Linguistic Flows: Hip Hop Cultures, Youth Identities, and the Politics of Language*, ed. H. Samy Alim, Awad Ibrahim, and Alastair Pennycook (New York and London: Routledge, 2009), 1–22.

[40] See, for instance, Keyes, *Rap Music and Street Consciousness*; Jeff Chang, *Can't Stop Won't Stop: A History of the Hip-Hop Generation* (London: Ebury Press, 2005); Mickey Hess, ed., *Icons of Hip Hop: An Encyclopedia of the Movement, Music, and Culture* (Westport, CT and London: Greenwood Press, 2007); Reiland Rabaka, *Hip Hop's Amnesia: From Blues and the Black Women's Club Movement to Rap and the Hip Hop Movement* (Lanham, MD: Lexington Books, 2012); Kathy Iandoli, *God Save the Queens: The Essential History of Women in Hip-Hop* (New York: HarperCollins, 2019).

[41] Bryan Pfaffenberger, '"If I Want It, It's OK": Usenet and the (Outer) Limits of Free Speech', *The Information Society* 12, no. 4 (November 1996): 365–386.

[42] Megan Sapnar Ankerson, *Dot-Com Design: The Rise of a Usable, Social, Commercial Web* (New York: New York University Press, 2018); Manuel Castells, *Communication Power* (Oxford: Oxford University Press, 2009); Michael Mandiberg, 'Introduction', in *The Social Media Reader*, ed. Michael Mandiberg (New York: New York University Press, 2012), 1–10.

[43] Christina Ortner, Philip Sinner, and Tanja Jadin, 'The History of Online Social Media', in *The SAGE Handbook of Web History*, ed. Niels Brügger and Ian Milligan (London: SAGE, 2019), 372–384; José van Dijck, Thomas Poell, and Martijn de Waal, *The Platform Society: Public Values in a Collective World* (New York: Oxford University Press, 2018).

26 Digital Flows

promote their materials and tour listings; home video stores offered online VHS listings for postal distribution. As internet speeds increased, the circulation of hip hop media became more common, in forms such as engaging videos hosted on YouTube and WorldStarHipHop (launched months apart in 2005). Video-sharing sites gradually drew viewers away from music video television channels like MTV, Video Music Box, and BET Hip-Hop. OnSMASH hosted popular forums for discussing rap, while independent blogs posting all kinds of opinion, review, and interview material rapidly blossomed.

Popularly known as hip hop's 'blog era', this period thrived at the intersection of independent blogs, mixtape hosting sites, music journalism, forums, and audio file-sharing. The importance of this era cannot be understated for hip hop's development in the early 2000s,[44] not least for how it ushered in changes in artist promotion and audience engagement. Myspace in particular enabled virtual, parasocial connections between artists and listeners in a more ostensibly direct form than ever before.[45] A handful of online platforms soon provided centralized spaces for sharing various audiovisual media artefacts and, by the late 2000s, the internet was fast becoming one of the main ways that people around the world first interacted with hip hop. They did not always do so on legal terms.

Ever since CDs could be ripped to computer storage, people have shared recorded music online. File transfer protocols facilitated this process for early adopters of the internet, with dial-up modems straining to grab a couple of megabytes' worth of compressed audio at a time. As internet speeds increased near-exponentially, peer-to-peer software like Napster and LimeWire enabled quick, easy, and anonymous file-sharing—so-called 'piracy'—of vast archives of MP3s worldwide.[46] Vinyl and CD stores with websites provided access to a significant catalogue of records—far larger than the record stores within local reach—albeit leaving the buyer waiting to receive the music in physical form through the mail, and often facing high postage costs. Seeking to provide a

---

[44] This period is being historicized by a podcast called *The Blog Era*, billed as telling 'the story of hip-hop's Internet revolution in the 2000s'. Jeff Ihaza, 'A New Podcast Shows How the Rise of Blogs Changed Hip-Hop Forever', *Rolling Stone* (blog), 19 April 2023, https://www.rollingstone.com/music/music-featu res/blog-era-rap-podcast-interview-1234719834/. See also Reggie Ugwu, 'On "The Blog Era," Resurrecting Rap Media History', *New York Times*, 18 May 2023, https://www.nytimes.com/2023/05/18/arts/blog-era-podcast-drake.html.

[45] Nancy Baym, *Playing to the Crowd: Musicians, Audiences, and the Intimate Work of Connection* (New York: NYU Press, 2018), 10–11; Jabari Evans, 'Old Hits Verzuz New Technology: How a Pandemic Ushered Legacy Artists into Monetizing the Clout Economy', in *Sustaining Black Music and Culture during COVID-19: #Verzuz and Club Quarantine*, ed. Niya Pickett Miller (Lanham, MD: Lexington Books, 2021), 83–84.

[46] Adam Haupt, *Stealing Empire: P2P, Intellectual Property and Hip-Hop Subversion* (Cape Town: HSRC Press, 2008), 95; Jonathan Sterne, *MP3: The Meaning of a Format* (Durham, NC: Duke University Press, 2012), 187–188.

legal alternative to peer-to-peer file-sharing and beat online record stores for speed and convenience, iTunes and competing digital download stores offered standardized prices and easy access to an extensive archive of music.[47] Countless hip hop songs have been bought on digital download stores and transferred to iPods, and other MP3 players, over hours of frustrating USB connections.

In the mid-2010s, on-demand audio streaming became the dominant format of music consumption.[48] This period has been labelled the 'streaming era', marked by streams quickly overtaking digital downloads as the largest source of performance revenue.[49] It has taken place in a context where, in the most digitally connected countries, the main way of listening to music is using an internet-connected computer (including smartphones) to access songs stored in a database owned by a platform.[50] Stream listeners do not pay to own a copy of the files, though they are temporarily stored on the device, and can be downloaded for 'offline' listening in some cases. Instead, listeners pay a recurring subscription fee to access all files currently hosted by the platform. Free access tiers provide limited samples of music, allow the choice of albums but not songs, and/or bombard the user with adverts.

As of 2022, the most-used music streaming services are YouTube, in about half the world's countries; Spotify, Apple Music, Amazon Music, Deezer, and Tidal, predominantly in the US and Europe; KuGou, QQ Music, Kuwo, AliMusic, and NetEase Cloud Music in China; Joox and KKBox in Southeast Asia; Melon and Genie in South Korea; Boomplay across ten countries in Sub-Saharan Africa; Yandex in Russia and Eastern Europe; Anghami in the Middle East and North Africa; JioSaavn and Gaana in India; and Patari in Pakistan. Much research on the streaming era has focused on Spotify (and a couple of other English-language services),[51] for good reasons. The Swedish platform is

---

[47] Jeremy Wade Morris, *Selling Digital Music, Formatting Culture* (Berkeley and Los Angeles: University of California Press, 2015), 146.

[48] I base this claim on streaming revenues overtaking other digital formats and physical sales for the major labels Sony, Warner, and Universal. Sony Corporation, *Supplemental Information of the Consolidated Financial Results for the First Quarter Ended June 30, 2016* (Sony Corporation, 2016), 11, https://www.sony.com/en/SonyInfo/IR/library/presen/er/16q1_supplement.pdf; Warner Music Group, *Warner Music Group Corp. Reports Results for Fiscal Second Quarter Ended March 31, 2015* (Warner Music Group, 2015), https://www.wmg.com/news/warner-music-group-corp-reports-results-fiscal-second-quarter-ended-march-31-2015-20696; Vivendi, *Financial Report and Unaudited Condensed Financial Statements for the Half Year Ended June 30, 2016* (Vivendi, 2016), 14, https://www.vivendi.com/wp-content/uploads/2016/08/20160825_VIV_PDF_Vivendi_Financial_Report_H1_2016.pdf.

[49] David Hesmondhalgh, 'Is Music Streaming Bad for Musicians? Problems of Evidence and Argument', *New Media & Society* 23, no. 12 (December 2021): 3593–3615.

[50] David Arditi, *Itake-Over: The Recording Industry in the Streaming Era*, 2nd ed. (London: Lexington Books, 2020), 8.

[51] Lee Marshall, '"Let's Keep Music Special. F—Spotify": On-Demand Streaming and the Controversy over Artist Royalties', *Creative Industries Journal* 8, no. 2 (July 2015): 177–189; Robert Prey, Marc Esteve Del Valle, and Leslie Zwerwer, 'Platform Pop: Disentangling Spotify's Intermediary Role in the Music Industry', *Information, Communication & Society* 25, no. 1 (January 2022): 74–92; Rasmus Fleischer,

28 Digital Flows

highly prominent in media discourse and everyday interaction with hip hop music in the US and Europe. Well-publicized statements by founder Daniel Ek and debates over artist royalties often provide useful starting points for academic investigation. Despite its prevalence in certain places, however, it is worth remembering that Spotify and streaming are not synonyms. Many other streaming services provide national alternatives, offer various functions, and are experienced differently by listeners. A notable outsider is SoundCloud,[52] which has gained notoriety for helping the development of a particular genre of hip hop and which I address in the next chapter.

In the streaming era, hip hop as a genre has held a major presence among all genres of music as undoubtedly one of, if not *the* most, popular. Industry statistics are unreliable and incomplete but provide useful indications of its prevalence. In 2014 in the US, the media research firm Nielsen placed the category dubbed R&B/Hip-Hop the second largest genre by total consumption (behind Rock, which subsumes metal), but already the most-streamed genre.[53] In mid-2017, Nielsen saw R&B/Hip-Hop surge to the top spot, cornering a quarter of the total market and beating Rock, Pop, Country, and their other categories.[54] In 2018, this lead had increased to well over a third, 37.5 per cent, of all on-demand audio streams: three in every eight streamed tracks labelled hip hop (or hip hop-adjacent).[55] The same year, all of Spotify's most streamed artists made hip hop music of one variety or another.[56] Focusing solely on the US market may slightly overstate hip hop's prominence: IFPI's 2019 survey of 34,000 people in twenty-one countries reported hip hop/rap/trap in fourth place behind pop, rock, and oldies (though around a quarter of young people across the globe report it as their favourite genre).[57] In any case, it is clear

---

'Universal Spotification? The Shifting Meanings of "Spotify" as a Model for the Media Industries', *Popular Communication* 19, no. 1 (January 2021): 14–25.

[52] Ian Dunham, 'SoundCloud Rap: An Investigation of Community and Consumption Models of Internet Practices', *Critical Studies in Media Communication* 39, no. 2 (March 2022): 107–126.

[53] Nielsen Music, *2014 Nielsen Music Report* (The Nielsen Company, 2014), 2, https://www.nielsen.com/wp-content/uploads/sites/3/2019/04/nielsen-2014-year-end-music-report-us-1.pdf. Note that Nielsen's audience measurement methods have been disputed by Jennifer Hessler, at least in the domain of television ratings between 1980 and 1995. Jennifer Hessler, 'Peoplemeter Technologies and the Biometric Turn in Audience Measurement', *Television & New Media* 22, no. 4 (May 2021): 400–419.

[54] Nielsen Music, *Mid-Year Report U.S. 2017* (The Nielsen Company, 2017), 14, https://training.nielsen.com/wp-content/uploads/sites/3/2019/04/music-us-mid-year-report-2017.pdf.

[55] Nielsen Music, *Mid-Year Report U.S. 2018* (The Nielsen Company, 2018), 30, https://www.nielsen.com/wp-content/uploads/sites/3/2019/04/us-midyear-music-report-2018.pdf.

[56] Drake, Post Malone, and XXXTentacion are widely considered to be hip hop artists. I include artists combining hip hop with other Black music styles in the Latin music context: J Balvin in this instance. Ed Sheeran is more likely thought of as a pop artist, but both J Balvin and Ed Sheeran regularly rap and have released collaboration albums with hip hop artists.

[57] IFPI, *Music Listening 2019: A Look at How Recorded Music Is Enjoyed around the World* (IFPI, 2019), 15, https://www.ifpi.org/wp-content/uploads/2020/07/Music-Listening-2019-1.pdf.

that hip hop as a recorded genre of music has major audiences around the world, retaining (and gaining) significant popularity alongside the growth of streaming as a format.

The dominance of streaming has been claimed to cause a range of changes in how music is produced, accessed, and used. There are many academic research projects dedicated to studying streaming platforms and their effects on music culture. Some of the major developments associated with streaming have been addressed by David Hesmondhalgh, who urges critical reflection and investigation rather than assuming that streaming has precipitated entirely new practices of engaging with recorded music.[58] Anxieties abound, for example, concerning the relationship of streaming to attention, user choice, and the quality of listening experiences.[59] David Arditi makes the point that streaming is an economic model resembling a wider development in capitalism towards near-constant, endless consumption.[60]

Meanwhile, other strands of inquiry have focused on accelerated cycles of production,[61] with hip hop a particularly important case in point. Artists have been criticized for churning out large bodies of cookie-cutter material. Media articles have taken aim at trap music in particular for releasing long albums of short, repetitive songs: musically uninspired but well-suited to the model that streaming services demand.[62] If my use of the word 'demand' seems excessive, it is worth highlighting Daniel Ek's comment that sustaining a professional career in recorded music is 'about putting the work in', advising artists to create 'a continuous engagement with their fans'.[63] These statements place the responsibility for artists' financial sustainability purely

---

[58] Hesmondhalgh, 'Is Music Streaming Bad for Musicians?'.

[59] David Hesmondhalgh, 'Streaming's Effects on Music Culture: Old Anxieties and New Simplifications', *Cultural Sociology* 16, no.1 (June 2021).

[60] David Arditi, *Streaming Culture: Subscription Platforms And The Unending Consumption Of Culture* (Bingley: Emerald Group Publishing, 2021).

[61] Jeremy Wade Morris, 'Music Platforms and the Optimization of Culture', *Social Media + Society* 6, no. 3 (July 2020): 2. For a point of comparison with the broader content creator economy (of which musicians are now arguably a part), see Arturo Arriagada and Francisco Ibáñez, ' "You Need At Least One Picture Daily, If Not, You're Dead": Content Creators and Platform Evolution in the Social Media Ecology', *Social Media + Society* 6, no. 3 (July 2020), doi:10.1177/2056305120944624.

[62] Though exacerbated in the streaming era, hip hop has previously been accused of bloated releases. Memories of the heyday of CDs vary, however: music critic Alexis Petridis suggests that certain 'rappers confused quantity with quality in the CD era, when every hip-hop album came stretched out to a disc's maximum playing time', whereas culture writer Adam Aziz comments that a 2021 twenty-minute album 'harked back to a golden era of rap when shorter albums were commonplace and quality was prioritized over quantity'. Alexis Petridis, 'Kendrick Lamar: Mr Morale & the Big Steppers Review', *The Guardian*, 13 May 2022, https://www.theguardian.com/music/2022/may/13/kendrick-lamar-mr-morale-the-big-stepp ers-review; Adam Aziz, 'The Coming Battle over Rap Album Lengths', *Andscape* (blog), 1 October 2021, https://andscape.com/features/the-coming-battle-over-rap-album-lengths/.

[63] Stuart Dredge, 'Spotify CEO Talks Covid-19, Artist Incomes and Podcasting (Interview)', *Music Ally*, 30 July 2020, https://musically.com/2020/07/30/spotify-ceo-talks-covid-19-artist-incomes-and-podcast ing-interview/.

30 Digital Flows

on producing cultural products on Ek's platform's terms. The system is thus one where artists' ability to sustain a successful career relies on generating significant value for streaming platforms and receiving a minute percentage of the overall revenue. The hip hop producer Birocratic eloquently described this to me as a 'hypercapitalist' model. Many artists have spoken publicly about feeling pressure to constantly create and release music, compared to earlier eras of carefully crafted, complete creative works. This surely involves some mythologizing of prior decades—for example, in its heyday Motown Records was modelled on the automobile industry's assembly line, rapidly producing highly marketable records[64]—but it may be that certain artistic freedoms have been curtailed by the external demands of a more precarious and fast-paced distribution market.

Yet hip hop has kept afloat of these trends. It boasted wide popularity when many of the technological and cultural changes to how music is accessed and listened to took place over the 2000s and 2010s. Throughout these decades, it has only become ever more popular, and some form of the audience excitement around 'Rapper's Delight' can still be seen accompanying new releases today. Granted, such a response looks different: far less calling radio stations or purchasing vinyl takes place, but many will enthusiastically tap or scroll through a streaming platform to access the hottest hip hop hits. Since the genre has not been harmed by technocultural developments in music consumption, and even took centre-stage in the streaming era, I suspect there is something about the music and its typical cultural circulation that lends itself so well to this format. Why are hip hop and streaming such a good fit?

Hip Hop's Cultural Charm Online: Borrowing, Exchange, and Sharing

In Chapter 1, I mentioned how sharing sits at the core of hip hop culture. Justin Williams' work provides a useful precedent for seeing *borrowing* at the heart of many of hip hop's creative practices. Williams' theory is fundamentally a text-based approach, tracing references, quotations, and samples between different performances, verses, and tracks: hence, forms of *intertextuality*. Borrowing is not an uncontroversial term given the histories of white appropriation of Black creative expression (as I explore in Chapter 6). However, it mostly serves to recognize that hip hop aesthetics centre around

---

[64] Suzanne E. Smith, *Dancing in the Street: Motown and the Cultural Politics of Detroit* (Cambridge, MA: Harvard University Press, 2001), 103–107.

using pre-existing materials to create something new, and thereby expand the total body of creative work associated with the culture.[65] Using a prescient turn of phrase to introduce this idea, Williams comments that 'hip-hop music celebrates and flaunts its "open source" culture'.[66]

Mary Fogarty's research on breaking makes a similar observation. Hip hop dance practices highlight the significance of *exchange* at the level of musical tastes and values, for instance through discourse on what beats might best accompany a breaking cypher.[67] Hip hop exchanges also take place more literally through the transfer of original media such as videotapes.[68] The local distribution of mixtapes among a given community serves as another useful example of sharing among the culture. A third sense in which hip hop emphasizes exchange takes the form of cross-cultural intermediation, as examined by Jason Ng in the Asia-Pacific region.[69] The same line of thinking informs Mark Katz's view of hip hop as a model for fostering global connections and even diplomatic relations.[70]

In André Sirois' work on hip hop DJs, the term 'exchange' refers to processes of communal participation and creative reuse.[71] Socioeconomic factors underlie such practices, at least historically: Harrison and Arthur highlight that, 'emerging from a context of scarcity, hip hop promotes borrowing, sharing, and above all else creative renovation'.[72] Malcolm James' study of grime videos on YouTube (alongside reggae and jungle, Black music traditions antecedent to and adjacent to hip hop) concludes that principles of sharing resist dominant neoliberal social norms. In these sonic cultures, 'mutuality, care and gifting operate as alternatives to cruelty, property ownership and privatization'.[73]

There is also more in common between peer-to-peer sharing and hip hop than initially meets the ear. Sampling, a key creative principle of hip hop

---

[65] Margie Borschke, *This Is Not a Remix: Piracy, Authenticity and Popular Music* (New York and London: Bloomsbury Publishing, 2017).

[66] Justin A. Williams, *Rhymin' and Stealin': Musical Borrowing in Hip-Hop* (Ann Arbor: University of Michigan Press, 2013), 1.

[67] Mary Fogarty, 'Sharing Hip-Hop Dance: Rethinking Taste in Cross-Cultural Exchanges of Music', in *Situating Popular Musics: IASPM 16th International Conference Proceedings*, ed. Ed Montana and Carlo Nardi (Umeå, Sweden: IASPM, 2011), 127–131.

[68] Mary Fogarty, 'Breaking Expectations: Imagined Affinities in Mediated Youth Cultures', *Continuum* 26, no. 3 (June 2012): 449–462.

[69] Jason Ng, 'Connecting Asia-Pacific Hip-Hop: The Role of the Cross-Cultural Intermediary' (PhD diss., Monash University, 2019).

[70] Mark Katz, *Build: The Power of Hip Hop Diplomacy in a Divided World* (Oxford, New York: Oxford University Press, 2019).

[71] André Sirois, *Hip Hop DJs and the Evolution of Technology: Cultural Exchange, Innovation, and Democratization* (New York: Peter Lang, 2016).

[72] Anthony Kwame Harrison and Craig E. Arthur, 'Hip-Hop Ethos', *Humanities* 8, no. 1 (March 2019): 7.

[73] Malcolm James, *Sonic Intimacy: Reggae Sound Systems, Jungle Pirate Radio and Grime YouTube Music Videos* (New York: Bloomsbury Publishing Inc, 2021), 117.

32 Digital Flows

production, is in itself an act of creative reuse. In the contemporary period, sampling more often than not relies upon the digital extraction and alteration of audio files. This exists alongside the widespread use of unlicensed audio software. In peer-to-peer networks, users provide software for others to download by seeding downloads on torrenting networks. Many of the beatmakers I interviewed nonchalantly suggested it was normal for amateur and aspiring musicians to pirate 'cracked' software like DAWs, plugins, and unlicensed sounds until they can afford them. In my decade working with a digital audio plugin developer, the number of hip hop producers asking for software licenses in exchange for artist endorsements or social media promotion indicates that the expectation of trading resources persists at every level of professionalization.

I want to draw these lines of thinking together to suggest that hip hop is not only a participatory culture but essentially a *sharing culture*, and argue that this contributes to its success in adapting to (even influencing) the logic of the platform economy.[74] This is not an uncontroversial argument given that hip hop is a form of expression tightly interwoven with the politics of identity and intersecting forms of marginalization and oppression.[75] I am by no means suggesting that hip hop is universally accessible, open to all, *free for the taking*. But there is undeniably a spirit of generosity and an ethos of sharing that manifest in many of the major practices commonly thought of as hip hop. Hip hop studies has been profoundly influenced by this characteristic, positioning ideas of sampling and sharing as key to understanding how ideas circulate in the culture.[76] Graffiti is one clear instance of producing publicly accessible art, making creative expression freely visible (leaving aside the political subversion of state or private property).[77] Equally, Kyra Gaunt's work posits that sampling may have a basis in, or commonality with, Black girls' musical games, a form of behavioural sharing and performance that informs public music culture in much the same manner as hip hop.[78]

Ideas of sharing similarly inform thinking about cultural interactions on the internet, first through file-sharing and later through sharing on social

---

[74] Nicholas A. John, *The Age of Sharing* (Cambridge and Malden, MA: Polity, 2017).

[75] Rose, *Black Noise*; Gwendolyn D. Pough, *Check It While I Wreck It: Black Womanhood, Hip-Hop Culture, and the Public Sphere* (Lebanon, NH: Northeastern University Press, 2004); Marc Lamont Hill, *Beats, Rhymes, and Classroom Life: Hip-Hop Pedagogy and the Politics of Identity* (New York: Teachers College Press, 2009).

[76] Nick J. Sciullo, *Communicating Hip-Hop: How Hip-Hop Culture Shapes Popular Culture* (Santa Barbara, CA: Praeger, 2018), 4.

[77] Harrison and Arthur, 'Hip-Hop Ethos', 11.

[78] Kyra Gaunt, *The Games Black Girls Play: Learning the Ropes from Double-Dutch to Hip-Hop* (New York: New York University Press, 2006), 14.

media.[79] Sharing originally referred to the free peer-to-peer transfer of files like MP3s, which I mentioned among early developments of the digital music economy. Recordings are still frequently exchanged in this way, though nowadays this is thought of most prominently in terms of torrenting and/or the alarming music-industry-anathema 'illegal downloads'.[80] Sharing has gradually gained more positive associations thanks to buzzword-like rebranding by the internet's dominant content owners. Commenting on Nicholas John's monograph on the topic, Margie Borschke notes that 'sharing',

> a word with both distributive and communicative meanings, offers a versatile rhetorical framework for making sense of a wide range of participatory practices enabled and encouraged by social media platforms (e.g., sharing your opinions, your photos, links to stories, etc.) and other digital and network technologies and media.

Major social media platforms use the term to refer to both posting original media and signal-boosting existing content. In this context, sharing can be 'both supportive and subversive of hegemonic (digital) culture'.[81] At the broadest level, to share is to contribute to online space. Thus, making a video and uploading it to YouTube is sharing, as is posting the link on Facebook to an assumed audience, and so is retweeting someone else's YouTube link. Sending that same link to a group chat on WhatsApp, Telegram, or Signal could also be called sharing. Remember to like and share!

Much like the hip hop notion of borrowing, sharing, in this definition, can transform media through commentary and recontextualization. In the act of sampling, artists usually make a clear statement on their relationship to the original material.[82] For example, Kanye West's famous 'chipmunk soul'[83] chops demonstrated admiration for the cultural lineage of Black music.[84] By contrast, UK grime's extracts of scornful news commentary often mock

---

[79] Matthew David, *Peer to Peer and the Music Industry: The Criminalization of Sharing* (London: SAGE, 2010); Graham Meikle, *Social Media: Communication, Sharing and Visibility* (New York and London: Routledge, 2016).

[80] The moral panic concerning music piracy reached its peak following the well-known case of Metallica suing Napster over the use of copyrighted material. See, for example, Joanna Demers, *Steal This Music: How Intellectual Property Law Affects Musical Creativity* (Athens: University of Georgia Press, 2006), 2–4.

[81] John, *The Age of Sharing*, 2.

[82] Schloss, *Making Beats*, 13.

[83] L. Burns, A. Woods, and M. Lafrance, 'Sampling and Storytelling: Kanye West's Vocal and Sonic Narratives', in *The Cambridge Companion to the Singer-Songwriter*, ed. K. Williams and J. A. E. Williams (Cambridge: Cambridge University Press, 2016), 169; Jeremy Tatar, 'Injury, Affirmation, and the Disability Masquerade in Ye's "Through the Wire"', *Music Theory Online* 29, no. 2 (June 2023): 1.7.

[84] Williams, *Rhymin' and Stealin'*, 53.

white audiences' ignorance of cultural contexts.[85] Comparably, writing Facebook posts that link to pre-existing content, quoting tweets, and captioning images on Reddit are all forms of making explicit comment on other media.[86] The epitome of making something new by performatively judging something else is the genre of reaction videos, which involve a commentator watching something while providing criticism and responding entertainingly.[87] Hip hop and social media therefore demonstrate similarities as cultures of critical reuse.

Given that hip hop itself prioritizes sharing alongside layers of commentary, it is an ideal fit for the logic of the social media ecosystem. This is only one of many reasons that hip hop experiences such popularity, but until now it has been under-explored. People may feel especially encouraged to circulate music and media in which the expression of values and judgements on prior media is already a key feature.[88] Just as Kanye's cut-up and sped-up samples of Nina Simone show appreciation for and recontextualize her artworks, someone sharing and commenting on the Ye track also contributes to the larger discursive arena around that artefact. Social media encourages the development of layer upon layer of cultural commentary, and something so richly embedded with a similar process of intertextual reference becomes a prime target for posting. As a consequence, hip hop enjoys an astoundingly lively presence on social media platforms as sound, video, and image.

This is both a blessing and a curse for the culture. It is perhaps obvious to suggest that artists, especially up-and-coming creatives, want their work shared and consumed. Hip hop texts teem with cultural critique, as voices, often from the margins of society, provide unique expressions of surviving and thriving. But there are also many dangers associated with such easy shareability. One is quite how easily hip hop can be misused (i.e., reused in undesired ways) or misunderstood (e.g., shared and received in unexpected contexts). These risks expose the original poster of any given media artefact to criticism more readily than in earlier forms of cultural mediation. Another

---

[85] Justin A. Williams, *Brithop: The Politics of UK Rap in the New Century* (Oxford: Oxford University Press, 2021), 15.

[86] Limor Shifman, *Memes in Digital Culture* (Cambridge, MA: MIT Press, 2014), 43.

[87] Yeran Kim, 'Globalization of the Privatized Self-Image: The Reaction Video and Its Attention Economy on YouTube', in *Routledge Handbook of New Media in Asia*, ed. Larissa Hjorth and Olivia Khoo (London and New York: Routledge, 2016), 333–342; Lewis Kennedy, '"I Grew up in Streatham": Rap, Reactions, Comments, and Capital on YouTube'. *London Calling*, 19 May 2020, https://london-calling-iaspm2020.com/lewis-kennedy-independent-scholar-uk/.

[88] Drawing on the critical theories of Jürgen Habermas, Michael Warner's work contends that reflexive commentary, maintained in 'a concatenation of texts through time', are crucial to the circulation of discourse in a public sphere. See Michael Warner, *Publics and Counterpublics* (New York: Zone Books, 2005), 90.

downside is the ephemerality of the social media timeline.[89] A hip hop hit popular today may be forgotten tomorrow.

Furthermore, one of the major debates about the digital media economy has been the reduction of various artistic practices and creative works to a monolithic body of 'content'.[90] With social media platforms economically sustained by attention and advertising revenues, artistic and cultural artefacts come increasingly to be seen as an undifferentiated mass, casting a net to attract the widest possible group of users. Thus any artist who makes anything that can be shared online—hip hop musicians, poets, dancers, graffiti artists, comedians, and livestreamers among them—becomes redefined as a 'content creator'.[91] Creative practitioners rarely like to think of themselves as low-level workers in a quasi-feudal relationship with social media megacorporations.[92] Yet there is currently a significant power imbalance that risks undermining hip hop as a cultural practice when it takes a digitally mediated, share-friendly form.

'Sound bite packaging': Hip Hop and/as Meme Culture

Tricia Rose used the term 'sound bite packaging'[93] to refer to hip hop's concision and catchiness, its ability to reduce complex local knowledges, along with value judgements, to small units of cultural currency. Griff Rollefson has similarly deployed the vernacular word 'gems', referring to miniature creative artefacts—turns of phrase, samples, dance steps—that express critical knowledge in a specific context or from a particular viewpoint.[94] These

---

[89] Brady Robards et al., 'Remembering Through Facebook: Mediated Memory and Intimate Digital Traces', in *Digital Intimate Publics and Social Media*, ed. Amy Shields Dobson, Brady Robards, and Nicholas Carah (Cham: Springer International Publishing, 2018), 77–87. Regarding the impermanence and precarity of hip hop archives in less-connected communities like Makhanda, South Africa, see Alette Schoon, '"Makhanda Forever?": Pirate Internet Infrastructure and the Ephemeral Hip Hop Archive in South Africa', in 'It's Where You're @: Hip Hop and the Internet', special issue, *Global Hip Hop Studies* 2 (November 2021): 199–218.

[90] Keith Negus, 'From Creator to Data: The Post-Record Music Industry and the Digital Conglomerates', *Media, Culture & Society* 41, no. 3 (April 2019): 367–384.

[91] Negus, 'From Creator to Data'.

[92] Though notions of informational feudalism are quite popular in vernacular commentary and cultural criticism, Christian Fuchs suggests that monopolistic informational capitalism is a more appropriate framing of the present-day computer technology economy. See Christian Fuchs, *Internet and Society: Social Theory in the Information Age* (New York: Routledge, 2008), 171; M. R. McGuire, 'Crime, Control and the Ambiguous Gifts of Digital Technology', in *The SAGE Handbook of Digital Society*, ed. William Housley et al. (London: SAGE, 2023), 35–54.

[93] Rose, *Black Noise: Rap Music and Black Culture in Contemporary America*, 3.

[94] J. Griffith Rollefson, 'Hip Hop Interpellation: Rethinking Autochthony and Appropriation in Irish Rap', in *Made in Ireland: Studies in Popular Music*, ed. Áine Mangaoang, John O'Flynn, and Lonán Ó Briain (New York and London: Routledge, 2021), 224.

36 Digital Flows

localized expressions typically relate to broader themes of hip hop knowledge that may be more widely understood or acknowledged. Though the neocolonial associations of the term 'gems' are problematic, the precious and valuable knowledges they invoke recalls Imani Perry's work on performance 'tropes', referring to intertextual lineages of Black music and expressive culture.[95] What might be a small feature of one artist's creative expression becomes taken up and transformed by others, as in the case of a travelling lyric, an iconic sound, or even a hairstyle.

An example is instructive, by way of comparison to the social web's conventions of sharing and transforming cultural knowledge. While sound is often the primary domain people associate with hip hop, studies of the web typically emphasize the visual and textual,[96] and so I focus here on image. It is a truism to state that clothing, fashion, and style are important to hip hop. Consider the commercial relationships between hip hop stars and sportswear brands, or the iconic imagery of high-top sneakers, tan boots, caps, jewellery, polo shirts, and backpacks. Just as much careful attention is given to how hip hop artists wear their hair.[97] Hair is a key domain of visual expression in hip hop, not least because of the politicization of natural Black hair and Rastafarian influences.[98] And to drive home the point that referentiality in hip hop is not purely sonic, hair provides an obvious way of representing influence and heritage.

Ol' Dirty Bastard's *Return to the 36 Chambers: The Dirty Version* has become an iconic record, not only for the album's post-Wu-Tang impact but also for the artwork,[99] featuring a fictionalized public assistance card where the rapper appears off-centre, head tilted, wearing spiked braids. Since then, other artists have adopted a similar fashion inspired by the look, twisting their locs up from the scalp and the top of the neck roughly towards the crown of the head. One such example is rapper 21 Savage, who in a 2017 ESPN interview appeared with freeform dreads. Whether a knowing allusion or passing

[95] I. Perry, *Prophets of the Hood: Politics and Poetics in Hip Hop* (Durham, NC: Duke University Press, 2004), 33–38.

[96] Jeremy Wade Morris, 'Hearing the Past: The Sonic Web from MIDI to Music Streaming', in *The SAGE Handbook of Web History*, by Niels Brügger and Ian Milligan (London: SAGE Publications Ltd, 2019), 492.

[97] See, for example, the connections between hip hop, diaspora cultures, and barbershops in Christopher Vito, 'Shop Talk: The Influence of Hip Hop on Filipino-American Barbers in San Diego', *Global Hip Hop Studies* 1, no. 1 (June 2020): 13–23.

[98] Chang, *Can't Stop Won't Stop*, 23–26; Ayana D. Byrd and Lori L. Tharps, *Hair Story: Untangling the Roots of Black Hair in America*, rev. ed. (New York: St Martin's Griffin, 2014).

[99] *The New Yorker*'s eulogy for designer Brett Kilroe described the album cover as 'iconic', while Atlantic Records' Creative Director placed it among his favourite '90s album covers. See Alexandra Schwartz, 'Portrait of a Friendship in the Face of Cancer', *The New Yorker*, 31 May 2016, http://www.newyorker.com/culture/photo-booth/portrait-of-a-friendship-in-the-face-of-cancer; Richard 'Treats' Dryden, 'Greg Burke's 10 Favorite Rap Album Covers of the '90s', *Complex*, 29 January 2014, https://www.complex.com/style/2014/01/greg-burkes-favorite-rap-album-covers-of-the-90s/.

The Digital Streaming Era 37

Figure 2.2 21 Savage supervillain meme reposted by Justin Bieber, from Instagram

similarity to ODB, his look references a legacy of spiked natural hair—akin to a soundbite, a gem, or a trope—in hip hop. This example also demonstrates how internet culture adopts aspects of borrowing and versioning. In the TV interview, 21 Savage sat in front of a city skyline, grinning and occasionally rubbing his hands. One viewer screenshotted the image and posted it with an accompanying caption suggesting the rapper resembled a villain announcing his dastardly plan in a superhero movie. The Twitter post quickly went viral.[100] Others compared the rapper's look to Edward Scissorhands, *Phineas and Ferb*'s Dr Doofenshmirtz, and *The Simpsons*' Sideshow Bob, reinforcing the socially embedded relationship between unkempt hair and villainy. Many others tweaked the caption, with reference to Batman and Gotham, or imagined a time limit—21 days, of course—until this fictional villain might execute his masterstroke. Pop megastar Justin Bieber reposted it on Instagram to over a million likes, cropping the username of the original captioner out, and adding: 'hillarious [sic]' (Figure 2.2).

---

[100] For a sense of the meme's spread, see, for example, Sidney Madden, '21 Savage Super Villain Memes Take Over the Internet', *XXL Magazine*, 10 March 2017, https://www.xxlmag.com/21-savage-meme-taking-over-internet/; Adam Roper, 'The Internet Can't Stop LOLing at This 21 Savage Supervillain Meme', *Gossip On This* (blog), 11 March 2017, https://gossiponthis.com/2017/03/10/21-savage-supervillain-meme-viral-twitter-facebook-social-media-internet-espn-highly-questionable/; Ben Dandridge-Lemco, 'The Internet Loves This Picture Of 21 Savage As A Batman Supervillian', *The FADER*, 9 March 2017, https://www.thefader.com/2017/03/09/21-savage-batman-gotham-supervillian-meme.

38 Digital Flows

In internet culture, the conventional term for any instance of versioning is 'meme'.[101] Just like hip hop's ability to recontextualize local and specific forms of expressive knowledge, the social web revolves around shareable, iterative chunks of cultural commentary like images, text posts, and short videos. It might seem disrespectful to compare hip hop's practices of borrowing, reference, and reuse to internet memes, since they are sometimes dismissed as relatively insignificant, short-lived, frivolous online in-jokes.[102] But to think of memes this way is to understate their importance as a contemporary communicative norm.

Internet memes have given rise to a rich body of scholarly thought with earlier links to (now largely defunct) memetics and, more recently, remix culture, digital communication, and participatory media studies. Definitions of internet memes variously attend to the similarity, intertextuality, replicability, circulation, appropriation, discursivity, virality, and participatory nature of digital artefacts (items, objects, texts) in specific contexts (network societies, public spheres, digital communities, internet infrastructures).[103] Rather than stick by a rigorous definition, I adopt a relatively vernacular approach to memes, trying to take them on the admittedly inconsistent and shifting terms that many internet users do. For it is the human agency involved in meme creation and sharing practices—emphasized by work on participatory culture[104]—that matters most to how hip hop thrives online. Memes are digital instances of referentiality with in-built, context-dependent, cultural commentary. They can manifest variously as political activism,[105] as creative and humorous linguistic play,[106] as displays of flagrantly racist and neocolonial power,[107] and more.

---

[101] Shifman, *Memes in Digital Culture*; Anastasia Denisova, *Internet Memes and Society: Social, Cultural, and Political Contexts* (New York: Routledge, 2019).

[102] Shifman, *Memes in Digital Culture*, 2.

[103] Shifman, 41; Victoria Esteves and Graham Meikle, '"Look @ This Fukken Doge": Internet Memes and Remix Cultures', in *The Routledge Companion to Alternative and Community Media*, ed. Chris Atton (Abingdon and New York: Routledge, 2015), 564; Denisova, *Internet Memes and Society*, 10; Patrick Davison, 'The Language of Internet Memes', in *The Language of Internet Memes* (New York: NYU Press, 2012), 122; Laine Nooney and Laura Portwood-Stacer, 'One Does Not Simply: An Introduction to the Special Issue on Internet Memes', *Journal of Visual Culture* 13, no. 3 (December 2014): 249; Bradley E. Wiggins, *The Discursive Power of Memes in Digital Culture: Ideology, Semiotics, and Intertextuality* (New York: Routledge, 2019), 11.

[104] Henry Jenkins and colleagues have argued repeatedly against the assumed passivity of terms like 'viral', and the gene metaphors, since people play active roles in spreading digital content. See Henry Jenkins, Sam Ford, and Joshua Green, *Spreadable Media: Creating Value and Meaning in a Networked Culture* (New York and London: New York University Press, 2013), 16–23. For a productive counterargument emphasizing corporate control over user content and retaining ideas of virality, see Paula Clare Harper, 'Unmute This: Circulation, Sociality, and Sound in Viral Media' (PhD diss., Columbia University, 2019), 9–27.

[105] Denisova, *Internet Memes and Society*, 54–171.

[106] Camilla Vásquez and Erhan Aslan, '"Cats Be Outside, How about Meow": Multimodal Humor and Creativity in an Internet Meme', *Journal of Pragmatics* 171 (January 2021): 101–117.

[107] Lisa Nakamura, '"I WILL DO EVERYthing That Am Asked": Scambaiting, Digital Show-Space, and the Racial Violence of Social Media', *Journal of Visual Culture* 13, no. 3 (December 2014): 257–274.

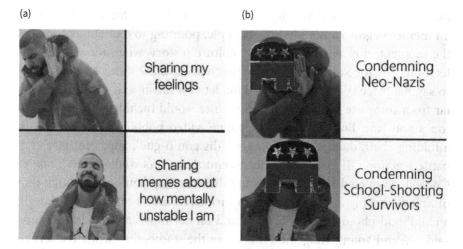

Figure 2.3 Examples of Drakeposting, from Know Your Meme
Source: Know Your Meme, 'Drakeposting: Image Gallery', *Know Your Meme*, accessed 6 July 2023, https://knowyourmeme.com/memes/drakeposting/photos

The term meme is itself a meme of sorts. It was coined by ethologist Richard Dawkins to refer to a cultural idea that spreads and mutates over time: a symbolic parallel to the biological 'gene', with a touch of 'mimesis'.[108] However, the word was adopted in digital popular culture to describe trends in discourse, and later any kind of viral media phenomenon: a particular image format, a video trope, or a craze. By now, uses of the word have little in common with Dawkins' original writing.[109] Moreover, an academic distinction between memes and meme formats[110]—individual instances of a broader trend, and the trend itself—has become somewhat eroded in contemporary online parlance. Hence, Drake's 'Hotline Bling' image template showing preference for one thing over another (sometimes called Drakeposting) and any given instance of it are both, simply, memes (Figure 2.3).

Memes express aspects of identity, indicate personal values, and make sociopolitical commentary. The Drake example is slightly outdated, though it is telling that these screenshots of the rapper's dance moves—stills from the 'Hotline Bling' video—so pertinently capture users' judgements about various aspects of everyday behaviour, culture, and politics. Hip hop, specifically its most popular and internationally recognized representative in the mid-2010s, became a cultural touchstone for the sharing of cultural commentary

---

[108] Shifman, *Memes in Digital Culture*, 9–10.
[109] Esteves and Meikle, '"Look @ This Fukken Doge"', 562–564.
[110] Shifman, *Memes in Digital Culture*, 41.

40 Digital Flows

through these reproducible digital forms. Indeed, Ryan Milner's 2016 book on memes begins with a hip hop example, pointing to digital mutations of the moment, now enshrined in pop culture history, when Kanye West interrupted Taylor Swift's acceptance speech at the 2009 Video Music Awards to say his piece.[111] In addition to 'I'ma let you finish' and Drakeposting, a far from complete list of hip hop in memes would include: a dancer in Jim Jones and Ron Browz' 'Pop Champagne' video bobbing into frame with a folding chair, dubbed—troublingly—'dis gon b gud'; Supa Hot Fire's rap battle reaction GIF, aka 'I'm about to end this man's whole career'; rapper Conceited's pursed-lips GIF and still (also from rap battle contexts); a shot of Xzibit cracking up in laughter with various recursive captions ('yo dawg'); a childhood photo of Cardi B, one hand on her hips, captioned 'my mama said . . .'; and Young Thug and Lil Durk in the studio, the former concerned and focused (seemingly on a computer), the latter watching on.[112] More will be made every day.

In audiovisual form, hip hop breathes life into a range of dance crazes amassed over YouTube channels, Instagram profiles, and TikTok hashtags. They also collide in a less-than-equitable way with video game platforms, which rapidly feed into the new media ecosystem.[113] Hip hop and internet memes (in their current instantiation and flow) both share a heritage in Black and Afrodiasporic oral culture.[114] In making this comparison, I aim not to replace but to add to the historical record that hip hop has hosted aspects of a meme culture since before internet memes existed. It is no coincidence that many of the most popular, wittiest, and politically urgent producers of new media are Black creatives providing perfectly honed commentary on—and thereby enhancing—various cultural artefacts with extreme shareable potential. Yet Black social media users are disproportionately compensated and recognized for their contributions, as demonstrated by the Bieber crop

---

[111] Ryan M. Milner, *The World Made Meme: Public Conversations and Participatory Media* (Cambridge, MA: MIT Press, 2016).

[112] The list goes on. For one example, Justin Burton briefly mentions the 'Drake the type' format. See Justin D. Burton, *Posthuman Rap* (New York: Oxford University Press, 2017), 65.

[113] Wayne Marshall, 'Social Dance in the Age of (Anti-)Social Media', *Journal of Popular Music Studies* 31, no. 4 (December 2019): 3–15; Cienna Davis, 'Digital Blackface and the Troubling Intimacies of TikTok Dance Challenges', in *TikTok Cultures in the United States*, ed. Trevor Boffone (London and New York: Routledge, 2022), 28–38.

[114] André Brock, *Distributed Blackness: African American Cybercultures* (New York: New York University Press, 2020), 203–208; Sarah Florini, *Beyond Hashtags: Racial Politics and Black Digital Networks* (New York: New York University Press, 2019), 17–19; Catherine Knight Steele, 'The Digital Barbershop: Blogs and Online Oral Culture Within the African American Community', *Social Media + Society* 2, no. 4 (October 2016); Catherine Steele and Jessica Lu, 'Defying Death: Black Joy as Resistance Online', in *A Networked Self and Birth, Life, Death*, ed. Zizi Papacharissi (New York: Routledge, 2018), 146–150.

The Digital Streaming Era **41**

above.[115] The vast, varied, and separate spaces that comprise the social web make it difficult to trace the originators of memes: even where sites like Know Your Meme attempt to pin down the origins of particular viral trends, there is the risk of obscuring multiple origins and citing only what lingers and can be referenced. The appearance of cultural authority and codification are risks associated with how the internet is historicized more broadly.[116]

The creative and transformative reuse of material now forms a major part of digital interaction, especially on social media sites, and thereafter among various communities: online collectives, instant message group chats, in-person sharing of media, and so on. Just as memes can be shared, so can music. The infrastructure of streaming platforms trivializes the sharing of songs.[117] One or two clicks of a button or, more commonly, taps on a smartphone screen, will open a share menu from any track on most of the major platforms and link to the user's preferred forum: a social media profile, an instant message, or a communication platform. Hip hop has thrived in this context because it has pervaded profiles and platforms since the birth of this technological feature. Hip hop, and Black popular culture more generally, is already entrenched in the discursive contexts of the social web, with individuals keen to offer their opinions in response. Often, the sounds and lyrics of hip hop tracks themselves encourage sharing (as I address in Chapter 3). This has often been the case throughout the history of hip hop music, but now the platforms have adapted to facilitate the circulation of the culture with ease.

Platformized Hip Hop Music Consumption

The YouTube music video era has had knock-on effects on the format in which music is consumed. In particular, critics have focused attention on the so-called (and typically exaggerated) 'death of the album'.[118] There are broad

---

[115] Catherine Knight Steele, 'Black Bloggers and Their Varied Publics: The Everyday Politics of Black Discourse Online', *Television & New Media* 19, no. 2 (February 2018): 112–127; Catherine Knight Steele, *Digital Black Feminism* (New York: New York University Press, 2021), 140; Francesca Sobande, *The Digital Lives of Black Women in Britain* (Cham: Palgrave Macmillan, 2020), 65–100; Marisa Parham, 'Sample | Signal | Strobe: Haunting, Social Media, and Black Digitality', in *Debates in the Digital Humanities 2019*, ed. Matthew K. Gold and Lauren F. Klein (Minneapolis and London: University of Minnesota Press, 2019), 101–122.

[116] Whitney Phillips, *This Is Why We Can't Have Nice Things: Mapping the Relationship Between Online Trolling and Mainstream Culture* (Cambridge, MA: MIT Press, 2015), 139; Ben T. Pettis, 'Know Your Meme and the Homogenization of Web History', *Internet Histories* 6, no. 3 (August 2021): 1–17.

[117] Anja N Hagen and Marika Lüders, 'Social Streaming? Navigating Music as Personal and Social', *Convergence: The International Journal of Research into New Media Technologies* 23, no. 6 (December 2017): 643–659.

[118] Adam Behr, 'The Album at 70: A Format in Decline?', *The Conversation*, 11 July 2018, http://theconversation.com/the-album-at-70-a-format-in-decline-99581; Kelley Newman, 'The End of an Era: The Death

concerns about the predominance of individual songs and the sustainability of traditional album cycles in the age of streaming. Instead, playlists take centre stage, whether curated by staff at a streaming service, assembled algorithmically, or created by individual users.[119] Though playlists have various functions, and essentially work like any other data container (think of a folder storing files), the playlists most troubling to critics are groupings of individual songs from several artists: ready-made, custom-built compilations that can span hours or even days. Playlists are usually themed according to particular criteria: genre, era, mood, intensity, BPM, and so on.[120] Given how crucial playlists have become to the architecture of most streaming platforms, many have queried whether artists' release schedules have been affected, albums (and songs) are being written differently, and playlists might constrain how listeners discover music.[121] In a system where songs can be easily extracted from the context of a broader album, and find their way to all manner of new contexts, it is understandable to worry about the artistic status of the conventional album.

However, there has never really been a conventional album, a form spanning from the sprawling progressive rock concept albums of the 1970s to split records by two (or more) independent punk bands. Even in the pre-streaming popular music industry, hit singles were often what made most artists' names, and what were promoted widely enough to sell albums (where listeners might be dismayed by a number of 'filler' tracks).[122] Hip hop has its own unique format: mixtapes, which traditionally acted as independently produced, locally distributed samplers of an artist's output. These could build hype for a rapper or producer, with music released more rapidly than waiting to record a major label-backed album.[123] As Jared Ball points out, mixtapes provide a low-cost way of supporting local community organizing and underground media which bypasses traditional industry gatekeepers (and undermines capitalist logics).[124]

---

of the Album and Its Unintended Effects', *Gnovis Blog* (blog), 28 February 2014, https://gnovisjournal.geo rgetown.edu/the-gnovis-blog/the-end-of-an-era-the-death-of-the-album-and-its-unintended-effects/.

[119] Tiziano Bonini and Alessandro Gandini, '"First Week Is Editorial, Second Week Is Algorithmic": Platform Gatekeepers and the Platformization of Music Curation', *Social Media + Society* 5, no. 4 (October 2019).

[120] Anja Nylund Hagen, 'The Playlist Experience: Personal Playlists in Music Streaming Services', *Popular Music and Society* 38, no. 5 (October 2015): 625–645.

[121] Hesmondhalgh, 'Streaming's Effects on Music Culture'.

[122] Mark Harvey, 'Politics and Power in the Record Industry: The Beatles, the Beach Boys, and the Album as Art Form', *Musicology Australia* 38, no. 2 (July 2016): 157.

[123] Anthony Kwame Harrison, '"Cheaper than a CD, Plus We Really Mean It": Bay Area Underground Hip Hop Tapes as Subcultural Artefacts', *Popular Music* 25, no. 2 (May 2006): 283–301.

[124] Jared A. Ball, *I Mix What I Like!: A Mixtape Manifesto* (Oakland, CA: AK Press, 2011), 138–140.

The Digital Streaming Era   **43**

Now, given that the most immediate way musicians release new work is to upload digital files to a streaming platform, hip hop artists (as a subset of popular musicians) have considered how their music would best suit the forum.[125] It may not be beneficial, financially or otherwise, to record full albums in this context. A hit single, with plenty of potential for placements on popular playlists, will often produce more tangible benefits. Musicians and labels alike have taken issue with the opaque decision-making and algorithmic sorting that determines how songs are playlisted, which is a fair concern given many artists' reliance on recording revenues from streams.[126] The 'black box' image of streaming platforms and the corporations maintaining them certainly does not help garner support for this system.[127] Still, it is possible that, due to the increasing power given to proprietary algorithms in the curation of music on streaming platforms, new and independent artists face fewer traditional gatekeepers like talent scouts and radio programmers compared to the music industry of previous decades. The platforms serve gatekeeping functions instead, constraining creative activities to suit their terms.[128]

There are clear instances of hip hop artists making tracks to fit the contours of streaming. This might be partly based on the not-so-secret industry knowledge that Spotify counts one stream as any listening period of thirty seconds or more.[129] To make money, artists therefore need to hold listeners' attention for at least half a minute. While research of an appropriate scale and adequate methodology is still in progress, it seems like this payout policy has led to more songs positioning a catchy chorus or hook earlier in the track, avoiding lengthy introductions, and eschewing interludes clocking in under the thirty-second time window. There may also be a tendency towards shorter songs overall.[130] Mainstream hip hop does well in this context, for it has long adopted pop song structures and gravitated towards three-to-four-minute runtimes. Obvious losers in this format include short skits and long-form works: the fifteen-minute cut of 'Rapper's Delight', for example, alongside

---

[125] Jeremy Wade Morris, Robert Prey, and David B. Nieborg, 'Engineering Culture: Logics of Optimization in Music, Games, and Apps', *Review of Communication* 21, no. 2 (April 2021): 164–166.

[126] Robert Prey, 'Locating Power in Platformization: Music Streaming Playlists and Curatorial Power', *Social Media + Society* 6, no. 2 (April 2020): 2–4.

[127] Maria Eriksson et al., *Spotify Teardown: Inside the Black Box of Streaming Music* (Cambridge, MA: MIT Press, 2019).

[128] Bonini and Gandini, ' "First Week Is Editorial, Second Week Is Algorithmic" '; Dunham, 'SoundCloud Rap'; Holly Rogers, ' "Welcome to Your World": YouTube and the Reconfiguration of Music's Gatekeepers', in *YouTube and Music: Online Culture and Everyday Life*, ed. Holly Rogers, Joana Freitas, and João Francisco Porfírio (London: Bloomsbury Academic, 2023), 1–38.

[129] Thomas Hodgson, 'Spotify and the Democratisation of Music', *Popular Music* 40, no. 1 (February 2021): 10.

[130] Kristopher R. K. Ohlendorf, ' "No Friends in the Industry": The Dominance of Tech Companies on Digital Music', in *Virtual Identities and Digital Culture*, ed. Victoria Kannen and Aaron Langille (New York: Routledge, 2023), 235–236.

44 Digital Flows

other genres such as jazz fusion and most of the Western European art music tradition. In many ways, streaming is designed for the consumption of popular genres like hip hop, where there is significant interest in hit singles with engaging sounds, dynamic opening sections, and catchy hooks. Rap music in particular has often prioritized memorable vocals, loop-based beats with constant forward motion, and attention-drawing punchlines.

If songs are getting shorter, it may be that albums are getting longer. Album charts have been subject to a constant shift over the last few years as industry bodies struggled to shift from a model based on record sales to one based on streams. In the late 2010s, Billboard and RIAA equated 1,500 song streams with one album sale, implying that anyone who buys an album is going to listen to it at least 100 times.[131] As such, the impetus to place more songs on an album, thereby helping it chart higher, sits alongside the incentive to churn out a bunch of playlist-viable songs. Hip hop may be the leading genre in this era partly because it is most pliable to produce a lengthy stream of variable-quality content for constant consumption.

The critical response to Migos' albums *Culture* and *Culture II* is instructive. The group's first record was lauded as 'packed with colour',[132] 'memeable, archetypal Migos, distilled and well-sanded',[133] and most tellingly as a 'taut, infectious, reliable, no-bullshit collection of 12 songs, almost all of which could be singles'.[134] However, reactions to *Culture II* a year later were far less enthusiastic, and most bemoaned an unnecessarily long runtime. It is 'unfocused . . . elongated', with 'commercial-ready performances – as in perfect for any streaming service'.[135] It is 'bloated and boring', comprising 'lengthy songs, unnecessary verses, redundant choruses, and forgettable bridges'.[136] One review opened by positing that 'ever since the chart rules were adjusted to count streams alongside sales, commercially-minded artists have been padding out

---

[131] Steve Collins and Pat O'Grady, 'Off the Charts: The Implications of Incorporating Streaming Data into the Charts', in *Networked Music Cultures: Contemporary Approaches, Emerging Issues*, ed. Raphaël Nowak and Andrew Whelan, Pop Music, Culture and Identity (London: Palgrave Macmillan UK, 2016), 155.

[132] Paul A. Thompson, 'Migos: Culture', *Pitchfork*, 31 January 2017, https://pitchfork.com/reviews/albums/22777-culture/.

[133] Winston Cook-Wilson, 'Review: It's Worth Listening to the Rest of Migos' Culture, Too', *SPIN*, 27 January 2017, https://www.spin.com/2017/01/review-migos-culture-a-story-of-perseverance-tests-the-if-it-aint-broke-dont-fix-it-thesis/.

[134] Christopher R. Weingarten, 'Review: Migos Up Their Game, Take Thrilling Victory Lap on "Culture"', *Rolling Stone* (blog), 26 January 2017, https://www.rollingstone.com/music/music-album-reviews/review-migos-up-their-game-take-thrilling-victory-lap-on-culture-126305/.

[135] Trent Clark, 'Review: Migos' "Culture II" Is an Unfocused, Unworthy Sequel to the Original', *HipHopDX*, 2 February 2018, https://hiphopdx.com/reviews/id.3085/title.review-migos-culture-ii-is-an-unfocused-unworthy-sequel-to-the-original.

[136] Yoh Phillips, 'Migos "Culture II" 1 Listen Album Review', DJBooth, 12 February 2018, https://djbooth.net/features/2018-01-26-migos-culture-ii-album-review.

The Digital Streaming Era **45**

their albums with filler to get those numbers up'.[137] Another noted that Migos promoted a specific playlist on their Spotify artist page which comprised the album back-to-back three times, further trying to game the stream counting system through repeat listens.[138]

Streaming platforms sometimes appear like spaces for the presentation of artworks, with artists offering up their selection of digital goods in the hopes of 'discovery'.[139] Consequently, the relationship between hip hop music and synchronization for other media is changing.[140] Popular artists may be able to rely upon their fanbases listening to their releases directly whereas others seek the placement of songs on playlists to provide support and build an audience. Another route for generating revenue is the extension of the discovery pipeline to relevant TV, film, games, and advertising media corporations. Synchronization licensing can provide significant benefits, providing a direct payout to the artist, airing a given track to a large audience, and steering potential fans back to the streaming platforms for further engagement. The promise of song playlisting for upcoming artists lies partly in the belief that someone who would otherwise never encounter your music might stumble upon a particular track, and that person might be seeking something for the soundtrack of their new hit Netflix show.

The significance of music video has also transformed during the transition to streaming.[141] The popularity of YouTube in the mid-2010s led to serious investments in hip hop music videos, bolstered by promotional campaigns on social media platforms. Many music videos produced today are expensive, extravagant, and culturally significant productions, as I address in Chapter 5. However, the 'golden age' of YouTube videos may be approaching its end. Artists increasingly shoot videos in both horizontal (TV or laptop screen) and vertical (smartphone) orientations. There has also been an increase in the production of visualizers: short loops providing some aesthetically appropriate visual accompaniment but without the expenses and logistical overheads of shooting a full video. These are increasingly embedded within audio streaming platforms, which are keen not to miss out on other modes of mediation that might capture user attention.

---

[137] Davy Reed, 'Migos: "Culture II" Review', *Crack Magazine* (blog), 31 January 2018, https://crackmagazine.net/article/album-reviews/migos-culture-ii/.

[138] Meaghan Garvey, 'Migos: Culture II', *Pitchfork*, 30 January 2018, https://pitchfork.com/reviews/albums/migos-culture-ii/.

[139] Morris, 'Music Platforms and the Optimization of Culture', 2.

[140] Leslie M. Meier, *Popular Music as Promotion: Music and Branding in the Digital Age* (Cambridge and Malden, MA: Polity, 2016), 62–64.

[141] Carol Vernallis, *The Media Swirl: Politics, Audiovisuality, and Aesthetics* (Durham, NC: Duke University Press, 2023), 212.

46   Digital Flows

By the early 2020s, consumption habits shifted towards short-form vertical video-sharing apps—predominantly TikTok, the current global leader, alongside YouTube's imitative Shorts and Instagram's Reels—where audio can be uploaded or reused for all sorts of purposes. Some songs have found significant new leases of life, becoming reborn, on such platforms. Increasingly, songwriters and producers discuss writing *for* TikTok. Dance challenges are a well-known format whereby users record themselves performing a set of intricate dance moves, with hip hop tracks commonly, even typically, featuring as the soundtrack. At launch, TikTok permitted videos of up to fifteen seconds. Later, this grew to a minute, and then three minutes. In early 2022, this was expanded to ten minutes. Still, the emphasis on shorter content lingers (though it varies significantly by video genre), and many hip hop dance videos clock in at around twenty seconds, accompanying a hook or half a verse. Artists are keenly aware of such trends. Some choreograph and perform dances themselves, as in Lil Nas X's now infamous 'yeehaw challenge' in support of 'Old Town Road', or Megan Thee Stallion's promotion for 'Savage'.[142] Consider also Drake's 'Toosie Slide', an explicit collaboration with social media dancers aiming to organically build buzz for the single release. The wild popularity of TikTok, especially among young users, is partly why competing social media and audio streaming platforms are attempting to reproduce its endless-scroll feed interface.

Several hip hop artists have gained their commercial breakthrough due to TikTok dancers using their songs. Many still pursue success through this means. Viewers of dance crazes may be motivated to find tracks in full or explore other songs by any given artist, such that short video sharing now forms a major part of the streaming pipeline. In some ways, this manner of using music bears comparison to TV synchronization. However, prior to agreements with record labels in 2018, processes to recognize copyright on TikTok were ineffective, and misattribution continues to run rife.[143] Now, artists are compensated according to a less-than-transparent algorithm based on the sliver of a stream of any given song featured in a video, scaling with the number of uses in TikTok videos rather than views.[144] Moreover, copyright owners are individually responsible for issuing take-down notices for

---

[142] Melissa Avdeeff, 'Lil Nas X, TikTok, and the Evolution of Music Engagement on Social Networking Sites', in *Virtual Identities and Digital Culture*, ed. Victoria Kannen and Aaron Langille (New York: Routledge, 2023), 226–227; Davis, 'Digital Blackface and the Troubling Intimacies of TikTok Dance Challenges', 28–29.

[143] D. Bondy Valdovinos Kaye et al., 'You Made This? I Made This: Practices of Authorship and (Mis) Attribution on TikTok', *International Journal of Communication* 15 (2021): 3196–3197.

[144] Allan Watson, Joseph B. Watson, and Lou Tompkins, 'Does Social Media Pay for Music Artists? Quantitative Evidence on the Co-Evolution of Social Media, Streaming and Live Music', *Journal of Cultural Economy* 16, no. 1 (January 2023): 35.

unauthorized use of licensed material.[145] In an earlier era of underpaying musicians (and artists more generally), there was a popular joke about being 'paid in exposure'. At present, it is attention, rather than the fractional income gleaned from views and listens, that determines the success of hip hop artists breaking through, a line of thinking that Chapter 3 will advance.

Conclusion

So goes the story of hip hop, media technologies, and the internet. From its very first appearance on record, hip hop has rapidly become a global phenomenon. It was immensely popular in an earlier era of globalizing media economies, as shown by its presence on radio, music television, and record sales. It sparks so much commentary and is used as a form of commentary itself. But it was not until most individuals connecting to the culture were able to voice their opinions and express their preferences among others, to share and to meme via online networks, that it soared to the very forefront of popular music culture.

I have focused in this chapter on the relationships between hip hop music and consumption technologies, especially streaming platforms. This has necessarily meant emphasizing mainstream hip hop in the US at the cost of what hip hop means around the globe and beyond the sonic. There are necessarily international fluctuations in the patterns I outline here. By drawing attention to the most visible, accessible, and pervasive instances of hip hop's digital evolution, I aim to have shown how these cultural flows are backlit by major forces of economic, technological, and social power. It does appear that many streaming services worldwide are adopting similar principles modelled on (for instance) Spotify's success in Europe and North America, not to mention Western platform giants expanding to new territories: to what end is yet to be seen.[146] China has a distinct system although, similarly, media megacorporations like Tencent have concentrated significant power over national music consumption, tying hip hop inexorably to internet technologies with platform-based market logic.

What I have suggested in this chapter is that hip hop began life as an offline form and remained a relatively stable entity that adapted as it migrated to the

---

[145] Melissa K. Avdeeff, 'TikTok, Twitter, and Platform-Specific Technocultural Discourse in Response to Taylor Swift's LGBTQ+ Allyship in "You Need to Calm Down"', *Contemporary Music Review* 40, no. 1 (January 2021): 84.

[146] Spotify, with its vast catalogue of American music, only expanded to India in 2019, and South Korea in 2021.

48 Digital Flows

internet. But as with the vast expansion of cultural activity on the internet throughout the 2000s and 2010s, new practices, conventions, and values associated with hip hop have emerged. There is still a clear basis in the culture that originated it, but there are also aspects of contemporary hip hop that distinctly bear marks of internet culture, born in the contexts of platformization and the attention economy. The next chapter focuses on these developments, homing in on the controversial genre of internet rap emerging from Soundcloud.

3

Internet Rap and Generational Tensions in Hip Hop's SoundCloud Era

'Famous on the Internet'

Introduction

Saturday Night Live's 2020 'Rap Roundtable' sketch stages a fight for the spirit of hip hop.[1] On one side, Queen Latifah (played by Punkie Johnson) and ?uestlove (starring as himself) are guardians of the culture, keen to sustain what the latter calls 'the lyrical tradition of America'. On the other side, the fictional rap duo Xan Mob offer youthful gibberish, from 'yeet' to 'skrt',[2] and mumble impressions of Black slang (see Figure 3.1). By citing the group's record-breaking '3 billion streams' on SoundCloud, the sketch invents Xan Mob with a clear point of reference. Guaplord (Pete Davidson) and $mokecheddathaassgetta (Timothée Chalamet), two skinny young white men with face tattoos and brightly dyed hair, represent the SoundCloud generation of hip hop. Though the host (played by Ego Nwodim) admits that 'the sound has changed', ?uestlove is nothing if not magnanimous, still appreciating 'the party side of hip hop'. 'There's space for all of us', he says. 'Hip hop is constantly evolving and I have respect for y'all doing your own thing'. His patience does not last more than twenty seconds of Xan Mob's song. They give an impromptu performance of a bumping trap track with more 'yeet' and 'skrt' ad-libs, and an exaggerated, full-voiced, '00s Midwest emo-pop vocal a la 'Fall Out Boys [*sic*]' (cited as the group's biggest inspiration). ?uestlove slaps them both and $mokecheddathaassgetta whinily phones his father to come pick them up. The show's argument is clear: young rap stars who blow up online are inane, incoherent, and inauthentic, making viral pop music with a complete disregard for hip hop's origins.

---

[1] *Rap Roundtable—SNL*, YouTube, 13 December 2020, https://www.youtube.com/watch?v=3sxR Aeh8f7w.

[2] One transcription renders their catchphrase 'yee', and their enunciation makes it tricky to pin down the word one way or another, but the youth-associated meme slang 'yeet' seems a more likely point of reference for SNL.

Digital Flows. Steven Gamble, Oxford University Press. © Oxford University Press 2024.
DOI: 10.1093/oso/9780197656389.003.0003

50 Digital Flows

Figure 3.1 Cast of Saturday Night Live's fictionalized 'Rap Roundtable', screenshot from YouTube

If there was a competition for the most derided aspect of contemporary hip hop, the winner would almost certainly be 'SoundCloud rap'. A series of terms emerged in the mid-to-late 2010s, mostly in online music journalism and culture writing, to characterize a range of new hip hop sounds jostling alongside the youthful energy of mainstream pop, punk, and metal.[3] These are often confused and quickly conflated. In the mid-2000s, Soulja Boy set the blueprint for breaking through online with his persistent promotion of 'Crank That'.[4] Shortly after, the psychedelic beats and stream-of-consciousness rap popularized by Lil B was dubbed 'cloud rap'. Next, it was the rise of the 'mumble rapper', aimed mostly at the laid-back Atlanta rap style characterized by triplet flow, slurred articulation, and distinct vocal production styles (reductively described as 'autotune'). Then came 'SoundCloud rap'—by far the most prevalent term—named after the music platform which enabled young artists to freely upload music and reach hip hop audiences.[5] Artists drawing

[3] Missy Scheinberg, 'Understanding SoundCloud Rap', *LNWY*, October 2017, https://web.archive.org/web/20191224225722/https://lnwy.co/read/meet-soundcloud-rap-hip-hops-most-punk-moment-yet/; Carrie Battan, 'The Messy Story of How SoundCloud Rap Took Over Everything', *GQ*, 31 January 2019, https://www.gq.com/story/soundcloud-rap-boom-times; Alphonse Pierre, 'How Rap's SoundCloud Generation Changed the Music Business Forever', *Pitchfork*, 27 February 2019, https://pitchfork.com/thepitch/how-raps-soundcloud-generation-changed-the-music-business-forever/.

[4] Tom Breihan, *The Number Ones: Twenty Chart-Topping Hits That Reveal the History of Pop Music* (New York: Hachette, 2022), 264–274.

[5] Ian Dunham, 'SoundCloud Rap: An Investigation of Community and Consumption Models of Internet Practices', *Critical Studies in Media Communication* 39, no. 2 (March 2022): 108–110.

Internet Rap and Generational Tensions   **51**

more conspicuously on the style of emo music were associated with the terms 'emo rap' and 'sad rap'. Those more influenced by metal were making 'trap metal'. Eventually the frame of reference became broader, with something like 'internet rap' both pointing to the born-digital nature of the music and implicitly distinguishing an 'internet rapper' from a *real* rapper. Some have also written about 'meme rappers'.[6] By the end of the 2010s, so-called SoundCloud rappers had accrued additional subgenre labels including 'plugg' and 'rage'.[7] More importantly, they were by now some of the biggest names in hip hop. No longer merely an online oddity, internet rap is well entrenched in the rap mainstream, a state of affairs which warrants closer examination.

Whatever one may call it—I will mostly use 'internet rap' and save the more commonplace 'SoundCloud rap' to specifically invoke the platform—this kind of rap music is intensely online, associated with a generation of young artists who spent their childhood and adolescence on the web.[8] As these artists have 'grown up alongside social media and thus have a wholly organic relationship with its communicative, distributive and participatory methods',[9] internet-specific interactions, inclinations, and in-jokes are part of the social fabric of this music culture. It is net-native: not only natively digital,[10] but a cultural formation developed primarily on the internet that carries traces of the medium in its expression. Yet this raises some tensions with other manifestations of hip hop, a culture, as I have established, physically and spiritually tied to the streets.[11] Accordingly, rappers have made various viewpoints on the internet clear. At one extreme, some artists swear it off altogether as a surveillant technology to be avoided or a vacuous stage for clout-chasing. At the other, artists passionately communicate their immersion in internet culture through their new media practices and productions.[12]

---

[6] Sheldon Pearce, 'A Guide to Meme Rappers', *Pitchfork*, 9 October 2017, https://pitchfork.com/thepi tch/a-guide-to-meme-rappers/; Michael Waugh, '"Every Time I Dress Myself, It Go Motherfuckin' Viral": Post-Verbal Flows and Memetic Hype in Young Thug's Mumble Rap', *Popular Music* 39, no. 2 (May 2020): 226.

[7] Brandon Callender, 'Popstar Benny Wants to Make Your Favorite Artist Get Weird', *The FADER*, 20 December 2021, https://www.thefader.com/2021/12/20/popstar-benny-interview; Kieran Press-Reynolds, '6 Years Ago a College Student Made a Fan Video for His Favorite Rapper. Now He's at the Forefront of the YouTube Hip-Hop Scene, Helping Boost Artists into Internet Stardom', *Insider*, 7 May 2022, https://www. insider.com/dotcomnirvan-interview-youtube-yeat-trippie-redd-plugg-soundcloud-rap-2022-5.

[8] Dunham, 'SoundCloud Rap', 116.

[9] Waugh, '"Every Time I Dress Myself, It Go Motherfuckin' Viral"', 226.

[10] Christopher Haworth and Georgina Born, 'Music and Intermediality after the Internet: Aesthetics, Materialities and Social Forms', in *Music and Digital Media: A Planetary Anthropology*, ed. Georgina Born (London: UCL Press, 2022), 381.

[11] Richard Bramwell and James Butterworth, 'Beyond the Street: The Institutional Life of Rap', *Popular Music* 39, no. 2 (May 2020): 169–186.

[12] Kai Arne Hansen and Steven Gamble, 'Saturation Season: Inclusivity, Queerness, and Aesthetics in the New Media Practices of Brockhampton', *Popular Music and Society* 45, no. 1 (2021); Steven Gamble and Justin Williams, 'Analyzing Hip-Hop Hacktivism and Automobility in Injury Reserve's (2019) "Jailbreak

Digital Flows

This chapter surveys a new wave of hip hop culture amplified along the networked flows of online media platforms. I first analyse rap lyrics addressing the internet since it became an integral part of everyday life, to identify dominant strands of thought that hip hop artists express about the web. I then turn my attention to the mid-2010s, particularly a class of young rappers who became popular through independent online releases, predominantly thanks to the platform SoundCloud. The creative output of these artists raises significant distinctions from previous eras of hip hop in relation to age, attitude, and alternative aesthetics. I examine examples of music, music videos, and new media to tease out why internet rap has been received with such suspicion and scorn. Its aesthetic differences from earlier forms of hip hop are hard to ignore, especially for heads of an older generation or a more conservative outlook on the culture. Throughout the chapter I am therefore concerned with the question: is it really hip hop? To answer this, I elaborate on the attention economy of the internet, where the strategic use of social media and audiovisual media platforms has become integral for the promotion and professionalization of upcoming artists. In the final section, I show that internet rappers use online self-promotional techniques, adeptly riding the waves of web-based communication, to grow their audiences. Using technology innovatively, deploying cultural capital, and producing provocative media to make their voices heard? Sounds pretty hip hop to me.

Rappers on the Internet: An Overview of Lyrics

Since the intrusion of the internet into so many aspects of daily life, hip hop artists have articulated various stances towards it.[13] Rappers reference the internet lyrically just as MCs at the dawn of the culture commented on whatever was part of their social fabric: their neighbourhoods, friends, faith, jobs, cars, comic books, TV shows, and so on. Since attitudes to the web are diverse, I divide them into themes for clearer discussion. I use a corpus of rap songs with lyrics including terms that specifically invoke the web.[14] The semantic

---

the Tesla" (Feat. Aminé)', in *Analyzing Recorded Music*, ed. William Moylan, Lori Burns, and Mike Alleyne (London and New York: Routledge, 2022), 38–55.

[13] Sarkar suggests that in contemporary Indian hip hop, 'one invertedly finds the discussion of platform capitalism seeping into the tracks'. Debarun Sarkar, ' "Azadi's Political until You're Pressing Play": Capitalist Realism, Hip-Hop, and Platform Affordances', *Convergence* 29, no. 6 (May 2023): 5.

[14] The full list of terms is: 'internet', 'online', 'the gram', 'IG', 'Instagram', 'SoundCloud', 'Snapchat', 'Twitter', 'Facebook', 'YouTube', and 'TikTok'.

Internet Rap and Generational Tensions **53**

focus here inevitably reinforces a logocentrism—privileging words over music—that haunts the study of hip hop,[15] but aims to explore how artists express their views towards the internet through their raps and broader media productions. I encountered around two-thirds of the lyrics in the dataset as part of my everyday listening, transcribed them, then cross-referenced with crowdsourced hearings on Genius. I found the remaining third by querying Genius's search engine for specific keywords. The five broad trends in lyrics about the internet are:

1. embracing the internet as an educational, performative, or everyday space;
2. dismissing social platforms as fake, inauthentic places of activity (usually contrasted with 'offline', 'real' life);
3. viewing the web as an arena for meaningless confrontation;
4. using social platforms to pursue or maintain sexual relationships;
5. criticizing the internet as a source of privacy violations or producing negative psychological effects.

Addressing these in turn paints an interesting picture of hip hop's complex stance towards the web and provides important context for understanding the tensions that follow in rap music of the online generation.

Logging On and Coming Up

For people who spend a lot of time online, it's tempting to see the internet as the default environment for various daily activities. Many rappers describe the web as a place they live, with various platforms—a term metaphorically emphasizing place—providing opportunities for self-development and career progression. Injury Reserve's classification of their music as not 'jazz rap' (as critics claimed) but 'raised by the internet ain't had no dad rap' on 'Oh Shit!!!' speaks volumes about the time spent online during childhood and adolescence. The responsibility ascribed to the web here also warrants consideration of how much young hip hop heads rely on internet technologies. Rich Brian adopts a similar line of thinking in 'Amen': 'I don't need no education, internet's my favourite teacher'. Praising the internet's educational potential is

---

[15] Richard Bramwell, *UK Hip-Hop, Grime and the City: The Aesthetics and Ethics of London's Rap Scenes* (New York and London: Routledge, 2015), 2.

54 Digital Flows

interesting given the special place of 'street knowledge' in hip hop's mythos,[16] but it also resounds with a young, globalized audience.

Rappers also laud the web's potential for them to distribute music and thereby professionalize. In his feature on Drake's 'In the Bible', Lil Durk makes it sound easy: 'I did my dance one time on TikTok and went viral with it'. This is a bit of a flex, of course, but others aren't so keen to tie their success to online platforms. 'Bleed' by A Boogie wit da Hoodie references his own reputation using the couplet, 'they call me a SoundCloud boy / They stealing my sound now, boy'. The capacity of SoundCloud to help grow artists' careers is significant (as I'll go on to discuss in this chapter), but it also generates some derision and—according to Boogie—a wave of derivatives. Being unoriginal is associated with hip hop's cardinal sin of inauthenticity.[17] For some artists, therefore, the internet couldn't be further from reality.

'The Internet a Fairy Tale'

There is a general attitude expressed by hip hop lyrics that online communication is inferior—or altogether fake—compared to face-to-face interaction. In her apt 'On the Internet', Kari Faux could hardly be more direct: 'I don't give a fuck if you're famous on the internet'. Distinguishing herself from 'internet people' who are 'mad sus in real life', she decries follower metrics as meaningless.[18] This is a common lyrical trend since the heyday of social media where artists downplay the significance of followings. Yet academic research has shown that social media and streaming platform metrics are crucial indicators of audience size and engagement,[19] assessed by brands for partnership deals.[20] Rappers suggest they simply don't care, that the deep musical connections sought by their art can't be measured in numbers, or that these figures are all artificially inflated anyway. Not only is having an online presence widely devalued, but rappers frequently assert their authenticity by establishing their distance from the internet, as exemplified by the lyrics in Table 3.1.

---

[16] Travis L. Gosa, 'The Fifth Element: Knowledge', in *The Cambridge Companion to Hip-Hop*, ed. Justin A. Williams (Cambridge: Cambridge University Press, 2015), 56–70.

[17] Lee Watkins, 'Keeping It Real: amaXhosa Iimbongi Making Mimesis Do Its Thing in the Hip-Hop and Rap Music of the Eastern Cape', *African Music: Journal of the International Library of African Music* 8, no. 4 (2010): 27–28.

[18] The term 'internet people' would later be used—ostensibly reclaimed in a positive light—for a Spotify playlist highlighting hip hop tracks doing the rounds online.

[19] Nancy K. Baym, 'Data Not Seen: The Uses and Shortcomings of Social Media Metrics', *First Monday* 18, no. 10 (2013).

[20] Gil Appel et al., 'The Future of Social Media in Marketing', *Journal of the Academy of Marketing Science* 48, no. 1 (January 2020): 82–83.

Internet Rap and Generational Tensions   55

Table 3.1 Sample of hip hop lyrics that position the internet as fake

Lyric	Artist and Song
'You [are] famous on the internet, I'm real life hot'	J. Cole, 'Villuminati'
' "Fake it till you make it", that's the internet code'	GloRilla, 'Internet Trolls'
'I'm rich in real life, not Instagram'	Kyle, 'Girls'
'Told me you was a big fan, but the first thing you said when you saw me was, "can I get a pic for the gram?" '	Skepta, 'Man'
'I am the real deal, not some SoundCloud ho'	Princess Nokia, 'Receipts'
'I drops every blue moon, to separate myself from you kings of the YouTube'	Pusha T, 'Untouchable'

The conspicuous performance of wealth on image- and video-sharing platforms is seen as especially distasteful. Jay Z derides those 'on the 'gram holding money to your ear / There's a disconnect: we don't call that money over here'. Yet the 'money phone' pose predates Instagram and has long been a display of rappers' wealth.[21] It evidently looks more superficial in its online form, and sometimes it is.[22] Still, rappers, including Jay Z, have hardly stopped rapping about being rich or flashing cash in their videos. Instagram may have become the subject of particular vitriol because of how intensely it encourages self-promotional performances of self, wealth, or popularity. In platform-based cultural production, authenticity and self-promotion always sit in tension,[23] with social media in particular 'perceived to be superficial, narcissistic and alienating'.[24] Even though songs and music videos may be just as staged as social media posts, online platforms betray hip hop's ideological emphasis on realness.[25] Furthermore, social media posts frequently lack the explicit local specificities so important to the performance of hip hop authenticity.[26] The internet is therefore positioned as a domain of pretence and vain

---

[21] Peter A. Berry, '13 Rappers Talking on the Money Phone', *XXL*, May 2015, http://www.xxlmag.com/news/2015/05/rappers-money-phone-pose/.

[22] 6ix9ine—more on him later—has admitted to using 'prop money' in Instagram videos, reasoning in one interview that 'I'm an entertainer, and obviously we're talking about it, so I did a pretty good job in entertaining people'. See TMZ Staff, 'Tekashi 6ix9ine Claims He's Flashing Fake Cash in Videos, Still Owes Robbery Victims', *TMZ*, 18 April 2022, https://www.tmz.com/2022/04/18/tekashi-6ix9ine-money-owe-lawsuit-rap/.

[23] Thomas Poell, David B. Nieborg, and Brooke Erin Duffy, *Platforms and Cultural Production* (Medford: Polity, 2021), 153.

[24] Trine Syvertsen and Gunn Enli, 'Digital Detox: Media Resistance and the Promise of Authenticity', *Convergence* 26, nos. 5–6 (December 2020): 1272. For a contrasting argument, see Kreling et al. on how users feel that they present themselves authentically on Instagram: Rebekka Kreling, Adrian Meier, and Leonard Reinecke, 'Feeling Authentic on Social Media: Subjective Authenticity Across Instagram Stories and Posts', *Social Media + Society* 8, no. 1 (January 2022).

[25] Murray Forman, ' "Things Done Changed": Recalibrating the Real in Hip-Hop', *Popular Music and Society* 44, no. 4 (August 2021): 451–477.

[26] My thanks to Kai Arne Hansen for highlighting this point.

56 Digital Flows

flexing, which underscores perhaps the most famous take on the internet's inauthenticity, Kendrick Lamar's 'Element': 'I don't do it for the 'gram, I do it for Compton!'.

Internet Gangsters

When Mark Anthony Neal was writing about hip hop's authenticity crisis in 1999, he could have been describing the exhibitionistic conventions of social media: 'the authenticity of the critical discourse of the hip-hop community remains a central tension, particularly given the use of spectacle by both corporate entities and black artists themselves to caricature and stylize the reality of the black urban experience'.[27] Conventional discourses of self-representation also apply powerfully to online confrontation. Time and time again, rappers have used the web to face off against one another. Rap beefs in the internet era are avidly documented by web journalists, blogs, and commentary and reaction videos. However, lyrics express a range of opinions about how seriously to take online interpersonal conflict. At one end, rappers treat such conflict as valid and meaningful, and at the other end, they mock those who make (or even acknowledge) web-based threats. A good touchpoint for taking things seriously is Stormzy's 'Shut Up': 'mention my name in your tweets: oi, rudeboy, shut up'. The track appears dismissive of receiving disrespect online, but then the rapper does spend almost thirty seconds of the song with bars focused on social media comments. He reaches a point of exasperation before cutting off his flow ('how the fuck can I–?') and, shortly after, intensifies the threat by pointing out his armed 'man over there with the pouch'. For someone claiming not to be affected by criticism circulated on the internet, there is evidently a lot at stake for an artist trying to protect their reputation against shit-talkers.[28]

In contrast, some artists refuse to engage with online conflict, treating it as artificial. Given the importance of urban geography to legitimacy and authenticity in hip hop, it is easy to view the internet as fake, false, or faulty representation.[29] Brockhampton's 'Chick' mocks 'all these internet gangsters . . , aiming with their keyboard, they're shooting uppercase'. Young M.A makes the contrast between urban gang warfare and the web crystal clear in 'Eat', rapping 'my goons in the fields, not the internet'. The perceived inauthenticity of acting

[27] M. A. Neal, *What the Music Said: Black Popular Music and Black Public Culture* (New York and London: Routledge, 1999), 161.

[28] Forrest Stuart, *Ballad of the Bullet* (Princeton, NJ: Princeton University Press, 2020), 9.

[29] Bramwell and Butterworth, 'Beyond the Street'.

Internet Rap and Generational Tensions **57**

like a gangster on social media platforms is addressed with some vitriol by Dave East in his track with Method Man, 'Unbelievable':

> most the killers that I know ain't got no Instagram; most the hitters that I know ain't got no Twitter; most the gangsters that I know don't be on TikTok; claiming you a killer, every day you posting pictures: it's unbelievable.

Drake, whose authenticity is especially open to question by other rappers,[30] has got in on the trend, ridiculing how 'trigger fingers turn to Twitter fingers' in 'Back to Back'. Of course, the viral potential of combative call-outs being spotlighted by platform algorithms and amplified by online audiences is not lost on media celebrities like Drake. JID, by comparison, distances himself altogether from social media disputes with the snappy line 'online beef, not my motif' in 'Off Deez'. Having significantly influenced rap's onlining in his early YouTube music videos, Lil B expresses his hallmark 'based'[31]—that is, carefree—attitude to online criticism in 'Wonton Soup': 'suckers stay talking on them internet comments'. He simply brushes them aside.

Getting It Online

Although lyrics on fame and conflict share the notion that online interactions are questionably real, there is one domain of online activity that rappers view as having tangible effects on their social lives: pursuing romantic and sexual relationships. Social media platforms are widely understood as places made for the performance of sexuality, often alongside glamour, wealth, and personal authenticity.[32] Meanwhile, expressions of misogyny are normalized both in hip hop and across social media,[33] although women in hip hop are doing sex-positive feminist work to publicly reclaim agency over their bodies and desires (see Chapter 5). With conventions around relationships and

---

[30] Alexandra Boutros, 'The Impossibility of Being Drake: Or, What It Means to Be a Successful (Black) Canadian Rapper', *Global Hip Hop Studies* 1, no. 1 (June 2020): 95–114.

[31] Sal Hagen and Daniël de Zeeuw, 'Based and Confused: Tracing the Political Connotations of a Memetic Phrase across the Web', *Big Data & Society* 10, no. 1 (2023).

[32] Crystal Abidin, 'Communicative ❤ Intimacies: Influencers and Perceived Interconnectedness', *Ada: A Journal of Gender, New Media, and Technology*, no. 8: Gender, Globalization and the Digital (November 2015): 1–16; Brooke Erin Duffy, *(Not) Getting Paid to Do What You Love: Gender, Social Media, and Aspirational Work* (New Haven, CT and London: Yale University Press, 2017), 104–111.

[33] Brittney C. Cooper, Susana M. Morris, and Robin M. Boylorn, 'Hip Hop Generation Feminism: A Manifesto', in *The Crunk Feminist Collection*, ed. Brittney C. Cooper, Susana M. Morris, and Robin M. Boylorn, xix–xxii (New York: The Feminist Press at CUNY, 2016); Moya Bailey, *Misogynoir Transformed: Black Women's Digital Resistance* (New York: New York University Press, 2021).

58 Digital Flows

technological affordances changing in tandem, rappers have addressed a variety of social and sexual interactions taking place online.

Quite a lot of Childish Gambino's album *because the internet* focuses on the ramifications of social media on intimate relationships. Three extracts will show the breadth of this commentary. In the song 'III. Telegraph Ave. ("Oakland" by Lloyd)', Childish Gambino reflects on approaches to casual hook-ups facilitated by swipe-to-match dating apps: 'Two dates and he still wanna get it in / And they're saying it's because of the internet / Try her once and it's on to the next chick'. The artist comments on trading sensitive photos with a potential lover: 'send them pics to my phone, GPOY [gratuitous picture of yourself]' ('II. Earth: The Oldest Computer (The Last Night)'). Finally, he provides a pun about online dance videos, contextually sexualized: 'showing off her ass, that's a net twerk' ('II. Worldstar').

Other rappers have offered lyrics ranging from the innocuous to the insulting. In 'George Jeff', Jaden uses Instagram as a straightforward exchange of personal information: 'you know she know I'm the man, I got her number on the 'gram'. The platform has also helped Tyga court women: ''fore I had the 'gram, I couldn't get at 'em' ('1 of 1'). YG puts this more crudely in 'Don't Tell 'Em', recalling 'some Twitter pussy I met on the internet'. This kind of sexist objectification spans languages and platforms, as heard in the German rapper Kollegah's boast, 'Ich kläre Internetschlampen bei Facebook' ('Halleluja').[34] Cardi B flips the script on such derogation, demanding a serious commitment before presenting herself with a partner on social media: 'if ain't no ring on my finger, you ain't going on my 'gram'. Other female artists describe sexual activities enabled by internet technologies with light-hearted glee, as in Doja Cat's 'Cyber Sex'. On 'Ungrateful', Megan Thee Stallion teases, 'boy, stop liking all my pics before you get in trouble'. Suggesting that her apparently irresistible profile might make men sexually unfaithful, she points to the wider ramifications of social media liking conventions on everyday relationships.

'Internet Got No Chill'

So says Rapsody, on 'Nobody'. She's right, for a number of reasons. Rappers have cited various negative effects of the internet. Childish Gambino takes aim at those motivated by the quantified affirmation of social media metrics: 'Never forget this feeling, never gonna reach a million / Eventually all my followers realize they don't need a leader' ('III. Life: The Biggest Troll

---

[34] His claim is, 'I sort out internet bitches on Facebook'. Thanks to Surma for reviewing my translation.

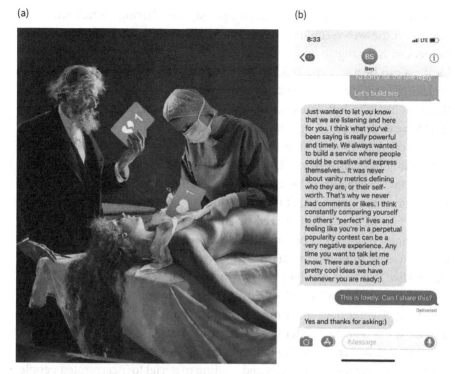

Figure 3.2 Kanye West's posts critiquing the value ascribed to social media like counts, from Instagram

[Andrew Auernheimer]'). Kanye West voices a similar complaint in 'Saint Pablo', confessing to 'checking Instagram comments to crowdsource my self-esteem'. In 2018, he argued for the removal of the public display of follower and like metrics on social media platforms, which Snapchat's then-Senior Vice President Ben Schwerin calls 'vanity metrics' (Figure 3.2).[35]

The internet is claimed to not only affect Kanye West's self-esteem, but also to infringe on his legal rights, as he notes that 'a million illegally downloaded my truth over the drums' ('Saint Pablo'). Post Malone shares Ye's concern about the public release of unfinished material, claiming he's 'paranoid since they've been leaking my shit . . . fuck the internet, and you can quote that' (Post Malone, 'Internet').

It is not only the sharing of music, but also images and location data, that rappers distrust. In 'Send the Addy', Flo Milli expresses concerns about people sharing photos of her without permission: 'I can't let him post me on

---

[35] This feature was later implemented as the default option for Instagram users viewing others' posts, though the setting can be changed to reveal the numbers.

60 Digital Flows

the internet'. Others, like Saba, warn against over-sharing: 'watch what you put up on the web / You don't want everyone aware' ('Beautiful Smile'). For rappers with a gangsta image, or genuine connections, publicly stating their location can be a security risk. Jay Rock explains it clearly: 'I don't post a lot on Instagram / That's the quickest way they'll get you, man' ('U.O.E.N.O'). On 'Internet Trolls', GloRilla works the other way, tracking someone down who 'ain't have to drop the lo', I got it from his Snapchat'.

Political themes regarding the internet as a source of disinformation or groupthink have also emerged, as in Run The Jewels' reworking of a Gil Scott-Heron classic: expanding his critique of mass media to the internet, 'goonies vs E.T.' gives the couplet 'ain't no revolution is televised and digitized / You've been hypnotized and Twitter-ized by silly guys'. Their position is somewhat contradictory, of course, because Run The Jewels also promote political discourse widely in online media like the Netflix show *Trigger Warning with Killer Mike*. Noname similarly decries those 'Twitter ranting for martyrdom, unified as capitalists' ('Regal') and, in another track, encourages the listener to 'check my Twitter page for something holier than Black death' ('Yesterday'). Similarly, her take on Twitter is complex and nuanced. Although she has not referenced it in her lyrics, Noname also uses Twitter to publicize her Book Club, which provides POC-authored reading material to incarcerated people, links to Black- and collectively owned bookstores, and puts funds towards community projects. There may yet be hope for radical hip hop artists to do political work using social media platforms.[36] For the most part, however, the web is a thorny topic for artists, seen by varying degrees to be artificial, superficial, and exhibitionistic.

Internet Rap Defined by Three Fissures

Enter into these online contexts a new wave of young artists, sensitive to the cultural influence of the internet on everyday life. In his 2014 track 'Here We Go', Mac Miller summarized the typical stance hip hop heads took to

---

[36] This is to say nothing of the significance of hip hop to online aspects of the Movement for Black Lives (sometimes conflated with specific organizations under the banner Black Lives Matter), which has been well addressed in academic literature and beyond. See, for example, Fernando Orejuela, 'Introduction', in *Black Lives Matter and Music: Protest, Intervention, Reflection*, ed. Stephanie Shonekan and Fernando Orejuela (Bloomington: Indiana University Press, 2018), 1–4; Elaine Richardson and Alice Ragland, '#StayWoke: The Language and Literacies of the #BlackLivesMatter Movement', *Community Literacy Journal* 12, no. 2 (2018): 27–56; Steven Gamble, *How Music Empowers: Listening to Modern Rap and Metal* (London: Routledge, 2021), 164–167; Lakeyta M. Bonnette-Bailey et al., 'The Bigger Picture: Hip-Hop, Black Lives, and Social Justice', in *Black Popular Culture and Social Justice*, ed. Lakeyta M. Bonnette-Bailey and Jonathan I. Gayles (London and New York: Routledge, 2023), 109–124.

net-native stars: 'internet rappers ain't shit when no computers work'. As I—
and SNL's 'Rap Roundtable' sketch—have suggested, gaining success purely
with online hits betrays a core hip hop principle in its apparent rejection of
locality. It is clear from the work of Murray Forman near the dawn of hip hop
studies that representing for specific geographical spaces is a defining feature of the culture. In the music TV station era of the genre's media circulation, references to space and place helped distinguish hip hop artists through
lyrics, music, and music video. There was no 'TV rapper': musicians explicitly
stand for their localities 'in order to provide a vehicle for the representation
of their city or urban neighbourhood', which became 'a standard component
of hip-hop's symbolic systems'.[37] Internet rappers, by virtue of their come-up
in the cloud, appear to reject this tradition. Reports of such rappers' emergence in spotlight often overstate the perceived placelessness of their work,[38]
replacing referents like East Coast and Compton with the online platforms
where they first gained wide popularity, whether SoundCloud or TikTok.[39]
Their apparent emergence from the internet underscores three more ideological tensions concerning their position in hip hop culture: a generational divide, tension between hip hop and rap, and punk influences.

Generational Tensions

The sounds of the internet rap scene have been classed pretty uniformly as
youthful. Over and above rap's historical reputation, they are vibrant, energetic, and raw. They are the sounds of a new, fresh-faced generation of rap
stars. Many internet rappers were indeed young when they broke through
online,[40] but this is not unusual for hip hop: LL Cool J signed to Def Jam
aged only sixteen (in 1985); Gangsta Boo was just fifteen when *Mystic Stylez*
dropped (1995); Chief Keef was sixteen when the 'I Don't Like' video flung
him into the spotlight (2012). Fans, too, are just as young as—sometimes

---

[37] Murray Forman, *The 'hood Comes First: Race, Space, and Place in Rap and Hip-Hop* (Middletown, CT: Wesleyan University Press, 2002), 245.

[38] Many of the best-known SoundCloud rappers—though undoubtedly exploding in popularity by posting media online—derive from particular rap scenes, such as Atlanta (Playboi Carti, Trippie Redd, MadeinTYO), New York (6ix9ine, $not, Lil Tecca), and South Florida (Lil Pump, Ski Mask the Slump God, Denzel Curry, SpaceGhostPurrp and the rest of his Rvidxr Klvn). Denzel Curry, XXXTentacion, and Ronny J briefly lived together, in a manner reminiscent of traditional hip hop collectives. *DENZEL CURRY x MONTREALITY* \\ *Interview*, YouTube video, 24 January 2018, https://www.youtube.com/watch?v=jiNLTGt4A4M.

[39] Daniel Allington, Byron Dueck, and Anna Jordanous, 'Networks of Value in Electronic Music: SoundCloud, London, and the Importance of Place', *Cultural Trends* 24, no. 3 (July 2015): 219–220.

[40] Concurrent with the SoundCloud scene, other viral rappers have broken through at even younger ages, like Bhad Bhabie (aged fourteen) and Matt Ox (twelve).

62 Digital Flows

younger than—the artists.[41] The actual ages of artists and audiences aside, it is more the *youthfulness* of internet rap that is noted by music critics, many of whom represent an older listening public peering into a community of on-line youth creativity. It is this music's perceived immaturity by people who are no longer young that may have earned it such a bad reputation. To quote Lil Yachty's debut album title, internet rap has gained a reputation for being full-to-bursting with *Teenage Emotions*.

Pressingly, this appears to be the first generation of rap artists to which older hip hop heads simply cannot relate. When NWA honed gangsta rap for a mainstream audience, even its detractors could still detect the lineage of Black political resistance among its violence and vulgarity. Yet internet rap is often painted as music for and by drugged-out teens with no respect for the cul-ture.[42] Conventionally, hip hop is associated with sexual maturity, used by art-ists to signal a step-change in their career,[43] which may make the perception of immaturity especially uncomfortable in the hip hop context. Some internet rappers further compound the issue by explicitly refusing to pay dues to hip hop's elder statesmen, a formerly inviolable custom. Critics shocked to hear Lil Yachty dismiss Pete Rock as an 'old head',[44] or Lil Xan describe Tupac's music as 'boring',[45] however, are focusing on the traditional value of conspicu-ously recognizing hip hop lineage and legacy.[46] They overlook that it is, simul-taneously, a quintessential hip hop attitude to rebel from orthodox thinking (the thinking now common among an older generation of heads), and to not respect people simply because others tell you that you should.

This tension came to a head in a now-iconic 2016 Hot 97 interview with Lil Uzi Vert.[47] Longstanding radio DJ Ebro gives the artist—then half his age—a hard time about not wanting to rap on a classic DJ Premier beat, which he describes as a mandatory test for all young rappers. 'I'm not into that', says Lil Uzi Vert, to incredulity and laughter. Pete Rosenburg chimes in, describing 'a huge disconnect between the adults and kids of hip hop' forged in the wake of Kanye West's *808s and Heartbreak*. Co-host Laura Stylez points out that its 2008 release coincided with artists' teenage 'emo' phase. Lil Uzi Vert shrugs it

---

[41] Battan, 'The Messy Story of How SoundCloud Rap Took Over Everything'.

[42] Jon Caramanica, 'The Rowdy World of Rap's New Underground', *New York Times*, 22 June 2017, https://archive.is/b6MX4.

[43] Kai Arne Hansen, *Pop Masculinities: The Politics of Gender in Twenty-First Century Popular Music* (Oxford and New York: Oxford University Press, 2021), 49–52.

[44] Matthew T. Phillips, 'Soundcloud Rap and Alien Creativity: Transforming Rap and Popular Music through Mumble Rap', *Journal of Popular Music Studies* 33, no. 3 (September 2021): 133.

[45] Jacque-Corey Cormier, 'I Stank I Can, I Know I Can, I Will: Songwriting Self-Efficacy as an Expression of Identity Orchestration', in *Identity Orchestration: Black Lives, Balance, and the Psychology of Self Stories*, ed. David Wall Rice (Lanham, MD: Lexington Books, 2022), 41–42.

[46] J. A. Williams, *Rhymin' and Stealin': Musical Borrowing in Hip-Hop* (Ann Arbor, MI: University of Michigan Press, 2013), 140–144.

[47] *Lil Uzi Vert Talks Hating Interviews, Starting To Rap For Attention + Drops Bars!*, YouTube video, 24 February 2016, https://www.youtube.com/watch?v=Bq6IsU390E0.

Figure 3.3 Hot 97 hosts and Lil Uzi Vert reflect generational tensions in hip hop, screenshots from YouTube
Source: *Lil Uzi Vert Talks Hating Interviews*

off, unwilling to rap on 'one of them old beats'. 'Why?', asks Ebro. The answer is stated simply: 'I am a rockstar'. Ebro ups the stakes, suggesting that young rappers fall off as they reach their late twenties and look to re-engage with the classic sounds of hip hop. Lil Uzi Vert is unwavering: 'I'm going to be all the way a rockstar by then' (Figure 3.3).[48]

By dismissing respected forebears and gatekeeping traditions, internet rappers actively contest ideas central to proving oneself within the cultural traditions of hip hop. They introduce new frameworks for authenticity that contest conventional paradigms of how rappers represent themselves. As Forman identifies, understandings of hip hop authenticity have evolved over several generations, 'with younger individuals growing up in a more intricately networked sharing culture and older hip-hop heads arriving at the realization that over a lifetime they have consistently repressed a multitude of complex thoughts, feelings, and emotions'.[49] Earlier generations may resent their own repression and can slip into envying or resenting the more emotionally effusive younger generation. For the internet rap cohort, their emphatic (albeit still mediated and performative) expression of self, along with their rebelliousness in the face of elder wisdom, becomes associated with not only youth but also immaturity and oversentimentality. This new wave of hip hop risks reducing political consciousness to puerile complaint.

Of course, the music bears a lot of weight for judgements about internet rap's immaturity, too. Short tracks suggest short attention spans. Distorted bass, prominent kick drums, and off-kilter mixes imply amateurism. Frantic, repetitive, or complex-pitched[50] vocals afford an explosive—as if

---

[48] In case it was in any doubt whose predictions were more accurate: at the 2023 Grammy Awards, aged twenty-seven, Lil Uzi Vert closed the fifteen-minute, fiftieth-anniversary tribute to hip hop organized by the Roots.
[49] Forman, '"Things Done Changed"', 470.
[50] This is an analytical term encapsulating screaming and some kinds of shouting—vocal expressions prominent in extreme styles of metal and punk—to distinguish 'distorted' and 'harsh' vocals from 'clean'

64   Digital Flows

hormonal—energy. From the beats to the bars, this is evidently rap music. However, its relationship to hip hop is not always clear.

The Hip Hop–Rap Betrayal

The distinction between hip hop and rap can be laid out very simply, but only by concealing some complexities. In the introduction to this book, I described hip hop as a culture, articulated through creative practices like graffiti and breaking and some styles of music. One kind of music born from hip hop is rap. All rap music has some basis in hip hop, but not all hip hop music is rap. That's the simplest way of making the distinction. In the current era, there is a new fissure between artists and fans who describe their music as both hip hop and rap, and those who are happy to omit the hip hop inheritance and commit to making, simply, rap music.

Frequently, this distinction is determined by the role of commercialism. It suffices to say that hip hop has never been completely free of economic incentives, and in fact the need to make a little extra money motivated the very earliest parties in the Bronx. Still, the explicit intervention of music industry executives during the 1980s led to a conceptual split in the culture. On the one hand, heads carried forward the sociopolitically 'conscious', progressive, community-oriented ethos of the culture in its original conception. On the other, artists making hardcore rap, gangsta rap, or pop rap—tracks for partying and driving to, political message be damned—seemed to sell the culture short (or dumb it down) with corporate-backed mainstream music. The latter form is better known in popular culture and mass media to this day, the former largely relegated to the 'underground'. Granted, elements of 'real' hip hop have remained visible in mainstream popular music, albeit understood as 'conscious' characteristics of a few celebrated artists—Kendrick Lamar, Rapsody, J. Cole, Little Simz—who still need to make bangers for the club or the car as well.[51]

It was this split that Tricia Rose's *The Hip Hop Wars* addressed, decrying the direction hip hop had taken since the publication of her groundbreaking book *Black Noise*. Gone was the 'locally inspired explosion of exuberance and

---

vocals like singing and rapping. See E. T. Smialek, 'Genre and Expression in Extreme Metal Music, ca. 1990–2015' (PhD diss., McGill University, 2015), 209–211.

[51] My thanks to Jabari Evans for emphasizing this point.

political energy tethered to the idea of rehabilitating community,[52] replaced in the spotlight by 'a breeding ground for the most explicitly exploitative and increasingly one-dimensional narratives of black ghetto life.'[53] In its migration to the internet, hip hop turns away from the significance of local specificity, and towards a more commercialized, spectacular vision of rap popular in mainstream online culture. Internet rap invests thoroughly in inflated imagery of conspicuous consumption, gangbanging, sexist violence, and patriarchal Black masculinity from the legacy of the most 'self-destructive . . . disproportionately celebratory . . . [and] hyper-gangsta-iz[ed]'[54] versions of rap music.

Though Rose's concern is understandable, there may be alternative readings of these admittedly narrow representations of Black self-expression. Justin Burton's work on trap, especially the party-friendly pop-rap of Rae Sremmurd—not a world away musically from some internet rap, I should note—points out that the music evokes an earlier era of hip hop hustling through tropes like 'a 24/7 grind, innovative production techniques, and a bootstrap mentality that allows trappers to achieve financial success against social and political odds.'[55] However, Rae Sremmurd do not celebrate upward mobility in the ways white middle America expects and enjoys: an entrepreneurial, rags-to-riches-to-white-picket-fence, American Dream fantasy (respectability politics, basically[56]). Instead, 'trap stays in the trap.'[57] Contemporary young Black rap artists reject the terms of the socio-economic contexts that Others, represses, and marginalizes them. They advance an alternative political project by 'partying, enjoying yourself, when the world intends you to suffer.'[58] Such readings are not always obvious to the mass media or public at large, who may write this kind of rap off as hedonistic, self-destructive, and misogynistic, thereby validating Rose's critique. Still, trap artists' refusal to comply with neoliberal American expectations—that is, entrepreneurship aimed at becoming ordinary productive citizens (and thus serving hegemonic, white-directed agendas)—exemplifies an ethos that Burton describes as 'perhaps as central to hip hop as anything else.'[59]

---

[52] Tricia Rose, *The Hip-Hop Wars: What We Talk about When We Talk about Hip-Hop and Why It Matters* (New York: Basic Books, 2008), ix.

[53] Rose, *The Hip-Hop Wars*, 3.

[54] Rose, *The Hip-Hop Wars*, 3.

[55] Justin D. Burton, *Posthuman Rap* (New York: Oxford University Press, 2017), 101.

[56] Kyesha Jennings, 'City Girls, Hot Girls and the Re-Imagining of Black Women in Hip Hop and Digital Spaces', *Global Hip Hop Studies* 1, no. 1 (June 2020): 47–70.

[57] Burton, *Posthuman Rap*, 96.

[58] Burton, *Posthuman Rap*, 109.

[59] Burton, *Posthuman Rap*, 109.

66   Digital Flows

The antisocial resonances of this ethos can be felt fully in internet rap. Here the generational divide appears again. Without either blaming or excusing SoundCloud's teenage superstars for their unpolished political purviews, it is clear that a sense of rebellion predominates. It may be articulated crudely, like 'fuck authority', compared to Burton's poststructuralist reading of trap as postwork, but I suggest we should not rush to dismiss it as strictly antithetical to hip hop's social consciousness. The anger, sadness, or urgency so widely interpreted in internet rap is a kind of performative resistance. For marginalized and burnt-out young people, concern for social justice and inequality—key issues of intergenerational politics—may manifest more like emotionally reflective resentment (hence accusations of oversentimentality in 'emo rap').[60] This may lead to more reductive expressions of selfhood and suffering than the calls for community, solidarity, or revolution found in earlier hip hop. But in streamlining rebelliousness to digitally distributed soundbites, it also makes political resistance widely digestible for young, pissed-off, online audiences.

Punk Influences

This raises the third issue associated with internet rap in the hip hop context: its proximity to punk. The music culture memelords NEOPUNKFM began a June 2023 YouTube video by stating,

> Internet rap has been moving in a heavily punk rock influenced direction ever since Playboi Carti dropped *Whole Lotta Red*, an album that shook up the entire [hip hop] underground by using '80s punk rock aesthetics, aggression, and the moshing culture that you see at shows today.[61]

This is a sound summary. Both musically and visually, internet rap artists add to hip hop a heady cocktail of emo, metal, and pop punk influences. They perform as web-literate rockstars designed for smartphone screens.

Among the visual signifiers of internet rap, face tattoos, piercings, and brightly dyed hair feature prominently. Lil Wayne provides a clear precedent

---

[60] Jing Zeng and Crystal Abidin, ' "#OkBoomer, Time to Meet the Zoomers": Studying the Memefication of Intergenerational Politics on TikTok', *Information, Communication & Society* 24, no. 16 (December 2021): 2461.

[61] *Internet Rap Fans Go Outside For First Time*, YouTube video, 18 June 2023, https://www.youtube.com/watch?v=jiFcOcXsmRc.

for these fashions, with his range of bold clothing choices, thoroughly inked body and face, and bleached dreads. Some years later, 6ix9ine takes transgressive self-expression to the logical extreme, encompassing almost every possible hair colour, rainbow grills, and '69'—the sex number!—inked all over his face and hands in nearly every conceivable rendering of digits and letters. The prevailing narrative goes that this kind of look—face tattoos in particular—symbolizes commitment to the rap lifestyle, preventing artists from giving up and getting regular jobs. Internet rappers' conventional visual styles express rebellion and difference, rejecting norms of socially acceptable self-presentation.

Tattoos and vivid hair colours aside, the look itself is not always distinctly punk (at least not in terms of well-known signifiers like tartan, leather, or flannel), but the ethos is. For emerging artists, a striking look helps as a means of differentiation. Clothing tends towards hip hop style in the era of hyperconspicuous consumption: streetwear and high fashion designer brands; jewellery and grills; a vast spread of shoes, hats, and accessories. However, internet rap artists also dabble in ostentatious clothing associated with queer and hybrid masculinities.[62] They exhibit their wardrobes across their multimedia productions—in music videos, interviews, social media posts—sometimes seeming desperate to be seen.

But while trying to have one's unique style noticed is a core trait of hip hop, internet rap appears to try a bit too hard, earning critiques about its aesthetic excess. Musically, it seems almost designed to outrage heads of an older generation, diminishing hip hop production conventions in favour of prominent features of '00s punk and metal. The basis for most tracks is through and through trap, itself already a modern distortion (sometimes literally) of hip hop's 'old-school chime and rhyme, the bounce and jazziness of Nineties production'.[63] Alongside heavy 808s, wavy synths, and iconic drum sounds, internet rap also features shouted and screamed vocals, prominent distortion or overdrive effects, electric guitars, sparse textures, poppy vocal melodies, and sentimental lyrics. These influences can sometimes be difficult to place, spanning the gamut from pop punk à la Blink 182 to nu metal in the vein of Slipknot. Notably, these are alternative and extreme music genres, but in their most pop-friendly forms.

---

[62] James Whittaker and Ashley Morgan, '"They Never Felt These Fabrics before": How SoundCloud Rappers Became the Dandies of Hip Hop through Hybrid Dress', in 'Black Masculinities: Dress, Fashion and Style as Gendered Racialized Experiences', special issue, *Critical Studies in Men's Fashion* 9 (April 2022): 99–118.

[63] Jesse McCarthy, 'Notes on Trap', *N+1*, no. 32 (2018), https://www.nplusonemag.com/issue-32/essays/notes-on-trap/.

68   Digital Flows

Three approximate modes of influence can be identified. In emo rap, one finds the most melodic (usually sung-through), sentimental, and pop-derived internet rap. Juice Wrld's 'Lucid Dreams' takes a reverberant, minor-key guitar line from Sting—not the most common source of hip hop samples, but a well-chosen one for this immensely popular track nonetheless—and adds busy trap drums and prominent 808 bass. The vocals are ever-present,[64] as Juice Wrld spills line after catchy line of emotionally effusive lyrics. The rapper briefly faced a lawsuit from pop punk band Yellowcard over accusations he had copied one of their melodies. This was an unsurprising turn of events, given that Juice's vocals are textbook pop punk, incredibly tuneful, with a singsong quality. The emo staples are all there, full of teenage angst, love, and betrayal: his first verse rhymes 'all in my head', 'you in my bed', and 'better off dead'.

At the other—the heaviest—end of the spectrum, rappers invoke various distortions from metal music. Though he worked across many genres in his brief, controversial career,[65] XXXTentacion gave extreme music hip hop's most conspicuous embrace in many decades. His '#I'mSippinTeaInYoHood' pushes trap production to its limits, centred around a wildly distorted bass synth that grinds up and down by a semitone (a tonally dark harmonic shift inherited from metalcore breakdowns).[66] His vocals are mostly shouted, just on the edge of overdriving to a scream, as he simulates violent fantasies: 'bitch, I'll skin your face'; 'stab a body'; 'put that shit right in your spleen'. This is a distinct and contemporary meeting between rap and metal, influencing the emergence of trap metal artists Scxrlxrd, Ghostemane, and City Morgue, as well as a new wave of horrorcore spearheaded by artists like Bones, Night Lovell, and $uicideboy$. It also coincided with the development of a viral sub-genre known as drift phonk, combining Memphis rap influences with four-to-the-floor beats and distorted 808 cowbell patterns.

---

[64] Dai Griffiths' spatial frame for analysing vocal phrasing would characterize this as extremely verbally dense. Dai Griffiths, 'From Lyric to Anti-Lyric: Analyzing the Words in Pop Song', in *Analyzing Popular Music*, ed. A. F. Moore (Cambridge: Cambridge University Press, 2003), 39–59.

[65] It is more than a little concerning how many of the internet rap superstars mentioned in this chapter have been accused of sexual assault or misconduct. Patriarchal attitudes are normalized in the music and ostensibly inform artists' real lives. These attitudes seem to derive from the marketability of misogyny mixed with conventions around conspicuous consumption, which portray women's bodies as desirable yet exploitable. Moreover, hip hop fans hold a remarkably diverse set of values about online sexual miscon-duct allegations, informed by the #MeToo movement. See Jenessa Williams, 'Music Fandom in the Age of #MeToo: Morality Crowdsourcing, Racialised Cancellation and Complicated Listening Habits in Online Hip-Hop and Indie-Alternative Communities' (PhD diss., University of Leeds, 2023).

[66] Steven Gamble, 'Breaking down the Breakdown in Twenty-First-Century Metal', *Metal Music Studies* 5, no. 3 (September 2019): 342.

Somewhere in the middle, the mumble rules supreme. Quite often, those accused of being mumble rappers are really experimenting with different vocal performance styles. Just predating internet rap proper (in the early 2010s) are the pioneering triplet-flow trap singers: Young Thug, Future, and Migos. A few years later, SoundCloud was buzzing with a wave of artists playing around with catchy vocal phrases and ad-libs over hazy trap beats. The punk influence here is sometimes less tangible musically but clear in visual branding and lyrical references, crystallized by Lil Uzi Vert's spiked hair and Playboi Carti's *Whole Lotta Red*: this album includes songs titled 'Rockstar Mode', 'Punk Monk', and 'F33l Lik3 Dyin'. On the latter track, with a stop-start sung flow sounding barely squeezed out of his throat, Playboi Carti rhymes 'rockstar shit like I'm Jimi Hendrix' with 'Light my cigarette up like an incense'. This is a relatively lyrical example of this kind of music, sometimes called 'rage', where verses can sound more like collections of experimental ad-libs strung together and looped endlessly (well, at least until the end of a track's two-minute runtime).[67] Sometimes this music is derided for its perceived simplicity, inanity, or lean-motivated lethargy. But to hear a lack of complexity as contradictory to hip hop is to overlook its earworm potential.[68] As well as singing and rapping, artists gasp, squeak, and play around with pitch-corrected melodies to produce snappy soundbites in short bursts of energy.[69] The beats often have an airy tone, with buzzy synth pads and ultra-catchy sequenced loops, sometimes topped with retro-game soundtrack distortion.

With these new conventions laid bare, we are some way from the smoothness, the wit, the groove of Golden Age hip hop. The generational divide looms large once more: this new wave of artists is equally inspired by hip hop and alternative/extreme music, perhaps the two most prevalent genres among youth throughout the '90s and '00s.[70] Hip hop's conscious core is also nowhere to be seen next to the self-serving excess of rapstar life. The punkish attitude of rappers who broke through online in the 2010s is therefore a problem for

---

[67] Sometimes songs *are* experimental ad-libs strung together, in fan productions built around leaked studio recordings and more. See Jamie Ryder, 'Chopped and Screwed? How Studio Leaks Are Creating a New DIY Rap Music', *The Guardian*, 3 January 2020, https://www.theguardian.com/music/2020/jan/03/chopped-and-screwed-how-studio-leaks-are-creating-a-new-diy-rap-music.

[68] Many of the most derided artists are described as perfectionists in the studio, suggesting material is carefully crafted for popular appeal. See, for example, Stephen Witt on 6ix9ine and Stephen Kearse on Playboi Carti: Stephen Witt, 'Tekashi 69: The Rise and Fall of a Hip-Hop Supervillain', *Rolling Stone* (blog), 16 January 2019, https://www.rollingstone.com/music/music-features/tekashi-69-rise-and-fall-feature-777971/; Stephen Kearse, 'Playboi Carti, Rap Iconoclast', 2 March 2021, https://www.thenation.com/article/culture/playboi-carti-whole-lotta-red/.

[69] Waugh, '"Every Time I Dress Myself, It Go Motherfuckin' Viral"'.

[70] Gamble, *How Music Empowers*, 1–2.

70   Digital Flows

other hip hop factions, who deride or dismiss this music as a strange anomaly of kids who spend too much time on the internet.

Internet Rap as Viral Online Media

For de Paor-Evans, mumble rap manifests 'creativity born out of boredom'.[71] I have already introduced Justin Burton's contrasting reading of trap as a commitment to hustling that resists conventional upward mobility. A third understanding, which I raise here, emphasizes the importance of the online cultural contexts which birthed the scene.

This youthful, dynamic, and hedonistic music relies on the contours of the attention economy. Compared to a traditional economy based on factors of scarcity in the *production* of material goods, an 'attention economy is based on the scarcity of the capacity for the *reception* of cultural goods'.[72] Though the term has a long history (longer than that of the internet),[73] it helpfully characterizes the landscape of social media content since the early 2010s. In contrast to an earlier era of corporate-owned media production, a glut of social media creators vie for the valuable attention of platform users. Since there is an overabundance of cultural products available online,[74] where one directs their attention is an important and value-laden decision. Media products themselves are presented freely—in the foundational logic of YouTube, for example, preserved to this day—in exchange for user attention, which can be transformed into economic and informational value for advertisers, sponsors, and platforms.

A dominant feature of the attention economy is that, since there is no shortage of media products, they are in increased competition, and their form has developed driven by desire to capture audiences. Some developments suggested by observers are oversimplified or exaggerated,[75] but align with the priorities of media platforms. Recall Chapter 2, in which I suggested that on-demand streaming platforms' playlist infrastructure has prompted

---

[71] Adam de Paor-Evans, 'Mumble Rap: Cultural Laziness or a True Reflection of Contemporary Times?', *The Conversation*, October 2017, http://theconversation.com/mumble-rap-cultural-laziness-or-a-true-reflection-of-contemporary-times-85550.

[72] Yves Citton, *The Ecology of Attention*, trans. Barnaby Norman (Cambridge: Polity Press, 2017), 2. Italics preserved.

[73] Jonathan Crary, *Suspensions of Perception: Attention, Spectacle, and Modern Culture* (Cambridge, MA and London: MIT Press, 2001); Ann Blair, *Too Much to Know: Managing Scholarly Information Before the Modern Age* (New Haven, CT and London: Yale University Press, 2010).

[74] Ian Milligan, *History in the Age of Abundance?: How the Web Is Transforming Historical Research* (Montreal: McGill-Queen's University Press, 2019).

[75] David Hesmondhalgh, 'Streaming's Effects on Music Culture: Old Anxieties and New Simplifications', *Cultural Sociology* 16, no.1 (June 2021).

some musicians to focus on single releases, and how the significant popularity of video-sharing apps encourages artists to try to create dance crazes. It is ultimately the technology companies who stand to profit most from this paradigm, selling the audience time and attention that artists generate to advertisers. For artists, it is hard to break away from—or altogether refuse to participate in—this system, because streaming platforms and video-sharing apps are where the vast majority of their potential audiences already pay their attention.

Internet rappers are fierce competitors for attention on audiovisual and social media platforms. They actively brand themselves as young, controversial rockstars to help them stand out among other musicians, influencers, and micro-celebrities on social media. It is essential for aspiring professionals to produce and distribute—once again, share—media content to promote oneself as an individual creative. Hence rappers fill Instagram feeds, promote their work on TikTok, and record Facebook Live videos, affording kinds of access and intimacy that audiences crave and now expect.[76] At a professional level, most rappers outsource the bulk of this work to dedicated staff among their creative teams. However, aspiring artists across the music industry typically do all of this themselves, moving 'seamlessly between making art, creating brands, running small businesses, and selling their cultural capital, all while working to retain status as radical, and sometimes street, artists'.[77] Internet rap is an especially intense example of such work, which can be understood as a form of visibility labour[78] or relational labour.[79] Emerging rappers compete for clout online to attract prospective fans, expand their social media followings, and enter online public discourse (whether with some viral content, as a trending topic, or as a meme).

Throughout the 2010s, DIY-aligned 'new amateurs'[80] and 'produsers'[81] have managed to undercut traditional music industry gatekeepers by strategically

---

[76] Chris Rojek, *Presumed Intimacy: Para-Social Relationships in Media, Society and Celebrity Culture* (Cambridge: Polity, 2016); Nancy Baym, *Playing to the Crowd: Musicians, Audiences, and the Intimate Work of Connection* (New York: New York University Press, 2018).

[77] Sarah Banet-Weiser, *Authentic™: The Politics of Ambivalence in a Brand Culture* (New York: NYU Press, 2012), 98.

[78] Crystal Abidin, 'Visibility Labour: Engaging with Influencers' Fashion Brands and #OOTD Advertorial Campaigns on Instagram', *Media International Australia* 161, no. 1 (November 2016): 86–100; Jabari M. Evans and Nancy K. Baym, 'The Audacity of Clout (Chasing): Digital Strategies of Black Youth in Chicago DIY Hip-Hop', *International Journal of Communication* 16 (May 2022): 19.

[79] Baym, *Playing to the Crowd*, 173–176.

[80] Nick Prior, 'The Rise of the New Amateurs: Popular Music, Digital Technology and the Fate of Cultural Production', in *Handbook of Cultural Sociology*, ed. J. R. Hall, L. Grindstaff, and M. Lo (London and New York: Routledge, 2010), 398–407.

[81] Axel Bruns, 'Prosumption, Produsage', ed. Klaus Bruhn Jensen and Robert T. Craig, *The International Encyclopedia of Communication Theory and Philosophy* (Chichester and Noboken, NJ: Wiley-Blackwell and the International Communication Association, 2016).

72   Digital Flows

Figure 3.4 6ix9ine with his prominent rainbow hair and grills, and extensive '69' tattoos, with text caption dubbing him the final boss of SoundCloud rappers, from Know Your Meme

deploying online promotion techniques to gain the valuable attention of social media users.[82] However, Ian Dunham points out that SoundCloud 'simultaneously functions as a traditional gatekeeper and as a space for artists to circumvent gatekeeping'.[83] It is worth distinguishing between media platforms in their capacity to streamline creatives' engagement with potential audiences. The upload process on SoundCloud is freer and easier than enlisting a third-party distributor to publish music on on-demand streaming services, giving rise to a sense that SoundCloud is more 'producer-oriented' than the consumer-oriented market leaders like Spotify.[84]

6ix9ine is perhaps the most social media-savvy breakthrough artist of the internet rap generation. His eccentric look is readymade meme fodder, leading to a viral image that dubs him the 'final boss' of SoundCloud rappers (Figure 3.4).

In combining ostentatious visual aesthetics to attract attention, his public image seems to scream 'look at me' (which, incidentally, was the apt title of XXXTentacion's breakthrough single). Furthermore, it recalls a kind of nonchalant and unapologetic attitude of self-representation from earlier hip hop

---

[82] Evans and Baym, 'The Audacity of Clout (Chasing)', 2677–2681.
[83] Dunham, 'SoundCloud Rap', 112.
[84] David Hesmondhalgh, Ellis Jones, and Andreas Rauh, 'SoundCloud and Bandcamp as Alternative Music Platforms', *Social Media + Society* 5, no. 4 (October 2019).

Internet Rap and Generational Tensions **73**

fashion. Think of Kanye with the pink polo and backpack, Danny Brown's skinny jeans, or back to Flavor Flav's silly-sized clock necklace. 6ix9ine describes his persona[85] as an act of representation for young people who are treated like 'some type of joke to . . . society'.[86]

He is also an online provocateur who has started shit—or retaliated to others, always upping the stakes—with what seems like half of hip hop's major players. Rap beefs used to rely on traditional media circulation, which operated at a slower pace and within more disparate fora than the rapidly centralizing forces of social media platforms. Goading figures with large fanbases is therefore a strategy well designed for the social media climate, inspiring impulsive reactions, likes, shares, downvotes: anything to gain an audience. Hip hop artists have typically sought co-signs and endorsements based on mutual respect; 6ix9ine instead links himself to famous rappers through antagonism, though both sides arguably benefit from the virtual sparring. Alongside other 'viral techniques' deployed on social media,[87] his confrontational music is also finely attuned to the conventions of online media circulation.

His breakthrough 'Gummo' video stages a series of remarkable ambiguous contrasts.[88] Set on the stoop of a Brooklyn apartment block (and, in a few scenes, an off-street van with large bags of marijuana on the hood), a couple dozen Black men dressed in Bloods colours dance, pose, rap along, drink, cook, and throw signs. These are all archetypal hardcore rap tropes. Now add to the mix 6ix9ine: breaking the clothing colour palette, he totes a green tracksuit or parades around topless, revealing his prominent '69' stomach tattoo (Figure 3.5). His rainbow hair hangs low, sometimes partly concealed by a red-and-white bandana, thus contrasting an ostensible silliness, perhaps even post-ironic queerness, with the street coding of gang headwear.[89]

The beat is sparse, slightly creepy in its narrow pitch intervals, but with an airiness in the synth timbres and uninflected, clicky trap drums. There is locomotion, but no explosive energy, to this unlicensed Pi'erre Bourne

---

[85] Kai Arne Hansen, '(Re)Reading Pop Personae: A Transmedial Approach to Studying the Multiple Construction of Artist Identities', *Twentieth-Century Music* 16, no. 3 (October 2019): 501–529.

[86] *Open Space: Tekashi69 (6ix9ine)*, YouTube video, 11 May 2017, https://www.youtube.com/watch?v=12f9v1_9K_E.

[87] Paula Harper, 'BEYONCÉ: Viral Techniques and the Visual Album', *Popular Music and Society* 42, no. 1 (January 2019): 63.

[88] 'Remarkable' understood quite literally, as something that makes internet users want to remark on it and share it within their cultural networks. Karine Nahon and Jeff Hemsley, *Going Viral* (Cambridge: Polity, 2013), 61. See also Justin Kirby and Paul Marsden, eds., *Connected Marketing: The Viral, Buzz and Word of Mouth Revolution* (Oxford and Burlington, MA: Butterworth-Heinemann, 2007), xxv–xxvii.

[89] Two and a half years later, 6ix9ine would appear to give up members of the Nine Trey Gangsta Bloods as part of court testimony, which resulted in many hip hop artists distancing themselves from him. His widely publicized legal disputes also serve to promote his viral profile.

Figure 3.5 6ix9ine stands out in 'Gummo' video, screenshots from YouTube

production. 6ix9ine pairs it with seemingly excessive, high-pitched and hoarse shouted vocals—drenched in reverb to give an inflated sense of size—and hyper-aggressive lyrics.[90] The Mexican-Puerto Rican rapper is relatively light-skinned, especially by contrast with the Black crowd in the video, yet consistently uses Black-exclusive slang as though racially assimilated.[91] He offers a fierce rap performance and some brilliant mean mugging,[92] but his rainbow grills also shine from his mouth, belying his belligerence. His stance is serious but his look is frivolous, resulting in a music video always open to question, inviting reaction of whatever form. Alongside the structures of networked communication that drive virality, 'information characteristics, like humor, surprise, novelty, resonance, and quality, can influence our decision to share'.[93] To my mind, 6ix9ine's 'Gummo' is tailor-made to garner online remarks and reposts: it carries many shareworthy features as attention-grabbing, smartly contradictory, and controversial media content.

Three years later, on 'Gooba', he acknowledges his provocative stance, putting down his rap opposition who 'always wanna chase clout', stating simply, 'I am clout'. Whereas rappers of a previous generation might cite clout-chasing pejoratively—trying too hard to be heard, or failing to gain *real* fans—6ix9ine instead mocks other clout-chasers because *he is the best at it*.[94] Yet he always relates his social media stardom to a hip hop sensibility, especially by way of his Brooklyn roots, lest he appear entirely inauthentic to the culture. From video

---

[90] His vocal performance style on this track seems inherited from another of rap's most controversial stars, Eminem, at his shoutiest.

[91] This critique does not mean to reinforce colourism (as if to say, 6ix9ine would get a pass if he were darker), but to problematize the longstanding issue concerning Hispanic and Latinx artists' entitlement to particular elements of African American Vernacular English.

[92] Miles White, *From Jim Crow to Jay-Z: Race, Rap, and the Performance of Masculinity* (Urbana: University of Illinois Press, 2011), 43–44.

[93] Nahon and Hemsley, *Going Viral*, 63.

[94] See also Evans and Baym, 'The Audacity of Clout (Chasing)', who avoid judgements about clout-chasing, positioning it instead as an integral part of platform logics concerning exposure, audience engagement, and capital.

Internet Rap and Generational Tensions   75

Figure 3.6 6ix9ine suggesting his 2-million-strong Instagram Live audience makes him the King of New York, from Twitter

locations to his lyrical references, he thoroughly ties his work to his home city, dubbing himself a New York legend (another claim that seems designed to anger old school heads, given his conspicuous visual and musical differences). Regardless of his real-life connections, the artist 6ix9ine is clearly more of an online phenomenon, developed strategically for viral impact some way from a traditional hip hop artist on the come-up. In the era of social media, however, the online audience is a new metric of success that overshadows the significance, and even the veracity, of local connections. Displaying some conceptual sleight-of-hand, his record-breaking Instagram Live viewership of two million—a purely online audience—is captioned with the tweeted text: 'I'm still the King of New York' (Figure 3.6).

It may be 6ix9ine's ability to bridge the gap between traditional hip hop's local specificity and the internet's wide-reaching placelessness that garners him the reputation of internet rap's provocateur par excellence. He remains just recognizably hip hop enough, while channelling youthful punk-rap energy into online media primed with viral potential.

Conclusion

If the urgency to have one's voice heard—no matter the social, financial, critical, or legal cost—is beginning to sound kind of hip hop after all, you may see why I have suggested internet rap continues its legacy as a new generation of

76 Digital Flows

the culture. Despite artists' dismissal of older heads,[95] the addition of alternative and extreme styles, and the web-savvy clout-chasing, the hip hop lineage shines through. Just as the 'creative misuse' of turntables to loop dance breaks birthed hip hop as a live performance form,[96] internet rap best reflects its hip hop ethos through the strategic use of internet technologies for personal and professional gain.

Internet rap may be a short-lived phenomenon. In much the same way as its role model, punk, was pronounced dead, critics have also claimed the end of the SoundCloud generation,[97] with good reason. For one, three of its key players—Lil Peep, XXXTentacion, and Juice Wrld—have passed away. For another, changes to how SoundCloud functions as a platform—essentially bringing it more in line with other on-demand streaming services—seem to have reduced opportunities for the independent breakthroughs it enabled just a few years earlier. At the time of writing, all eyes are on TikTok, which functions less like a music distribution platform and relies more on audio-visual content to make or break specific songs. We had the era of 'SoundCloud rappers', and now we have 'TikTok rappers', as musicians vie for moments of viral attention that can be leveraged into careers in the industry. Old school heads may squirm at the thought of the culture being harvested for profit, visibility, and clout among social media audiences. Yet hip hop is continually adapted on the internet to suit the conditions of the attention economy.

There is no better example of such viral achievement than Lil Nas X's breakthrough, which has been well covered by scholars.[98] His 'Old Town Road' was born of internet culture fluency, and, like internet rap, exacerbated friction between traditional and contemporary music industry gatekeepers. It was intensely catchy, widely appealing, and highly shareworthy to boot. The song also heightened tensions around stylistic and genre conventions by combining elements of country, pop, and trap. In particular, Lil Nas X subverted expectations associated with country music and condensed recognizable hip hop

---

[95] I have mentioned Lil Yachty and Lil Xan as artists that disregard their hip hop forebears, but many of their peers—other internet rappers—show a deep respect for hip hop legacy. Regarding Juice Wrld and XXXTentacion, see, for example, *Juice WRLD Breaks Down Tupac & Eminem's Influence on His Music*, YouTube video, 23 July 2018, https://www.youtube.com/watch?v=fsaolirWIKQ; Jonathan Reiss, *Look at Me!: The XXXTENTACION Story* (New York: Hachette Books, 2020).

[96] Richard Elliott, '"The Most Annoying Noise of All Time"', *Australian Humanities Review*, no. 70 (2022): 60.

[97] Jon Caramanica, 'Juice WRLD and the Tragic End of the SoundCloud Rap Era', *New York Times*, 9 December 2019, https://archive.is/W9SpT; Pierre, 'How Rap's SoundCloud Generation Changed the Music Business Forever'.

[98] Hansen, *Pop Masculinities*, 66–99; Mel Stanfill, 'Can't Nobody Tell Me Nothin': "Old Town Road", Resisting Musical Norms, and Queer Remix Reproduction', *Popular Music* 40, no. 3–4 (December 2021): 347–363; Natalie Collie and Caroline Wilson-Barnao, 'Playing with TikTok: Algorithmic Culture and the Future of Creative Work', *The Future of Creative Work*, September 2020, 172–188.

aesthetics into a humorous, meme-oriented, and viral video trend. Though he may have a good claim to the legacy of internet rap, 'Old Town Road' is just one example of the integration of hip hop in mainstream online culture. Elsewhere online, audiovisual media associated with hip hop generates communities that form and shift according to audience demands. The next chapter provides an in-depth study of lofi hip hop, a YouTube phenomenon lambasted for its attentional demands,[99] to examine how the affordances and reception of online hip hop continue to evolve.

---

[99] Amanda Petrusich, 'Against Chill: Apathetic Music to Make Spreadsheets To', *The New Yorker*, 10 April 2019, https://www.newyorker.com/culture/cultural-comment/against-chill-apathetic-music-to-make-spreadsheets-to.

4
Lofi Hip Hop and Community in YouTube Comments During the COVID-19 Pandemic

Chill Beats to Quarantine to

Introduction

There's a strange feeling evoked by seeing someone else's YouTube homepage. Behind the scenes of the world's second-most popular website, recommendation algorithms operate on user data about viewing activity, subscriptions, and location (derived from an IP address) in service of personalization. If you're logged in, YouTube is trying to suggest videos you are likely to watch at any given time. As such, a visit to YouTube presents very different content—thumbnails, titles, topics, uploader names—to different users. If this has passed you unnoticed, try opening YouTube in a private or 'incognito' window on your web browser. Since no cookies are stored in this mode, this will show you a version of YouTube that is less informed by your personal data but instead emphasizes trending content that performs well with first-time users.[1] In standard day-to-day viewership of online video, however, users leave significant traces of previous engagement with YouTube.

Much has been written about the personalization of media platforms in general,[2] but this chapter jumps off from the appearance of a particular YouTube thumbnail among someone's video recommendations: an anime-inspired drawing of a young woman, seated and facing left, working away at a desk while wearing headphones. This is an image of the character popularly dubbed 'lofi girl' (Figure 4.1), who serves as a visual emblem for an entire genre of popular music and its associated community of internet sociality. The video

---

[1] I write less informed rather than uninformed because YouTube can still make some data-driven predictions using your location, device, time of day, and so on.

[2] Eli Pariser, *The Filter Bubble: How the New Personalized Web Is Changing What We Read and How We Think* (New York: Penguin, 2011); José van Dijck, Thomas Poell, and Martijn de Waal, *The Platform Society: Public Values in a Collective World* (New York: Oxford University Press, 2018), 31–48.

Digital Flows. Steven Gamble, Oxford University Press. © Oxford University Press 2024.
DOI: 10.1093/oso/9780197656389.003.0004

Lofi Hip Hop and Community   79

Figure 4.1 'Lofi girl', from 'lofi hip hop radio - beats to relax/study to', courtesy of Stanislas Somoguy at Lofi Records

represented is a constant livestream titled 'lofi hip hop radio - beats to relax/study to', hosted on the channel Lofi Girl, which rebranded from ChilledCow in March 2021 due to the iconic status of the character.[3] Catching sight of the thumbnail implies the use of music for specific functions (accompanying studying, computer-based work, and repose), with particular genre aesthetics (hip hop), and to encourage or support a certain state of mind (such as concentration or relaxation).

Although Lofi Girl appears especially prominently in YouTube's recommendation algorithms, there are many videos like 'lofi hip hop radio'. Searching for keywords such as 'lofi', 'beats', 'chill', 'study', and 'relax' will return thousands of video results, from popular channels including (at the time of writing) Chillhop Music, STEEZYASFUCK, The Jazz Hop Café, Homework Radio, and the bootleg boy. The videos appearing under these search terms can be usefully divided into three types. The first, real-time livestreams, emulate an enhanced form of radio and, aptly, often include 'radio' in their titles. While live, they are constantly broadcasting songs back-to-back, although a user can also skip backwards in time up to twelve hours and change the playback speed. The second type of video is a prepared playlist, commonly referred to as a mix (distinguishing it from what YouTube calls playlists—like a folder—of individual songs).[4] Mixes are YouTube videos formed of pieces of music sequenced

---

[3] Lofi Girl, 'Lofi Hip Hop Radio - Beats to Relax/Study To', YouTube livestream, 22 February 2020, https://www.youtube.com/watch?v=5qap5aO4i9A.

[4] João Francisco Porfírio, 'YouTube and the Sonification of Domestic Everyday Life', in *YouTube and Music: Online Culture and Everyday Life*, ed. Holly Rogers, Joana Freitas, and João Francisco Porfírio (London: Bloomsbury Academic, 2023), 214, 220.

80 Digital Flows

punkz
@PUNKZBUNNY

And the Grammy goes to....... Lo–Fi Hip Hop Anime Chil Beats To Study and Relax To

11:57 am · 29 Jan 2018 · Twitter for iPhone

49.8K Retweets   **1.2K** Quote Tweets   **136.4K** Likes

Figure 4.2 Tweet comically awarding lofi hip hop YouTube videos a Grammy award, courtesy of user

one after the other, usually lasting anywhere from thirty minutes up to about two hours. They make up a large part of all music listening on the platform, whether comprising major popular songs (e.g., Top Hits 2020), specific genres (Rock Ballads), or functions (Focus Music). The third kind of lofi video is a standalone track lasting around three minutes. This chapter focuses on the first and second types of lofi hip hop video—streams and mixes—since they are central to the culture of lofi listening. Individual tracks are still interesting artefacts of online instrumental hip hop, of course, but they are much less commonly consumed, for a range of factors such as the prevailing plural term beats and automated recommendations of the most popular livestreams and mixes.

Lofi hip hop in its current instantiation emerged in the mid-2010s.[5] Sometimes referred to as 'YouTube lofi', 'chill beats', or 'beats to study/relax to'—employing an ironic mishmash of common video title terms, as highlighted by Figure 4.2—livestreams and mix videos are now a popular staple of YouTube musical activity. Some of the most popular channels have developed into record labels, such as Lofi Records and Chillhop Music, complete with vinyl releases and merchandise. A Wikipedia entry and Know Your Meme page indicate wide online recognition of the lofi hip hop phenomenon. And while lofi mixes have long referenced popular cartoons, a 2020 episode of *BoJack Horseman* referenced lofi back. The character Pickles, who is obsessed with social media, comically states that her favourite *recording artist* is the Lofi Girl livestream: 'I love Lo-Fi Chill-Hop Beats to study/relax to!'[6] Moreover,

---

[5] Emma Winston and Laurence Saywood, 'Beats to Relax/Study To: Contradiction and Paradox in Lofi Hip Hop', *IASPM Journal* 9, no. 2 (December 2019): 40.

[6] Amy Winfrey, dir., *BoJack Horseman*, season 6, episode 11, 'Sunk Cost and All That', Netflix (2020), https://www.netflix.com/watch/81026969. I took the punctuation and capitalization from Netflix's subtitles.

a number of media publications have profiled lofi hip hop and interviewed some of the best-known uploaders, particularly in relation to the music's increasing popularity during the COVID-19 pandemic.

Throughout 2020, lofi hip hop went on a wild ride. Lofi mixes advertising music to accompany studying, coding, or relaxing—the latter partially a euphemism for recreational drug use, typically smoking marijuana—already comprised a very popular category on YouTube, with millions of views on the most popular mixes and an active audience on non-stop livestreams. After being live for 548 consecutive days, the 'lofi hip hop radio - beats to relax/study to' stream came to an end when YouTube mistakenly banned the ChilledCow account based on a terms of service violation. It was reinstated within a day and quickly regained its position as the most viewed lofi radio. The sudden ban, however, led to a mass outcry on social media platforms and made headlines for transforming the livestream up to that point into one of the longest-ever YouTube videos. That took place at the end of February 2020.

With the threat of the novel coronavirus (SARS-CoV-2) looming, March saw the worldwide introduction of public health measures, variously referred to as quarantine, lockdown, and stay-at-home orders. Most educational institutions and businesses transitioned to internet-based communication, with those privileged in homes typically working remotely, that is, online, for several months. Lofi hip hop became well-used and well-loved during this period, as web journalists widely reported.[7] How might this influx of new listeners have changed the conventions of engagement with the music on YouTube? In short, how did lockdown affect lofi listening?

This chapter investigates the genre aesthetics of lofi hip hop and the virtual community built around commenting on YouTube lofi mixes. This is achieved through a data-driven method comparing word association thematic analysis of around 182 thousand video comments with close readings of popular comments and online cultural journalism. The focus is on lofi hip hop as a contemporary net-native music culture that combines the internet-based activity of functional music listening with lofi aesthetics and hip hop beats. I am principally concerned with changes in lofi hip hop commentary during the COVID-19 pandemic, a period marked by a surge in audience growth. This is

---

[7] Julia Alexander, 'Lo-Fi Beats to Quarantine to Are Booming on YouTube', *The Verge*, 20 April 2020, https://www.theverge.com/2020/4/20/21222294/lofi-chillhop-youtube-productivity-community-views-subscribers; Sophie Atkinson, 'The "24/7 Lo-Fi Hip Hop Beats" Girl Is Our Social Distancing Role Model', *Dazed*, 23 March 2020, https://www.dazeddigital.com/music/article/48486/1/the-24-7-lo-fi-hip-hop-beats-girl-is-our-social-distancing-role-model; Torry Threadcraft, 'Lo-Fi Hip Hop YouTube Channels Reporting Significant Boost During Quarantine', *Okayplayer*, 27 April 2020, https://www.okayplayer.com/culture/lo-fi-hip-hop-quarantine.html.

82   Digital Flows

an exemplary case study revealing how people interact with hip hop on the internet to experience—or at least report experiencing—feelings of communal belonging, affirmations of personal identity, and social connection to others. My findings also reveal how hip hop can be transformed by online mediation and commercialization, and how the culture is understood differently by distinct user groups.

Audiovisual Aesthetics of Lofi Hip Hop

The most common colloquial name for lofi hip hop is the abbreviation 'lofi'. Of course, numerous kinds of music have historically been referred to as lofi, or indeed 'lo-fi', referring to the opposite of the sound technology advertising term high-fidelity.[8] The term 'low-fidelity' appeared popularly in the 1990s music press, referring to the 'raw' and 'minimal' production aesthetics of particular styles of rock music.[9] In his study of the topic, Adam Harper finds appreciation for lo-fi aesthetics associated with perceived imperfections in recorded music. Over time, he argues, the ideologies determining listeners' tastes for such sounds have varied between primitivism (think of artists portrayed as amateur, poor, racially or colonially coded as 'simple'), realism ('authentic', everyday), postmodernism (tending towards being pretentious), and archaism (using older technologies). Such systems of value—and the associated term, originally written 'low-fi'—have been applied to musics such as rockabilly, indie rock, and punk, and especially associated with cassette culture.

The word lofi continued to refer to aesthetics highlighting sonic imperfections when music started to be released on CDs and later as digital audio files. As such, lofi hip hop has a handful of more direct progenitors than 1980s rock: hypnagogic pop, chillwave, and vaporwave. Hypnagogic pop has been described as evoking 'the state between sleep and wakefulness', featuring nostalgic sounds influenced by 1980s US cassette tape recordings.[10] As YouTube developed a publicly accessible archive of audiovisual material throughout the late 2000s, the platform became a rich resource for the

[8] Bo Nilsson and Kerstin Edin, ' "It Has Seldom Been So Difficult to Try to Dress Up a Sound Experience in Words": Technology and the Rhetoric of Sound and Music Reproduction in Hi-Fi Magazines', *PULS: Musik- Och Dansetnologisk Tidskrift* 7 (2022): 121–140.

[9] Adam Harper, 'Lo-Fi Aesthetics in Popular Music Discourse' (DPhil diss., University of Oxford, 2014), 11.

[10] Georgina Born and Christopher Haworth, 'From Microsound to Vaporwave: Internet-Mediated Musics, Online Methods, and Genre', *Music and Letters* 98, no. 4 (2017): 629.

development of hypnagogic pop's genre aesthetics. This genre label was somewhat superseded by chillwave, which developed a stricter musical focus on conventional pop song structure. Chillwave's genre identity is based on retrofuturistic references to 1980s electronic dance music and the visual imagery of classic video games, especially arcade racing games like *Pole Position*. Its rhythmic consistency and lightly distorted timbres evoke the feeling of driving. Developing on chillwave's sample-heavy aesthetics and cultural nostalgia, vaporwave is understood as a more ironic, politically engaged genre that principally critiques consumer capitalism.[11] Perhaps the most emblematic image for vaporwave is the disused shopping mall, what with its affordances of garish 1990s corporate marketing, the popularity of the personal computer, the ubiquitous presence of Muzak, and the technological optimism of then-rapidly evolving markets like Japan.[12] Each of these kinds of music embrace low-fidelity audio aesthetics and reference outdated technologies, but are sometimes characterized as microgenres,[13] which implies limited popularity.

By contrast, the contemporary flag-bearer for the term lofi—the hip hop broadcast by Lofi Girl and others on YouTube—has become extremely well known in mainstream online culture. The number of remix videos with a title ending 'but it's lofi' demonstrates a stable set of meme conventions and expectations based around the music (Figure 4.3).[14] It has also been appropriated in other forms of media, such as the 'Lo-Fi Player' developed using Google's Magenta machine learning models.[15] The artwork for the rhythm game *lofi ping pong* is ripe with genre signifiers, such as a drawing of a woman wearing earphones and visual imperfections like paint chips (not to mention the lower-case title).[16] Similarly, a third-party listing for the defunct 'lo-fi block breaker' game *Hiatus* invokes a number of terms in common with the discourse surrounding lofi music, promoting the game as 'endless', 'casual', and 'relaxing', all couched within soft pastel-coloured animations.[17]

[11] Andrew Whelan, '"Do You Have a Moment to Talk About Vaporwave?" Technology, Memory, and Critique in the Writing on an Online Music Scene', in *Popular Music, Technology, and the Changing Media Ecosystem*, ed. Tamas Tofalvy and Emília Barna (Cham: Springer, 2020), 187.

[12] Laura Glitsos, 'Vaporwave, or Music Optimised for Abandoned Malls', *Popular Music* 37, no. 1 (January 2018): 100–118.

[13] Guillaume Loignon and Philippe Messier, 'Vaporwave Pedagogy: Multimodal Learning with an Internet Music Microgenre', *Liminalities* 16, no. 3 (2020): 1–23.

[14] Limor Shifman, *Memes in Digital Culture* (Cambridge, MA: MIT Press, 2014).

[15] Vibert Thio and Douglas Eck, 'Lo-Fi Player', *Magenta*, 1 September 2020, https://magenta.tensorflow.org/lofi-player.

[16] eastasiasoft, 'Lofi Ping Pong Trailer (Nintendo Switch)', YouTube video, 1 April 2021, https://www.youtube.com/watch?v=nLZ8CcAXTAQ; Adam Harper, 'What Is Lo-Fi? A Genealogy of a Recurrent Term in the Aesthetics of Popular Music Production', research seminar, City University of London, December 2020.

[17] Shrine Studio Ltd, AppAdvice, 'Hiatus', January 2021, https://appadvice.com/app/hiatus/1493350890. .

Figure 4.3 'X but it's Y' meme of Bernie Sanders filibustering combined with lofi audiovisual aesthetics, screenshot from YouTube

As well as a stabilizing set of genre conventions, lofi hip hop can also be thought of as a distinct music style (more on this distinction in Chapter 6).[18] Tracks in YouTube mixes and livestreams have many musical characteristics in common. Lofi hip hop is built around looped passages of piano, guitar, or a synthesized instrument. This is sometimes referred to by lofi producers as 'the sample' of any given track, a more style-specific use of the term compared to general sampling practices that lie at the foundation of hip hop production.[19] A lofi sample usually cycles through between two and four chords, typically

---

[18] See Allan F. Moore, 'Categorical Conventions in Music Discourse: Style and Genre', *Music & Letters* 82, no. 3 (January 2001): 432–442.
[19] J. G. Schloss, *Making Beats: The Art of Sample-Based Hip-Hop* (Middletown, CT: Wesleyan University Press, 2004).

Lofi Hip Hop and Community **85**

using or implying extended chords, which also form the basis of jazz harmony. Most tracks begin with this sample, or loop, playing once or twice before percussive sounds enter: kick, snare, and sometimes hi-hats. These sounds are all more muffled than conventional hip hop percussion, with a low-pass filter applied to reduce high-frequency content. This effect dampens the sound character while retaining the drums' impact and therefore the track's rhythmic motion: hence, they are 'chill beats'. In addition, a number of other sounds inhabit the lofi soundworld: voice extracts (often lengthy samples from cartoons or anime which play out over looped sections without the drums), harmonic filler layers in the form of synthesized timbres and other samples, and a range of adornments such as filter effects, turntable scratching, and rhythmic stutters.

Most lofi beats resemble a relaxed take on boom bap, the East Coast style predominantly emphasizing the kick on beats one and three and the snare on beats two and four of each four-beat bar.[20] However, the specific placement of these elements plays a significant role.[21] Lofi beats gain their characteristic sound through careful consideration of microrhythm, with producers placing percussive elements slightly outside the metronomic grid to produce unique grooves variously experienced as 'hazy'[22] and 'lazy',[23] or inciting 'head-bobbing'.[24] It is common to hear conspicuous reverb or delay effects added to samples, although drums tend to remain relatively dry. A final prominent feature is the constant presence of analogue audio imperfections, emulating the hiss and flutter of cassette tape or the crackling of vinyl on a turntable.[25] Lofi producers I spoke to described these effects as the 'glue' that holds a lofi beat together, and indeed some of the style's most identifiable features. The stylistic conventions identified here will be recognizable in the vast majority of lofi tracks, which draw upon the work of celebrated instrumental hip hop producers Nujabes, J Dilla,[26] and Madlib.[27]

---

[20] Michail Exarchos, 'Boom Bap Ex Machina', in *Producing Music*, ed. Russ Hepworth-Sawyer, Jay Hodgson, and Mark Marrington (New York: Routledge, 2019), 32–51.

[21] R. Brøvig-Hanssen and A. Danielsen, *Digital Signatures: The Impact of Digitization on Popular Music Sound* (Cambridge, MA: MIT Press, 2016), 101–115.

[22] Kemi Alemoru, 'Inside YouTube's Calming "Lofi Hip Hop Radio to Relax/Study to" Community', *Dazed*, 14 June 2018, https://www.dazeddigital.com/music/article/40366/1/youtube-lo-fi-hip-hop-study-relax-24-7-livestream-scene.

[23] Luke Winkie, 'How "Lofi Hip Hop Radio to Relax/Study to" Became a YouTube Phenomenon', *VICE*, 13 July 2018, https://www.vice.com/en/article/594b3z/how-lofi-hip-hop-radio-to-relaxstudy-to-became-a-youtube-phenomenon.

[24] Michael Wu, 'What Are Lofi Hip Hop Streams, and Why Are They So Popular?', *Study Breaks*, 2 December 2018, https://studybreaks.com/culture/music/lofi-hip-hop-streams-popular/.

[25] Adam Scott Neal, 'Lo-Fi Today', *Organised Sound* 27, no. 1 (April 2022): 33.

[26] Rhythmic characterizations of Dilla's beats are closely aligned with descriptions of lofi: '*sloppy. Drunken. Limping. Lazy. Dragging. Off*' (italics preserved). Dan Charnas, *Dilla Time: The Life and Afterlife of J Dilla, the Hip-Hop Producer Who Reinvented Rhythm* (New York: Farrar, Straus and Giroux, 2022).

[27] Madlib was widely cited by my interviewees as an important influence, although I must admit I hear few traces of his iconic ruptures and carefully crafted abrasiveness in lofi's gentler musical conventions.

86   Digital Flows

My interviewees often suggested that lofi is an 'old school' hip hop style. It is perhaps the emphasis on looped melodies and dampened drums which led to this impression, as well as the presence of audio samples with nostalgic affordances. Like many other forms of internet music sociality tinged with irony and post-irony,[28] the hissing and crackling analogue imperfections are predominantly produced in digital audio workstations. This is an aesthetic endorsement of archaism, emulating the iconic qualities of earlier audio production using contemporary technologies. The limited high-frequency content of lofi recordings—a more vintage sound—persists alongside modern techniques such as the quality of digital side-chain compression and reverb effect plugins.[29] So why 'lofi'?

The name lofi appears to carry emotional resonances above and beyond low-fidelity audio imperfections. In the mid-1990s, low-fi gained a close association with DIY practices, with one music critic that Harper cites describing a particular indie rock release as 'casual and unadorned'.[30] Despite including some more sophisticated production conventions, lofi hip hop seems like low-effort music, resonating with critical ideas about 'chill'.[31] Given the downbeat tone of many lofi comments, the term can imply aspects of poor personal wellbeing: low mood or even lo-neliness. Indeed, lofi listeners frequently express their feelings and memories in striking detail, and discuss them with other commenters on YouTube. This understanding of lofi hip hop as the soundtrack to an emotionally reflective, relaxed, even somewhat lazy virtual space ('lo-afing around'?) gives rise to affordances of domestic activity that were intensified during the pandemic, as user comments reveal.

Listening During Lockdown

With a sense of the genre conventions and stylistic norms of lofi in mind, I turn to an analysis of changes in YouTube commentary on mixes during the COVID-19 pandemic. I did not include 'chill beats to quarantine to', a mix uploaded by actor and musician Will Smith (taken as this chapter's subtitle), in this dataset, but will address it towards the end of the chapter.[32] It is also

---

[28] Adam Trainer, 'From Hypnagogia to Distroid: Postironic Musical Renderings of Personal Memory', in *The Oxford Handbook of Music and Virtuality*, ed. Sheila Whiteley and Shara Rambarran (Oxford: Oxford University Press, 2016), 419–427.

[29] Neal, 'Lo-Fi Today', 32.

[30] Jon Pareles, 'Low-Fi Rockers', *The New York Times*, 11 April 1993.

[31] Robin James, 'Toned Down for What? How "Chill" Turned Toxic', *The Guardian*, 2 July 2018, http://www.theguardian.com/music/2018/jul/02/toned-down-for-what-how-chill-turned-toxic.

[32] Will Smith, 'Chill Beats to Quarantine To', YouTube video, 20 March 2020, https://www.youtube.com/watch?v=rA56B4JyTgI.

important to mention that no livestream videos were used in the data sample because static comments are disabled and replaced by a live chat box. The following thematic analysis is therefore exclusive to lofi mixes. I return to lofi as radio in the subsequent section.

I compared 97,000 comments posted prior to March 2020 with 85,000 comments posted in the subsequent nine months, a period which included national lockdowns affecting half of the global population.[33] Although provinces in mainland China announced quarantine measures in January 2020 and the World Health Organization did not declare COVID-19 a pandemic until 11 March, many major countries launched lockdowns throughout March. 1 March was chosen as the cut-off point as a neat division between pre-pandemic conditions and the period in which widespread public health measures were active.[34] Using the software Mozdeh, I determined statistically significant differences in the proportions of words used in comments posted during each period.

Mozdeh uses chi-squared tests to determine significant differences in term use between two subsets (in this case by time period, in Chapter 5 by commenter gender). It then controls the occurrence of false positives using the Benjamini-Hochberg procedure, which adjusts p-values (the measure of statistical significance) by comparing them to a threshold based on the number of chi-squared tests conducted.[35] These processes provide a more robust method than simply comparing frequencies. To further improve the statistical power of my analysis, I only considered terms to be significant only if the likelihood of identifying false positives was 0.1 per cent or lower. Additionally, I excluded terms that were used too infrequently to provide a statistically significant result. I then carried out a process of thematic analysis, reading terms in the context of up to 100 randomized comments and applying thematic labels.

---

[33] Gerry F. Killeen and Samson S. Kiware, 'Why Lockdown? Why National Unity? Why Global Solidarity? Simplified Arithmetic Tools for Decision-Makers, Health Professionals, Journalists and the General Public to Explore Containment Options for the 2019 Novel Coronavirus', *Infectious Disease Modelling* 5 (January 2020): 442–458.

[34] In May 2023, the World Health Organization reduced their classification of COVID-19 from a public health emergency of international concern to an established and ongoing health issue. The disease continues to affect people worldwide and in disproportionate ways. I mostly write in past tense about comments that were posted during 2020, or specific quarantine recommendations that no longer stand. In doing so, I am not implying that there are no longer health risks or outstanding issues associated with disability justice, unequal access to vaccinations, and so on. See, for example, Emily M. Lund and Kara B. Ayers, 'Ever-Changing but Always Constant: "Waves" of Disability Discrimination during the COVID-19 Pandemic in the United States', *Disability and Health Journal* 15, no. 4 (October 2022).

[35] For a slightly more detailed description of Mozdeh's statistical method, see Mike Thelwall, 'Can Museums Find Male or Female Audiences Online with YouTube?', *Aslib Journal of Information Management* 70, no. 5 (January 2018): 487–488; Mike Thelwall and Saheeda Thelwall, 'Covid-19 Tweeting in English: Gender Differences', arXiv preprint, arXiv.2003.11090 (2020), 3–4.

88   Digital Flows

Table 4.1 Thematic analysis of term frequency in lofi YouTube comments before and during the COVID-19 pandemic

Theme	Subtheme	Terms more frequent before COVID-19	Terms more frequent during COVID-19
Listening context	COVID-19		quarantine, corona, covid, virus, pandemic
	Studying and working		online, doing, module, assignment, study
	Time and place	during	night, Monday, summer
Identity	Witches and ghosts		witch, ghost, witchcraft, wizard, spell
	a e s t h e t i c	[Individually spaced letters]	
	Music references	mix, genre, vaporwave, chillhop, music	lofi
	Media references	Bebop, Morty, Duskwood	
Social connection	Appraisal	love, dope, good, first, beautiful	
	Conversation	man	vibing, hi, comment
	Memes		zooted, homer, plot, pov, twist
	Emotional expression	life, shit, feel, alone, depressed	safe

Reading the terms that had substantially increased and declined in use between these periods revealed a variety of changes in the reported contexts of listening, performances of identity, and social connections. Table 4.1 provides a summary of the themes, subthemes, and terms that saw significant changes in word frequency. My discussion follows.

Listening Context

Unsurprisingly, there were no mentions of 'covid' or 'pandemic' before 1 March 2020, so the most significant changes in term frequency appear around new terms like 'covid-19'.[36] Users tended to emphasize the social and public health implications of the pandemic, with terms like 'lockdown' and 'quarantine' appearing in thousands of comments among people keen to report their

---

[36] Individual words in inverted commas are the specific terms appearing in my analysis.

specific listening circumstances. Some indicative statements include:[37] 'the songs in this playlist help me get through quarantine', 'who else is listening to this in quarantine?', and 'my teacher says to quarantine at home because of coronavirus'.

There is a notable chunk of commentary dedicated to expressing gratitude for the music. It apparently brought comfort during periods of lockdown, alongside a sense of solidarity, urging that lofi listeners would, for example, 'get through this together'. The word 'stay' saw a large increase in usage—even more significant than 'covid-19'—perhaps because it has several meanings relevant to the pandemic. It often appeared in lofi commentary before COVID-19, in phrases like 'stay awake', posted by tired students, and 'stay alive', advocated by emotionally supportive users. During the early period of the pandemic, however, 'stay safe' became perhaps the most popular platitude in everyday communication, which is reflected in comments on lofi mixes. Users also reflected on health and safety concerns, recommending (or having received the recommendation to) 'stay inside'.

Beyond the extraordinary circumstances of the pandemic, listeners increasingly reported accompanying periods of study with lofi mixes. Numerous terms speak to the pervasiveness of studying while listening, with 'online', 'doing',[38] 'module', 'assignment', 'study', 'finished', 'homework', 'session', and 'classes' all seeing greater use. There is a clear precedent for lofi listeners using the music alongside schoolwork or studying, which Winston and Saywood, in the best academic treatment of lofi to date, associate with the frame of Jonathan Crary's '24/7 capitalism'.[39] They describe lofi hip hop as an appropriate soundtrack for a social context where the time spent in school and doing homework has continuously increased since the 1980s, and where periods formerly used for leisure and relaxation have been filled with more work.[40] These developments certainly account for the lofi audience's fondness for mixes encouraging activities like a '1 A.M Study Session'.[41]

---

[37] Note that comments quoted as examples are abbreviated or rearranged to preserve poster anonymity. However, I avoid introducing new words to maintain an accurate portrait of the sentiments expressed. This approach communicates a 'general feeling' of each comment while protecting the privacy of individual social media users. Helen Kennedy, *Post, Mine, Repeat: Social Media Data Mining Becomes Ordinary* (London: Palgrave Macmillan, 2016), 118. See also Steven Gamble, 'Towards an Ethical Model of Data Analysis for Research on Online Music Cultures', in *Music and the Internet: Methodological, Epistemological, and Ethical Orientations*, ed. Christopher Haworth, Daniele S. Sofer, and Edward Katrak Spencer (Abingdon: Routledge, 2023).

[38] While the term 'doing' might seem too broad to consistently indicate education, the vast majority of uses occurred in relation to another word in this theme, especially 'homework', 'online school', or 'online class'.

[39] Jonathan Crary, *24/7: Late Capitalism and the Ends of Sleep* (London: Verso Books, 2014).

[40] Winston and Saywood, 'Beats to Relax/Study To', 49.

[41] Lofi Girl, '1 A.M Study Session 📚 - [Lofi Hip Hop/Chill Beats]', YouTube video, 8 December 2019, https://www.youtube.com/watch?v=1TRiuFIWV54.

90   Digital Flows

Describing study periods has always been a popular trope in lofi comments sections. Now, one purported function of the music—to study to—evidently became indispensable, as students had more time for listening during distance learning and posting about it. With educational institutions the world over shifting to remote learning, students working from home gained unprecedented control over their background music while studying. They discuss enjoying lofi mixes to accompany online lectures or while working through e-learning courses, a privilege usually denied during in-person education. The term 'school' only became slightly more popular, failing to reach the benchmark for statistical significance, and evidencing the novelty and sudden ubiquity of 'online' learning in particular. The trend towards constant work that Winston and Saywood observe might have intensified during the pandemic, as suggested by lofi comments' abundant references to schoolwork during the pandemic. That said, the idea of undertaking a well-organized study 'session' or reporting being 'finished' with a specific 'module' indicates that students were successfully putting boundaries around periods of study, accompanied, of course, by beats to study to.

With quarantine and studying largely occupying the minds of commenters during the pandemic, it follows that there are fewer references to other times and places than there used to be. The terms 'night', 'Monday', and 'summer' are much more frequent in the sample of texts prior to the pandemic, in reflections such as, 'it's 1am here, a perfect night to forget about everything' and 'this takes me back to the summer of 2015'. I had assumed that listeners' memories of better times would be a more common topic of conversation during the pandemic, but this is not reflected in the commentary. One simple explanation for this might be that so much attention was focused on COVID-19 that it took precedence over writing about other times and places. For instance, users in the later period posted things like 'I'm still awake listening in lockdown' rather than 'I'm still awake listening late at night'. Interestingly, the word 'during' appeared much more frequently after March 2020, prompted by describing the contexts of the pandemic: 'here during quarantine', 'I love having this on in the background during my classes on zoom', and 'kept me going during hours of homework'.

Arguably, comments reflecting on the poster's current environment and activities resemble a miniature form of diarizing.[42] Sentiments range from trivial remarks to strikingly specific microfiction. While personal blogging on YouTube typically appears in the videos themselves—as vlogging—many comments on lofi mixes chronicle the present moment in miniature. Not

---

[42] Jill Walker Rettberg, *Blogging*, 2nd ed. (Cambridge: Polity, 2014).

only did individuals posting during COVID-19 seem eager to acknowledge their living through an important period of history, but often asked questions seeking conversation or solidarity: 'who else is vibing to this during lockdown?', 'the covid situation here is bad, have schools in your country reopened yet?', and 'anyone else listen to this to calm down?'. It is tempting to dismiss this altogether as reassurance-seeking, but the implied forms of communality— and the number of responses people tend to give and receive—suggest a kind of collective identity shared among lofi listeners.

Identity

There is limited demographic data about the lofi audience, aside from Cherie Hu (2020) noting the most popular channels are managed by 'white European men in their twenties',[43] and Winston and Saywood suggesting that a large proportion of commenters are school and university students.[44] My data shows a close to even split between male and female participants (inferring binary user gender by name, a methodological limitation discussed in Chapter 5). In her *New Yorker* commentary, Amanda Petrusich draws a generational division between herself and her lofi-listening university students, though she also conflates the music with SoundCloud rap, mischaracterizing that wildly dynamic genre (the subject of Chapter 3) as 'chill'.[45] The Jazz Hop Café's viewers are 'for the most part' aged under thirty-five, with a geographically diverse viewership; similarly, representatives of Chillhop Music stated that almost three-quarters of their audience is under thirty-five.[46] Beyond categorical demographics, however, new associations and expressions of personal identity emerged among the lofi audience during the pandemic, some of which are rather surprising, even spooky.

The most statistically significant increased terms in the entire sample are 'witch' and 'ghost'. There is a simple surface-level explanation for this. Two of the most popular lofi mixes of 2020 were Homework Radio's 'Lo-fi for Ghosts

---

[43] Cherie Hu, 'The Economics of 24/7 Lo-Fi Hip-Hop YouTube Livestreams', *Hot Pod News*, 11 January 2020, https://web.archive.org/web/20230531122716/https://hotpodnews.com/the-economics-of-24-7-lo-fi-hip-hop-youtube-livestreams/.

[44] Winston and Saywood, 'Beats to Relax/Study To', 41.

[45] Amanda Petrusich, 'Against Chill: Apathetic Music to Make Spreadsheets To', *The New Yorker*, 10 April 2019, https://www.newyorker.com/culture/cultural-comment/against-chill-apathetic-music-to-make-spreadsheets-to.

[46] Bill Hochberg, 'Chill Hop, Jazz Hop, LoFi, Whatever You Call It, It's Catching On With Gen-Z', *Forbes*, 8 September 2020, https://www.forbes.com/sites/williamhochberg/2020/09/08/chill-hop-jazz-hop-lofi-whatever-you-call-it-its-driving-gen-z-mild/.

92 Digital Flows

(Only)',[47] uploaded in August 2019, and 'Lo-fi for Witches (Only) [lofi / calm / chill beats]',[48] which went live on 27 March 2020. Understandably, there are few references to witches and ghosts prior to these videos. Alongside 'witch' and 'ghost', the terms 'witchcraft', 'wizard', 'spell', 'warlock', and 'wiccan' also saw major surges in use. Two videos with characterful variations on the typical lofi title, prompting commenters to use these marked terms, might seem like an uninteresting finding at first glance. However, the mystical imagery and fantastical identities invoked by these popular mid-COVID mixes are worth some consideration.

Many individuals introduce themselves in the comments section of 'Lo-fi for Witches' as a witch, often indicating a process of self-discovery: 'I first knew I was a witch when . . .', 'I want to be a witch', 'listening to this as a witch makes me feel . . .', and so on. Ghosts are similarly discussed in the corresponding video—'I'm a ghost on the inside'—though occasionally the title provokes dry humour: 'YouTube recommended this mix to me so I guess that makes me a ghost'. Lofi listeners increasingly identified with such figures during the pandemic, and it may be easy to see why. Loneliness and social isolation have been the topics of much research examining the impacts of quarantine and lockdown measures.[49] One particular term used in public health advice, 'self-isolation', promotes staying at home by oneself as conscientious civic behaviour. This is not lost on journalist Sophie Atkinson, who describes the lofi girl character as 'the poster girl for responsible coronavirus behaviour for Gen Z and millennials alike'.[50] The practical consequences of self-isolation, however, align closely with the emotionally isolated, otherworldly imagery of ghosts and witches. Consider how ghosts and witches are portrayed in popular media as invisible or outcast loners removed from social connections, typically situated indoors, and committed to domestic hobbies. With the absence of everyday social interactions during COVID-19, lofi listeners began positively associating with such supernatural figures. Vaporwave, lofi's ancestor,

---

[47] Homework Radio, 'Lo-Fi for Ghosts (Only)', YouTube video, 6 August 2019, https://www.youtube.com/watch?v=2GjPQfdQfMY.

[48] Homework Radio, 'Lo-Fi for Witches (Only) [Lofi / Calm / Chill Beats]', YouTube video, 27 March 2020, https://www.youtube.com/watch?v=4Hg1Kudd_x4.

[49] Tzung-Jeng Hwang et al., 'Loneliness and Social Isolation during the COVID-19 Pandemic', *International Psychogeriatrics* 32, no. 10 (October 2020): 1217–1220; Jing Xuan Koh and Tau Ming Liew, 'How Loneliness Is Talked about in Social Media during COVID-19 Pandemic: Text Mining of 4,492 Twitter Feeds', *Journal of Psychiatric Research*, November 2020; Yuval Palgi et al., 'The Loneliness Pandemic: Loneliness and Other Concomitants of Depression, Anxiety and Their Comorbidity during the COVID-19 Outbreak', *Journal of Affective Disorders* 275 (October 2020): 109–111; Ben J. Smith and Michelle H. Lim, 'How the COVID-19 Pandemic Is Focusing Attention on Loneliness and Social Isolation', *Public Health Research & Practice* 30, no. 2 (June 2020).

[50] Atkinson, 'The "24/7 Lo-Fi Hip Hop Beats" Girl Is Our Social Distancing Role Model'.

Figure 4.4 Original artwork for 'Lo-fi for Witches' by Anaïs Maamar, courtesy of artist

has similarly evoked the ghost as a figure produced by online communication, which leads to feeling 'social while alone, thronged with invisible entities'.[51] As for the frequent use of 'wizard' and 'warlock', the number of comments like 'what about lofi for wizards?' imply that witch was received as a feminine or female-gendered term which apparently required parity.

Given lofi's young, student audience, there may be additional resonances given the associations between witchcraft and studying popularized in film and television. The tropes of studiousness and spellcasting inform characters like Hermione Grainger in the *Harry Potter* universe, Willow in the TV show *Buffy the Vampire Slayer*, and the cast of the anime *Little Witch Academia*. The video of 'Lo-fi for Witches' plays on these tropes through visual references, replacing lofi girl with a cartoon witch leant over a desk, complete with pointed hat, open spell books, wand, and so on (Figure 4.4). For all the students working away, confined to bedrooms and dorm rooms in self-isolation, the image of a lonely witch practising an arcane craft evidently feels relatable. The video title also prompted some discussion of contemporary mysticism and neopaganism, coinciding with the growth of a TikTok community dedicated

---

[51] Grafton Tanner, *Babbling Corpse: Vaporwave and the Commodification Of Ghosts* (Winchester: Zero Books, 2016).

94 Digital Flows

to witchcraft, known as WitchTok.[52] Connotations of alternative medicine, shamanism, and New Age thought more broadly are troubling given the info-demic precipitated by COVID-19,[53] although the comments on YouTube are generally innocuous. Almost all of the discussion in this section comes from comments on the 'witches' video, so evidently mixed titles and visuals can strongly sway the topic of conversation. Homework Radio's attempts to brand lofi for other characters (vampires, demons, mermaids, angels, insomniacs) have not (yet) proven as successful, indicating the imagery of witches and ghosts in popular culture fit a particular niche aligning with lofi's listener identities during the pandemic.

There are broader conventions adopted by participants in lofi mix comments sections. A prominent feature since the earliest appearances of the genre on YouTube is the use of full-width characters, known as an 'aesthetic' font or simply 'aesthetic text'. This convention originated in online vaporwave culture, when it was more commonly used for capital letters along-side kana and kanji typography. For example, tracks now considered to be vaporwave classics, from albums like フローラルの専門店 ('Floral Shoppe') by Macintosh Plus and *FINAL TEARS* by INTERNET CLUB, are commonly rendered in capitals and include Japanese characters. The artist t e l e p a t h テレパシー能力者, first active using that title around 2013, solidified the trend of spaced-out text in vaporwave. Fullwidth lettering, or simply placing a space between each letter, now appears in many lofi mix titles and comments, such as 'h o m e w o r k & s t u d y（ミュージック）'.[54] However, in-dividually spaced letters were used in a greater proportion of comments prior to March 2020, suggesting that this kind of typing—formerly an integral part of lofi's aesthetic identity—appears to be going out of style.

A straightforward explanation for the decrease in 'aesthetic text' is that the genre's rising popularity during the pandemic brought many new listeners to the YouTube mixes, who were not familiar with—or chose not to adopt—the typographical convention. The arrival of new listeners leaving comments without spaces may have therefore skewed the dataset towards standard text. However, there may be a larger cultural shift at play, with users viewing the typing style as somewhat tired, overused, or basically dissolved into meme

---

[52] Lauren McCarthy, 'Inside #WitchTok, Where Witches of TikTok Go Viral', *Nylon*, 6 July 2020, https://www.nylon.com/life/witchtok-witches-of-tiktok.

[53] Matteo Cinelli et al., 'The COVID-19 Social Media Infodemic', *Scientific Reports* 10, no. 1 (October 2020).

[54] R L I F E, 'H o m e w o r k & S t u d y（ミュージック）', YouTube video, 5 April 2018, https://www.youtube.com/watch?v=mUeZDu9rBH8.

fodder. For example, it is museumized by a Know Your Meme page on 'aesthetic' (the date of this article implying it was already passé during vaporwave's peak).[55] It nonetheless serves as an indicator of genre aesthetics, and can even identify lofi mixes without the usual title keywords, as in the highly popular videos 'N O S T A L G I C'[56] and 'F e e l i n g s'.[57]

Aesthetic text is not lofi's only inheritance from vaporwave. Winston and Saywood also identify nostalgia as a central theme of lofi hip hop. For fans, the genre provides 'hyper-specific memories of popular media which may have been consumed during, or at least associated with, a listener's childhood'.[58] I found new identifications with witches and ghosts, but references to several pop-culture figures precede the pandemic as a form of identity construction. In the dataset, we find mentions of the animated TV series *Cowboy Bebop*, *Rick and Morty*, and *The Simpsons*. Like aesthetic text, however, these references see declining use. Yet particular playlists from the pre-pandemic period, especially from around 2016–2018, help to identify the core of lofi hip hop as an online community built upon shared nostalgic references.

Uploader the bootleg boy's series of twenty-minute mixes entitled 'Volumes' has an aesthetic identity strongly informed by specific cartoons. In these videos, images of familiar characters like *Spongebob Squarepants*, *Futurama's* Fry, and Jake the Dog of *Adventure Time* appear downcast or crying. With music commissioned around audio samples from specific shows (a different series for each video in the series), the mixes serve as indexes of childhood memory combined with nostalgic sadness.[59] For instance, in the thirty-second opening 'B A D F E E L I N G S',[60] a video loop of Bart Simpson crying (Figure 4.5) is complemented by audio from *The Simpsons* drenched in reverb, an effect widely used to evoke memory and emotional significance. In the clip, Marge encourages Lisa to suppress her sadness: 'take all your bad feelings, and push them down . . . I want you to smile today'. After a pause,

---

[55] Know Your Meme, 'Aesthetic', *Know Your Meme*, 12 August 2021, https://knowyourmeme.com/memes/aesthetic.

[56] NEOTIC, 'N O S T A L G I C', YouTube video, 14 February 2017, https://www.youtube.com/watch?v=hQyzEyIf7P0.

[57] Cabvno, 'F e e l i n g s', YouTube video, 8 August 2017, https://www.youtube.com/watch?v=0cKzCUdtRh8.

[58] Winston and Saywood, 'Beats to Relax/Study To', 41.

[59] This is a trend found in other YouTube music compilations. Joana Freitas observes that 'epic music compilations convey a set of tropes pre-established in other media to activate audiovisual memory'. Joana Freitas, ' "Only People With Good Imaginations Usually Listen to This Kind of Music": On the Convergence of Musical Tags, Video Games and YouTube in the Epic Genre', in *Remediating Sound: Repeatable Culture, YouTube and Music*, ed. Holly Rogers, Joana Freitas, and João Francisco Porfírio (London: Bloomsbury Academic, 2023), 161.

[60] the bootleg boy, 'B A D F E E L I N G S', YouTube video, 25 June 2017, https://www.youtube.com/watch?v=_z442kpDbUY.

Figure 4.5 Bart Simpson crying animation in YouTube mix B A D F E E L I N G S by the bootleg boy, screenshot from YouTube

Lisa responds, 'But I don't feel like smiling', which echoes out as the first beat begins. Instances like this exemplify both the referential and the nostalgic qualities of lofi, contributing to a sense of collective identity among listeners of a similar age and shared childhood media experiences. Still, 'Simpson' is mentioned twice as often prior to March 2020, which indicates the diminishing popularity of cartoons as shared cultural touchpoints in lofi comments. This is perhaps influenced by the declining use of visual imagery and audio samples in mixes themselves.

However, some visual elements encouraged more discussion in the comments. Mixes using looped animations of a character studying, in the model of lofi girl, warranted increased discussion of 'balcony', 'cat', and 'typing'. This indicates that listeners continue to respond to the content of the videos, but that the visual aesthetics of lofi have developed over time. Whereas cartoons are no longer as popular (or perhaps not as popular among the expanding audience), visual signifiers and titles that reinforce the advertised functions of studying and relaxing appear more appealing. It is tempting to posit a shift in uses of lofi from leisure time (including emotional reflection and nostalgia prompted by cartoons) towards more labour (working using a constant stream of lofi as a motivating factor), which certainly correlates with the late capitalist contexts of listening.[61] We should not forget, however, that new leisure practices emerged, such as the identity formations based around witchcraft. I will return to these considerations in a discussion of the future of lofi listening at the end of the chapter.

Discussion of lofi as music developed rapidly. The declining use of the terms 'mix', 'genre', 'vaporwave', 'chillhop', and 'beat' suggest earlier uncertainties around what such music might be called. Indeed, the only increasingly frequent term about music is 'lofi', clearly showing the genre coalescing around this label. Earlier exchanges show the collegial, conversational spirit of lofi even when the terminology was unstable. For instance, one query on a hip hop-based mix, 'what is this genre called?', garnered the response 'vaporwave', dubiously suggesting that the term originated from 'a bunch of guys who vape'.[62] As lofi became codified separately from vaporwave, such confusion appears less commonly. Personal exchanges between participants nonetheless remain a key feature of lofi mix comments sections. It has been claimed that such interactions represent 'one of the kindest communities on the internet',[63] one characterized by 'overall supportiveness'.[64]

Social Connection

As well as a genre, lofi is popularly understood to be a community. It is one that centres around YouTube but also spills out across record labels that run Discord servers, artists' SoundCloud pages, and fan encounters on subreddits like r/lofi and r/lofihiphop. The text-based interactivity of these platforms is key to lofi's cultural identity and the perceived virtual community formed around listening to the music. I align with Jessa Lingel's assessment that defining community, especially in the online context, is tricky, variously referring to ties between people who 'are bound by a shared set of knowledge about doing something . . . share a collective sense of identity that stems from shared geography . . . [or share] conditions of otherness'.[65] I deploy the term here to refer to perceived commonalities in practice, aligning people with an appreciation for lofi music, commenting about it online, undertaking similar

---

[61] Crary, *24/7: Late Capitalism and the Ends of Sleep*.

[62] The name is a play on 'vaporware': long-promised software that fails to materialize or live up to the standard advertised, much like (as the genre's proponents would claim) late capitalism altogether.

[63] Alemoru, 'Inside YouTube's Calming "Lofi Hip Hop Radio to Relax/Study to" Community'.

[64] Winston and Saywood, 'Beats to Relax/Study To', 49.

[65] Jessa Lingel, *Digital Countercultures and the Struggle for Community* (Cambridge, MA: MIT Press, 2017), 5–7.

98   Digital Flows

everyday activities (like studying and working, of course), and exchanging personal reflections and recollections. Since most internet interactivity is pseudonymous, one cannot easily know what aspects of identity and culture they share with others in online communities, yet the imagination of common conventions and assumed affinities can contribute to a powerful sense of belonging.[66] Given its friendly reputation, how did the arrival of newcomers during COVID-19 reinforce or challenge popular notions of lofi as a kind and supportive community?

Conversations accompanying lofi mixes typically span a variety of topics, including appreciation for the music, personal stories, and internet memes. However, words based on a positive appraisal of the music—'love', 'good', and 'beautiful'—appear less often after March 2020. The related drop-off of 'dope', a word derived from hip hop slang, indicates a distancing of lofi from its hip hop origins. Moreover, fewer listeners inquired about the 'first' track of a mix, a formerly common trend where users tried to track down particular pieces of music. On the whole, it seems that YouTube users, stumbling upon lofi from outside the typical cultural spaces of hip hop during the pandemic, pay less attention to the music (or at least discuss it less). This waning interest in music appreciation might support Petrusich's critical reading of lofi as 'apathetic' background music that is not worth aestheticizing.[67] However, such surface engagement struggles to see how lofi listening nonetheless facilitates congenial interactions, with the lofi audience highly expressive about their appreciation for others posting in the comments sections.

The community became increasingly conversational during the pandemic, with more use of the terms 'hi', 'comment', 'reading', and 'vibing'. A representative example combining these terms is: 'hi to everyone reading my comment while vibing along'. General greetings, often directed to 'whoever reads this', seemingly act as a substitute for direct social connection that nonetheless helps to provide ontological security (i.e., 'I am saying hello! I still exist!').[68]

---

[66] For more on how communities can be constituted imaginatively, see Benedict Anderson, *Imagined Communities: Reflections on the Origin and Spread of Nationalism*, rev. ed. (London and New York: Verso, 2006), and work that has previously applied Anderson's ideas to an imagined hip hop community, such as Friederike Frost, 'Breaking the Limits? Exploring the Breaking Scene in Havana, Cuba and Belonging in a Global (Imagined) Breaking Community', *Global Hip Hop Studies* 2, no. 1 (June 2021): 15–36 and Christina Higgins, 'From Da Bomb to Bomba: Global Hip Hop Nation Language in Tanzania', in *Global Linguistic Flows: Hip Hop Cultures, Youth Identities, and the Politics of Language*, ed. H. Samy Alim, Awad Ibrahim, and Alastair Pennycook (New York and London: Routledge, 2009), 95–112.

[67] Petrusich, 'Against Chill'.

[68] Aside from individual gratification, Varis and Blommaert found that 'phatic' online commentary—like small talk or seemingly trivial memes—help to produce conviviality, which may underlie the communal resonances of lofi on YouTube. Piia Varis and Jan Blommaert, 'Conviviality and Collectives on Social Media: Virality, Memes, and New Social Structures', *Multilingual Margins: A Journal of Multilingualism from the Periphery* 2, no. 1 (2015): 31–45.

Participants announcing their presence to an imagined community affords 'security in the sense of self and confidence in the continuity of one's being-in-the-world'.[69] The comments section not only provided an opportunity for staving off isolation but also held the potential for encouraging wellbeing practices in others. Many individuals offered advice to the crowd, such as, 'hi everybody ♥ make sure to drink enough water and have regular meals today', and 'Hi to everyone studying for exams, we'll get through this, keep going!'. As I previously mentioned, the desire to share activities with others—'who's still vibing to this in 2020?'—further affirms feelings of belonging united by common behaviours expressed on YouTube. Lofi thus exemplifies danah boyd's conception of a networked public as 'the imagined collective that emerges as a result of the intersection of people, technology, and practice'.[70]

Despite the increase in cursory terms, longer sentences dwindled somewhat. There was an overall reduction in the use of common sentence words such as 'I', 'of', 'these', 'it', 'the', and so on. One might suggest this trend indicates that lengthy comments formerly used for diarizing individual feelings have been superseded by general introductions. Though typing at length about personal situations may be on the decline, specific self-reflections remain popular. Two thousand users liked a post detailing an apparently relatable scenario: 'anyone else vibing to this in bed waiting for the coast to be clear at 2am to go grab some cereal?'. This is a vivid image: a young person who lives in their parental home (or dorm) with a private bedroom, listening to lofi in the early hours using a personal laptop or smartphone, and awaiting a quiet time when others in the house are asleep so they can sneak to a (shared) kitchen for a late-night snack. Though it is wise not to over-generalize about lofi listeners' identities, this comment—and its significant positive response—reveals a great deal about the typical circumstances of individuals tuning in.[71]

In addition to common listening practices, users also partook in a series of popular in-jokes across lofi comments sections. These are highly repetitive

---

[69] Lynn Jamieson, 'Personal Relationships, Intimacy and the Self in a Mediated and Global Digital Age', in *Digital Sociology: Critical Perspectives*, ed. Kate Orton-Johnson and Nick Prior (London: Palgrave Macmillan, 2013), 15.

[70] danah boyd, 'Social Network Sites as Networked Publics: Affordances, Dynamics, and Implications', in *A Networked Self*, ed. Zizi Papacharissi (New York and London: Routledge, 2011), 39.

[71] This individualized, domestic listening contrasts with earlier reflections on YouTube as a shared experience *in situ*. Christopher Schneider found users who 'recounted their experiences watching [a video posted in 2005] with family and friends', suggesting the existence of 'a *participatory culture* that extends into various offline spaces'. Christopher J. Schneider, 'Music Videos on YouTube: Exploring Participatory Culture on Social Media', in *Symbolic Interactionist Takes on Music*, ed. Christopher J. Schneider and Joseph A. Kotarba (Bingley: Emerald, 2016), 108, italics preserved. Perhaps this tracks with developments in consumer technology, from owning a single family desktop computer to a household possessing a range of personal laptops and smartphones.

100 Digital Flows

and formulaic text posts—copypasta[72]—whose playful ubiquity forms part of the humour.[73] A user scrolling down the page will be met by identical comment after identical comment.[74] After March 2020, there was a major increase in the terms 'zooted', 'homer', 'plot', 'pov', and 'copying'. In the comments of one particular mix, uploaded by GEMN Chill Out & Lofi Music, such memes run rampant.[75] It features an oversaturated animation of Homer Simpson in a car, endlessly nodding his head from side to side, his eyelids heavy, as clouds pass him by. Listeners interpreted the visual accompaniment to the mix as showing Homer high on psychoactive drugs, just sitting in his car as time passes, hence the repeated phrase 'Homer is so zooted he's not even driving. The clouds are moving not him.' This exact text comprised a significant proportion of all comments on the video. Commenters occasionally varied on the theme, imagining a first-time viewer's perspective when approaching the YouTube page using the 'POV' meme format: 'POV: You're looking for a comment that doesn't say "Homer is so zooted he's not even driving. The clouds are moving not him"'. This repeats at increasingly meta levels to refer even to the 'POV' comment. There could hardly be a clearer example of Carol Vernallis' assertion that 'reiteration reigns supreme on YouTube'.[76]

The 'POV' format works similarly to 'plot twist', again speaking in the tone of a narrator instructing the reader to imagine the surprising scenario which follows. For instance, poking fun at the Lofi Girl animation, users posted, 'plot twist: she is actually right handed and has just been practicing writing with her left all this time'. The social interaction involved in these meme trends is far from conversational in any deep sense and barely related to lofi music itself. However, 'getting the joke' and then playing along manifests as an exercise in social bonding. It resembles the 'uncreativity' found in other growing online communities, as new members stick to established scripts.[77] That said, the removal of the zooted Homer video[78]—and the entire GEMN channel—as

[72] Elizabeth F. Chamberlain, '"Our World Is Worth Fighting for": Gas Mask Agency, Copypasta Sit-Ins, and the Material-Discursive Practices of the Blitzchung Controversy', *Computers and Composition* 65 (September 2022): 9.

[73] Shifman, *Memes in Digital Culture*, 78–79.

[74] Denisova and Herasimenka identified similarly repetitive commentary in their study of Russian rap on YouTube, describing it as 'indirect' and 'reciprocal' social interaction. Anastasia Denisova and Aliaksandr Herasimenka, 'How Russian Rap on YouTube Advances Alternative Political Deliberation: Hegemony, Counter-Hegemony, and Emerging Resistant Publics', *Social Media + Society* 5, no. 2 (April 2019): 8.

[75] GEMN Chill Out & Lofi Music, 'Chill Lo-Fi Hip-Hop Beats FREE | Lofi Hip Hop Chillhop Music Mix | GEMN', YouTube video, 2 May 2020, https://web.archive.org/web/20201220171946/https://www.youtube.com/watch?v=qvUWA45GOMg.

[76] Carol Vernallis, *Unruly Media: Youtube, Music Video, And The New Digital Cinema* (New York: Oxford University Press, 2013), 131.

[77] Edward Katrak Spencer, 'When Donald Trump Dropped the Bass: The Weaponization of Dubstep in Internet Trolling Strategies, 2011–2016', *Twentieth-Century Music*, forthcoming.

[78] It has since been rehosted on another channel. It may be yet taken down again, then put up again, then removed once more, in an endless battle of user persistence and platform moderation.

of mid-2021 suggests the lofi mix did not comply with YouTube's regulations around copyrighted material.[79] Regardless, the tendency towards meme spam indicative of internet culture at a more general level shifted the emphasis away from lofi's formerly tight-knit social connections.

Emotionally sincere commentary has been a hallmark of lofi mixes since their earliest days on YouTube, reminiscent of Tumblr's personally expressive mode of discourse. Winston and Saywood write of the 'emotional narrative microfiction' that characterizes much lofi commentary, which they observe in relation to 'affective labour'.[80] However, words related to personal feelings appeared less commonly since around the time that COVID-19 measures were enacted. Such terms include 'life', 'feel', 'make', 'alone', 'depressed', 'nostalgic', 'sad', 'childhood', 'everything', 'nostalgia', and 'lonely'. There was also less recourse to the swear words 'shit' and 'fuck', even where they simply serve as intensifiers ('I love this shit'). The only emotional term that significantly increased in use was noted earlier—'safe'—which relates to conventional, conversational expressions during the pandemic.

Like many of the terms I analyse here, there is a sense that more diverse commentary from newcomers to the lofi comments sections increased the amount of chatter, revealing a reduction in emotional language. At a broader level, an earlier manifestation of the lofi community on YouTube resembles a form of internet subculture or digital counterculture that has now been dissolved by an influx of general YouTube music viewers.[81] It could also be argued that the emotional mode of expression that used to widely accompany lofi mixes simply ran its course, with users finding different outlets for discussing their feelings. I propose a third explanation for the decline in emotional commentary. Taking the prevalence of 'safe' into account alongside the maintenance of other conversational norms, perhaps public health messaging inhibited commentary on everyday feelings, with listeners attempting to demonstrate resilience in the face of the grave global circumstances. As such, commenters provide less personal reflection on experiences of low mood or nostalgia, even though the feelings themselves may persist. Moreover, a crisis of COVID-19's scale might make day-to-day woes seem fairly insignificant, leading individuals to post something positive—'stay safe everyone reading!'—rather than wallowing in negative feelings.

---

[79] There has been an associated shift in lofi beat production away from using lengthy samples requiring clearance, which is beyond the means of independent record labels, and towards creating original samples by recording guitars, keyboards, synths, and so on.

[80] Winston and Saywood, 'Beats to Relax/Study To', 47–48.

[81] Lingel, *Digital Countercultures and the Struggle for Community*.

Livestream Listening and Commercial Appropriations of Lofi Hip Hop

The increasingly surface-level conversation that my analysis uncovered aligns with a broader shift away from lofi mixes and towards radio-style livestreams. Use of lofi primarily as a study aid might make livestreams more attractive. They are always on and always there, offering a kind of reliability: one can 'tune in' at any point and gain accompaniment for an undefined (even unlimited) period of time, with no risk of being interrupted by a mix video ending while in the flow of things. Lofi livestreams are well-promoted by YouTube's recommendations, often appearing on a user's homepage—as anecdotally discussed in the introduction—and require only a single low-commitment click before consistent background music begins playing. These videos have live chat, rather than persistent comments displayed below the video, a technical feature which has major consequences for listener discussion. On popular channels, the pace of chat makes back-and-forth conversation between individuals difficult, with several languages, emojis, and links flying across the screen. This transience means it is unlikely that users will write personal reflections with any hope of preservation or response. Users are also limited to 200 characters per post, preventing lengthier comments. Certain social connections are lost in this format, which privileges constant activity over in-depth discourse preserved over time.

Lofi livestreams have received criticism for appearing to endorse non-stop work rather than merely offering flexibility. In other words, they encourage listeners to study *all the time*, not just at any time. If the animated lofi girl is a 'role model' for social distancing,[82] does she also endorse studying constantly, without breaks, while the sun sets and rises outside like it does behind her? Petrusich's *New Yorker* profile of lofi construes it as reconfiguring music as 'a tool for productivity'.[83] Winston and Saywood are similarly concerned about the genre's relationship to post-Fordism, with the music used as 'a tool for self-regulation to increase productivity'.[84] Relatedly, Robin James sees chill music as a gendered form of self-regulation: with emotional excess culturally considered something feminine, 'chill' acts as a celebration of masculine restraint.[85] Critiques of students' increasing workloads and neoliberal pressures towards productivity typically position lofi as symptomatic of the

---

[82] Atkinson, 'The "24/7 Lo-Fi Hip Hop Beats" Girl Is Our Social Distancing Role Model'.

[83] Petrusich, 'Against Chill'.

[84] Winston and Saywood, 'Beats to Relax/Study To', 49.

[85] Robin James, 'Chill Pop & Feminine Excess: A "Sign of the Times"', *It's Her Factory* (blog), May 2017, 201, https://www.its-her-factory.com/2017/05/chill-pop-feminine-excess-a-sign-of-the-times/.

Lofi Hip Hop and Community   103

political problems evoked. I would suggest instead that the music is used actively, and with agency, by young hip hop listeners as an attempt to ameliorate such issues. Since excessive labour demands are already entrenched in contemporary capitalist societies,[86] it is quite understandable for young people to try to enjoy such experiences of unavoidable work. The conflation of studying and relaxing, as though they are interchangeable, was not *originated* by 'beats to study/relax to', though music is often typecast as the cause of social ills.[87] Rather, lofi hip hop *emerges from* social conditions which have already elided self-managed work and leisure time.

In this reading, lofi streams might act as a partial corrective to the individualized labour of isolated students who, while listening, can imagine working collectively in real-time, united by a common soundtrack. The idea of tuning in to an event taking place synchronously worldwide (which I explore further in Chapter 7) encourages communal expressions of support and mutual motivation. While the live chat minimizes the opportunity for longer conversation, this may actually be beneficial for people trying to study without distraction. I can attest to losing a good deal of time reading comments on mixes! Furthermore, YouTube's live chat provides a space for users to post links and liaise elsewhere for less ephemeral discussion. Lofi channel owners clearly recognize the kinds of communication that are lost when using real-time chat and rectify this by linking through pinned chat posts and the video description to associated Discord servers. These servers, usually hosted by record labels like Lofi Girl and Chillhop Music, enable closer engagement with the community of listeners, untethered from expectations of studying or working.

Besides, the more recent popularity of livestreams does not mean that mixes have stopped being accessible. Mixes remain popular, as demonstrated by the recent success of 'Lo-fi for Witches'. Alongside Lofi Girl's leading livestream, which averages 25,000 real-time listeners as of early 2023, the channel continues to upload new mixes monthly. These videos receive hundreds of comments rather than thousands, but they show evidence of lofi's former tendencies towards microfiction, diarization, and emotional expression. The variety of referential contexts that new playlist videos evoke—cartoons, video games, cities, environments, moods, times of day—suggests that the lofi mix tradition is far from over. Users enthusiastically navigate mix thumbnails

---

[86] Peter Fleming, *The Mythology of Work: How Capitalism Persists Despite Itself* (London: Pluto Press, 2015); Malcolm Harris, *Kids These Days: Human Capital and the Making of Millennials* (New York: Little, Brown and Company, 2017).

[87] Adam L. Perry, 'From the McCarthy Era to "Gangsta Rap": The Rhetoric of Popular Music and Moral Panic in America' (PhD diss., Pennsylvania State University, 2013), https://etda.libraries.psu.edu/catalog/19541.

104 Digital Flows

and titles, create their own playlists of mix videos, or even create and upload their own compilations in conventional produser practice, as seen across YouTube.[88] They may be guided by YouTube's recommendation algorithms, or allow lofi videos to auto-play as a sort of meta-radio, but we should be wary about claims that listeners have lost all agency over their engagement with the platform.[89]

One unexamined consequence of lofi's growing mainstream popularity is its openness to commercial appropriation. Some channels are run as a hobby and others have developed into independent record labels founded by community members.[90] However, broader commercial and political incentives have motivated the production of videos using the aesthetic veneer of lofi as a popular point of reference. Just as the first American states imposed stay-at-home orders, rapper-turned-actor Will Smith uploaded the lofi mix 'chill beats to quarantine to'.[91] The ninety-minute video features an animation of Smith himself in the style of lofi girl, working at a desk, complete with a cat on the windowsill and an urban skyline visible out the window. The logo on his headphones reads 'Fresh', a reference to his rap persona the Fresh Prince, and he wears a hoodie with the logo 'Bel-Air'. The first line of the video description encourages listeners to buy merchandise from his clothing company Bel-Air Athletics. While an advertisement like this might seem like an intrusion into lofi conventions, it is not the first attempt to capitalize on lofi by selling physical products. The Australian clothing company Cool Shirtz, which specializes in meme-heavy and internet culture branding, printed t-shirts combining a pastiche of Universal Music Group's *Now That's What I Call Music* compilations with lofi mix title keywords (Figure 4.6).

The community-born lofi record labels also sell merchandise and vinyl releases. Once again, a sense of nostalgia pervades such products: even Will Smith could be seen as trading in the cachet of his starring role in NBC's 1990s hit *The Fresh Prince of Bel-Air*.

Still, the commercial presence of external companies can be seen in wider uses of the lofi mix format, as exemplified by the 'code-fi' video uploaded in association with the web development framework Accelerated Mobile Pages

---

[88] Porfírio, 'YouTube and the Sonification of Domestic Everyday Life', 213.

[89] Jose van Dijck, *The Culture of Connectivity: A Critical History of Social Media*, The Culture of Connectivity (Oxford: Oxford University Press, 2013), 113; Vinícius de Aguiar, 'Musical Playlisting and Curation on YouTube: What Do Algorithms Know about Music?', in *YouTube and Music: Online Culture and Everyday Life*, ed. Holly Rogers, Joana Freitas, and João Francisco Porfírio (London: Bloomsbury Academic, 2023), 204.

[90] Hu, 'The Economics of 24/7 Lo-Fi Hip-Hop YouTube Livestreams'.

[91] Smith, 'Chill Beats to Quarantine To'.

Figure 4.6 Cool Shirtz's t-shirt combining iconic popular music format titles, from company website

(originally owned by Google).[92] A number of new uploaders produced mixes or livestreams in 2020 to advertise virtual product placements and affiliate links, such as Code Pioneers' 'mysterious cup of coffee that seems to stay hot forever'[93] as the lofi girl stand-in continues to sip it on loop, or to encourage traffic towards another website. The apparent functions of lofi—to code to, to draw to, to sleep to—conveniently expanded in tandem (further pushing back against the claim that the music bears responsibility for manipulating

---

[92] The AMP Channel, 'Code-Fi / Lofi Beats to Code/Relax To', YouTube video, 24 April 2020, https://www.youtube.com/watch?v=f02mOEt11OQ.
[93] Code Pioneers, 'Coding in Chicago | 🎧 LoFi Jazz Hip-Hop [Code - Relax - Study]', YouTube livestream, 24 November 2020, https://www.youtube.com/watch?v=esX7SFtEjHg.

106 Digital Flows

listeners into endless studying). Commercial interests continue to encroach upon lofi, perhaps compelled by web journalism reporting on the growth of the phenomenon. That said, established channels maintain a hold over the existing audience.

The potential for political appropriations of lofi was identified at an earlier point in the genre's emergence on YouTube. In late 2019, playing on vaporwave and lofi titles, the UK Conservative Party uploaded 'lo fi boriswave beats to relax/get brexit done to' (quoting a then-widespread party slogan).[94] The video mostly features beats from Audio Network, a commercial music library, overdubbed with lengthy samples from Boris Johnson speeches. Johnson is lightly animated perusing a folder while on a moving train, with a copy of the British conservative newspaper *The Daily Telegraph* on the table. Given that the video uses a Creative Commons Attribution license, one can assume that these tracks have been purchased outright, and one may wonder whether the mix is a good use of taxpayers' money. The promotional benefits of such propaganda, with links encouraging listeners to join the Conservative Party, are evidently worthwhile when tied into the wildly popular lofi mix template. This example develops upon earlier traditions like 'sovietwave', which creatively remixed Soviet anthems with the electronic sounds of synthwave. Such variations on the mix format both demonstrate the wide accessibility of YouTube music mixes and indicate the risks associated with lofi's increasing popularity in a period of global social upheaval.

Conclusion

Many core conventions of lofi commentary have changed since the onset of the COVID-19 pandemic. Some trends can be directly related to the health crisis, with listeners reflecting on the current circumstances or accompanying periods of at-home study with lofi mixes, leading many to relate to isolated fantastical figures like witches and ghosts. Other shifts in discussion indicate developing formations of identity and community among listeners. An influx of new listeners has both displaced standard practices like the use of aesthetic text and imported new memes from wider internet culture. Across the comments, there are fewer references to music and cartoons—this genre of hip hop's preferred sample material—just as the music has stabilized around the label 'lofi'. More users greet others and make general chitchat, while fewer

---

[94] Conservatives, 'Lo Fi Boriswave Beats to Relax/Get Brexit Done To', YouTube video, 25 November 2019, https://www.youtube.com/watch?v=cre0in5n-1E.

are writing posts full of long sentences, which used to carry a distinct, emotionally reflective tone. In sum, a smaller, more intimate community forged around personal, nostalgic expression has become overshadowed by what lofi now represents in mainstream online culture: a category of YouTube content encouraging studying or relaxing, with users reporting their current circumstances through brief check-ins with the wider audience.

While commercial and political interests have encroached upon lofi hip hop as a popular form of cultural media hosted on YouTube, there remains a good deal of communal expression that demonstrates the use of music to alleviate challenging sociopolitical contexts. Viewing the genre reductively as something easily transferable, repurposable, and approaching meme status would fail to see the rich expressions of self, community, and sociality still present in the comments sections. Beyond changes in the terms of discourse, however, hip hop expressivity is subject to all kinds of value judgments in online contexts, as the following chapter on feminist rap YouTube videos investigates.

5

Online Hip Hop Feminism, Rap Music Videos, and Gender in YouTube Comments

Responses to Black Women Rappers on Their Hot Girl Shit

Introduction

This chapter gives recognition to a wave of Black women rappers making music aligned with hip hop feminism, demonstrating savvy digital sensibilities through social media activity, and achieving success in the mainstream music industry.[1] In particular, I focus on the rap music video as a site of online hip hop performance. Drawing on an existing literature that is focused on representations of Black women in rap videos, I provide a complementary study that homes in on YouTube users' comments: what do people post in response to music videos by Black women rappers? I am especially interested in how the values expressed in posts vary depending on the gender of the commenter. This is a crucial concern for the reception of Black women's creative performances, uncovering how identity dynamics significantly inform discourse about hip hop feminism and Black womanhood in mainstream online culture.

To reiterate my positionality in relation to this subject, I am writing as a white man whose thinking is entrenched in Black feminist thought. I spoke to Black women in various roles related to hip hop—rapper, producer, fan—in formal interviews as well as informal discussions among friends. The aim is to provide a scholarly contribution to hip hop feminism through a data-feminist lens.[2] My analysis offers new insights on problems such as male

---

[1] I use the slightly clunky term 'woman rapper' as a neutral alternative to 'female rapper', a label that carries misogynistic associations. The latter term implies a 'rapper' is (or should be) male by default, requiring the prefix when identifying women as though they are lesser or atypical. See, for example, Dan Hyman, 'Little Simz Has Flow, But Don't Call Her a "Female Rapper"', *Shondaland*, 1 March 2019, https://www.shondaland.com/inspire/a26541464/little-simz-grey-area-dont-call-her-female-rapper/; Nadirah Simmons, 'What Are We to Do with the Term "Female Rapper?"', *The Gumbo*, 8 August 2019, https://thegumbo.net/blog/2019/8/8/what-are-we-to-do-with-the-term-female-rapper.

[2] Catherine D'Ignazio and Lauren F. Klein, *Data Feminism* (Cambridge, MA: MIT Press, 2020).

Digital Flows. Steven Gamble, Oxford University Press. © Oxford University Press 2024.
DOI: 10.1093/oso/9780197656389.003.0005

discrimination towards Black women (afforded by a degree of critical distance) to better understand and be able to combat online misogynoir. This issue is not only gendered but racialized, with patriarchy fundamentally sustained by white supremacy.[3] In other words, misogynoir is a problem rooted in white male attitudes and behaviours,[4] so it should be white men's work to expose and challenge it.[5]

While it is sometimes helpful to describe hip hop as a masculinist or patriarchal culture, it is also a simplification. Doing so risks reinforcing those ideas as fact, as though a male stranglehold on the culture has been so restrictive that women have never played a part. This would be patently untrue. To accept that simplification would mean overlooking the vast significance of women (and people of other genders) throughout the history of hip hop. We can point to figures like Cindy Campbell and Sylvia Robinson, without whom hip hop as party soundtrack and recorded music respectively would not exist. Describing hip hop as male-dominated means acknowledging that, more often than not, it is men who are visible, celebrated, and in positions of power (for example, in the hip hop record industry). This situation is not helped by the exacerbation of misogynistic, sexist, and objectifying tropes in gangsta rap—hip hop in perhaps its most mainstream (i.e., white-recognized) form. Hip hop's normative degradation of women reached a peak in public discourse around 2003–4, after the release of Nelly's 'Tip Drill' video. The rapper cancelled his charitable foundation's bone marrow drive at Spelman College after a feminist group raised reasonable questions about his simultaneous representations and demands of Black women.[6]

As artists, fans, industry professionals, and more, Black women play a huge part in the culture, although their participation is frequently limited, or *invisibilized*, by patriarchal structures. Kyra Gaunt's work, for one example, shines a spotlight on the important ways that young Black girls' self-expressive

---

[3] bell hooks, *Ain't I A Woman: Black Women and Feminism* (Boston, MA: South End Press, 1982); Patricia Hill Collins, *Black Feminist Thought: Knowledge, Consciousness, and the Politics of Empowerment*, 2nd ed. (New York: Routledge, 2000).

[4] I am referring to white men here in the manner of Sara Ahmed, more as an institution than a way of grouping people who share certain identities. See Sara Ahmed, *Living a Feminist Life* (Durham, NC: Duke University Press, 2017), 148–158.

[5] We must also be conscious that in some contexts white social justice activists' behaviours can recentre whiteness, reinforce power imbalances, and cause burnout among activists of colour. Work on effective allyship continues to develop at pace. See Terese Jonsson, 'The Narrative Reproduction of White Feminist Racism', *Feminist Review* 113, no. 1 (July 2016): 50–67; Reni Eddo-Lodge, *Why I'm No Longer Talking to White People about Race* (London: Bloomsbury Publishing, 2018), 213–224; Paul C Gorski and Noura Erakat, 'Racism, Whiteness, and Burnout in Antiracism Movements: How White Racial Justice Activists Elevate Burnout in Racial Justice Activists of Color in the United States', *Ethnicities* 19, no. 5 (October 2019): 784–808.

[6] Moya Bailey, *Misogynoir Transformed: Black Women's Digital Resistance* (New York: New York University Press, 2021), i–iii.

110   Digital Flows

play includes 'a unique repertoire of chants and embodied rhythms ... that both reflects and inspires the principles of black popular music-making'.[7] At the same time, Black women are often made *hypervisible* in hip hop, typically in music videos, where portrayals of stereotypical figures like the Jezebel (i.e., animalistically sexual, always-available, eroticized), gold digger, or baby mama abound.[8] Only recently has media appeared in mainstream online culture that speaks more accurately to—and, importantly, from the perspective of—a diversity of Black women's experiences.[9] Though not without precedent, these relatively recent, more authentic audiovisual representations of Black womanhood reveal hip hop feminism in action.

Hip Hop Feminism

Hip hop feminism refers to both a body of literature and an ethos. In its original conception—one less inflected by the onlining of everyday life—hip hop feminist studies combined Black and intersectional feminist theory, Black women's creative writing, and complex affections towards hip hop culture.[10] Histories of racial relations in the US traditionally focused on post-Emancipation political gains made by Black men (especially when recalled through 'Great Man' figures like Martin Luther King Jr. and Malcolm X). Second-wave feminism, spearheaded predominantly by white women, overlooked political struggles distinct to women of colour. It was therefore Black feminist writing that drew attention to Black women's 'double burden' of race- and gender-based

---

[7] Kyra Gaunt, *The Games Black Girls Play: Learning the Ropes from Double-Dutch to Hip-Hop* (New York: New York University Press, 2006), 1.

[8] Dionne P. Stephens and April L. Few, 'Hip Hop Honey or Video Ho: African American Preadolescents' Understanding of Female Sexual Scripts in Hip Hop Culture', *Sexuality & Culture* 11, no. 4 (December 2007): 48–69.

[9] Regina N. Bradley, 'Awkwardly Hysterical: Theorizing Black Girl Awkwardness and Humor in Social Media', *Comedy Studies* 6, no. 2 (July 2015): 148–153; Apryl Williams and Vanessa Gonlin, 'I Got All My Sisters with Me (on Black Twitter): Second Screening of How to Get Away with Murder as a Discourse on Black Womanhood', *Information, Communication & Society* 20, no. 7 (July 2017): 984–1004; Francesca Sobande, *The Digital Lives of Black Women in Britain* (Cham: Palgrave Macmillan, 2020); Adeerya Johnson, 'Hella Bars: The Cultural Inclusion of Black Women's Rap in Insecure', *Open Cultural Studies* 6, no. 1 (January 2022): 76–87.

[10] Joan Morgan, *When Chickenheads Come Home to Roost: A Hip Hop Feminist Breaks It Down* (New York: Simon & Schuster, 1999); shani jamila, 'Can I Get a Witness? Testimony from a Hip-Hop Feminist', in *Colonize This!: Young Women of Color on Today's Feminism*, ed. Daisy Hernández and Bushra Rehman (New York: Seal Press, 2002), 382–394; Gwendolyn D. Pough, *Check It While I Wreck It: Black Womanhood, Hip-Hop Culture, and the Public Sphere* (Lebanon, NH: Northeastern University Press, 2004); Gwendolyn D. Pough et al., eds., *Home Girls Makes Some Noise: Hip Hop Feminism Anthology* (Mira Loma, CA: Parker Publishing, 2007); T. D. Sharpley-Whiting, *Pimps Up, Ho's Down: Hip Hop's Hold On Young Black Women* (New York and London: New York University Press, 2007); Whitney A. Peoples, ' "Under Construction": Identifying Foundations of Hip-Hop Feminism and Exploring Bridges between Black Second-Wave and Hip-Hop Feminisms', *Meridians* 8, no. 1 (September 2008): 19–52.

discrimination.[11] Even pioneering work, such as that of Patricia Hill Collins,[12] has more recently been argued to espouse 'uplift' or respectability politics—that is, urging Black women to meet traditional expectations about white matriarchal and domestic femininity—when it comes to subjects such as pornography.[13] Joan Morgan was now-famously concerned with a Black feminism that would instead 'fuck with the grays': nuancing simplistic stereotypes about Black women, embracing contradictions, and exploring sexuality and Black joy through a politics of pleasure.[14] Thereafter, important developments emerged from working-class, Southern, and 'ratchet' perspectives.[15] As a field of study, hip hop feminism challenges the culture's patriarchal status quo while embracing elements of its expressive practices. The internet has recently received particular attention concerning online mediations of Black womanhood in hip hop.[16]

Hip hop feminism is also a lived practice with varied expressions and representations in hip hop culture. Since the mid-2010s, several Black women rappers have espoused principles inherited from the original generation of hip hop feminism. At the same time, they make commercially successful music and have become highly visible in popular culture. An inevitably incomplete list of such artists includes Nicki Minaj, Megan Thee Stallion, Cardi B, Saweetie, Young M.A, Ice Spice, Coi Leray, Latto, City Girls, Flo Milli, Sexyy Red, and GloRilla.[17] Doja Cat, Lizzo, Janelle Monáe, Princess Nokia,

---

[11] Yanick St. Jean and Joe R. Feagin, *Double Burden: Black Women and Everyday Racism* (Armonk, NY: M.E. Sharpe, 1998).

[12] Hill Collins, *Black Feminist Thought*.

[13] Mireille Miller-Young, *A Taste for Brown Sugar: Black Women in Pornography* (Durham, NC: Duke University Press, 2014), ix.

[14] Morgan, *When Chickenheads Come Home to Roost*, 59; Aria S. Halliday and Nadia E. Brown, 'The Power of Black Girl Magic Anthems: Nicki Minaj, Beyoncé, and "Feeling Myself" as Political Empowerment', *Souls* 20, no. 2 (April 2018): 228.

[15] Aisha Durham, 'Class Formation: Beyoncé in Music Video Production', *Black Camera* 9, no. 1 (2017): 200; Bettina L. Love, *Hip Hop's Li'l Sistas Speak; Negotiating Hip Hop Identities and Politics in the New South* (New York: Peter Lang US, 2012); L. H. Stallings, 'Hip Hop and the Black Ratchet Imagination', *Palimpsest: A Journal on Women, Gender, and the Black International* 2, no. 2 (2013): 135–139; Regina Bradley, *Chronicling Stankonia: The Rise of the Hip-Hop South* (Chapel Hill: University of North Carolina Press, 2021).

[16] For example, Erica B Edwards and Jennifer Esposito, 'Reading the Black Woman's Body Via Instagram Fame', *Communication, Culture and Critique* 11, no. 3 (September 2018): 341–358; Kyesha Jennings, 'City Girls, Hot Girls and the Re-Imagining of Black Women in Hip Hop and Digital Spaces', *Global Hip Hop Studies* 1, no. 1 (June 2020): 47–70; Jabari Evans, 'Link in Bio: Exploring the Emotional and Relational Labour of Black Women Rappers in Sexual Dance Economies on OnlyFans', in 'It's Where You're @: Hip Hop and the Internet', special issue, *Global Hip Hop Studies* 2 (November 2021): 179–198; Catherine Knight Steele, *Digital Black Feminism* (New York: New York University Press, 2021).

[17] Nicki Minaj (who I have included in this list but who could also be positioned as a predecessor), Rihanna, and Beyoncé are important recent forebears who continue to innovate and inspire this wave of artists. Of course, many more—Queen Latifah, Erykah Badu, Lauryn Hill, Foxy Brown, Lil Kim, Missy Elliott (for too few examples)—paved the way.

112 Digital Flows

and Doechii (among others) overlap this sensibility with pop stardom.[18] Though this wave of artists is most distinct in the US, hip hop feminist rappers breaking through since the 2010s from other countries include Little Simz (UK), Sampa the Great (Zambia/Australia), Denise Chaila (Ireland), Yeboyah (Finland), Dope Saint Jude (South Africa), and Tkay Maidza (Australia), and may extend to some non-Black rappers like Silvana Imam (Sweden) and VaVa (China).

The principles of hip hop feminism are complex and contested in the contemporary era. Like other aspects of hip hop I have discussed, its feminist strand is affected by online conventions such as social practices played out on internet media platforms and the digitalization of the music economy. Despite some inclusive spaces and tendencies,[19] it is now perhaps a truism to state that internet cultures are widely plagued by racist and misogynistic attitudes,[20] summarized by Adrienne Massanari as 'toxic technoculture'.[21] Intersectional experiences integral to Blackness and womanhood led Moya Bailey to coin the term misogynoir, referring to 'co-constitutive racialized and sexist violence that befalls Black women as a result of their simultaneous and interlocking oppression at the intersection of racial and gender marginalization', especially in digital media.[22]

Though discriminatory attitudes are pervasive, 'social media platforms like Twitter and Instagram have created unique spaces where perpetrators [of misogynoir] risk being called out'.[23] The collective mobilization of internet users has been dubbed 'callout culture' or 'cancel culture': the former typically aligned with social justice, the latter a pejorative term used by defenders of free speech.[24] Hip hop feminism is evidently (albeit not only) a frame for resisting misogynoir, though an ethos or attitude by itself surely cannot surmount the

---

[18] Other artists connecting with themes of hip hop feminism, but mostly outside of the rap mainstream, include Tierra Whack, Noname, Rapsody, Azealia Banks, Rico Nasty, and Cookiee Kawaii, as well as a host of R&B stars like SZA, Jhené Aiko, Kehlani, H.E.R, Solange, and Summer Walker.

[19] Jessa Lingel, *Digital Countercultures and the Struggle for Community* (Cambridge, MA: MIT Press, 2017).

[20] For just two examples of entire fields of research into online inequities, see André Brock, 'From the Blackhand Side: Twitter as a Cultural Conversation', *Journal of Broadcasting & Electronic Media* 56, no. 4 (October 2012): 529–549; Sarah Banet-Weiser and Kate M. Miltner, '#MasculinitySoFragile: Culture, Structure, and Networked Misogyny', *Feminist Media Studies* 16, no. 1 (January 2016): 171–174.

[21] Adrienne Massanari, '#Gamergate and The Fappening: How Reddit's Algorithm, Governance, and Culture Support Toxic Technocultures', *New Media & Society* 19, no. 3 (March 2017): 329–346.

[22] Bailey, *Misogynoir Transformed*, 1.

[23] Jennings, 'City Girls, Hot Girls and the Re-Imagining of Black Women in Hip Hop and Digital Spaces', 60.

[24] Lisa Nakamura, 'The Unwanted Labour of Social Media: Women of Colour Call Out Culture As Venture Community Management', *New Formations* 86, no. 86 (December 2015): 106–112; André Brock, *Distributed Blackness: African American Cybercultures* (New York: New York University Press, 2020), 219–220; Jenny Janssens and Lotte Spreeuwenberg, 'The Moral Implications of Cancel Culture', *Ethical Perspectives* 29, no. 1 (2022): 89–114.

structural inequities facing Black women.[25] However, the emergence of hip hop feminist expressions in mainstream rap music—and, by extension, visibly in popular culture—have opened new discourses on expressions and representations of Black womanhood in the internet era. Simultaneously, there has been a call for research into Black technoculture beyond traditional emphases on resistance, oppression, and labour. André Brock uses the term 'libidinal economy' to draw attention to online Black joy, desire, pleasure, and play, which aligns with hip hop feminist work on pleasure politics.[26] More specifically, Kyesha Jennings' introduction of a 'digital hip hop feminist sensibility' dismantles precepts of respectability politics, observing that 'with an increase of women demanding visibility as rappers, there has been a reimagining or more so a redefining of black women's identities'.[27] I support these lines of scholarship here by analysing how contemporary Black women rappers represent Black womanhood in music videos on YouTube, as well as how commenters understand such representations in a context marked by both misogynoir and callout culture.

Rap Music Videos and Representations of Black Women

Music videos made for rap songs are undoubtedly a vibrant and diverse form of artistic expression. However, hip hop heads would be the first to point out that mainstream rap visuals have become fairly homogenous, highlighting a limited range of settings, characters, and performance tropes. Since the heyday of music video television channels, rap videos have been dominated by the 'booty video', which Mako Fitts Ward defines as 'formulaic video imagery that emphasizes rappers' accumulated wealth and property [alongside] overwhelming representation of women's posteriors'.[28] In the narrative world of booty videos, men—usually the performing artists themselves—are hypermasculine heroes living lavish lives, sometimes mixed in with urban

---

[25] That said, I have written extensively on the potential for rap music to afford empowerment for listeners. Through acts of individual and collective listening and cultural participation, people undergo embodied and cognitive experiences that can stimulate changes in mood, behaviour, and social action. The key issue is distinguishing the buzzword 'self-empowerment' (placing the onus on the powerless) and collective, social, structural change. See Steven Gamble, *How Music Empowers: Listening to Modern Rap and Metal* (London: Routledge, 2021).

[26] Brock, *Distributed Blackness*, 31–34.

[27] Jennings, 'City Girls, Hot Girls and the Re-Imagining of Black Women in Hip Hop and Digital Spaces', 59–60.

[28] Mako Fitts, '"Drop It Like It's Hot": Culture Industry Laborers and Their Perspectives on Rap Music Video Production', *Meridians* 8, no. 1 (September 2008): 211–212.

114 Digital Flows

sensibilities. Women are staged around these men like sexually available accessories, reductively portrayed as quasi-pornographic and positioned for the male heterosexual gaze. Such videos commonly provide close-ups of women's body parts, displaying them as eroticized, 'pleasurable objects'.[29] When women appear in a similar fashion to money, cars, and opulent locations, they act as a means of demonstrating male material power (rather than independent, individual human beings). This has contributed to a norm whereby 'women's bodies are a requisite component of self-promotion' in hip hop,[30] forming an integral part of male rappers' competitive sexual bravado and machismo.[31] As Fitts Ward points out, this trend articulates precisely the sexual, cultural, and economic dynamics embedded in T. Denean Sharpley-Whiting's 'pimps up, hos down' equation.[32] Hip hop helps reinforce male control over women's sexuality—it reaffirms patriarchal gender roles—and thereby succeeds as a commercial enterprise due to the exploitation of young women of colour. Music video is perhaps the most visibly striking example of this power imbalance in action.

The extent to which actors and dancers—sometimes called 'video vixens' or 'video girls'—have control over their self-representation has been a major point of contention in scholarship.[33] To assume that all women starring in sexually objectifying videos are exploited, passive, and powerless both excuses their participation and denies their agency in such labour. In the late 2000s, Tricia Rose took the commercialized, stereotypical representations of Blackness in hip hop to task. Mainstream rap music videos played a primary role in fuelling the sexual objectification of young Black women, she argued, where 'what appears to be expression of sexual freedom is, in fact, participation in an industry that reinforces male sexual fantasy and power'.[34] More recent hip hop feminist scholars have nuanced this work, with Adeerya Johnson critiquing 'the notion that Black women in hip-hop were victims of the genre, lacked agency, and were solely seen as props to the male rappers to be objectified'.[35] This nuancing is a clear example of fucking with the greys. As Patricia

---

[29] Matthew Bannister, 'Funny Girls and Nowhere Boys: Reversing the Gaze in the Popular Music Biopic', in *Rethinking Difference in Gender, Sexuality, and Popular Music*, ed. Gavin Lee (New York: Routledge, 2018), 118.

[30] Fitts, '"Drop It Like It's Hot"', 212.

[31] Diane Railton and Paul Watson, *Music Video and the Politics of Representation* (Edinburgh: Edinburgh University Press, 2011), 128.

[32] Sharpley-Whiting, *Pimps Up, Ho's Down*.

[33] Aria S. Halliday, 'Envisioning Black Girl Futures', *Departures in Critical Qualitative Research* 6, no. 3 (September 2017): 69–70.

[34] Tricia Rose, *The Hip-Hop Wars: What We Talk about When We Talk about Hip-Hop and Why It Matters* (New York: Basic Books, 2008), 177.

[35] Adeerya Johnson, 'Dirty South Feminism: The Girlies Got Somethin' to Say Too! Southern Hip-Hop Women, Fighting Respectability, Talking Mess, and Twerking Up the Dirty South', *Religions* 12, no. 11 (November 2021): 6.

Hill Collins sagely noted years earlier, it is difficult to clearly identify between 'representations of Black women who are sexually liberated and those who are sexual objects, their bodies on sale for male enjoyment'.[36]

From outside hip hop feminist writing, it has been all too easy to point to women's cooperation in producing sexualized videos as a form of self-objectification and internalized misogyny.[37] This ignores, however, that expressions of sexuality through dance and performance can be pleasurable and make women feel liberated and powerful. Furthermore, such performances reclaim practices of sexuality that have been socially denied, stereotyped, and stigmatized. Amber Johnson has stressed how hip hop helps women—especially women of colour—feel like both respectable and sexual beings.[38]

Hill Collins noted a shift from the *celebration* to the *objectification* of Black women's bodies in early 1990s popular culture.[39] Earlier, she had argued that 'when self-defined by Black women ourselves, Black women's sexualities can become an important place of resistance. Just as harnessing the power of the erotic is important for domination, reclaiming and self-defining that same eroticism may constitute one path toward Black women's empowerment'.[40] A key distinction for music videos therefore concerns where agency can be interpreted in sexualized performances. When video models occupy a male rapper's imaginary harem and are cinematically presented as desirable objects, patriarchal and misogynistic representations of women may be reinforced. However, when it is women running the show, self-representing as—to quote some current framings—hot girls, bad bitches, or super freaky girls, such expressions are more likely perceived as empowering expressions of liberatory and sex-positive feminism.[41] From the mid-2010s, I see signs of a reversal of Hill Collins' celebration-to-objectification trend in women rappers' videos, which celebrate Black women's bodies and pursuits of sexual pleasure.

[36] Patricia Hill Collins, *Black Sexual Politics: African Americans, Gender, and the New Racism* (New York and London: Routledge, 2004), 126.

[37] Cynthia M. Frisby and Jennifer Stevens Aubrey, 'Race and Genre in the Use of Sexual Objectification in Female Artists' Music Videos', *Howard Journal of Communications* 23, no. 1 (January 2012): 66–87.

[38] Amber Johnson, 'Confessions of a Video Vixen: My Autocritography of Sexuality, Desire, and Memory', *Text and Performance Quarterly* 34, no. 2 (April 2014): 189–191.

[39] Hill Collins, *Black Sexual Politics*, 128.

[40] Hill Collins, *Black Feminist Thought*, 128.

[41] There are rich precedents for women (and others) staging a variety of subversive tactics in music videos. Consider the reversal of gendered sexualization (i.e., objectifying male video models), visual disembodiment, and (female) homoerotic desire. See, for example, Shana L. Redmond, 'This Safer Space: Janelle Monáe's "Cold War"', *Journal of Popular Music Studies* 23, no. 4 (2011): 393–411; Savannah Shange, 'A King Named Nicki: Strategic Queerness and the Black Femmecee', *Women & Performance: A Journal of Feminist Theory* 24, no. 1 (January 2014): 29–45; Brad Osborn, 'Resistance Gazes in Recent Music Videos', *Music and the Moving Image* 14, no. 2 (2021): 51–67.

116 Digital Flows

With this important context in mind, I turn now to online audiences, who may not share the same liberatory views about Black women's sexuality. As I have suggested, Black women rappers' productions, while subversive, are nonetheless mediated into contexts rife with sexist, racist, and objectifying logics of reception.[42] This was undoubtedly true in the music video television era, and it remains true today as artists explore 'socially unsanctioned sexualities' in their music videos on YouTube.[43] The difference is that today viewers publicly share their thoughts in the form of comments for other users to see. I could point to many brilliant commentaries, blog posts, and reviews that establish the empowering potential of Black women rappers' music videos. Their ability to inspire is not in doubt. What we know less about is the broader reception at a large scale, especially how people of different genders respond to these music videos and thereby 'dictate cultural norms related to gender performance'.[44] With a concern for how patriarchal, misogynistic, objectifying, racist, and white supremacist logics may be upheld, my study aims to shed light on how Black women rappers are received in online contexts.

Comments on Black Women Rappers' Music Videos

To carry out this analysis, I identified twenty popular videos by Black women rappers associated with contemporary hip hop feminism (listed in Table 5.2). I selected videos that are well known in mainstream popular music culture, preferring those that generate significant online discussion (more than ten thousand comments) to those that articulate more subtle, nuanced, or alternative feminist themes. The sample therefore emphasizes spectacular,[45] visually striking, and sex-positive performances of Black womanhood, including perhaps the most-discussed example of raunchy hip hop feminism ever, 'WAP' by Cardi B feat. Megan Thee Stallion. The videos span from August 2014 (the first is Nicki Minaj's 'Anaconda') to October 2022 (GloRilla and Cardi B's 'Tomorrow 2' remix), with the greatest concentration around 2019 and 2020.

---

[42] In the comments sections of Russian rap YouTube videos, for example, 'racist attitudes prevail on the symbolic, hegemonic level. The predominance of White men in the discourse coincided with continuous belittling or stereotyping of the ethnic minorities'. Anastasia Denisova and Aliaksandr Herasimenka, 'How Russian Rap on YouTube Advances Alternative Political Deliberation: Hegemony, Counter-Hegemony, and Emerging Resistant Publics', *Social Media + Society* 5, no. 2 (April 2019): 9.

[43] Carol Vernallis, *The Media Swirl: Politics, Audiovisuality, and Aesthetics* (Durham, NC: Duke University Press, 2023), 211.

[44] Della V. Mosley et al., 'Hashtags and Hip-Hop: Exploring the Online Performances of Hip-Hop Identified Youth Using Instagram', *Feminist Media Studies* 17, no. 2 (March 2017): 135–136.

[45] For Carol Vernallis, spectacle sits at the core of online audiovisual mediation. Vernallis, *The Media Swirl*, 1–5.

Following the other steps of the method outlined in Chapter 4, I collected around 750,000 YouTube comments from a potential three million (removing duplicates and spam).

I applied Mozdeh's gender filtering, which on YouTube is limited to the interpretation of male and female posters. This is perhaps the largest methodological limitation: Mozdeh infers gender heuristically by matching commenters' usernames to a comprehensive list of names from the 1990 US census.[46] Each name on the list is used at least 90 per cent of the time by either male or female people, and Mozdeh associates commenters' gender accordingly. This method risks the erasure of non-binary people and those of other genders, implying that names either fall into one of two cis categories or cannot be determined.[47] That said, a substantial proportion of YouTube commenters do indeed have a username that associates accurately with the gender with which they identify (typically their preferred given or taken name). Though Mozdeh's gender filter emphasizes Anglophone names, YouTube is predominantly an English-language platform, and the videos mostly appeal to Anglophone audiences. Finally, the large size of the dataset also reduces the risk of incorrectly assuming gender by username, as it is more effective at scale.[48] In my sample, 15.6 per cent of comments (116k) are likely to be posted by female commenters and 13.5 per cent (100k) likely by males. I mostly refer to these as being made by 'women' and 'men' to avoid the misogynistic associations of the noun 'female',[49] though I did not gather age information and cannot assume commenters are adults.

I developed eight themes to classify gendered terms in commentary on Black women rappers' music videos, displayed in Table 5.1. The themes called value, body, and respectability were most relevant to my focus on attitudes towards Black womanhood and hip hop feminism.

---

[46] Mozdeh classifies names commonly used by people of various genders and usernames that do not resemble real names as unknown.

[47] One methodological improvement worth noting is that Mozdeh *can* identify gender-neutral pronouns (variations of the text 'they/them') when these are stated in Twitter bios. However, the extortionate paywall placed around Twitter's API for research purposes in early 2023 has made Twitter less viable as a platform for data analysis.

[48] Manual checks of this method of gender association by name show it to be between 96.5 and 96.8 per cent accurate on a sample of US academic authors. See Mike Thelwall, 'Gender Differences in Citation Impact for 27 Fields and Six English-Speaking Countries 1996–2014', *Quantitative Science Studies* 1, no. 2 (June 2020): 599–617.

[49] Elizabeth Ann Hintz and Jonathan Troy Baker, 'A Performative Face Theory Analysis of Online Facework by the Formerly Involuntarily Celibate', *International Journal of Communication* 15, no. 2021 (2021): 3049; Andrew Ferley, 'The Semantic Derogation of Female' (Masters thesis, York University, 2022), https://yorkspace.library.yorku.ca/xmlui/bitstream/handle/10315/39771/Ferley%20A%20-%20MRP.pdf?sequence=1&isAllowed=y.

118 Digital Flows

Table 5.1 Thematic analysis of term frequency in recent rap music videos by Black women comparing posts by male and female users

Theme	Subtheme	Terms more frequent among men	Terms more frequent among women
References	Gendered subject	dude, guy, chick, female	
	Lyrics	rola, munch	friend, bestie, Tessie, bestfriend
	Reference	Anitta, Montana, Eminem, Drake	Kylie, tik, tok, Hezo, Kehlani
Appraisal	Originality	Bobby, flow, Kodak, Shmurda	
	Opinion	beat, music, is, rap, this	I, my, outfit, omg, yes
	Value	trash, garbage, shit, mute, worst	love, cute, best, obsessed
Black womanhood/ hip hop feminism	Body	ass, smell, hot, ugly, garbage	natural, twerk, beautiful, butt
	Respectability	porn, society, nut, culture, America	mom

The terms listed in this table appear more frequently in comments by male users compared to overall comments (not male compared to female), and the same for female users.

I'll first briefly address the other themes (the first five rows in Table 5.1). The gendered subject theme found that men used gendered terms referring to performers and other commenters more frequently than women. I would suggest that the music videos evoked gender and sexual politics in a way that made men eager to reaffirm gendered categories, especially male ones. The lyrics theme simply contains lyrics that commenters posted, with a predominance of women writing out lyrics from Saweetie's 'Best Friend feat. Doja Cat'. Commenters often described how they found a given video or pointed out the appearance of famous performers, which I bundled under the reference theme.

Originality is a more meaningful theme given the importance of original, authentic self-representation in hip hop. Men were far keener than women to point out when they thought women rappers 'stole' other—notably male—rappers' 'flow'.[50] The opinion theme also encourages brief consideration, as it captures a diverse range of commenters' thoughts about the videos. Women tended to post about how the videos inspired, excited, or empowered them: noting a particular 'outfit'; whether a rapper 'ate'; performers looking

---

[50] All terms in quotation marks are significant terms found in the analysis. Some appear in Table 5.1.

Online Hip Hop Feminism 119

Table 5.2 YouTube music videos used for comment analysis, formatted as artist and song title (not the exact video title) for consistency

Artist	Song title
Cardi B	WAP feat. Megan Thee Stallion
Megan Thee Stallion	Body
Nicki Minaj	Anaconda
Doja Cat	Juicy feat. Tyga
Ice Spice	Munch (Feelin' U)
Coi Leray	Blick Blick! feat. Nicki Minaj
GloRilla	Tomorrow 2 feat. Cardi B
Latto	Bitch From Da Souf feat. Saweetie and Trina
Saweetie	Best Friend feat. Doja Cat
City Girls	Twerk feat. Cardi B
Megan Thee Stallion	Hot Girl Summer feat. Nicki Minaj and Ty Dolla Sign
Cardi B	Bodak Yellow
Cardi B	Up
DeJ Loaf	Try Me
Young M.A	OOOUUU
Flo Milli	In The Party
Nicki Minaj	Good Form feat. Lil Wayne
City Girls	Pussy Talk feat. Doja Cat
Saweetie	My Type
Megan Thee Stallion	Big Ole Freak

'pretty' and 'confident'; and using exclamations like 'omg' and 'yesss'. In particular, it is interesting to note that women were more likely to share opinions in terms of their subjective feelings ('I' and 'my') whereas men posted as if their views were facts ('this' and 'is'). Men more often worded their opinions in terms of the objective value of the music video in question, which I examine in more detail throughout the following discussion.

Value

The value theme is distinguished from the opinion theme by highlighting particularly value-laden terms used in the comments. The most significantly gendered term in the whole sample, and by a striking margin, is 'love' (including 'loved' and 'loves'), which appears in 8.2 per cent of all women's comments and just under 4 per cent of men's. Women were significantly more effusive than men in their praise for rappers, the songs, and the videos. In other words, they value them (Figure 5.1). In addition, women more commonly described things as 'cute' and 'best' (the latter also prominent in 'Best Friend' lyrics, though many comments refer to other songs or videos using the adjective), or referred to being 'obsessed'. By contrast—and I suggest readers brace themselves now for an outpouring of male misogynoir—men far more frequently used negative terms that suggest the videos lack value (Figure 5.2).

Some of these terms are adjectives, like 'trash' and 'garbage', whereas others expressed disdain about the videos existing at all. 'Shit' appeared again and again in men's posts as a derogatory noun, typically like 'what is this shit' (though men also more commonly use the phrase 'this shit is . . . ' in a range of senses, positive or negative). Men frequently joked about preferring to watch

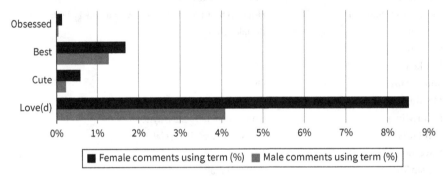

Figure 5.1 Terms with significant gender differences in the 'value' theme used more frequently by female commenters

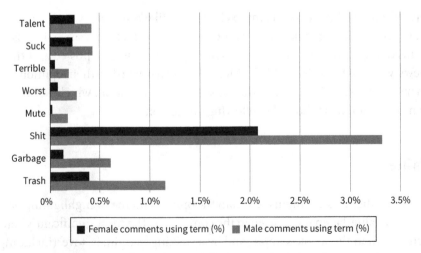

Figure 5.2 Terms with significant gender differences in the 'value' theme used more frequently by male commenters

Online Hip Hop Feminism   121

'on mute', as if the songs were worthless and that the raunchy videos were the main attraction. It is surprising how often men's apparent dislike for a given video was articulated by decrying the worth of the performers, who they claim 'suck' and lack 'talent'. Unfortunately, such comments barely scratch the surface of male outrage over these expressions of hip hop feminism.

Body

In 2014, the 'Anaconda' video saw Nicki Minaj 'asserting her power, not as a sexual object but a sexual subject', setting a new twenty-four-hour streaming record for Vevo in the process.[51] Retrospectively, I view this as a break-through moment in Black women rappers' production of raunchy, fun, and provocative videos. 'Anaconda' flipped the script on the male objectification of women both musically and visually. Sir Mix-A-Lot's 'Baby Got Back' had already questioned the racial dynamics of how women's bodies are awarded social value. By sampling that track, Nicki Minaj queries the significance of men posing these questions, celebrating—as her outro puts it—'big fat ass bitches' on her own terms. In the 'Anaconda' video, Nicki Minaj is shown to be fully in control of her body and her actions, for example by leading a lap dance and leaving the male recipient (label-mate and frequent collaborator Drake) wanting more. In doing so, the song and its video generated a gender-polarizing debate at the intersection of sexual propriety, feminine beauty ideals, and racialized fetishism with a history reaching back to—and beyond—Josephine Baker and Saartje Baartman. The song dramatically disrupted popular representations of Black women's bodies at the time, which included Taylor Swift's 'Shake It Off' video, Miley Cyrus's 2013 'We Can't Stop' video and MTV Video Music Awards performance (which effectively introduced twerking—with a lot of harmful baggage—to a white public), and Kim Kardashian's 'Break the Internet' *Paper* magazine cover (a recreation of Jean-Paul Goude's 'Carolina Beaumont', originally in his 1983 book *Jungle Fever*).[52]

---

[51] Molly Lambert, 'Nicki Minaj Reclaims the Twerk in the "Anaconda" Music Video', *Grantland* (blog), 20 August 2014, https://grantland.com/hollywood-prospectus/nicki-minaj-reclaims-the-twerk-in-the-anaconda-music-video/; Hilary Lewis, 'Nicki Minaj's "Anaconda" Video Breaks Vevo Record', *Billboard* (blog), 22 August 2014, https://www.billboard.com/music/music-news/nicki-minaj-anaconda-vevo-record-6229110/.

[52] Jody Rosen, 'The 2013 VMAs Were Dominated by Miley's Minstrel Show', *Vulture*, 26 August 2013, https://www.vulture.com/2013/08/jody-rosen-miley-cyrus-vmas-minstrel.html; Bethonie Butler, 'Yes, Those Kim Kardashian Photos Are about Race', *Washington Post* (blog), 21 November 2014, https://www.washingtonpost.com/blogs/she-the-people/wp/2014/11/21/yes-those-kim-kardashian-photos-are-about-race/.

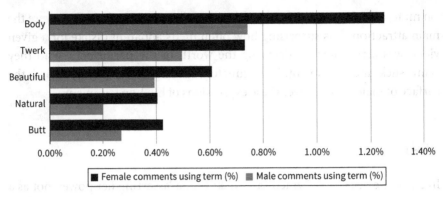

Figure 5.3 Terms with significant gender differences in the 'body' theme used more frequently by female commenters

Contemporary rap music videos that continue these discourses show women and men are divided in their responses to the physicality of Black women. In YouTube comments, women opted for the softer term 'butt' to describe buttocks and lauded the 'natural' 'body' on display, as well as finding it 'beautiful' (Figure 5.3). It appears that women also focused on the dancing or described their own desires to 'twerk'. This finding reinforces work on how, for many Black women and girls, twerking acts as a self-determining and public performance of embodied pleasure that disrupts the broader social denigration or erasure of Black bodies.[53] By contrast, men can be seen to reinforce white supremacist patriarchal ideas about the body (Figure 5.4). They more frequently deployed a coarser term for the backside, 'ass', and described such videos—and the bodies performing in them—as 'hot'. Worse, there is a small collection of explicitly degrading terms wielded significantly more often by men than women: 'ugly', 'fat', and 'smell'. This is a striking and upsetting trend that provides clear evidence of misogynistic and sexist attitudes in response to feminist hip hop, supporting Sam de Boise's observation that 'music which embodies masculinist themes often, in fact, frames women as repulsive rather than objects of desire'.[54]

---

[53] Aria S. Halliday, 'Twerk Sumn!: Theorizing Black Girl Epistemology in the Body', *Cultural Studies* 34, no. 6 (November 2020): 882–884.

[54] Sam de Boise, 'Music and Misogyny: A Content Analysis of Misogynistic, Antifeminist Forums', *Popular Music* 39, no. 3–4 (December 2020): 474.

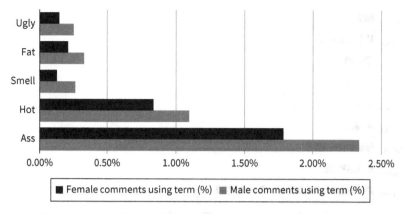

Figure 5.4 Terms with significant gender differences in the 'body' theme used more frequently by male commenters

Respectability

Men's devaluation of these videos and derogation of women's bodies are surely caused by underlying sociopolitical values. I aim to unpack those with reference to terms under the respectability theme, which were all used more frequently by men than women (Figure 5.5). There are three subthemes to address in turn: pornography, patriarchy, and wider society.

First, for men much more than women, these videos are perceived as pornographic.[55] Men used the terms 'porn', 'nut' [ejaculate], 'pornhub' [pornography website], and 'fap' [masturbate] to suggest what these videos bring to mind, thereby treating them as though designed purely for male erotic pleasure. This voyeurism evidently acts as a gendered means of control, attempting to re-objectify sexually suggestive performances. I am tempted to joke that only in pornography could such men experience sexual displays like these: it's funny to mock men aligned with incel values thus,[56] but doing so ultimately reinforces conventional expectations around heteronormative masculinity. Regardless, this comment trend demonstrates the ongoing fetishization of Black women's bodies. It also suggests that mostly male viewers

---

[55] This over-sexualization resembles when young Black girls' twerking videos are flagged as age-restricted content (i.e. perceived as explicitly sexual), based on white misunderstandings of 'normative behavior and values associated with erotic (not pornographic) displays of dance common across the African diaspora'. Kyra D. Gaunt, 'The Disclosure, Disconnect, and Digital Sexploitation of Tween Girls' Aspirational YouTube Videos', *Journal of Black Sexuality and Relationships* 5, no. 1 (2018): 111.

[56] On incels and their values, see Winnie Chang, 'The Monstrous-Feminine in the Incel Imagination: Investigating the Representation of Women as "Femoids" on /r/Braincels', *Feminist Media Studies* 22, no. 2 (February 2022): 254–270.

124 Digital Flows

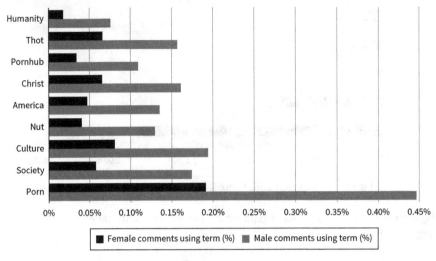

Figure 5.5 Terms with significant gender differences in the 'respectability' theme used more frequently by male commenters

were not purely aroused, but also shocked, by the explicit female sexuality on display, hence several comments like 'did I open Pornhub by mistake?'.

Second, commenters used terms implying that the women in these videos—rappers, dancers, extras—lack worth. Their personhood is attacked, not just their music or dancing. Men were almost twice as likely to use disrespectful stereotypes to describe women, like 'thot', gold 'digger[s]', and 'feminist[s]'. Granted, 'thot' has become a pervasive term in contemporary rap lyrics, wielded by artists of all genders, though it clearly carries more patriarchal judgment about acceptable femininities in the mouths of men.[57] The gender imbalance of 'feminist' as a term, three times more common in posts by men than women, might be surprising, especially given that these rappers are often identified as feminists in blogs and fan commentaries.[58] However, the

---

[57] Megan Thee Stallion has led the charge in reclaiming 'thot', associated with expressing sexual freedoms, just like 'bitch' was reclaimed in decades prior. She explains that 'it used to [have a negative connotation]. That's old news . . . I see it so much on the Internet, guys that's probably still living in like 2012 . . . get online bitching and complaining about girls twerking and having fun . . . If I want to do thot shit, I could do that . . . If y'all still using it as a negative word, y'all need to grow up because we all doing thot shit'. See *Megan Thee Stallion - Thot Shit Song Breakdown*, YouTube video, 13 July 2021, 3:18–4:08, https://www.youtube.com/watch?v=aJSkbTC-4I8. For more on reclaiming shaming terms, see Diana Khong, '"Yeah, I'm in My Bag, but I'm in His Too": How Scamming Aesthetics Utilized by Black Women Rappers Undermine Existing Institutions of Gender', *Journal of Hip Hop Studies* 7, no. 1 (July 2020): 92–93.

[58] For example, Mahina Adams, 'The Feminine Musique: Cardi, Megan, and Black Feminism', *afterglow*, 6 December 2021, https://www.afterglowatx.com/blog/2021/12/6/the-feminine-musique-cardi-megan-and-black-feminism; Taylor Hosking, 'Rappers Like Megan Thee Stallion Are Writing a New Feminist Canon', *Vice* (blog), 20 August 2019, https://www.vice.com/en/article/evjnnk/rappers-like-megan-thee-stallion-are-writing-a-new-feminist-canon-cardi-b-city-girls-princess-nokia-rico-nasty-saweetie.

Online Hip Hop Feminism **125**

term is used pejoratively by men—'is this what feminists wanted?'—whereas women express genuine feminist sentiments more casually, such as the posts celebrating natural bodies, butts, and twerking I highlighted under the body theme. This observation aligns with the sense that feminism is a dirty word in the online context of the Manosphere.[59]

Third and finally, there is a medley of terms gesturing towards developments in wider social norms. Placed together, they tell a story of male expectations about the status quo: 'society', 'culture', 'America', 'Christ', 'humanity', 'generation', and 'nowadays'. Reading such comments, one might get the impression that Black women making tracks about sex and dancing to them represent the decline of Western civilization. Men post about 'losing my faith in humanity' or 'the corruption of society', a line of thinking also found in de Boise's work on misogynistic antifeminist forums, where there exists 'an affective sense that white, "traditional masculinity"—regarded as a cornerstone of "Western civilization"—is in decline'.[60] If these rap videos and their expressions of sex-positive hip hop feminism represent the downfall of society, one can assume that these commenters value traditional white domestic, sexually-repressed and subservient femininity. By loudly and proudly rejecting such normative gender roles, Black women rappers challenge patriarchal or idealized masculine expectations,[61] which is evidently more noteworthy to male than female viewers.

The Politics of Raunchy Rap Videos in the Internet Age

Men making reactionary comments about social decline form part of the audience for these music videos alongside the Black women viewers who feel recognized and empowered by them. In fact, the attention of mostly male conservative viewers is easy to capture and can even be very profitable for the artists. City Girls' 'Pussy Talk feat. Doja Cat' and Saweetie's 'My Type', for example, strategically use direct, anatomically precise, and smutty lyrics which both express Black women's pursuits of pleasure and afford shock value for audiences with puritanical gender politics. By doing so, these releases gain attention from surprised listeners and mainstream media alike, who feel compelled to

---

[59] Angela Nagle, *Kill All Normies: Online Culture Wars from 4Chan and Tumblr to Trump and the Alt-Right* (Winchester: Zero Books, 2017), 86.

[60] De Boise, 'Music and Misogyny', 463.

[61] Johnson, 'Dirty South Feminism', 2–5.

signal boost the songs as typifying what's wrong with America today, or some such framing. The videos, often with tantalizing visuals to match, have viral potential in circulation on the politically polarized, clickbait-driven climate of social media platforms (described in further detail in Chapter 3).[62]

A clear case in point is the 'self-own' of conservative troll Ben Shapiro, who described 'WAP' as 'what feminists fought for' and ended up suggesting that vaginal lubrication is an abnormal medical condition.[63] In taking the bait and responding to Megan Thee Stallion and Cardi B's punchy, provocative song, he ends up tacitly revealing that at the heart of this public outcry lies (reactionary, white) male discomfort with (radical, Black) female sexuality. In YouTube comment sections and wider cultural commentary, the crux of such critique is men's inability to *manage*—both in the sense of dealing with one's own experience of, and to have dominion over—the bodies of the women expressing Black joy, desire, and 'erotic power'.[64]

In her study of Black women in pornography, Mireille Miller-Young introduced the term 'illicit eroticism' to describe a strategy by which Black women use erotic capital, which is marked by racial fetishism and hypersexual stereotypes, to gain economic and cultural power.[65] Women rapping today are savvy internet users who creatively deploy illicit eroticism in their music and videos to generate attention in the digital media economy. In other words, men fear their sexual freedom, and they know it. Men show this fear by being more likely to leave hateful comments. It is disheartening to encounter misogynoir in the comments section, but it is worth the reminder that this exists among a small minority highlighted in contrast to women's posts. Moreover, I have suggested that riling men with significant online audiences can both profit the artists through the wider circulation of their songs and reveal ideologies that uphold white supremacy and patriarchy.

What does this mean for hip hop? Black women rappers making subversive, sexually provocative tracks show the culturally expressive potential of hip hop in its internet era. This wave of new artists powerfully demonstrates that hip hop 'influences how individuals embody the self, and how they use media

---

[62] Joel Penney, *Pop Culture, Politics, and the News: Entertainment Journalism in the Polarized Media Landscape* (New York: Oxford University Press, 2022), 10.

[63] Rachel Handler, 'We Asked a Gyno About "WAP"', Vulture, August 2020, https://www.vulture.com/2020/08/we-asked-a-gyno-about-wap.html; Arwa Mahdawi, 'The WAP Uproar Shows Conservatives Are Fine with Female Sexuality – as Long as Men Control It', *The Guardian*, 15 August 2020, https://www.theguardian.com/commentisfree/2020/aug/15/cardi-b-megan-thee-stalion-wap-conservatives-female-sexuality; Heran Mamo, 'Ben Shapiro Reads the Censored Lyrics to Cardi B and Megan Thee Stallion's "WAP" & He Can't Handle It', *Billboard* (blog), 10 August 2020, https://www.billboard.com/music/rb-hip-hop/ben-shapiro-reads-censored-wap-lyrics-cardi-b-megan-thee-stallion-9432034/.

[64] Halliday, 'Twerk Sumn!', 880.

[65] Miller-Young, *A Taste for Brown Sugar*, 10.

and digital tools as a space to create meaning for themselves and others.'[66] Digital Black feminist practice in mainstream online culture provides prototypical images, videos, and new media expressions to which fans and users relate their own online practices.[67] In doing so, these artists make Blackness and womanhood points of unapologetic pride, as well as normalize displays of sexuality that contest stigmatized and stereotyped tropes. Their videos present structural challenges to the vectors of marginalization that limit Black women's full and free social participation.

However, the videos I have analysed may fall short of some radical political ideals. For the most part, they are committed to upholding capitalism as a prevailing economic order, expressing joy in reaping its benefits. This is wholly conventional for commercial hip hop, where resistant ideas coexist alongside neoliberal tenets such as conspicuous consumption and rags-to-riches fantasies.[68] Margaret Hunter and Alhelí Cuenca describe Nicki Minaj's work as adopting accommodationist politics, using her 'body-product' to appeal to the widest possible range of potential consumers.[69] What's more, Erica B. Edwards and Jennifer Esposito have identified that a politics of pleasure, despite emerging from Black feminist theory, is sometimes elided with postfeminist ideology by prioritizing 'individual desire and agency over collective action.'[70] Post-feminism suggests that gender equity has been achieved, just like post-racism (sometimes called colourblind racism) posits that no racial inequalities persist today.[71] Post-feminism aids and bolsters patriarchal structures. To view women as sexually liberated, empowered individuals free from oppression while they remain clearly subject to objectification, sexualization, and regulation denies such systemic subjugation.

Amy Shields Dobson's critique of postfeminist popular culture applies effectively to Black women rappers' videos. These videos perfectly exemplify 'powerful images of "active" rather than passive, desired and *desiring* female bodies [that] are now common across mediascapes and in certain cultural scenes.'[72] Yet it remains the case that presentations of desire, via pleasure politics or

---

[66] Crystal LaVoulle and Tisha Lewis Ellison, 'The Bad Bitch Barbie Craze and Beyoncé: African American Women's Bodies as Commodities in Hip-Hop Culture, Images, and Media', *Taboo: The Journal of Culture and Education* 16, no. 2 (April 2018): 79.

[67] Steele, *Digital Black Feminism*, 142–147.

[68] Travis L. Gosa, 'The Fifth Element: Knowledge', in *The Cambridge Companion to Hip-Hop*, ed. Justin A. Williams (Cambridge: Cambridge University Press, 2015), 56–70.

[69] Margaret Hunter and Alhelí Cuenca, 'Nicki Minaj and the Changing Politics of Hip-Hop: Real Blackness, Real Bodies, Real Feminism?', *Feminist Formations* 29, no. 2 (2017): 39–42.

[70] Edwards and Esposito, 'Reading the Black Woman's Body Via Instagram Fame', 342.

[71] Eduardo Bonilla-Silva, *Racism Without Racists: Color-Blind Racism and the Persistence of Racial Inequality in America*, 6th ed. (Lanham, MD: Rowman & Littlefield Publishers, 2021), xxii; Kalwant Bhopal, *White Privilege: The Myth of a Post-Racial Society* (Bristol: Policy Press, 2018).

[72] Amy Shields Dobson, *Postfeminist Digital Cultures* (New York: Palgrave Macmillan US, 2015), 31.

other means, at best exist alongside patriarchal oppressions and at worst reinforce individualizing, neoliberal ideals at the cost of a still-marginalized collective. As Rosalind Gill argues, 'just about anything in the mainstream media universe can be (re)signified as "feminist", highlighting 'feminism being championed as a cheer word, a positive value—yet in a way that does not necessarily pose any kind of challenge to existing social relations.'[73]

Furthermore, Shields Dobson notes that 'a relatively narrow range of young, slim, white, able bodies are still fetishized in postfeminist popular culture.'[74] Clearly the presence of curvy (albeit still slim), Black, and historically stigmatized bodies in mainstream rap is celebrated, as evident in both the 'body' theme I discovered and wider fan commentary. But it is an open question whether the participation of Black women in postfeminist media—a formerly white-dominated space—is cause for unconditional celebration, for it may resemble improved diversity without any structural change. In other words, it brings Black women into the same harmful frame that predominantly white women participate in. Such videos risk encouraging women 'to ascribe to a post-racist and/or post-sexist standpoint, as they come to believe that they have the economic and individual power to overcome racism and sexism', reinforcing inequalities that are especially prominent on social and digital media platforms.[75]

Conclusion

For all of the contradictions and complexities, it is undeniable that the creativity, the sisterhood, and the playful sexuality performed in these rap videos are powerful expressions of Black women's joy. This is something that has been historically silenced, stigmatized, or marginalized, even in hip hop spaces assumed to be progressive.[76] Now it is widely celebrated on YouTube and far beyond, as gendered terms in comments show that Black women rappers contest patriarchal control through the expression of desire and pleasure. In essence, my analysis shows that Black women rappers' music videos are at the

[73] Rosalind Gill, 'Post-Postfeminism?: New Feminist Visibilities in Postfeminist Times', *Feminist Media Studies* 16, no. 4 (2016): 619.

[74] Dobson, *Postfeminist Digital Cultures*, 31.

[75] Edwards and Esposito, 'Reading the Black Woman's Body Via Instagram Fame', 342.

[76] Denise Noble and Lisa Amanda Palmer, 'Misogynoir: Anti-Blackness, Patriarchy, and Refusing the Wrongness of Black Women', in *The Palgrave Handbook of Critical Race and Gender*, ed. Shirley Anne Tate and Encarnación Gutiérrez Rodríguez (Cham: Springer International Publishing, 2022), 233.

Online Hip Hop Feminism   129

forefront of online Black resistance. Rather than being sequestered in Black communities, these videos are widely visible music artifacts that

> celebrate Black life in ways that challenge mainstream media's attempts to fix Black people and Black life into a position of death and despair; assert Black people as fully human, capable of experiencing and expressing a full, dynamic range of emotion; and capture, share, and circulate expressions of Black life and joy[77]

for mass consumption in mainstream online culture. In doing so, Black women rappers deploy hip hop's 'Black rhetorical strategies and cultural practices to play with notions of publicity, daring to live freely in defiance of the dominant group's expectations and prejudices.'[78] Despite pushback from the most conservative and outspoken men, hip hop feminists refuse to be silenced. Their voices resonate loudly across racial boundaries and are celebrated by diverse audiences. Further exploration of how race affects responses to online hip hop is necessary, for white appreciation of hip hop can develop into the adoption of Black aesthetics and identities without sensitivity to sociocultural contexts, as the next chapter demonstrates.

---

[77] Jessica H. Lu and Catherine Knight Steele, ' "Joy Is Resistance": Cross-Platform Resilience and (Re) Invention of Black Oral Culture Online', *Information, Communication & Society* 22, no. 6 (May 2019): 829.
[78] Lu and Steele, 834.

6

Hip Hop and Online Cultural Appropriation Discourse

Trap, Pop, and Race

Introduction

Hip hop's onlining has had a profound impact on mainstream online culture. In previous chapters and elsewhere,[1] I have highlighted evidence about the intense global popularity of hip hop in the internet age. Hip hop today has large and diverse audiences, encompassing people of various races, ethnicities, and nationalities. Artists across the gamut of popular music genres and a range of social media platform users enthusiastically engage with hip hop aesthetics and Black culture more broadly. Such engagements demonstrate the changing politics of race, identity, and participation in online hip hop music and culture.

The history of non-Black musicians, particularly white Americans, performing Black music precedes the internet by over a century.[2] The digital music economy—perhaps in part due to hip hop's top spot—has exacerbated borrowings of Black popular culture. Contemporary pop music has taken significant influence from hip hop, to the extent that, as *The New Yorker* journalist Kelefa Sanneh puts it,

> in the 2010s . . . hip hop *was* popular music, with everything else either a subgenre or variant of it, or a quirky alternative to it. On streaming services especially, you might look at the chart and see that just about all the most popular songs . . . were hip-hop, or hip-hop-ish.[3]

[1] Steven Gamble and Raquel Campos Valverde, 'Editorial', in 'It's Where You're @: Hip Hop and the Internet', special issue *Global Hip Hop Studies* 2 (November 2021): 153–158.

[2] Eileen Southern, 'The Georgia Minstrels: The Early Years', in *Inside the Minstrel Mask: Readings in Nineteenth-Century Blackface Minstrelsy*, ed. Annemarie Bean, James Vernon Hatch, and Brooks McNamara (Hanover, CT and London: Wesleyan University Press, 1996), 163–178.

[3] Kelefa Sanneh, *Major Labels: A History of Popular Music in Seven Genres* (New York: Penguin Press, 2021), italics preserved.

Digital Flows. Steven Gamble, Oxford University Press. © Oxford University Press 2024.
DOI: 10.1093/oso/9780197656389.003.0006

Moreover, the politics of such borrowings are contentious, sparking online discourse about white appropriations of Black culture. Discussions unfold primarily on social networking services, where individuals passionately and publicly engage in heated debates. These are intensified by a range of features that encourage users to express their own views, adding fuel to the fire through interactions such as liking, sharing, and commenting.

In this chapter, I advance a critical technocultural inquiry into how social media platforms shape discourse about the appropriation of Black culture. My inquiry centres around accusations of Blackfishing levelled at the pop superstar Ariana Grande. Maha Ikram Cherid defines Blackfishing as actions of predominantly white women to convince others that they are Black using visual cues such as makeup, hairstyles, and fashion based in Black culture.[4] Ariana Grande is an illuminating example because of her immense popularity, the substantial incorporation of hip hop (especially trap) elements in her music, and the internet-mediated and extensively debated public image she presents. By listening to the musical and cultural values disputed by users on Reddit, Twitter (before its rebranding as X and associated changes to the platform), and Tumblr, I shed light on how pop music's adoption of trap's musical and visual aesthetics is both thoroughly normalized and contested online.

Part of the impetus for this inquiry is that students in music, media, cultural studies, and other disciplines frequently wish to write about cultural debates on social media but are not always well-equipped with how to start. This chapter therefore serves as a model for analysing online discourse about popular music and culture. As it pertains to the book's focus, the Ariana Grande reading also shows how different user groups disparage, dilute, or defend hip hop on the internet. I analyse the music and video of '7 rings', which provoked many of the online exchanges about the artist's borrowings from hip hop. Through a combined analysis of the music video and the online discourse, I provide insights into the evolving relationship between trap and pop in the internet age, as well as the racial conceptions that mainstream—which is to say largely white[5]—audiences articulate online about hip hop as an art form.

---

[4] Maha Ikram Cherid, '"Ain't Got Enough Money to Pay Me Respect": Blackfishing, Cultural Appropriation, and the Commodification of Blackness', *Cultural Studies ↔ Critical Methodologies* 21, no. 5 (July 2021): 1.

[5] Cedric D. Burrows, *Rhetorical Crossover: The Black Presence in White Culture* (Pittsburgh, PA: University of Pittsburgh Press, 2020), 5–9.

Borrowings of Black Music

As I addressed in Chapter 2, hip hop is a cultural form based on acts of borrowing.[6] Borrowing is not inherently bad: it can be consensual, equitable, or even encouraged. Hip hop music was created by the reuse and remixing of pre-existing records. Yet the history of borrowing in popular music is rarely so encouraging, not least because of how power imbalances affect processes of appropriation.[7] Racial inequities are especially prominent. The twentieth century is full of instances of Black musical creativity being emulated and repackaged by white artists to achieve greater popular and commercial success. Benny Goodman 'became the "King of Swing" leading a mostly white band'.[8] White 'rock 'n' roll' artists systematically covered and outsold Black 'rhythm & blues' songs.[9] Of course, at the turn of the millennium, hip hop gained its own white megastar, and one of the best-selling rap artists still to this day, Eminem.[10] Black scholars interpreting this pattern have observed that white audiences want to experience a kind of essentialized urban Black *culture*—signifying 'coolness, youth culture, and counternarratives of socioeconomic marginalization'—without Black *people*.[11]

White engagement with Black popular culture is frequently fleeting and extractive, yet wildly popular. Online, borrowing moves in ever more rapid and complex ways. Reaction GIFs, as in the use of an animated looping image as a form of commentary, exemplify how digital, cross-racial borrowings are pervasive. Drawing on Laur Jackson's writing, Rachel Kuo describes an 'overrepresentation of black people, vernacular and expression in GIFs and meme culture' leading to a status quo in which 'non-black uses of reaction GIFs puppeteer and playact through the black image'.[12] Non-Black users unthinkingly draw on animated, emotional, and joyful expressive performances

---

[6] J. A. Williams, *Rhymin' and Stealin': Musical Borrowing in Hip-Hop* (Ann Arbor: University of Michigan Press, 2013), 1.

[7] Lauren Michele Jackson, *White Negroes: When Cornrows Were in Vogue . . . and Other Thoughts on Cultural Appropriation.* (Boston, MA: Beacon Press, 2019), 1–6.

[8] Perry A. Hall, 'African-American Music: Dynamics of Appropriation and Innovation', in *Borrowed Power: Essays on Cultural Appropriation*, ed. Bruce H. Ziff and Pratima V. Rao (New Brunswick, NJ: Rutgers University Press, 1997), 31.

[9] Reebee Garofalo, 'Crossing Over: From Black Rhythm & Blues to White Rock "n" Roll', in *R&B (Rhythm & Business): The Political Economy of Black Music*, ed. Norman Kelley (New York: Akashic Books, 2002), 124–126.

[10] Loren Kajikawa, *Sounding Race in Rap Songs* (Berkeley and Los Angeles: University of California Press, 2015), 121.

[11] Imani Kai Johnson, 'Black Culture without Black People: Hip-Hop Dance beyond Appropriation Discourse', in *Are You Entertained?*, ed. Simone C. Drake and Dwan K. Henderson (Durham, NC: Duke University Press, 2020), 194.

[12] Rachel Kuo, 'Animating Feminist Anger: Economies of Race and Gender in Reaction GIFs', in *Gender Hate Online: Understanding the New Anti-Feminism*, ed. Debbie Ging and Eugenia Siapera (Cham: Springer International Publishing, 2019), 183.

by Black people in many forms of visual media. Hip hop features prominently within such conventions, as I demonstrated in Chapter 2's discussion of memes. I suggest here that, in a digital media economy with accelerated forms of intercultural borrowing, popular music is another site where the use of Black expressivity and adoption of Black aesthetics has become thoroughly normalized.

In the contemporary era, we hear the use of Black music all across pop, a genre rendered as a separate market category from hip hop and R&B. Yet such categorization is built on fraught racial and cultural distinctions. Black artists and their representatives have frequently expressed frustration surrounding the industry's racialized divisions.[13] The furore surrounding Lil Nas X's 'Old Town Road' provides the clearest recent example of sustained racial boundaries, with the song's removal from the Billboard country chart described by Robert Christgau as 'racist pure and simple'.[14] The history of racial segregation in the popular music market, placing Black performers in a category of race music, has hardly improved.[15] In the contemporary climate, Black artists making all varieties of pop music still frequently find themselves confined to R&B or hip hop, with their non-Black counterparts placed in pop.[16] Among discussions around award ceremonies' naming conventions in early 2020, Tyler, the Creator expressed this critique clearly:

> On one side I'm very grateful that what I made could just be, you know, acknowledged in a world like this, but also it sucks that whenever we—and I mean guys that look like me—do anything that's genre-bending or that's anything, they always put it in a rap or urban category, which is—and I don't like that urban word, it's just a politically correct way to say the N-word to me. So when I hear that, I'm just like, why can't we just be in pop?[17]

---

[13] Briana Younger, 'Black Musicians on Being Boxed in by R&B and Rap Expectations: "We Fit in So Many Things"', *Pitchfork*, 28 September 2017, https://pitchfork.com/thepitch/black-musicians-on-being-boxed-in-by-randb-and-rap-expectations-we-fit-in-so-many-things/.

[14] Robert Christgau, 'Xgau Sez', *Robert Christgau*, 18 June 2019, https://robertchristgau.com/xgausez.php?d=2019-06-18. See also Kai Arne Hansen, *Pop Masculinities: The Politics of Gender in Twenty-First Century Popular Music* (Oxford and New York: Oxford University Press, 2021), 66–68.

[15] Reebee Garofalo, 'Industrializing African American Popular Music', in *Issues in African American Music*, ed. Portia K. Maultsby and Mellonee Burnim (New York: Routledge, 2016), 90–109.

[16] The few counterexamples can be counted on one hand. For instance, paragons of Black music like Michael Jackson and Beyoncé have gained honorifics relating to pop. Another case in point: though working across pop, R&B, hip hop, and electronic dance music, the Weeknd tends to be nominated by his label as pop in genre-based award categories where possible. See Jem Aswad, 'Is the Weeknd Pop, R&B or Hip-Hop? Why the Distinction Matters at the Grammys', *Variety* (blog), 1 October 2020, https://variety.com/2020/music/news/weeknd-grammys-pop-hip-hop-category-1234789560/.

[17] *Tyler, The Creator TV/Radio Room Interview | 2020 GRAMMYs*, YouTube video, 27 January 2020, https://www.youtube.com/watch?v=j5a42MwoYsw. The Recording Academy removed the term 'Urban' in the months following this statement, though the point about the segregation of Black musicians to rap and R&B categories stands.

134 Digital Flows

This is a serious issue with industry structures that has thankfully received attention from a range of scholars as well as journalists and artists. If particular music categories have been racialized, with some implicitly coded Black, what does it mean for white musicians to participate in these genres? In this chapter, I am concerned with how white artists use Black musical and cultural aesthetics while retaining their association with pop as an industry category, their pop star status, and other privileges granted by their whiteness.

The Hip Hop–Pop Relationship in the Digital Media Economy

The apparent popularity of hip hop among all popular music genres is a strange thing. As I discussed in Chapter 2, statistics produced by Luminate Data (formerly Nielsen Music and MRC Data) have placed hip hop as the dominant genre among US listeners since 2017, when it first overtook rock—all forms of the vast and diverse category of rock, which also somehow includes all forms of metal—in association with a surge in streaming.[18] Throughout the 2010s, pop sat in third place to rock and hip hop. These classifications serve market purposes, to some extent, but in practice remain 'complex, possibly contentious, and difficult to escape'.[19]

The relationship between hip hop and pop operates on different levels. Allan Moore's division between the concepts of style and genre advances the idea that both terms are key to our ability to understand music as music.[20] Genre refers to musical gestures and their contexts ('what'), style to how listeners interpret their articulation ('how'). Put differently, genre focuses on music as social practice, whereas style provides a sonic emphasis that—imperfectly— 'brackets out the social'.[21] Megan Lavengood suggests the two concepts are 'too intertwined to untangle them in any practical context', yet she also provides a successful reading of ' "genres" as they exist as complex social phenomena and "styles" as they are deployed within . . . a polystylistic musical text'.[22] Paying

---

[18] Tricia Rose observed this trend even earlier, drawing on 1991 data by Soundscan, which featured 'rock and rap . . . showing the greatest actual sales and outstripping mainstream pop acts'. Tricia Rose, *The Hip-Hop Wars: What We Talk about When We Talk about Hip-Hop and Why It Matters* (New York: Basic Books, 2008), 15.

[19] David Brackett, *Categorizing Sound: Genre and Twentieth-Century Popular Music* (Berkeley and Los Angeles: University of California Press, 2016), 2.

[20] Allan F. Moore, 'Categorical Conventions in Music Discourse: Style and Genre', *Music & Letters* 82, no. 3 (January 2001): 441.

[21] Moore, 'Categorical Conventions in Music Discourse', 441.

[22] Megan Lavengood, 'Timbre, Genre, and Polystylism in Sonic the Hedgehog 3', in *On Popular Music and Its Unruly Entanglements*, ed. Nick Braae and Kai Arne Hansen, Pop Music, Culture and Identity (Cham: Springer International Publishing, 2019), 210.

attention to style does not need to imply that music exists in a vacuum, or that it can ever be separated from its social significance: it simply means a closer focus on *how* music is practised (performed, recorded, listened to). Genre instead implies starting from a social perspective—music as it is categorized by cultural understandings, that is, *what* it is—even when addressing musical gestures themselves.

Whereas style works at different hierarchical levels that vary in detail (from something as broad as 'rap' down to the details of a particular vocalist's timbre), genre implies a distinct level of categorization which places 'pop' and 'hip hop' in parallel. To make wider or narrower classifications by genre, umbrella terms like 'metagenre' and subdivisions like 'subgenre'—in linguistics, 'hypernyms' and 'hyponyms'—are typically used. Perhaps confusingly, Roy Shuker has applied the term metagenre to categories of music that most people would call genres, hip hop and pop among them.[23] Shuker suggests that thinking on the level of genre is not necessarily appropriate for subsuming the entire variety of musical practices that can be called hip hop. For example, the parties soundtracked by New Yorkers spinning disco and rock breaks were hip hop, yet so is the trap music currently thriving in Finland, a sound that has already travelled from Atlanta via the internet.[24] Rather than consider (what we would now call) old school hip hop and trap subgenres of the genre hip hop, it may be more useful to recognize them as genres of their own accord. Then, old school hip hop as a genre can cover both early East Coast and West Coast subgenres. Trap can divide into subgenres including plugg and rage (see Chapter 3). I do not see record labels, managers, and artists using the term metagenre any time soon. Yet Shuker's suggestion to shift hierarchical thinking up one level—hip hop as an overarching metagenre, its subcategories genres, and further differentiations as subgenres—helps to manage the incredible diversity of music labelled hip hop today (exemplified in Table 6.1).[25] This approach has already been successfully applied to other music, such as metal.[26]

With this concept in mind, we can see how genre acts as an important structuring device in the marketing, promotion, and classification of music. In an

---

[23] Roy Shuker, *Popular Music: The Key Concepts*, 4th ed. (London and New York: Routledge, 2017), 148–152.

[24] Inka Rantakallio, 'New Spirituality, Atheism, and Authenticity in Finnish Underground Rap' (PhD diss., University of Turku, 2019), 205.

[25] Note that hip hop is often subdivided according to geographical distinctions, reflecting a unique emphasis on space, place, and representation. See Murray Forman, *The 'hood Comes First: Race, Space, and Place in Rap and Hip-Hop* (Middletown, CT: Wesleyan University Press, 2002).

[26] For example, Deena Weinstein, 'Playing with Gender in the Key of Metal', in *Heavy Metal, Gender and Sexuality: Interdisciplinary Approaches*, ed. Florian Heesch and Niall Scott (London and New York: Routledge, 2016), 13.

136 Digital Flows

Table 6.1 Genre hierarchy with various examples of popular music

Metagenre	Genre	Subgenre
Hip hop	East Coast hip hop	Boom bap
	Southern hip hop	Memphis rap
	Drill	UK drill
		Brooklyn drill
	Trap	Latin trap
		Plugg
		Rage
Metal	Death metal	Melodic death metal
Pop	Easy listening	Lounge music
Electronic dance music	House	Tropical house
		Acid house

era where recorded music was more rigidly constrained by record labels, pop and hip hop were produced and consumed along stratified lines.[27] Indeed, how genre boundaries reinforce ideas about cultural tastes and identities is an important element of foundational work in popular music studies.[28] Artists in different genres are placed in different areas of record stores, reviewed in different magazines, and nominated in different awards categories. And, importantly, they are now also labelled with different metadata tags in the digital music landscape.

The relationship between genre and platform structures like tagging has transformed throughout the 2010s and continues to shift today.[29] Emerging artists—facing an increasingly broad set of career development demands[30]—compete for space and attention across a limited range of social media platforms. Platform affordances like tags may help posts reach desired audiences but collide within a range of collapsed contexts that 'blur

---

[27] Brackett, *Categorizing Sound*, 88–99. See also Anne Danielsen, 'The Sound of Crossover: Micro-Rhythm and Sonic Pleasure in Michael Jackson's "Don't Stop 'Til You Get Enough"', *Popular Music and Society* 35, no. 2 (May 2012): 151–168.

[28] Sara Cohen, 'Ethnography and Popular Music Studies', *Popular Music* 12, no. 2 (May 1993): 123–138; S. Frith, *Performing Rites: On the Value of Popular Music* (Oxford: Oxford University Press, 1996), 75–95.

[29] See, for example, Amelia Besseny, 'Lost in Spotify: Folksonomy and Wayfinding Functions in Spotify's Interface and Companion Apps', *Popular Communication* 18, no. 1 (January 2020): 1–17; Eric Drott, 'Why the Next Song Matters: Streaming, Recommendation, Scarcity', *Twentieth-Century Music* 15, no. 3 (October 2018): 325–357; Raphaël Nowak and Andrew Whelan, '"Vaporwave Is (Not) a Critique of Capitalism": Genre Work in An Online Music Scene', *Open Cultural Studies* 2, no. 1 (November 2018): 451–462; Tom Johnson, 'Chance the Rapper, Spotify, and Musical Categorization in the 2010s', *American Music* 38, no. 2 (2020): 176–196.

[30] Jo Haynes and Lee Marshall, 'Reluctant Entrepreneurs: Musicians and Entrepreneurship in the "New" Music Industry', *The British Journal of Sociology* 69, no. 2 (2018): 459–482.

boundaries between audiences'.[31] TikTok feeds, structured according to a dizzying array of user data and attention-optimizing algorithmic determinations,[32] are far more opaque than the record store or genre-coded magazine of an earlier era.

These developments also suggest that boundaries between hip hop and pop used to be more clear-cut. Cultural criticism and scholarship alike have examined the extent to which on-demand streaming services have challenged conventions of genre. For example, Spotify blurs typological distinctions between genre, mood, activity, decades, and more.[33] Classifications upheld by the streaming economy struggle to recognize artists performing in multiple (or hybrid) music genres, which often place the West at the centre of musical knowledges.[34] Meanwhile, songwriters and producers may be influenced by the algorithmic leanings of specific platforms.[35] Even the basic structure of streaming services— based on processes of centralizing data and users, as I described in this book's introduction—places formerly distinct genres like pop and hip hop significantly closer side-by-side within the platform interface, sometimes only a click away.

Contemporary hip hop, in its most commercial leanings, has undoubtedly embraced many features of pop.[36] There are also many artists who actively and explicitly combine elements of the two metagenres. Furthermore, there is a burgeoning body of research on racial representations in K-pop's appropriation of hip hop,[37] which influences my thinking here. In the internet age, the transnational flow of cultural materials has rapidly accelerated,[38] with hip hop's global influence an important case in point. With all this in mind,

---

[31] Nancy Baym, *Playing to the Crowd: Musicians, Audiences, and the Intimate Work of Connection* (New York: New York University Press, 2018), 161.

[32] D. Bondy Valdovinos Kaye, Jing Zeng, and Patrik Wikstrom, *TikTok: Creativity and Culture in Short Video* (Cambridge: Wiley, 2022), 58ff.

[33] Mads Krogh, 'Rampant Abstraction as a Strategy of Singularization: Genre on Spotify', *Cultural Sociology*, May 2023, 8.

[34] David Hesmondhalgh et al., *The Impact of Algorithmically Driven Recommendation Systems on Music Consumption and Production: A Literature Review*, (Department for Digital, Culture, Media & Sport, 2023), https://www.gov.uk/government/publications/research-into-the-impact-of-streaming-services-algorithms-on-music-consumption/the-impact-of-algorithmically-driven-recommendation-systems-on-music-consumption-and-production-a-literature-review.

[35] Liz Pelly, 'Streambait Pop', *The Baffler*, 11 December 2018, https://thebaffler.com/latest/streambait-pop-pelly.

[36] Amy Coddington, ' "Check Out the Hook While My DJ Revolves It": How the Music Industry Made Rap into Pop in the Late 1980s', in *The Oxford Handbook of Hip Hop Music*, ed. Justin D. Burton and Jason Lee Oakes (Oxford: Oxford University Press, 2018).

[37] Crystal S. Anderson, 'Hybrid Hallyu: The African American Music Tradition in K-Pop', in *Global Asian American Popular Cultures*, ed. Shilpa Davé, LeiLani Nishime, and Tasha Oren (New York: New York University Press, 2016), 290–303; Joyhanna Yoo Garza, ' "Where All My Bad Girls at?": Cosmopolitan Femininity through Racialised Appropriations in K-Pop', *Gender and Language* 15, no. 1 (March 2021): 11–41; Chuyun Oh, 'Performing Post-Racial Asianness: K-Pop's Appropriation of Hip-Hop Culture', *Congress on Research in Dance Conference Proceedings* 2014 (October 2014): 121–125.

[38] Henry Jenkins, Sam Ford, and Joshua Green, *Spreadable Media: Creating Value and Meaning in a Networked Culture* (New York and London: New York University Press, 2013), 284–285.

138 Digital Flows

I focus here on the pervasive trend of white US pop stars borrowing hip hop aesthetics, and how the social implications of such borrowings are debated among audiences on social media platforms.

Blackfishing Accusations against Ariana Grande on Social Media

In rapper and comedian Lil Dicky's 2019 climate charity music video 'Earth', Ariana Grande features among the ensemble cast as an animated zebra. She sings, 'am I white or Black?'. Though this is superficially a playful question about zebra stripes, allocating this voice part to Ariana Grande makes it funnier, and the Lil Dicky character accordingly gives the viewer a knowing shrug. Since the mid-2010s, the public image of singer, songwriter, and actor Ariana Grande has frequently prompted such questions. Her appearance in music videos and public events, combined with her use of Black musical aesthetics and her Italian American name, have contributed to racial ambiguity becoming a prominent aspect of her public profile. In the analysis that follows, I am concerned with Ariana Grande as a celebrity figure who is understood through the consumption of media texts and performances, and whose creative works are the product of many people's labour: a multiply constructed pop persona.[39] My references to the artist use this framing and do not assume anything about Ariana Grande as a person. This provides some critical distance from the parasocial connections that fans often form with artists on the mistaken—but strongly felt—belief that they know what they are 'really like'.[40]

My data collection focused on the search terms 'Ariana' and 'Blackfishing'. This approach may be open to criticism of bias, in that I looked specifically for what I hoped to find, rather than discovering such topics among general discourse on the artist. First, I read a variety of online texts—journalism, blogs, and social media posts—to familiarize myself with debates about accusations of cultural appropriation levelled at Ariana Grande. I then ran data collection pilots for these terms and others that I thought might prove pertinent, such as 'cultural', 'culture', 'Black', 'race', and 'tan', though these were used in highly varied contexts. Limiting the scope to 'Ariana' and 'Blackfishing' returned mainly relevant material and produced more apt sources than the larger set

---

[39] Kai Arne Hansen, '(Re)Reading Pop Personae: A Transmedial Approach to Studying the Multiple Construction of Artist Identities', *Twentieth-Century Music* 16, no. 3 (October 2019): 501–529.

[40] Kate Szer Kurtin et al., 'Parasocial Relationships with Musicians', *The Journal of Social Media in Society* 8, no. 2 (December 2019): 30–50. See also Riva Tukachinsky Forster, *Parasocial Romantic Relationships: Falling in Love with Media Figures* (Lanham, MD: Rowman & Littlefield, 2021).

Table 6.2 Sample of deidentified and obfuscated online comments about Ariana Grande's racially ambiguous appearance

'Hold on, she's white?'
'I thought she was Hispanic'
'Her family is Italian with partly North African lineage'
'Isn't she Asian-fishing now?'
'She's not "trying" to "look Black", she just tans easy'

spanning broad topics of commentary. This method therefore presents an alternative to the quantitative approach adopted in Chapters 4 and 5. Instead, I emphasize insights gleaned from small data,[41] listening to and 'acquiring knowledge of the online environment and (sub)cultural milieu' appropriate to the matter at hand.[42]

Online, there is a dizzying array of opinions about how Ariana Grande looks and performs (Table 6.2).[43] There is an overwhelming focus on skin colour over other phenotypic distinctions, echoing broader social tendencies in discussions about race (which give rise to the concept of colourism).[44] Images—press photos, candid shots, and stills from music videos—are prevalent within debates on Ariana Grande, which is unsurprising given the visuality of the topic and the image-sharing affordances of social media platforms. Users also frequently mention the artist's use of language and the audiovisual qualities of her music videos. There is a range of viewpoints expressed by commentators, who comprise fans, critics, and social media users interested in pop culture more generally.

Commentary posted on Twitter, Reddit, and Tumblr varies dramatically in form. The shortest (albeit not necessarily the simplest) posts are image memes with pithy captions (Figure 6.1). The longest are detailed investigations with repeated rounds of photo collages interspersed with commentary, discussing how Ariana Grande's skin colour compares to that of other white Americans and people with Italian ancestry. The latter are typically long-form Tumblr

---

[41] Lisa Blackman, *Haunted Data: Affect, Transmedia, Weird Science* (London and New York: Bloomsbury Publishing, 2019), 33.

[42] Edward Katrak Spencer, 'When Donald Trump Dropped the Bass: The Weaponization of Dubstep in Internet Trolling Strategies, 2011–2016', *Twentieth-Century Music*, forthcoming.

[43] Steven Gamble, 'Towards an Ethical Model of Data Analysis for Research on Online Music Cultures', in *Music and the Internet: Methodological, Epistemological, and Ethical Orientations*, ed. Christopher Haworth, Daniele S. Sofer, and Edward Katrak Spencer (Abingdon: Routledge, 2024).

[44] See, for example, Kamilah Marie Woodson, *Colorism: Investigating a Global Phenomenon* (Santa Barbara, CA: Fielding University Press, 2020).

Figure 6.1 A cropped Tweet (author account now suspended) comparing the colour difference between two images of Ariana Grande to mixing chocolate powder into milk

posts or threads that emphasize the platform's origin in cultures of blogging.[45] Posts about Ariana Grande and cultural appropriation also appeared on subreddits such as r/popheads (for those interested in popular music, an imperfectly-titled equivalent to r/hiphopheads), r/BadMUAs ('bad make up artists', showcasing examples of poor makeup practice by professionals), and r/Blackfishing, which invites users to 'call out all forms of ethnic/racial fishing... as well as posts about cultural appropriation'.[46]

Rather than thematically coding comments, I identified posts associated with common viewpoints and classified them into three topics: Blackfishing as an abstract concept, Ariana Grande as a public figure, and perceptions of Ariana Grande's use of Black aesthetics (or cultural appropriation more generally). Some of the most frequently expressed views are summarized in Table 6.3. Given the

---

[45] Allison McCracken et al., eds., *A Tumblr Book: Platform and Cultures* (Ann Arbor: University of Michigan Press, 2020), 4–6.
[46] r/blackfishing, 'Blackfishing', Reddit, 2023, https://www.reddit.com/r/blackfishing/.

Online Cultural Appropriation Discourse   141

Table 6.3 An indicative sample of common views online posters hold about Blackfishing and Ariana Grande

Views on Blackfishing	Views on Ariana Grande	Views on Ariana Grande's use of Black aesthetics
Widespread and harmful, akin to Blackface	Supports social justice	Just following trends
Widespread and permissible/normalized	Uses race like a costume	Understandable result of collaboration with Black friends and creative
Caused by beauty industry and mass media	Victim of media body shaming	Shows appreciation for/ spotlights Black culture
A rare abnormality, not a common trend	Fans fiercely defend her	Skin darkening not intentional/result of bad lighting
Long-standing critiques emerging from Black communities ignored	Not fooling public that she is not white	Co-opts Blackness to sell media products

nuanced, inconstant, and highly politicized nature of cultural appropriation discourse, it is helpful to talk of trends and tendencies rather than simple and static perspectives. While user statements may be brief and emphatic, they also conceal considerable depth about cultural values, which I aim to unpack through careful, time- and context-sensitive interpretation.[47]

Examining a few comments may be instructive. Take the following Tweet: 'I will never see the "Ariana is blackfishing" narrative and if people see her as anything but white, there's something wrong with them.' This post implies that Blackfishing is a real and negative phenomenon, emphasizes that Ariana Grande could never fool people that she is not white, and suggests that her visual investment in Blackness is therefore insignificant. It typifies a fairly defensive position and uses quite hostile language, though it is ambiguous in its stance towards Ariana Grande. Passionate fandom, sometimes associated with stan culture, is often more obvious. For example, people struggle to square their appreciation for the artist with accusations that she has caused social harm, as in the Reddit post: 'people always criticize Ariana for her skin tone because of that one fake picture [i.e., Figure 6.1] but most celebs just tan like that now to follow the trend'. The user—perhaps identifying as an Arianator—sees skin darkening as a broader, normalized issue for which Ariana Grande should not bear so much individual responsibility or receive

[47] André Brock, *Distributed Blackness: African American Cybercultures* (New York: New York University Press, 2020), 107.

142 Digital Flows

so much attention. However, they also argue that the images of her with deeply bronzed skin are edited,[48] misrepresenting the extent of her tanning and makeup and thereby excusing her racially ambiguous appearance.

Beyond her divisively dark skin tone, Ariana Grande also provokes a variety of perspectives concerning her broader engagement with Black culture. Black Twitter, 'Twitter's mediation of Black cultural identity, expressed through digital practices and informed by cultural discourses about Black everyday life,'[49] is generally sympathetic towards Ariana Grande, perceiving her to have a genuine appreciation for Black culture. In lighthearted and signifyin(g) fashion, Black users frame the artist as being invested in Black popular culture, albeit a little over-immersed in representations of Black womanhood. From this vantage point, Tweets variously defend and gently poke fun at the artist. Some refer to the artist as 'Arihanna', an ironic portmanteau of Ariana and Black megastar Rihanna, whereas one sarcastic caption on a photo of Ariana Grande and Nicki Minaj reads 'two powerful Black queens'. Another user excuses Ariana Grande more emphatically: 'shut up yall. Its instagram models actually blackfishing and taking opportunities from black women, meanwhile ariana has always obviously been white and actually uplifts black women whenever she can'. This view is far from unanimous, as others reply to say 'this joke is overdone', or to point out the consequences of this trend as it spread beyond Black Twitter: 'we started calling ariana black as a joke then non black people got mad and once they heard about "blackfishing" they FLIPPED'.

Indeed, it appears to be non-Black fans who most often debate the validity of Blackfishing accusations made of Ariana Grande. Some users align themselves with social justice, perceiving their social media activity as fighting on behalf of the Black community who suffer the indignity of Ariana Grande's transgressions. One Tumblr post lays it all out:

> people say she started using a 'blaccent' cause she's using African American Vernacular English. I love 7 rings like everyone does, but I realized the song and video are full of appropriation. Black artists say she stole their flow. We know her music is heavily inspired by Black artists and she appreciates the culture, but when you steal their flow it's not looking good for you.

---

[48] The user may be right, to some extent. The darker image in Figure 6.1 probably is photoshopped by someone to artificially emphasize her skin darkening (though other detractors frequently cite images from her official music videos). Still, this line of reasoning overlooks the fact that *all* photos of Ariana Grande are edited by virtue of being professionally produced as part of the artist's media package. The intensity of users' detailed investigations into images of the artist is striking.

[49] Brock, *Distributed Blackness*, 80–81.

Online Cultural Appropriation Discourse   143

This detailed kind of evaluation is relatively common, exemplifying the 'your fave is problematic' trope associated with the birth of callout culture.[50] As mentioned in Chapter 5, this discursive form of resistance was originally sparked by online communities of colour (especially Black women) holding public figures accountable, *calling them out* by publicizing evidence of misconduct or discrimination (i.e., showing the receipts).[51] Users like the above Tumblr poster aim to detail what they see as an injustice perpetrated by powerful figures to the detriment of another group of marginalized people. However, as Black Twitter's take on Ariana Grande shows, Black social media users do not necessarily feel the same way, nor do they need non-Black people to speak on their behalf.

Though the work of woke whites is usually well-intentioned, and often aligns with the views of many Black users, it may also be seen as a vacuous kind of performative activism.[52] This state of affairs, combined with the characteristically hostile, anti-discursive tone that some radical-progressive users (dubbed social justice warriors) adopt, has led to significant reactionary pushback, especially by the alt-right.[53] Callout culture evolved into cancel culture,[54] as calling powerful individuals out for wrongdoings became portrayed as—and in some cases began to resemble—a witch-hunt mob mentality that tried to punish people indiscriminately for past social transgressions. It was no longer about punching up, or exposing abuse, but acting as an apparently all-powerful force of surveillance and harassment with life-ruining potential. In this polarized framing, those fighting for social justice are portrayed as extremists unwilling to engage in dialogue, while free speech advocates endorse 'reasonable conversation', 'common sense', or, in the US context especially, conservative dog-whistles like 'traditional social values'.

Reactionaries may have a point—not a statement I ever thought I would write—in decrying the so-called woke lefty cancel-culture Twitter mob, for there can indeed be 'destructive effects of increasingly swift and bitter public

---

[50] Beth Tucker, '"That's Problematic": Tracing the Birth of Call-Out Culture', *Critical Reflections: A Student Journal on Contemporary Sociological Issues*, no. 2018 (April 2018): 4.

[51] Brock, *Distributed Blackness*, 219–220.

[52] Mariah L. Wellman, 'Black Squares for Black Lives? Performative Allyship as Credibility Maintenance for Social Media Influencers on Instagram', *Social Media + Society* 8, no. 1 (January 2022); Amira Abdalla et al., 'Social Media as a Stage: A Behind the Scenes Analysis of Performative Activism, "Cancel Culture," and Effective Allyship', *McMaster Undergraduate Journal of Social Psychology* 3, no. 1 (October 2022): 83–122.

[53] Sean Phelan, 'Neoliberalism, the Far Right, and the Disparaging of "Social Justice Warriors"', *Communication, Culture and Critique* 12, no. 4 (December 2019): 456; Adrienne L. Massanari and Shira Chess, 'Attack of the 50-Foot Social Justice Warrior: The Discursive Construction of SJW Memes as the Monstrous Feminine', *Feminist Media Studies* 18, no. 4 (July 2018): 525–542.

[54] Hervé Saint-Louis, 'Understanding Cancel Culture: Normative and Unequal Sanctioning', *First Monday* 26, no.7 (2021).

144 Digital Flows

shaming and factionalism amongst members of progressive groups online'.[55] Sometimes, as in the oft-cited case (following Godwin's Law) that Nazism was not overcome through civil conversation,[56] silencing people, shutting down conversation, and refusing to further engage can be effective defensive strategies against hatred. In other cases, however, users easily fall victim to dualistic thinking about right and wrong, misdirect anger about social injustice, and engage in abusive behaviours towards already marginalized people, as leftist YouTuber ContraPoints articulates in her video essay 'Canceling'.[57] 'Heated argumentation'[58] and direct harassment are not only features of social media platforms but key parts of what makes a 'hellsite'[59] like Tumblr or Twitter profitable and sustainable.[60] In summary, cancelling has transformed considerably, from the original mobilization of users of colour to hold powerful people to account, into sometimes misguided outpourings of rage which risk reinforcing conservative ideas that the left is unreasonable, obstinate, or even the real fascists in the equation.[61]

Ariana Grande is an important touchpoint for heated online discourse on the politics of identity and appropriation. Some consider her 'already cancelled', whereas others are willing to deliberate over issues with her use of Black culture. One Tumblr post laments that she gets away with it: 'its astounding how much she personally profits off black culture. peak white feminism, peak white privilege'. It is often revealing how social media users frame Black culture, frequently stereotyping it as some undifferentiated, monolithic thing. The crux of the issue appears to centre around how Ariana Grande positions herself in relation to women of colour. As users point out, 'her surname sounds Latina', some of her closest musical collaborators are Black women, and she got herself in hot water after reposting a sarcastic comment that suggested white women singing about weaves will rectify racism.[62] The

---

[55] Shakuntala Banaji and Ramnath Bhat, *Social Media and Hate* (Abingdon: Routledge, 2021), 117.

[56] Gabriele Fariello, Dariusz Jemielniak, and Adam Sulkowski, 'Does Godwin's Law (Rule of Nazi Analogies) Apply in Observable Reality? An Empirical Study of Selected Words in 199 Million Reddit Posts', *New Media & Society* 26, no. 1 (2021).

[57] *Canceling | ContraPoints*, YouTube video, 2 January 2020, https://www.youtube.com/watch?v=OjMPJVmXxV8.

[58] Mehitabel Glenhaber, 'Tumblr's Xkit Guy, Social Media Modding, and Code as Resistance', *Transformative Works and Cultures* 36 (September 2021).

[59] Kendra Calhoun, Review of *tumblr*, by Katrin Tiidenberg, Natalie Ann Hendry, and Crystal Abidin, *Visual Commnunication* (July 2022).

[60] Glenhaber, 'Tumblr's Xkit Guy, Social Media Modding, and Code as Resistance'; Calhoun, Review of *tumblr*.

[61] Dawn Wheatley and Eirik Vatnoey, ' "It's Twitter, a Bear Pit, Not a Debating Society": A Qualitative Analysis of Contrasting Attitudes towards Social Media Blocklists', *New Media & Society* 22, no. 1 (January 2020): 16.

[62] Chelsea Ritschel, 'Ariana Grande Apologises on Instagram for Misunderstanding Comment about "7 Rings" ', *The Independent*, 22 January 2019, https://www.independent.co.uk/arts-entertainment/music/ariana-grande-apology-ig-7-rings-instagram-weave-a8740651.html.

song in question was the 2019 single '7 rings', prompting users to pinpoint issues with the spectacularized representations of trap music that Ariana Grande's work adopts. I have focused on image and text posts that reveal a wide range of complex and intersecting perspectives on Ariana Grande's racial ambiguity. However, since it is mostly this era of Ariana Grande's career (and especially this single) that brought accusations of Blackfishing to a head, I turn now to analyse the music video, addressing what, exactly, social media users are debating.

Trap Aesthetics in Ariana Grande's '7 rings' (2019)

'7 rings'[63] was released in January 2019 as the second single of Ariana Grande's fifth album *Thank U, Next*. Along with many other awards, the song received Grammy nominations for Record of the Year and Best Pop Solo Performance, and its music video won the MTV Video Music Award for Best Art Direction. None of its official achievements mention hip hop, and Ariana Grande was later chosen as Billboard's Greatest Pop Star of 2019. Yet the presence—even predominance—of hip hop aesthetics in both the song '7 rings' and its music video is remarkable.

The introduction features audio of helicopters flying, as if overhead, and police sirens. These sounds are hip hop staples that carry associations of police surveillance or crime scene activity. The chorus and verses feature Ariana Grande singing in a rap-adjacent monotone, articulating short snappy rhymes and, in the final verse, accelerating into triplet flow.[64] Her voice is produced conventionally for rap, featuring layering, ad-libs, sample overdubs, and filtering. The beat comprises prominent trap drums: clicky hats, powerful bass drums, and clappy snares, alongside other digital artefacts. These are all features of contemporary hip hop production, where particular sounds, such as those suggested by the platform Splice, are increasingly reused by producers.[65] Building on Allan Moore's research on style and tone-setting, Kai Arne Hansen uses the term 'sonic styling' to how listener expectations and interpretations of songs and artists are shaped:

---

[63] The song title is rendered in lower case.

[64] Ben Duinker, 'Good Things Come in Threes: Triplet Flow in Recent Hip-Hop Music', *Popular Music* 38, no. 3 (October 2019): 423–456.

[65] Alexandria Arrieta, 'Splice and the Platformization of Hip Hop Production: Navigating the Online Music Platform for Royalty-Free Samples', in 'It's Where You're @: Hip Hop and the Internet', special issue, *Global Hip Hop Studies* 2 (2021): 232.

146 Digital Flows

> The sonic styling of the artist not only prepares listeners for how to respond to a singer's vocal performance, or the style of a track, but also shapes audiences' responses to the artist's persona more broadly ... an artist's sonic styling is key to how they are perceived, being integral to how listeners interpret meaning in musical or audiovisual texts.[66]

Using this framing, it is clear that '7 rings' is fully immersed in the style of trap music, a kind of hip hop that constructs 'rural Black Southern identity'.[67] The astute reader can predict what this means for how Ariana Grande is therefore interpreted. Musical characteristics that have been identified with trap include:

- prominent low-frequency bass,
- bright synth timbres and melodic loops,
- texturally sparse middle frequencies,
- a set of artificial-sounding—and now conventional—percussion samples developed from drum machines, such as the 'Young Chop' snare,
- syncopated or dotted-rhythm kick drums,
- busy rattling hi-hats,
- voice layering and copious ad-libs,
- uninflected, smoothly articulated ('mumbled' or 'slurred') vocals, and
- rapping with distinctive triplet rhythms.[68]

'7 rings' manifests all these features prominently: listeners may be hard-pressed to hear anything but trap in the track.[69] These musical affordances are supported by another trap mainstay in Ariana Grande's vocals, the use of African American Vernacular English. AAVE is described by Samy Alim as the language of the hip hop nation,[70] which is to say it is the standard

---

[66] Hansen, *Pop Masculinities*, 84.

[67] Corey Miles, 'Black Rural Feminist Trap: Stylized and Gendered Performativity in Trap Music', *Journal of Hip Hop Studies* 7, no. 1 (July 2020): 3. See also Seneca Vaught and Regina N. Bradley, 'Of the Wings of Traplanta: (Re)Historicizing W.E.B. Du Bois' Atlanta in the Hip Hop South', *Phylon (1960–)* 54, no. 2 (2017): 11–27.

[68] Justin D. Burton, *Posthuman Rap* (New York: Oxford University Press, 2017), 83–87; Anders Reuter, 'Who Let the DAWs Out? The Digital in a New Generation of the Digital Audio Workstation', *Popular Music and Society* 45, no. 2 (March 2022): 113–128.

[69] Ben Duinker notes the presence of triplet flow elsewhere on *Thank U, Next*, commenting that 'triplet flow-influenced singing has begun to make its way into mainstream popular music'. Duinker, 'Good Things Come in Threes', 28.

[70] H. Samy Alim, *Roc the Mic Right: The Language of Hip Hop Culture* (New York and London: Routledge, 2006).

linguistic form used in Anglophone hip hop music. With reference to sociolinguistic terms that identify AAVE, Ariana Grande rap-sings *negative concord* constructions—think double negatives—such as the lyric 'ain't gon' be no Mrs', uses the *habitual be*, as in 'my receipts be looking like phone numbers', and omits any form of 'to be'—a *zero copula*—in phrases like 'retail therapy my new addiction'.

As I mentioned in the social media commentary, the song's snappy vocal hook was subject to particular controversy for imitating the flow of other rap songs. Most notably—and darkly ironically—Princess Nokia called out Ariana Grande over the song's similarity to her track, 'Mine'. Princess Nokia's song repeats 'it's mine, I bought it' in reference to the cultural specificities of Black and Brown women's hair. I noted in Chapter 2 that hair is an important expression of Black cultural identity sustained in hip hop, with contemporary haircare practices aiming to disrupt the racial policing and politicization of Black hair.[71] Yet Ariana Grande uses the same vocal rhythm as Princess Nokia to celebrate her own weave-purchasing power with a similar lyric: 'you like my hair? Gee thanks, just bought it'. As Princess Nokia joked in a short (now deleted) video posted to Twitter: 'hmm . . . sounds about white'.

Furthermore, Ariana Grande's imitation of Black slang and grammar in '7 rings' is reinforced visually: the performance of the lyric 'when you see them racks, they stacked up like my ass' strategically aligns with a hard cut away from the artist to two Black women dancing. Seconds later, Ariana Grande switches into triplet flow, referencing The Notorious B.I.G.'s 'Gimme the Loot' to rhyme with 'nothing but net when we shoot', accompanied by a dunking motion. Like the recording, the music video spotlights trap music's performances of 'ratchet'—working-class or ghettoized, hustle-driven, mostly Southern, predominantly feminine[72]—Blackness. The '7 rings' video is set in a pink, glammed-up trap house with a pink '70s low-rider parked out front (imagery originated by 2 Chainz for the 2017 album *Pretty Girls Like Trap Music*, which also served community functions[73]). The song title appears tagged on the front door in spray paint. Ariana Grande wears stylized tracksuits with oversized ear hoops, her deeply bronzed skin lit in shades of pink and blue, screenshots of which abound in the accompanying social media discourse.

---

[71] Ayana D. Byrd and Lori L. Tharps, *Hair Story: Untangling the Roots of Black Hair in America*, rev. ed. (New York: St Martin's Griffin, 2014).

[72] Bettina L. Love, 'A Ratchet Lens: Black Queer Youth, Agency, Hip Hop, and the Black Ratchet Imagination', *Educational Researcher* 46, no. 9 (December 2017): 539–547; Montinique Denice McEachern, 'Respect My Ratchet: The Liberatory Consciousness of Ratchetness', *Departures in Critical Qualitative Research* 6, no. 3 (September 2017): 78–89.

[73] Rhana A. Gittens, 'Atlanta's Pink Trap House: Reimagining the Black Public Sphere as an Aesthetic Community', *Theory & Event* 24, no. 2 (April 2021): 434–455.

Figure 6.2 Trap visual aesthetics in Ariana Grande's '7 rings' music video, screenshots from YouTube

She is surrounded by a racially diverse group of dancers and friends. She dances using moves approximating twerking, descending to a squat position and sticking out her tongue. In contrast to the ostensibly impoverished exterior, the house interior drips with luxury, from chandeliers to champagne (Figure 6.2).

Jesse McCarthy meticulously outlines these visual features of trap as

> a strange Esperanto of gesture and cadence intended to signify the position of blackness. In the "lifestyle" videos, the tropes are familiar, establishing shots captured in drone POV: the pool party, the hotel suite, the club, the glistening surfaces of dream cars, the harem women blazoned, jump cuts set to tight-focus Steadicam, the ubiquitous use of slow motion to render banal actions (pouring a drink, entering a room) allegorical, talismanic, the gothic surrealism of instant gratification.[74]

---

[74] Jesse McCarthy, 'Notes on Trap', *N+1*, no. 32 (2018), https://www.nplusonemag.com/issue-32/essays/notes-on-trap/.

Online Cultural Appropriation Discourse **149**

These visuals are precisely used in the '7 rings' video to magnify Ariana Grande's lyrics, which flaunt wealth, conspicuous consumption, and financial independence, tropes drawn directly from this most commercial form of hip hop. From this, it is evident why social media users express discomfort with both Ariana Grande's representations of race and how she situates wealth. Not only does the artist take a trap beat, distinct vocal styles, visual aesthetics, and lyrical themes from hip hop, but she also boasts about her ability to afford anything she wants.

I have focused on the prominent trap borrowings of '7 rings', but there is one more overt musical reference in the song. The first part of each verse interpolates the melody and a few lyrics from 'My Favorite Things', originally from the 1959 Rodgers and Hammerstein musical *The Sound of Music*. This act of borrowing is perhaps the song's only notable connection to popular songs separate from contemporary hip hop aesthetics. If the song and the music video were the only media one knew of Ariana Grande, one would have no other reason to associate this work with the genre of pop: it is trap through and through, with a splash of singing and a sprinkle of *Sound of Music*. The song consistently symbolizes Blackness through its audiovisual aesthetics. What it means for white artists' work to do so clearly underlies the online debates I examined. Moreover, hip hop's harvesting by pop stars in the internet age compounds long-standing white appropriations and exploitations of Black music.

White Performances of Blackness in the Internet Age

'7 rings' is a prime example of not only trap, nor just contemporary hip hop more generally, but sonic Blackness.[75] Influenced by Nina Sun Eidsheim's work, Jennifer Stoever's analytical frame, the sonic colour line, 'produces, codes, and polices racial difference through the ear, enabling us to hear race as well as see it'.[76] She further describes it as 'a socially constructed boundary that racially codes sonic phenomena such as vocal timbre, accents, and musical tones'.[77] Ariana Grande's heavy bass, triplet flow, and AAVE lyrics connote Blackness, as do the more obvious visual signifiers of the '7 rings' video.

---

[75] Nina Sun Eidsheim, 'Marian Anderson and "Sonic Blackness" in American Opera', *American Quarterly* 63, no. 3 (2011): 641–671.

[76] Jennifer Lynn Stoever, *The Sonic Color Line: Race and the Cultural Politics of Listening* (New York: New York University Press, 2016), 11.

[77] Stoever, *The Sonic Color Line*, 11.

150 Digital Flows

Listening, writes Stoever, is a process by which 'particular sounds are identified, exaggerated, and "matched" to racialized bodies'.[78] While social media users raise concerns about Ariana Grande's racially ambiguous appearance, they also discuss the affordances of their listening, identifying her as a white artist performing sounds and styles that are coded Black.

The motivation behind Ariana Grande's—and many other white performers'—aesthetic borrowings is clear. The late cultural critic Greg Tate explains how 'the aura and global appeal of hip-hop lie in . . . its perceived Blackness (hip, stylish, youthful, alienated, rebellious, sensual)'.[79] Hip hop, as well as being an intensely popular and enjoyable genre, provides archetypes of Black masculine performance styles which Michael P. Jeffries terms 'complex cool'.[80] The trope of Black coolness is a modernization of earlier (predominantly white American) understandings of Black identity as soulful, proud, and strong. The pose of complex cool is, at its root, a 'strategy for survival in a hostile environment—a rational adaptation to structural restrictions' in white supremacist American society.[81] This functions in the manner of Du Bois's double consciousness,[82] which translated rather directly into hip hop performance practices. Performances in a cool mode also include sexist and homophobic—or simply anti-feminine—values. Nonetheless, this 'phallic black masculinity' often appeals to white artists of all genders, who are 'fascinated yet envious of black style'.[83]

It has become clear in recent years that Black complex cool, easily accessed and expressed through hip hop, is irresistible in popular culture. Yet users providing justifications for cross-racial borrowing based on 'cultural appreciation' implies a post-racial worldview, as if all cultural actors participate on a level playing field.[84] White artists, Jeremy Orosz points out, 'have greater liberty to become stylistic chameleons than do their black counterparts'.[85] Moreover, white pop stars like Ariana Grande are able to take influence from, inhabit, and perform Blackness without permanently embodying it. Indeed, a handful of the highest-rated social media posts about cultural appropriation

---

[78] Stoever, *The Sonic Color Line.*

[79] Greg Tate, *Everything But the Burden: What White People Are Taking from Black Culture* (New York: Broadway Books, 2003), 4.

[80] Michael P. Jeffries, *Thug Life: Race, Gender, and The Meaning of Hip-Hop* (Chicago: University of Chicago Press, 2011), 55–76.

[81] Jeffries, *Thug Life*, 56.

[82] W.E.B. Du Bois, *The Souls of Black Folk*, ed. B. H. Edwards (New York: Oxford University Press, 2007).

[83] bell hooks, *Black Looks: Race and Representation*, New (New York: Routledge, 2015), 160–161.

[84] Michael B. MacDonald, *Remix and Life Hack in Hip Hop: Towards a Critical Pedagogy of Music* (Rotterdam: Sense Publishers, 2016), 33–40.

[85] Jeremy Orosz, ' "Straight Outta Nashville": Allusions to Hip Hop in Contemporary Country Music', *Popular Music and Society* 44, no. 1 (January 2021): 55.

allegations cited photographs in *Vogue* magazine where Ariana Grande 'presented in her true [white] form'.[86] By temporarily adopting Black aesthetics, the artist reaps the benefits of racially ambiguous representation while living without the discrimination entailed by being Black in white supremacist society. Rather, artists trying out Black sonics and visuals delve into a cool and rebellious expressive mode that has always been a staple of hip hop, what William Cheng describes as a 'reputation of againstness'.[87] Non-Black artists inhabit a site of Otherness received as somewhat edgy and exotic by white audiences despite its familiarity in Black musical contexts. Thus, bell hooks suggests we can observe white artists'—in this case white women's—'interest in, and appropriation of, black culture as [a] sign of their radical chic. Intimacy with that "nasty" blackness good white girls stay away from is what they seek'.[88]

As the default language of hip hop, AAVE provides a widely beloved expressive form that renders its user cool and confident: sometimes a little conceited, sometimes confrontational.[89] Not only is such expression evidently popular, but it also sells well. In their work on Iggy Azalea's use of language, Maeve Eberhardt and Kara Freeman identify that 'linguistic commodification translates into tremendous fame and fortune for a white body performing blackness'.[90] The phenomenon of whites using AAVE has given rise to the term Blaccent (or Blackcent), which appeared in the social media discourse. Musical equivalents have been theorized in the form of Blackvoice and Blacksound.[91] In musical performance, white impersonation of stereotyped Black vernacular language resembles a modern form of minstrelsy. It reiterates a colonial, imperial dynamic where white performers (mis)represent the cultural lives of people of colour for the pleasure of predominantly white audiences. With sonic Blackness firmly entangled with Western social values of coolness, youthfulness, and exciting Otherness, white pop artists can

---

[86] Alicia Khan, 'What Ethnicity Is Ariana Grande? Whichever One Makes Her the Most Money', *Femestella* (blog), December 2021, https://www.femestella.com/ariana-grande-ethnicity-cultural-appropriation-blackfishing-asianfishing/.

[87] William Cheng, ed., *Loving Music Till It Hurts* (New York: Oxford University Press, 2019), 189.

[88] hooks, *Black Looks*, 157.

[89] YG encapsulates this quality of hip hop Blackness with his mantra (and 2016 song) 'Bool, Balm, and Bollective'. His play on 'cool, calm, and collected' swaps out Cs for Bs in iconic Bloods style.

[90] Maeve Eberhardt and Kara Freeman, '"First Things First, I'm the Realest": Linguistic Appropriation, White Privilege, and the Hip-Hop Persona of Iggy Azalea', *Journal of Sociolinguistics* 19, no. 3 (2015): 309.

[91] Gage Averill, *Four Parts, No Waiting: A Social History of American Barbershop Harmony* (New York: Oxford University Press, 2003), 33–34; Amanda Nell Edgar, 'Blackvoice and Adele's Racialized Musical Performance: Blackness, Whiteness, and Discursive Authenticity', *Critical Studies in Media Communication* 31, no. 3 (May 2014): 167–181; Matthew D. Morrison, 'Blacksound', in *The Oxford Handbook of Western Music and Philosophy*, ed. Tomás McAuley et al. (New York: Oxford University Press, 2021), 554–577.

152   Digital Flows

gain cultural and economic capital by taking marketable sounds and styles straight from hip hop.[92]

Users defending cultural appropriation sometimes offer the counterargument that all cultures borrow from one another and that cultural segregation would hardly be a viable or favourable alternative. Clearly, hip hop is not—never has been—a monoracial culture, as demonstrated by its multiracial origin in the Bronx and its global community today. However, there are a variety of ways by which non-Black artists can represent themselves faithfully while deploying Black musical and cultural practices. For a prominent example, the Beastie Boys' musical use of their New Yorker white Jewish accents—rather than mimicking their Black colleagues—exemplified a more authentic immersion in hip hop. Likewise, Eminem was generally welcomed in the genre both despite and because of how he strategically situated his working-class whiteness. Borrowings that belie performers' racial and class identities are more problematic. Recall when Vanilla Ice's shallow imitation of Black urban identity quickly saw him disgraced for violating hip hop's basic terms of authenticity.[93] Non-Black artists need to approach Black culture with understanding, respect, humility, and honesty. When sensitivity to authenticity is absent in artists' work, it becomes 'yet another trope manipulated for cultural capital.'[94]

Chiming with social media posts about how Ariana Grande's image and music fail to represent Black culture authentically, Maka Ikram Cherid has spelt out the harms of such white exploitation. By drawing on the sounds and styles of hip hop, white pop artists

> extract from its position in the North American cultural imagination the marketable and palatable parts of Black identity, without having to endure the systemic oppression that shapes it. In short, they benefit from blackness without ever having to give up the privilege of being White. As most other forms of appropriation, this causes harm to both individual Black creators, as their own work and craft is co-opted, and Black people as a collective, through the reproduction of racial hierarchies and power dynamics.[95]

---

[92] Danielsen, 'The Sound of Crossover', 165–166.

[93] Kajikawa, *Sounding Race in Rap Songs*, 121–125.

[94] E. Patrick Johnson, *Appropriating Blackness: Performance and the Politics of Authenticity* (Durham, NC: Duke University Press, 2003), 3.

[95] Cherid, '"Ain't Got Enough Money to Pay Me Respect"', 363.

Online Cultural Appropriation Discourse 153

Indeed, as online commenters point out, borrowings from Black music are a major facet of white privilege, demonstrating how white hegemony treats Black cultural practices as resources freely open for use and profit by dominant social groups. Recall the 'My Favorite Things' melody in '7 rings': I should now reveal that 90 per cent of the songwriting credits for '7 rings' were ceded to Rodgers and Hammerstein.[96] Since songwriting copyrights are based on vocal melody and lyric—a legal-economic framework privileging traditional, notated musical elements over less tangible aspects of style, like trap's iconic timbres—the majority revenue split goes to the white-owned Concord Music Group, which presides over the Rodgers and Hammerstein catalogue. A single-digit percentage will be shared among Ariana Grande's Black co-songwriters and producers, with no royalties granted to the beatmakers that originated the trap sound in underserved Black Southern communities. Appropriations like this are, therefore, not purely an issue of (mis)representing Black culture and identity, but in the worst cases funnel revenue predominantly to whites and reinforce white-dominated power structures. They use Black creative expression to reinforce white economic control over pop culture products mediated online.

For better or worse, Ariana Grande's extractive engagement with Black culture has been fleeting.[97] Critics noted the artist had 'shapeshifted'[98] for her stylistic development towards dance-pop on 2020's *positions*, evidencing 'maturity and sophistication'.[99] The implication that the hip hop on her earlier albums seems immature or unsophisticated is beside the point: Ariana Grande's use of trap on *thank u, next* makes hip hop seem disposable, something that can be dipped into and deployed for personal profit and career development. White artists taking from hip hop

---

[96] Ben Sisario, ' "7 Rings" Is a Hit for Ariana Grande, and a Knockout for Rodgers and Hammerstein', *The New York Times*, March 2019, https://www.nytimes.com/2019/03/19/business/media/ariana-grande-7-rings-rodgers-hammerstein.html.

[97] A noticeable strand of online discourse also discussed Asianfishing, or Ariana Grande's appropriation of East Asian beauty conventions, to further ambiguate her racial appearance. Building on Blackfishing discourse, Alicia Khan has argued that, with East Asian cultural media (like K-pop) gaining popularity in the West, Ariana Grande has switched tack from emulating Blackness towards emulating Asianness, motivated by commercial incentives. Alicia Khan, 'What Ethnicity Is Ariana Grande? Whichever One Makes Her the Most Money', *Femestella* (blog), December 2021, https://www.femestella.com/ariana-grande-ethnicity-cultural-appropriation-blackfishing-asianfishing/.

[98] Callie Ahlgrim and Courteney Larocca, 'Ariana Grande Finishes First on Her New Album "Positions"', *Insider*, 30 October 2020, https://www.insider.com/ariana-grande-positions-review-tracklist-breakdown-2020-10.

[99] Alexis Petridis, 'Ariana Grande: Positions Review – All-Night Romps but No Climax', *The Guardian*, 30 October 2020, https://www.theguardian.com/music/2020/oct/30/ariana-grande-positions-review.

154   Digital Flows

adopt aspects of African American culture when and how it is advantageous to do so, while ignoring all of what it means to be non-white in a culture that privileges whiteness. By extension, whites shed such behaviors when it suits them, and have no traces of their foray into blackness attached to them. Whites do not suffer the oppression of systemic racism . . . but rather benefit from its strictures and structures.[100]

This process is now thoroughly normalized since pop is 'increasingly assimilating the compositional practices of hip-hop'.[101] One of the producers I interviewed stated this clearly, echoing Kelefa Sanneh's point cited at the start of this chapter: 'hip hop is pop these days. Like, rap drums are just all throughout pop music, like, everywhere, and rap songs are number one charting songs'. Indeed, pop's borrowings from Black music can be seen and heard at all levels of the music industry, from the work of budding artists to hits by superstars. Sometimes this even seems like a recipe for success. To go by Spotify's most-streamed artists, the rankings of non-Black pop artists who have used hip hop sounds or styles in their work—Taylor Swift (#3), Ed Sheeran (#5), Justin Bieber (#6), Ariana Grande (#7), BTS (#9), Billie Eilish (13), Imagine Dragons (#17), Sam Smith (#28), Selena Gomez (#44), and Katy Perry (#55)—demonstrate just how widely Blackness appeals in contemporary popular culture.[102]

Conclusion

Loren Kajikawa once suggested that 'unlike rock and roll, rap never became "white"'.[103] This is a sound observation. Due to the technocultural force of hip hop, it might be more accurate to say that pop became Black.[104] White artists have harvested hip hop for its representations of Black complex cool, transforming popular music in the process. Similarly, in the early 1990s, Tricia Rose lampooned white conservative media responses to the popularity of hip hop, seen then as some kind of threatening Black presence that

---

[100] Eberhardt and Freeman, ' "First Things First, I'm the Realest" ', 321.

[101] Reuter, 'Who Let the DAWs Out?', 113.

[102] This list references ranks provided by Chartmasters as of July 2023. Without wanting to belabour the point about hip-hop's immense popularity, many of the gaps in this list of most-streamed artists are filled by hip hop artists themselves: Drake (#1), Bad Bunny (#2), Eminem (#8), Post Malone (#10), J Balvin (#11), ye/Kanye West (#12), Juice WRLD (#14), XXXTentacion (#19), Travis Scott (#24), and so on.

[103] Kajikawa, *Sounding Race in Rap Songs*, 5.

[104] By this I do not mean to essentialize either racial group, nor echo David Starkey's vile rhetoric about the apparent 'corruption' of the white British working class. See Ben Quinn, 'David Starkey Claims "the Whites Have Become Black" ', *The Guardian*, 13 August 2011, https://www.theguardian.com/uk/2011/aug/13/david-starkey-claims-whites-black.

would distort US culture.[105] Of course, who could have predicted that hip hop actually would change the state of popular culture among multiracial mass audiences, and that it would be through wilful—even joyful—appropriations by white artists?

From his vantage point two decades later, Kajikawa explains this development: 'new forms of black expressivity such as hip hop and rap music saturated mainstream culture without first having to be remade as white, redefining for a generation of youth what it meant to be "cool." '[106] Yet the Whiteness of Eminem, Kajikawa's main case study, is highly audible and visible, racially Othering the rapper in the context of hip hop. In contrast, contemporary white artists have been joyfully channelling Black aesthetics into pop while still retaining their mainstream status as white pop stars, as I have shown through the example of Ariana Grande's so-called 'sassy',[107] 'swaggering'[108] mid-career turn. Nonetheless, social media users, by and large, are not content to let Ariana Grande get away with it. I have shown how social media platforms provide users a forum in which to critique, discuss, and debate Ariana Grande's Blackfishing in highly polarized contexts. Who is entitled to use hip hop and its Black expressive orality, and in what ways, remain key points of contention among the heated online discourse. While users on platforms like Twitter, Reddit, and Tumblr generally resist exploitation of the culture, I examined a striking diversity of perspectives that connect to broader issues central to the online culture wars.[109]

Despite their intense manifestation online, debates about ownership, identity, and authenticity have run throughout the entire history of Western imperialism: of white extraction, representation, and commercialization of cultural practices taken from marginalized, exoticized, and Othered communities. From the pinnacle of pop, Ariana Grande flaunted the privilege to take whatever she likes from trap: 'I see it, I like it, I want it, I got it'. The final full-length chapter of the book, which follows, traces performances of hip hop within still more abstracted and contested contexts, situated within the virtual environments of video game platforms.

---

[105] Tricia Rose, *Black Noise: Rap Music and Black Culture in Contemporary America* (Middletown, CT: Wesleyan University Press, 1994), 130.

[106] Kajikawa, *Sounding Race in Rap Songs*, 120.

[107] Taylor Weatherby, 'Ariana Grande & Her Girlfriends Get Their Bling On In Sassy "7 Rings" Video: Watch', *Billboard* (blog), 18 January 2019, https://www.billboard.com/music/pop/ariana-grande-7-rings-video-8494008/.

[108] Stephen Thomas Erlewine, 'Ariana Grande – Thank u, Next', February 2019, https://www.allmusic.com/album/thank-u-next-mw0003246119.

[109] Angela Nagle, *Kill All Normies: Online Culture Wars from 4Chan and Tumblr to Trump and the Alt-Right* (Winchester: Zero Books, 2017).

7
Virtual Hip Hop Concerts in Video Games

One *Fortnite* only

Introduction

I began this book by suggesting that hip hop has a significant hold on mainstream online culture, especially among young audiences. The same could be said for video games, perhaps even more so. At the start of 2021, *The Guardian* reported that video games 'have replaced music as the most important aspect of youth culture'.[1] While this headline might reasonably be accused of sensationalism, it is easy to see how pervasive games have become. The remarkable cultural spread of youth-oriented franchises like *Fortnite Battle Royale* (hereafter *Fortnite*), *Minecraft*, and *Roblox* can be seen in the form of merchandise—especially children's clothing—across the globe. The growing economy of video games boasts a substantial proportion of young consumers (and a promising trend towards gender balance).[2] Politicians, too, are aware of the popularity of video games, as exemplified by Alexandria Ocasio-Cortez and Ilhan Omar's livestream of *Among Us*, the game *du jour* among young people during the run-up to the 2020 US presidential election. Video games predictably and consistently amass young people in online spaces, with significant potential for promoting other cultural products, modes of creative participation, and political messages.

Hip hop artists have taken notice of the young player base of video games, which often aligns with their own audiences. Video games are appealing to hip hop artists for the purposes of music synchronization revenues, cross-promotion, and brand development. For example, the professionally curated in-game radio channels of Rockstar Games' *Grand Theft Auto* are held in especially high esteem among gamers.[3] *Grand Theft Auto V*—second only to

---

[1] Sean Monahan, 'Video Games Have Replaced Music as the Most Important Aspect of Youth Culture', *The Guardian*, 11 January 2021, http://www.theguardian.com/commentisfree/2021/jan/11/video-games-music-youth-culture.

[2] Entertainment Software Association, *2020 Essential Facts About the Video Game Industry* (2020), https://www.theesa.com/wp-content/uploads/2021/03/Final-Edited-2020-ESA_Essential_facts.pdf.

[3] Nick Prior, *Popular Music, Digital Technology and Society* (Los Angeles: SAGE, 2018), 156.

Digital Flows. Steven Gamble, Oxford University Press. © Oxford University Press 2024.
DOI: 10.1093/oso/9780197656389.003.0007

Minecraft among the best-selling games ever[4]—featured a hip hop station, 'Radio Los Santos', hosted by Real 92.3's Big Boy. *Fortnite* follows the same model as *GTA*, licensing a rotating range of songs for its radio stations, which play automatically when player characters are inside vehicles. The station 'Beat Box Radio' is dedicated to hip hop, with an emphasis on US and Latin trap music. Whereas Rockstar's games use radio to flesh out the narrative world with a DJ offering humorous commentary between songs, *Fortnite* offers stripped-back musical compilations to accompany play. The latter game's stations essentially function just like playlists on streaming services,[5] popularizing contemporary songs and rotating tracks across in-game 'seasons'.

There have also been instances of active collaboration between game developers and artists. Many original hip hop songs have been created for game soundtracks, such as *Spiderman: Miles Morales*. *NBA Street Vol. 2*, released in 2003, which accompanied basketball action with a set of Just Blaze beats produced exclusively for the game. Games like the *Just Dance* series provide choreographed and animated dance sequences to popular hip hop tracks (alongside music in other genres). The most sustained collaborations have resulted in games like *50 Cent: Bulletproof*, an action shooter in which the player controls a rendering of the rapper 50 Cent as he navigates the criminal underbelly of New York. There have also been hip hop character models inserted into other popular games. For instance, Lil Wayne and Tyler, the Creator appeared as playable characters in *Tony Hawk's Pro Skater 5*. Playing with these figures offers an interactive mediation of their public personas,[6] helping to promote the artists' brands and potentially intensifying parasocial relationships. Fans know of these individuals as hip hop artists, then can also see or control their virtual forms in-game, 'bound up with their presentation of gendered and racialized kinesthetic repertoires' by shooting guns, dunking, and skateboarding.[7] Alongside direct collaboration, game developers have created animations of conspicuously unlicensed hip hop dances. Social dance crazes born on YouTube or TikTok have been appropriated for sale as 'emotes' in gaming platforms' virtual stores.[8]

---

[4] Manisha Singh, 'GTA V Becomes Second Best-Selling Game of All Time, Claims Publisher', *The Times of India*, 8 February 2022, https://timesofindia.indiatimes.com/gadgets-news/gta-v-becomes-second-best-selling-game-of-all-time-claims-take-two/articleshow/89434429.cms.

[5] Robert Prey, 'Locating Power in Platformization: Music Streaming Playlists and Curatorial Power', *Social Media + Society* 6, no. 2 (April 2020).

[6] Kai Arne Hansen, '(Re)Reading Pop Personae: A Transmedial Approach to Studying the Multiple Construction of Artist Identities', *Twentieth-Century Music* 16, no. 3 (October 2019): 501–529.

[7] Kiri Miller, *Playable Bodies: Dance Games and Intimate Media* (New York: Oxford University Press, 2017), 2.

[8] Wayne Marshall, 'Social Dance in the Age of (Anti-)Social Media', *Journal of Popular Music Studies* 31, no. 4 (December 2019): 3–15.

158 Digital Flows

Creative partnerships and character modelling have laid the groundwork for events mutually organized by artists and game developers. In April 2020, *Fortnite* announced a special in-game event called *Astronomical*. It was promoted as a 'virtual concert' featuring hip hop artist Travis Scott. The event was scheduled five times over three days, notably during a period when many cultural activities rapidly migrated to the internet due to COVID-19 public health guidelines (see also Chapter 4). In the days following *Astronomical*, Epic Games announced that the event series gained a global audience of nearly 28 million unique players.[9] Reviews agreed with the event's self-aggrandizing title (a play on Travis Scott's 2018 album title *Astroworld*), with journalists describing it as 'jaw-dropping,'[10] 'mind-blowing,'[11] and 'a gigantic, unprecedented success'.[12] However, its status as a 'virtual concert' is open to question.

It was developed as an online alternative to the annual Astroworld Festival usually held in Houston, inaugurated in association with Travis Scott's 2018 album launch and managed by ScoreMore shows. Supplanted to *Fortnite*, *Astronomical* may be understood more like a platform-wide ('global') limited-time event. Although it limited the typical play experience of the game, the event's spectacular audiovisual production led game journalist Patricia Hernandez (2020) to describe it as 'a totally new type of media experience'. It would be inaccurate to describe the music as live, given that the songs played via the game platform were identical to the studio recordings (many of them released on record a good two years prior). Moreover, the artist was not present during any point of the event, nor did he record motion capture for the visual performance. Epic Games' team of animators instead created a likeness of his body and movements, presumably using an in-house motion capture artist emulating Travis Scott's performance style. Given that *Astronomical* exhibited hip hop on perhaps its largest-ever online video game stage, it is worth some consideration of what exactly the event was, if not a live concert. To do that, I first address how virtual music concerts have previously been theorized.

---

[9] Fortnite (@FortniteGame), 'Thank You to Everyone Who Attended and Created Content around the Travis Scott Event! Over 27.7 Million Unique Players in-Game Participated Live 45.8 Million Times across the Five Events', Tweet, Twitter, 27 April 2020, https://twitter.com/FortniteGame/status/125481758467 6929537.

[10] Oscar Gonzalez, 'Fortnite: Travis Scott Astronomical Experience Seen by Almost 28 Million Players', *CNET*, 27 April 2020, https://www.cnet.com/news/fortnite-travis-scott-astronomical-experience-seen-by-almost-28-million-players/.

[11] Tatiana Cirisano, 'Game On: What Travis Scott Is Teaching Music Stars About the World's Biggest New (Virtual) Stage', *Billboard*, 24 July 2020, https://www.billboard.com/articles/business/9422287/travis-scott-fortnite-billboard-cover-story-interview-2020.

[12] die Makuch, 'Fortnite Sets New Records With Travis Scott Event', *GameSpot* (blog), 26 April 2020, https://www.gamespot.com/articles/fortnite-sets-new-records-with-travis-scott-event/1100-6476508/.

Virtuality, Mediation, and Liveness

The history of virtual concerts calls to mind phenomena such as the 2012 Coachella Festival hologram of Tupac, who appeared on the physical stage performing to a live audience. One may also think of Gorillaz, the virtual band whose animated performers appear on large screens at live shows. And there is hardly a more beloved virtual live performer than Hatsune Miku,[13] whose major arena concerts typically attract tens of thousands of fans across Japanese cities. In his work on virtual pop music performers, Thomas Conner identifies three factors that alter the quality of such simulations: animation, projection, and artificial intelligence.[14] The first depends on processing power and the second on holographic display technologies, whereas the third can be developed in a number of ways. Indeed, Conner queries the extent to which virtual performers would need to vary from a particular 'pre-programmed performance' to simulate a live experience.[15] This is a question well worth asking because concerts combining prepared visual projections with real performing musicians—most arena concerts, for example—provide many listeners with compelling, authentic experiences. For Shara Rambarran, the presence of a human band at one in-person Hatsune Miku concert successfully produced the 'feeling that it was a [fully] live concert'.[16]

Many physically situated concerts incorporate elements of virtuality. At their most technologically basic, gigs can incorporate projectors playing video footage on a screen behind the performers. At a more sophisticated level, visual effects can be generated in real- time, as well as lyrical overlays, animations, and images in complex interplay with stage lighting. Sonically, virtuality has been a feature of live events at least since the development of re-production technology. Backline equipment can make electric guitars appear louder than drumkits situated mere feet away. Through the act of amplification, guitars indeed *become* louder, an arguably virtual enhancement of the instrument's physical reality. Now-standard concert practices vary from in-visible yet audible backing vocalists—pre-recorded vocals incorporated into backing tracks—to reverb or echo effects that recall unreal environments in

---

[13] Prior, *Popular Music, Digital Technology and Society*, 139–140.

[14] Thomas Conner, 'Hatsune Miku, 2.0Pac, and Beyond: Rewinding and Fast-Forwarding the Virtual Pop Star', in *The Oxford Handbook of Music and Virtuality*, ed. Sheila Whiteley and Shara Rambarran (New York: Oxford University Press, 2016), 129–147.

[15] Conner, 'Hatsune Miku, 2.0Pac, and Beyond', 143.

[16] Shara Rambarran, *Virtual Music: Sound, Music, and* Image in *the Digital Era* (New York: Bloomsbury Academic, 2021), 123.

160 Digital Flows

real-time. Drum machines have long substituted for live drummers, and other virtual instruments are increasingly conventional across a range of genres.[17]

Hip hop as a live medium relies heavily upon sound reproduction, with the result being that much of the musical content is virtual. At live rap concerts, it is standard to hear prepared backing tracks with disembodied voices. The widespread nature of this convention compelled comedian Hannibal Buress, in a humorous skit, to plead: 'Stop rapping over your own vocals at your concert. Clear your goddamn instrumental and rap over it. I don't want to hear you rapping over your raps'.[18] This bugbear aside, the common presence of featured artists in rap songs can make live performances tricky, with absentee guest artists' voices left to sound out from the speakers. At concerts without a live DJ, backing tracks may be reproduced in full, creating the appearance of various virtual instruments. Taken to its extreme, the only live element of a hip hop show may be the rapper's microphone, and even then the effects chain may reduce the sense of realistic—and therefore less virtual—vocalizations. All hip hop concerts therefore incorporate virtuality to some extent, even though the conventional performative stance, being 'live and direct', remains a crucial part of hip hop authenticity.[19] In live settings, hip hop production managers must carefully balance the degree of conspicuous virtuality or premeditation on display.

My examples so far have focused on virtual performers in a physical concert setting. Alternatively, the virtuality may be associated not with the performer or performance but with the venue or medium: some kind of musical performance recorded and mediated on the internet. In this category, we can place portal shows, defined as 'a convergence between live music performance and digital media broadcast',[20] alongside livestreaming, and even some pre-recorded performances with specific airings. However, the conceptual boundaries of a virtual concert begin to stretch when audiences are present physically (is this an in-person concert where viewers are offered a supplementary online window into the event?) or performances do not take place in real-time (how does this vary from a premiere of a music video?).

---

[17] Steven Gamble and Lewis Kennedy, 'From the Studio to the Bedroom (and Back Again?): Distributed Production Practices in 21st Century Metal Music', in *The Routledge Handbook to Metal Music Composition: Evolution of Structure, Expression, and Production*, ed. Lori Burns and Ciro Scotto (New York: Routledge, forthcoming).

[18] Lil Dicky, 'Hannibal Interlude', featuring Hannibal Buress, *Professional Rapper*, track 7 (Commission Records, 2015), https://open.spotify.com/track/3xlxccjYAuqTFORC3shOSm?si=a0bc6932289b48d6.

[19] David Diallo, *Collective Participation and Audience Engagement in Rap Music* (Cham: Springer International Publishing, 2019), 65–84; Alex de Lacey, 'Live and Direct? Censorship and Racialised Public Morality in Grime and Drill Music', *Popular Music* 41, no. 4 (December 2022): 495–510.

[20] James Rendell, 'Staying in, Rocking out: Online Live Music Portal Shows during the Coronavirus Pandemic', *Convergence* 27, no. 4 (December 2020).

Take the Eurovision Song Contest for one well-known example. The annual instalments of Eurovision are performed in a physical venue with an avid audience, and simultaneously televised and broadcast online to a high production standard. Indeed the vast majority of the audience consume the concert virtually, but it is still very much a 'real-life' show. However, when Eurovision performances use real-time video production effects and overlays designed for the screen rather than the stage, the boundaries between real and virtual begin to blur.

Still, it is not especially useful to think in binary terms about virtual concerts, since conceptual lines can be drawn all over the place: real/virtual, real/physical, physical/digital, offline/online. For a more helpful approach, Rambarran approaches virtuality as 'exposing and transforming the unimaginable, unthinkable, and unexpected ideas into reality'.[21] Ranging from remixing to virtual reality headsets, her study of virtual music locates new phenomena in an era of cultural production enhanced by novel applications of digital technology. Certainly, concerts without a performer and an audience in the same physical location are easily understood as virtual. Rambarran identifies an increasing demand for online events,[22] with more participatory opportunities, greater potential income streams, and a diversity of consumer experiences on offer. True enough, the increase in online cultural participation incited by COVID-19 regulations has galvanized a surge of activity in this domain, as described in Ruth Lang's writing on extended reality and virtual event staging.[23]

Virtuality is one useful perspective for understanding concerts that do not take place in a shared physical space, but these events also implicate the concept of liveness. Philip Auslander points out that theatre and performance theorists have traditionally situated the live in simple opposition to the mediated.[24] Jacques Attali's influential book on the political economy of music draws a similar boundary between representation (as in the live performance of concert music) and repetition (as in the reproduction of recorded sound), where the latter is more promising for the ongoing production of capital.[25] Seeking to defend the value of live artistic performance from the dominance of the mass media, Auslander bemoans the intrusion of audiovisual and communication technology into live events, and thereby the loss of liveness. At

---

[21] Rambarran, 7.

[22] Rambarran, *Virtual Music*, 129.

[23] Ruth Lang, 'Livestreaming Sets', *Frame*, no. 138, pp. 102–109, January 2021. https://ualresearchonline. arts.ac.uk/id/eprint/16386/1/F138_NewTypology.pdf

[24] Philip Auslander, *Liveness: Performance in a Mediatized Culture*, 2nd ed. (London: Routledge, 2008), 3.

[25] Jacques Attali, *Noise: The Political Economy of Music*, trans. Brian Massumi (Minneapolis: University of Minnesota Press, 1985).

162 Digital Flows

some major pop stars' shows, for example, the goal of the concert production is to recreate the artist's music videos:[26] thus the live is in service of pre-existing audiovisual media. A live performance can be thoroughly rehearsed yet is still always spontaneous, improvisational, with (at least) minor variations in execution, and allowing feedback between performer and audience. The conventional music concert was ideally im-mediate, written as such to emphasize the etymological contrast with performances that are mediated.[27]

Hip hop has historically been understood as a set of creative practices and cultural priorities maintained through live events.[28] This is principally how it continues to thrive in underground hip hop music communities, such as open-mic freestyling workshops.[29] Hip hop heads may contend that the conventions of hip hop as a live performance art were transformed decades ago, when the music began appearing on record, and that hip hop recordings inevitably became mediated and non-live. However, David Diallo's book-length study of collective participation and audience engagement shows that hip hop retains a lyrical emphasis on immediacy and interactivity which is crucial to listeners' engagement with the music, even in recorded form.[30] It may therefore be necessary to distinguish face-to-face, real-time performance—what Paul Sanden calls 'classic' liveness[31]—from modes of musical interaction that continue to *feel* live for audiences, even when a range of media technologies are involved.

A case in point: what about performances that take place in real-time but are broadcast on the internet? Consider how a musical performance that is directly livestreamed compares to the premiere of a music video. Most listeners would describe the first but not the second as being live. Evidently, mediation is integral to online engagement with music, but how technologies of mediation affect perceptions of liveness varies in intensity. The extent to which different kinds of online music performance afford liveness can be placed along a spectrum (see Table 7.1).

A cover version of a song uploaded to YouTube is perhaps the least live format of online music performance. Yet, strangely, enough people watching it in real-time under the banner of a specific event can still give it an air of

---

[26] Auslander, *Liveness*, 34.

[27] Auslander, *Liveness*, 56.

[28] G. Dimitriadis, *Performing Identity/Performing Culture: Hip Hop as Text, Pedagogy, and Lived Practice* (New York: Peter Lang, 2001), 16–19.

[29] M. H. Morgan, *The Real Hiphop: Battling for Knowledge, Power, and Respect in the LA Underground* (Durham, NC: Duke University Press, 2009).

[30] David Diallo. *Collective Participation and Audience Engagement in Rap Music* (Cham: Springer International Publishing, 2019). https://doi.org/10.1007/978-3-030-25377-6.

[31] Paul Sanden, *Liveness in Modern Music: Musicians, Technology, and the Perception of Performance* (New York: Routledge, 2012), 13.

Virtual Hip Hop Concerts 163

Table 7.1 Indicative kinds of music performance mediated online ordered by perceived liveness

More live	Live, in-person performances ('concerts') with secondary online mediation
	Live, in-person performances without an audience, intended for online mediation ('portal shows')
	Livestreamed 'playthrough' performances ('e-busking', e.g., on Twitch)
	Virtual concerts as online multimedia experience (e.g., StageIt, WaveXR, and video game events)
Less live	Pre-recorded covers/'playthrough' performances (e.g., YouTube)

liveness. Take an early example of 'pandemic media',[32] the *One World: Together at Home* series organized by Global Citizen, which comprised performances pre-recorded at home by internationally celebrated artists including Lady Gaga, Stevie Wonder, Burna Boy, Lizzo, and Billie Eilish. The performances were assembled into an eight-hour livestream, divided into a six-hour pre-show and a simulcast two-hour television broadcast, which aired on 18 April 2021. It was billed as a benefit concert, although the disparate locations, diverse styles of audiovisual production, and composite editing of pre-recorded performance for televisual and online mediation surely stretch the boundaries of what can be considered a live event. Nonetheless, in a student seminar at my university the following day, someone asked, 'Who watched the gig last night?'

Just as this slippage between mediated and live performance intensifies, novel virtual events have been developed that situate music performance within the game-worlds of video games. These have been made increasingly feasible by advances in computer and internet technologies. For instance, a general improvement in upload speeds and a reduction in latency means that people living in areas with high-speed internet can communicate with very little audiovisual delay. Video game concerts are not the only beneficiary of improved online musical connectivity, of course. There has been mass adoption of video call functions (especially during the COVID-19 pandemic), with impressively fluid uses such as instrumental tuition and collaborative music production. Composers can sit in on orchestral recording sessions remotely,[33] and songwriters are able to collectively write lyrics using cloud-based word

---

[32] Philipp Dominik Keidl et al., *Pandemic Media: Preliminary Notes Toward an Inventory* (Lüneburg: meson press, 2020).

[33] Isabel Campelo, 'The "Virtual" Producer in the Recording Studio: Media Networks in Long-Distance Peripheral Performances', in *The Art of Record Production*, Simon Zagorski-Thomas, Katia Isakoff, Sophie Stévance, and Serge Lacasse, vol. 2, *Creative Practice in the Studio* (Routledge, 2019), 112–126.

164   Digital Flows

processors.[34] Twitch affords many varieties of streamer–audience feedback,[35] which implicate embodied 'action and participation on the part of the listener' and thereby emphasize live interactivity.[36] Since online video games have already resolved issues of simultaneous interaction through lag compensation (such as calculating which of two players shot the other first), there are especially exciting opportunities for musical performance with near-instant feedback.

Hip Hop Concerts in Online Video Games

In the current gaming climate, many of the major titles use the internet for gameplay features. Some games require an internet connection to be played at all. Most online-only games are multiplayer, relying on real-time interaction between players, whether competitive or collaborative. Scholarly literature on gaming has paid significant attention to massively multiplayer games like *Second Life*, *World of Warcraft*, and *Minecraft*.[37] Each of these provides virtual worlds for online communication and interaction with other players. The rise of massively multiplayer online games gave way to multiplayer online battle arenas and then a wave of battle royale games like *Fortnite*, which use server instancing to separate players into discrete matches. When players are not in matches, they interact with other systems housed by the game platform. These include a system for forming groups (or 'parties'), a friends list, chat channels, news on in-game events (and relevant real-world events like games conventions), a list of player achievements, cosmetic customizations, and a marketplace for purchasing digital assets. Some features, such as the ability to invite others to your party, are vital for playing with friends, whereas others, such as 'skins' (the character model the player controls in-game),[38] purely enhance the visual experience through cosmetic personalization.

---

[34] Matthew Clauhs, 'Songwriting with Digital Audio Workstations in an Online Community', *Journal of Popular Music Education* 4, no. 2 (July 2020): 237–252.

[35] Jason Ng and Steven Gamble, 'Hip-Hop Producer-Hosts, Beat Battles, and Online Music Production Communities on Twitch', *First Monday* 27, no. 6 (June 2022).

[36] Karen Collins, *Playing with Sound: A Theory of Interacting with Sound and Music in Video Games* (Cambridge, MA: The MIT Press, 2013), 5.

[37] Tom Boellstorff, *Coming of Age in Second Life, Coming of Age in Second Life* (Princeton, NJ: Princeton University Press, 2015); Hilde G. Corneliussen and Jill Walker Rettberg, eds., *Digital Culture, Play, and Identity: A World of Warcraft Reader* (Cambridge, MA: MIT Press, 2008); Nate Garrelts, ed., *Understanding Minecraft: Essays on Play, Community and Possibilities* (Jefferson, NC: McFarland & Company, Inc., 2014).

[38] This term is fraught yet entirely conventionalized within gaming culture. See, for example, Anne Mette Thorhauge and Rune K. L. Nielsen, 'Epic, Steam, and the Role of Skin-Betting in Game (Platform) Economies', *Journal of Consumer Culture* 21, no. 1 (February 2021): 52–67.

Such additions to the traditional game form have led critics to describe these games as platforms (bearing similarities to services for other media like music and television), known as games as a service (GaaS). Games which fall under this banner are continually updated with changing ('seasonal') content, game modes, maps (the play environments), and 'global' events. They often require paid subscriptions and typically solicit microtransaction payments for supplementary game content. Because of the recurring subscriptions, rotating content, and match-based style of play, they suit ongoing participation on behalf of gamers rather than traditional, linear, self-contained play experiences. The rotating content structure of GaaS lends itself well to time-limited experiences, such as so-called seasonal or global events, which offer opportunities for non-standard gameplay. For example, an earlier tie-in with *Star Wars: The Rise of Skywalker* aired one minute of original film footage on a virtual screen within *Fortnite*, bookended by director commentary from an animated J.J. Abrams and the appearance of the *Millennium Falcon*. To top it off, attendees' characters were given lightsabres to wield.

Because GaaS check so many of the boxes for real-time, online, mass-participatory, and one-off events, they provide fertile ground for the adaptation of communal experiences like music concerts. They can be used to host events that are virtual through and through, since there is no physical audience, and attendees at video game concerts are themselves represented virtually. The remainder of this chapter analyses three hip hop concert series held in video games in 2019 and 2020: two major corporate collaborations and one grassroots benefit. This is not a historical account of how music concerts entered video games per se, but a close study of specific instances which reveal how hip hop is implicated in another sphere of online cultural activity, gaming. I will conclude by considering how hip hop music transcends its typical auditory and audiovisual mediation to support new forms of cultural production, and finally examine what compromises are made when hip hop enters the virtual worlds of video games.

Fortnite and Travis Scott: *Astronomical*

As introduced at the start of this chapter, the Travis Scott *Fortnite* event represents a major collaboration between games and not only hip hop music but also commercial popular music more broadly. Travis Scott's fame exceeds recognition within the genre of hip hop, as indicated by collaborations with Justin Bieber and Rosalía, among many other leading pop stars. Epic Games (2020) announced *Astronomical* three days in advance, describing it variously

166 Digital Flows

as a 'journey', 'experience', 'tour', 'show', and 'event'. A range of Travis Scott-associated assets was added to the in-game store, such as a lifelike character model ($12), a 'back bling' asset (attached to the player's back) displaying the logo of Travis Scott's Cactus Jack record label ($12) and an 'Astro Jack' alter ego skin ($16). At the appropriate 'showtimes', *Astronomical* was accessed from a pre-game lobby within the platform interface where players could choose their skin, emotes, and equipment.

At the beginning of the event, players emerged in the standard 'Sweaty Sands' map but were presented with an unusual purple light beam illuminating a stage with a digital countdown floating above it. An approaching planet, with psychedelic visual stylings (developing on the imagined theme park of Travis Scott's *Astroworld* album cover), announced the start of the music. A small meteor orbited during the opening moments of 'SICKO MODE feat. Drake',[39] then crashed into the ground as the beat dropped. Emerging from the explosion of purple light, a giant Travis Scott figure lip-synced to the first verse. He teleported around the map, danced, and gestured along as though performing the music, while players were thrown around by various impacts timed with formal changes in the song. The Travis Scott model smashed two stars together to cause another explosion, which blasted players away as the second part of 'STARGAZING' played. Immediately the sky turned red, swirling in thunderous vortexes, with meteors falling, a ring of fire encircling the area, and holograms of giant dancers and rollercoaster tracks emerging on all sides (Figure 7.1). Players were granted significantly increased movement speed, free to dart about the place excitedly and take in all the sights and sounds.

The event continued with similarly dynamic and dramatic changes of environment to match the structure of the setlist. After 'STARGAZING', a tape-stop effect gave way to the chorus and first verse of 'goosebumps', accompanied by psychedelic, neon swirls of light. A sudden plunge into water debuted *Fortnite*'s swimming mechanic to the sounds of 'HIGHEST IN THE ROOM' while animated jellyfish passed by. One minute later, another eruption transported the players to a fluorescent environment for the third part of 'SICKO MODE', its sloping floor drawn with retrofuturistic 'outrun' gridlines. The ground rotated then dissipated, granting the players flight, and they shortly entered a sparse cosmos high above the planet, to the premiere of 'THE SCOTTS' (a Travis Scott project with Kid Cudi). The Astroworld planet burst into a flash of white light as the players sped through space and then found themselves falling through a rift back to the standard map. And the crowd . . . goes . . . wild!

---

[39] The song titles on the album *ASTROWORLD* are rendered in capitals, while those on *Birds in the Trap Sing McKnight* are in lowercase.

Virtual Hip Hop Concerts   167

Figure 7.1 Psychedelic spectacle, screenshots of *Travis Scott and Fortnite Present: Astronomical*, from YouTube

Source: *Travis Scott and Fortnite Present: Astronomical (Full Event Video)*, YouTube video, 26 April 2020, https://www.youtube.com/watch?v=wYeFAlVC8qU

Spectacle aside, the partnership between Travis Scott and *Fortnite* carries some tension regarding explicit content. Although demographic data on children (players under the age of eighteen) are not easily available, it is well known that *Fortnite*'s player base primarily comprises children and adolescents. Two reports published in 2018 give useful indications of the young audience. A survey by *Common Sense Media* reported six in ten teenagers in

168   Digital Flows

their sample play *Fortnite*.[40] Newzoo's study of 20 thousand gamers in six-teen countries reported over half of the game's player base to be aged between ten and twenty-five.[41] The game has a PEGI rating of twelve (recommended for players aged twelve and over) due to frequent scenes of mild violence. In the case of *Astronomical*, the young audience meant a number of lyrics were censored, albeit with some inconsistencies. Comparing the songs released on streaming platforms with their reproduction as part of the *Fortnite* event, it is thought-provoking to consider the cultural values informing hip hop's media-tion to an online audience dominated by children.

The common swear word 'fuck' was omitted, as were 'hoes' and 'bitches', explicit misogynistic terms for women. References to the drugs 'molly', 'Xan', and 'booch' were also removed or concealed through editing, but the lines 'she saw my eyes, she know I'm gone' and 'bring in the shots' avoided censor-ship despite their clear references to intoxication. Two specific instances of language implicating alcohol, 'bourbon' and 'mimosa'—a delightfully innoc-uous drink for a rapper to cite—were cut. (Strangely, 'off the Rémy [Martin]' slipped by.) The choices I have mentioned thus far are relatively common for 'clean' releases of songs with explicit lyrics. A range of other decisions invites consideration of how hip hop's lyrical imagery can be monitored and mod-erated. Racialized terms specific to African American Vernacular English and mentions of racist violence ('crackers' and 'noose') were obfuscated, even though the full line 'know the crackers wish it was a noose' clearly positions the performer as the victim, not perpetrator, of violently racist attitudes. Violent lyrics were toned down in general, which seems slightly redundant given that shooting guns is a primary component of *Fortnite* gameplay. The line 'keep the pistol on my side' was replaced altogether, two minutes before players were sent back to the map with their regular roster of destructive weapons.

Like violent language, sexual references were treated in a complex and somewhat contradictory manner. 'Pop that pussy' instead repeated as 'pop that, pop that' within one line, although the oblique lyric 'now I got her open' played in full. Later, the line 'now I got her in my room' curiously concealed the word 'her' with a tape-stop effect. The same sonic disruption obscured the first word in the phrase 'legs wrapped around my beard'. It appears that only

---

[40] Common Sense Media, 'Fortnite Frenzy: New Survey of Parents and Teens Reveals Concerns and Attitudes About the Video Game Everyone Seems to Be Playing', *Common Sense Media*, 6 December 2018, https://www.commonsensemedia.org/about-us/news/press-releases/fortnite-frenzy-new-survey-of-pare nts-and-teens-reveals-concerns-and.

[41] Orla Meehan, 'A Profile of the Battle Royale Player and How They Compare to Other Gamers', *Newzoo* (blog), 22 May 2018, https://newzoo.com/insights/articles/a-profile-of-the-battle-royale-player-and-how-they-compare-to-other-gamers/.

sexuality implicating the female body is treated as a problem ('pussy', 'her', 'legs'), although not with much consistency: Drake's suggestive line 'shorty in the back, she said she working on her glutes' rang out uncensored. In all, the performance of a medley of five songs cut down to under nine minutes seems to be carefully designed to balance lyrics most appropriate for children with those that enhance the euphoric tone of the event (bookended by the lyrics 'sun is down' and 'let's go'). For instance, 'STARGAZING' omitted a verse section referencing cocaine and overtly sexual activity, conveniently jumping ahead to 'this right here is astronomical'.

In addition to lyrical censorship and careful editing, other aspects of accessibility contributed to the success of the event. With *Fortnite* placing fewer restrictions than usual on livestreaming and re-broadcasting in-game footage, many (demonetized) videos of *Astronomical* recorded by gamers are available online. Widespread surprise and delight are evident in attendees' reactions to the subversion of staging expectations: jaws drop as the Travis Scott character stands about ten times the size of the stage, blasts the players around the map, and radically transforms the environment. To take a cynical view, one would expect such a positive response from full-time *Fortnite* streamers whose careers depend on the success of the game, and for whom celebrating the event is therefore mutually beneficial. In any case, *Astronomical* outclassed the prior example of a music event in *Fortnite*, hosted in partnership with the DJ Marshmello, whose avatar kept to his virtual DJ booth and remained contained within the stage area on the map.

In addition to having the former event as a basic model, *Astronomical* relied upon many of the principles and processes used to create other *Fortnite* content such as animated video trailers. The character of Travis Scott (as well as alter ego Cactus Jack) was animated using Unreal Engine 4, then the industry leader in game animation software. The character movements rely upon motion capture ('mocap'), a process that records actors' physical motions and codes these into animated figures in close to real-time. It results in highly fluid and realistic animations. The process has been used for many years in blockbuster films like *Avatar* and major games such as *The Last of Us*. Indeed, the same engine is used for *Fortnite*'s animated shorts, and it could be argued that *Astronomical* resembles a prepared animated film, albeit offering players the additional interactivity of moving around the game environment. Most *Fortnite* dance emotes also use motion capture of dancers, although it is unclear whether Travis Scott recorded the performance of *Astronomical*: I think it highly unlikely, and assume that another mocap artist was hired to perform in his style. Given the various resources created by Epic Games in the production of the event—the platform, the map and all the visual art assets, the

170 Digital Flows

animations, the effects, the user interface, and other player affordances—it is misleading to describe *Astronomical* as a live event featuring Travis Scott. It more closely resembles traditional music synchronization, such as a film licensing a song for its soundtrack. The artist's contributions to the event are limited to branding inspired by artwork originally developed for Travis Scott's other media products, the animated character in Travis Scott's likeness, and of course the recorded music.

Given the size and corporate nature of Epic Games, the negotiations behind the partnership are opaque.[42] It is possible that Travis Scott was highly invested and closely involved in the planning of the event, the virtual environments, and the flow of the nine-minute set. Moreover, *Fortnite*—not a music streaming platform like YouTube or Spotify—became the platform for debuting a new song and project ('THE SCOTTS'), as well as providing general cross-promotion for the artist. In terms of the event itself, however, and given conventions in game development, it seems most plausible that the bulk of the technical and creative work was done by Epic Games once the songs had been cleared for use. The developer essentially licensed Travis Scott's music (including four tracks which had already been released) and visual products to accompany their in-game event. And yet, because many players—who are used to assembling in virtual spaces for such events—were presented with the music and animated figure of Travis Scott, the experience has been widely understood and described as a virtual concert. Thus is the power of combining the physical likeness, the lip-synching animation, and the music within the game-world.

It may be useful to think of *Astronomical* more like an innovative music video. It can be seen as an enhancement of audiovisual media such as The Weeknd's 'interactive' 360-degree video for 'The Hills' remix featuring Eminem,[43] since players in the *Fortnite* event can also move their characters around and select emotes to perform. That said, the movement of players around the map is relatively limited given the environmental ruptures and 'stage' transitions of *Astronomical*. Epic Games described the event internally not as a 'concert' but a 'ride':[44] highly immersive but not freely interactive. This calls into question the extent to which attendees could feel surrounded by their friends, or among a crowd, compared to the archetypal concert experience, with the game developer retaining control over players' autonomy and

---

[42] Epic Games staff and representatives of Travis Scott did not respond to my requests for comment.

[43] Rambarran, *Virtual Music*, 103–105.

[44] Jordan Oloman, 'How Fortnite and Minecraft Virtual Concerts Kept Music Alive while We Weren't Allowed Outside', *Edge Magazine*, 7 July 2021, https://www.gamesradar.com/how-fortnite-and-minecraft-virtual-concerts-kept-music-alive-while-we-werent-allowed-outside/.

perspective. However, the multi-track setlist and the company's own framing of five 'tour dates'[45] complicate my comparison to music video. Besides, music video premieres do not usually attract audiences in the tens of millions: only a handful of the biggest-name pop stars debuting music videos on YouTube have achieved one million real-time viewers of new material. Evidently, *Fortnite's* limited-time event framing and the novelty of the in-game format provided an attractive sense of exclusivity.

Astronomical exemplifies a professionalized and polished collaboration between a major gaming platform and a mainstream hip hop artist. I have argued that, besides permissions granted by Travis Scott and his associated properties, it is primarily a multimedia production led by the game developer, with next to nothing in the way of a live performance by the artist. Indeed, Epic Games won a Cannes Lions Grand Prix award recognizing the company's 'Technological Achievement in Digital Craft', with no comparable recognition for Travis Scott. However, the production is not without its benefits for the artist. What's more, the collaboration also serves as a model for what future hip hop video game concerts might look like.

Roblox Presents the Lil Nas X Concert Experience

Six months after *Astronomical*, the hip hop and pop star Lil Nas X announced a similar event combining his music with a virtual performance animated in the game *Roblox*. As I mentioned in the conclusion to Chapter 3, the artist is known for his breakthrough hit (the RIAA-certified seventeen-times platinum song) 'Old Town Road feat. Billy Ray Cyrus' alongside number-one singles 'Montero (Call Me By Your Name)' and 'Industry Baby feat. Jack Harlow'. Much of the media discourse on Lil Nas X has characterized him as one of the most publicly visible, openly queer Black artists to date, and observed his successful deployments of social media. His *Roblox* partnership represents another step in that kind of online, youth-oriented promotional activity. Lil Nas X's 'concert' is not the first crossover media event in *Roblox*, although it is among the most high-profile collaborations. *Roblox* announced an attendance of 'more than 30 million visits' at his event,[46] which exceeded that of *Astronomical*. This is a striking figure, despite less enthusiastic media

---

[45] Epic Games, 'Fortnite and Travis Scott Present: Astronomical', Fortnite, April 2020, https://www.epicgames.com/fortnite/en-US/news/astronomical.

[46] Roblox, 'Explosive Lil Nas X Concert Paves the Way for Bold New Roblox Experiences', *Roblox Blog*, December 2020, https://web.archive.org/web/20220826072739/https://blog.roblox.com/2020/12/explosive-lil-nas-x-concert-paves-way-bold-new-roblox-experiences/.

172   Digital Flows

reportage (perhaps because it stands in the shadows of Travis Scott's event and *Fortnite* is a better-known game).

Roblox is essentially a platform for game development rather than a specifically structured gaming experience. It provides users with software (*Roblox Studio*) for creating their own games and publishing them in a large, searchable database which players can connect to and where the actual play takes place. Like *Fortnite*, *Roblox* was another media enterprise which grew its audience significantly as COVID-19 restricted children's leisure time to activities accessible from home. According to Roblox Corporation's SEC filing, around 17 million children under thirteen years old (of a total 31 million players) were active daily on the platform in 2020.[47] Like *Fortnite*, it has a virtual currency, Robux, and a vast marketplace of player avatars, where individual items range from the equivalent of a few cents to hundreds of dollars.

Lil Nas X's concert was accessed like any other *Roblox* game, although again, it had specific airing times (three instances over 14 and 15 November). The map also featured a virtual merch stand that linked to Lil Nas X-branded items purchasable with Robux. At the scheduled times, players were pulled into a new stage area with a Wild West theme (inspired by the music video backdrop for his breakthrough hit). Lil Nas X gave a spoken introduction to the event and motivated the audience with newly recorded dialogue. The following setlist reproduced his recorded songs 'Old Town Road', 'Rodeo' (without Cardi B's guest verse), 'Panini', and 'Holiday'. The event drew heavily from *Astronomical*, employing a giant-sized performer figure, brightly coloured thematic environments, and cut scenes transitioning between different virtual stages for each song, albeit in *Roblox*'s low poly visual style.

'Are you ready for my first ever virtual concert?', the disembodied voice of the artist called out, as if over a PA, at the start. Once again, however, the *Lil Nas X Concert Experience* contrasts with forms of media production previously described as a virtual concert. The game developers appear to value liveness in claiming that the concert was '*performed* entirely within Roblox'.[48] But what does performance mean in this context, which solely reuses existing song recordings? At the risk of belabouring the point, Lil Nas X's studio recordings took place months earlier and include the voice of a now-absent Billy Ray Cyrus alongside the production work of numerous other musicians. It would be more correct to say that the music was *reproduced* within *Roblox*. Lil Nas X recorded motion capture for his avatar's dancing and singing in the

---

[47] United States Securities and Exchange Commission, 'Form S-1 Registration Statement Under The Securities Act of 1933: Roblox Corporation', SEC Filing, November 2020, https://www.sec.gov/Archives/edgar/data/1315098/000119312520298230/d87104ds1.htm.
[48] Roblox, 'Explosive Lil Nas X Concert Paves the Way for Bold New Roblox Experiences', my italics.

game, although this was also produced long before the event aired. The absence of any real-time, live performance is therefore obscured by the 'concert' framing and the use of specific event times, a move representative of the wider platformization of cultural production.[49] Even a new pre-recorded musical performance (perhaps using original vocal tracks or additional instrumentation) would have made the event *feel* more live than the set of well-known, pre-existing sound recordings that were used in *Roblox*. In this way, Lil Nas X's video game appearance follows precisely in the footsteps of *Astronomical* by merely livestreaming his recorded songs with new visual accompaniment and in-game audience interactivity.

Perhaps to compensate for the lack of musical novelty, like Travis Scott, Lil Nas X debuted a new song: 'Holiday'. *Roblox* provided a platform to premiere the single, although a separate music video was released on YouTube on the same day. The partnership with *Roblox* fits Lil Nas X's typical release strategy, as he often iterates on past releases in the now-conventional manner of artists providing online content regularly and consistently (see my discussion of viral media and the attention economy in Chapter 3).[50] For instance, 'Old Town Road' has no fewer than nine YouTube videos, including an animated video, three remixes, and a five-minute extended version of the official music video (described as a 'movie' and featuring guest stars including Chris Rock and Rico Nasty). The *Roblox* 'concert experience' can therefore be seen as a contribution to a diversifying set of visual media accompanying Lil Nas X's music, thereby tapping into new platforms, new audiences, and—through virtual merchandise sales—new revenue streams.

Minecraft and Open Pit: *Lavapalooza*

When commercial profit and artist promotion are not the primary objectives of in-game music events, very different experiences can take place. In 2018, the design firm Parent Company developed a small production team named Open Pit, which began running virtual events in *Minecraft*. Owned by Microsoft and developed by Mojang (an early success story for independent game development), *Minecraft* is the best-selling video game globally[51] and

---

[49] David B Nieborg and Thomas Poell, 'The Platformization of Cultural Production: Theorizing the Contingent Cultural Commodity', *New Media & Society* 20, no. 11 (November 2018): 4275–4292; Gianni Sibilla, 'Alive & Digital: La performance musicale dal vivo alla piattaforma', *Fata Morgana Web*, 13 June 2020, https://www.fatamorganaweb.it/la-piattaformizzazione-della-performance-musicale-dal-vivo/.

[50] David Arditi, *Streaming Culture: Subscription Platforms and the Unending Consumption Of Culture* (Bingley: Emerald Group Publishing, 2021), 44.

[51] Tom Gerken, 'Minecraft Becomes First Video Game to Hit 300m Sales', *BBC News*, 16 October 2023, https://www.bbc.com/news/technology-67105983.

174 Digital Flows

has attained significant cultural spread, especially among young people and in popular culture. Its block-based sandbox environment affords considerable creativity in terms of world-building and online forms of participation. As I examine here, *Minecraft* also provides an engaging arena for virtual interaction among alternative online music communities.

Between September 2018 and August 2020, Open Pit ran eight events, called 'festivals', using the in-game world as an online interactive venue. For each event, the IP address or URL to access the server was circulated for players to join using *Minecraft*'s online multiplayer mode. Unlike *Fortnite* and *Roblox*, *Minecraft* has no capacity for playing specific music in-game, so participants relied upon a separate audio broadcast hosted on Twitch (and sometimes a mirror site like Mixlr). The idea was that attendees would open the music stream in a web browser in the background and then use *Minecraft* to virtually participate and interact with each other while listening simultaneously. Players were free to explore a custom-built server comprising virtual landscapes and blocky buildings, built with incredible sophistication and attention to detail. At many events, such as 2019's *Lavapalooza*, the nucleus of the server was a virtual venue building ('mosh pit') complete with custom game assets: a stage, speakers, and turntables rendered in *Minecraft*'s iconic, blocky style.

The line-up of artists for *Lavapalooza* included a range of metagenres spanning electronic dance music (EDM), hip hop, and pop. The majority of artists could be associated with the slippery label hyperpop (itself closely inspired by hip hop) and many are signed to the label PC Music, which helped originate the genre.[52] Few of the artists associated with Open Pit share the mainstream recognition of stars like Travis Scott or Lil Nas X, although several of them are well known among alternative hip hop audiences, such as 100 gecs, Flatbush Zombies, Tony Velour, Alice Longyu Gao, and Cali Cartier. Each artist provided a set of approximately twenty minutes which was recorded in advance and then streamed live, one after the other, by Open Pit. Many of these sets have been archived on SoundCloud in the model of EDM culture, where DJs commonly record and release full live mixes.

The nature of pre-recorded liveness is worth some examination, especially in highly electronic forms of popular music. The sets at *Lavapalooza* contained many original songs and remixes with newly developed effects, transitions, and other mashups typical of EDM DJ sets. While they were not performed live to an audience in real-time, they have a far stronger sense of originality

---

[52] Adam Harper, 'How Internet Music Is Frying Your Brain', *Popular Music* 36, no. 1 (January 2017): 86–97.

and novelty than the Travis Scott and Lil Nas X game events (perhaps even than the *One World* broadcast). Although DJs rarely deliver a complete render of their set ahead of time, most contemporary live performance involves significant musical preparation in a digital audio workstation. This has led to the derisive stereotype that major concert DJs simply 'press play' and then focus on energizing the crowd, dancing, and only miming changing musical equipment settings. This portrayal critiques the perceived inauthenticity of performing using computer technology, but more importantly, it bemoans a lack of liveness. In this context, premeditation rather than mediation is what disrupts the purity of classic liveness. However, because the Open Pit audience was aware that sets were pre-recorded—and partially because they were appeased by fresh remixes, transitions, effects, and so on—there was no such disdain for a lack of live performance.

The use of *Minecraft* as a virtual venue also made up for any absence of perceived liveness by providing a real-time meeting place for audiences to spontaneously celebrate the music livestream. Artists were free to appear in avatar form on the server during their sets and engage with the game-world as they wished. Limitations of the game engine meant that no performer could suddenly grow tenfold or send others flying with explosions. Their character models appeared the same size as everyone else's (which could be customized using third-party tools to load a particular skin into the game). Importantly, this is an appropriate metaphor for the politics of inclusion and social equality espoused by the event compared to its corporate equivalents, which retain deeply patriarchal resonances. In *Lavapalooza*, there was no celebration of one Great Man figure with complete control over the audiovisual environment, towering over his subservient audience. Instead, the performers controlled their own characters, just like every other attendee, and danced along, mime-like, to the prepared music performance (Figure 7.2). Some chose not to show up in-game at all.

The approaches to musical mediation and interactive staging aside, there are major organizational differences between Open Pit events and the other two examples addressed in this chapter. For the *Minecraft* events, no game environments, animations, or original content were produced by the game developer itself.

Consequently, *Lavapalooza* was not a produced multimedia experience so much as a scheduled virtual celebration, both liaising with artists to stream specially prepared music and developing an online space for attendees to collectively participate. Those facilitating the event were a grassroots collective of industry personnel, event managers, artists, and fans taking on responsibilities motivated primarily by interest and enthusiasm rather than revenue. Naturally, *Lavapalooza* and related 'festivals' helped to publicize the artists

Figure 7.2 Visual representations of equality among the pixelated chaos at *Lavapalooza*, screenshots from YouTube

Source: Open Pit LAVAPALOOZA Day 1, YouTube video, 22 April 2022, https://www.youtube.com/watch?v=rmV-TGRLBa4; *100 Gecs @ Lavapalooza 2020*, YouTube video, 23 December 2020, https://www.youtube.com/watch?v=lCrlKdHc7cU

and labels involved. Open Pit events also received sponsorships from Red Bull (who produced real T-shirts) and Pioneer DJ, who featured advertisements in-game and as stream overlays. The major motivating factor, however, was charity. *Lavapalooza* raised $20,000 in donations for the Okra Project, a 'community aid collective that seeks to support Black Trans people with the intention of alleviating barriers that the community faces'.[53]

---

[53] @TheOkraProject, 'TheOkraProject', Twitter feed, July 2023, https://twitter.com/TheOkraProject.

Commercial and Communal Dynamics

Comparing the charitable motivations of Open Pit concerts with the microtransaction-laden experiences of the *Fortnite* and *Roblox* events makes the contrast between the organizers' incentives crystal clear. The partnerships between artists and game platform corporations provide direct economic rewards and bidirectional cross-promotion. Many Travis Scott fans will have installed *Fortnite* and created new accounts specifically to experience his music in *Astronomical*. Equally, several *Fortnite* players attended the event with little to no prior recognition of Travis Scott (and, judging by YouTube reactions and commentary, most seemed appeased by the enjoyable game features). Travis Scott has similarly collaborated with corporations like McDonald's (the Travis Scott meal, widely available across US branches) and Nike (Travis Scott Air Force 1 shoes), representing a successful commercial model of hip hop promotion and enterprise encompassing new media forms.

Lil Nas X's work with Roblox Corporation clearly follows the model of *Astronomical*, although targeted strategically at a younger audience. This is sensible given his young fandom—recall this is the artist who wrote the hook 'Hey Panini, don't you be a meanie'—although there might have been eyebrows raised had he performed sexually explicit songs like 'MONTERO (Call Me By Your Name)' (as with the censorship of Travis Scott's lyrics in *Astronomical*). The *Lil Nas X Concert Experience* provides a useful example of how modern hip hop and pop artists are engaging with video game developers to create mocap-driven multimedia experiences alongside novel routes for music synchronization. These kinds of collaborations with major game platforms indicate the ever-intensifying corporatization of recorded hip hop music as well as its popularization among youth and gaming audiences. Mainstream hip hop music has long been criticized for its consumerist tendencies, but new streams for commercialization are now emerging through partnerships with game companies and the mutual exploitation of their player bases.

Open Pit pursues explicitly DIY-inspired, community-oriented outcomes. In comparison to the extensive production work of Epic Games and Roblox Corporation, Mojang and Microsoft were barely involved at all. The anti-corporate nature of Open Pit and the music genres it hosts were not necessarily undermined by the sponsorships from Red Bull and Pioneer DJ, since all money raised was directly provided to selected charities. However, a lot of volunteer labour is involved, which is surely unsustainable without reliable economic support. As these were essentially benefit concerts, all artists provided their work for free, and the limited income from sponsors barely covered the costs of the event production despite Open Pit's desire to compensate

178 Digital Flows

artists adequately.[54] They struck a compromise by promoting the performers through in-game hyperlinks to artist websites. As an offshoot of the design firm (ironically and aptly named) Parent Company, Open Pit has a vested interest in the commercial success of the artists that perform at their concerts, since that may lead to more paid design work in turn. *Lavapalooza* therefore functions as a charity event that also provides rewarding and mutually beneficial promotion for artists, brands, and the events team, not to mention entertainment for attendees.

Aside from global inequities in internet access, there are minimal barriers to entry for audiences at all three events. Whereas *Fortnite* and *Roblox* are free of charge to play (although the account sign-up involves parting with a little personal data), virtually attending an Open Pit event required a *Minecraft* license. The events themselves were accessible at no additional cost. The one-off event times of Open Pit festivals privileged a US audience on Eastern Time, whereas the other platforms' repeat broadcasts ensured more convenience and accessibility for participants across the globe. The Travis Scott and Lil Nas X events were entirely experienced within the game platforms, while Open Pit's use of a publicly available audio stream on Twitch meant advertising revenues went to the Amazon-owned platform. It is evidently difficult to escape the corporate shadow of commercial internet platforms altogether. Nonetheless, Open Pit demonstrates a promising model for future virtual hip hop concerts hosted in video games and maintains a cultural ethos of communality while still generating economic rewards for charities and promotion for the creators involved.

Open Pit has inspired a number of similar independent festivals and artist showcase events, although none so popularly attended as yet, to the best of my knowledge. There has been more use of Discord for streaming music (as an alternative to Twitch), retaining *Minecraft* as an interactive virtual meeting space. Events are promoted using social networking sites and accessed through private—albeit publicly distributed—Discord server codes. The young and Extremely Online[55] audience typically in attendance exhibits a kind of informal community participation rooted in the aesthetics and

---

[54] Oloman, 'How Fortnite and Minecraft Virtual Concerts Kept Music Alive while We Weren't Allowed Outside'.

[55] As I touched on in Chapter 1, Extremely Online (usually rendered like so, or sometimes as the problematic 'terminally online') is a pervasive vernacular term used by people who spend much of their time online and understand their identity as being shaped considerably by internet culture. See, for example, E. J. White, *A Unified Theory of Cats on the Internet* (Stanford, CA: Stanford Briefs, 2020), 12; Crystal Abidin, 'From "Networked Publics" to "Refracted Publics": A Companion Framework for Researching "Below the Radar" Studies', *Social Media + Society* 7, no. 1 (January 2021): 1; Fenwick McKelvey, Scott DeJong, and Janna Frenzel, 'Memes, Scenes and #ELXN2019s: How Partisans Make Memes during Elections', *New Media & Society* 25, no. 7 (July 2023): 1637; Taylor Lorenz, *Extremely Online: The Untold Story of Fame, Influence, and Power on the Internet* (New York: Simon & Schuster, 2023).

practices of internet culture. There is a delightful sense of immediacy to these events, even down to the organization (like set times shifting last-minute) and chaotic live chat channels. The DIY style of event management and relatively unmoderated server structure resonate with hip hop conventions, reminiscent of independently organized cyphers and casual communities of practice. Moreover, the music is highly indebted to contemporary hip hop production, especially the musical aesthetics of trap. At times, the specific signatures of online youth interaction—GIFs, emojis, abbreviations, irony, and text spam—may conceal the participatory sociomusical engagements at play here. Still, the spirit of hip hop culture shines through at the heart of these *Minecraft* concerts, supplanted by the contours of contemporary online interactivity.

In contrast to the communality observed at Open Pit concerts and subsequent *Minecraft* shows in the same model, the *Fortnite* and *Roblox* events privilege exciting in-game consumer experiences. With impressive animation of giant character models and gratifying game capacities like super speed as the stars of the show, hip hop music is relegated to an accompanying soundtrack. The sound recordings of the songs have already been distributed and are already known by fans: this is also true of what pulls audiences to in-person concerts, of course, although at least there the artist is physically present and performs some of the music in real-time. The pre-recorded virtualization of hip hop performance enables real-time player interaction with a multimedia production that sits alongside artists' other properties like music videos and merchandise. These are video game experiences using hip hop, rather than hip hop creativity taking place within a video game's virtual environment.

Conclusion

In coming to a close, it is worth re-examining the state of hip hop's liveness in the online video game context. Lil Nas X certainly helped to produce a slightly more original experience than Travis Scott by adding dialogue between songs and personally recording the motion capture. He did, in some virtual sense, perform the songs. Still, the music's lack of deviation from the recorded tracks limits the experience of immediacy expected of a concert. Open Pit found a promising middle-ground between liveness and mediation by having original sets produced in advance and broadcasting them at the time of the event alongside the possibility of spontaneous artist interaction. Broadcasting live motion capture, animation, and production as part of a simultaneous in-game audiovisual experience would be a technical challenge, although it is not altogether inconceivable using contemporary technologies. The feasibility

180 Digital Flows

of real-time, artist-to-audience performance has been demonstrated by the virtual entertainment company Wave, which uses mocap technology and sound recording to virtualize the performer, albeit with limited interactivity for audiences. Behind-the-scenes footage of *Fortnite* mocap recording shows screens displaying instant playback in animated form to help with direction, so the foundations for immediate online performance are evidently in place.

In any case, one would think that simultaneously recording and livestreaming sound is the least of the technological worries here. So why do none of the examples of video game hip hop concerts opt for live sound? This open question reveals an unresolved tension between internet (in this case video game) technologies and hip hop as a mode of live performance. Many hip hop practices have translated effortlessly to online formats, as this book has shown, and hip hop is at the forefront of exciting new media experiences that combine interactivity and audiovisual performance. Just like other on-line music concerts that pre-record performances (e.g., *One World*), however, virtual hip hop shows in video games tend to prioritize extensive control over event production rather than real-time connection between artist and audi-ence. In other words, a well-produced game experience is valued over musical liveness. In this way, hip hop's spontaneity and immediacy as a cultural form are compromised to comply with the commercial priorities of online media platforms. Less visible online are the alternative hip hop concerts placing communal motivations at the heart of participatory interactions. Whether they can persist in the face of an increasingly centralized and commercial-ized internet remains an open issue, one I tease out in the book's concluding chapter.

8
Conclusion

It's Where You're @

This book is a testament to the vitality of hip hop. Before starting this study, as a fan, producer, and scholar, I knew that hip hop was widespread, popular, and significant. Only in carrying out this research have I realized quite how uniquely hip hop is positioned in online cultures, and how instructive its position is for studying music, media, and culture in the internet age. But the culture knows it. In Chapter 3, I pointed to the presence of SoundCloud stars—rappers who broke through to the hip hop mainstream by online means, particularly Lil Uzi Vert—at the Grammys' celebration of the fiftieth anniversary of hip hop. The performance ended with LL Cool J describing hip hop's journey across the world and then the internet: 'It started in the Bronx and ever since it's gone everywhere: to the five boroughs, to the West Coast, to the heartland, overseas, to Europe, to Africa, to Asia, TikTok, whatever's next . . . hip hop is the global platform today'. I hope to have shown that this is no exaggeration.

In many ways, hip hop's onlining is reminiscent of its globalization. Studies of how hip hop flows globally can be characterized along a spectrum: at one extreme are studies that see the culture as an indiscriminate US commercial export; at the other are those that examine far-flung individuals' adoption of hip hop. Jumping off from studies of hip hop glocalization,[1] Griff Rollefson characterizes this as a binary between cultural imperialism and cultural appropriation.[2] He navigates between these extremes by suggesting that hip hop interpellates—that is, reveals, manifests, calls to attention—already-present local knowledges as it spreads worldwide. With a critical and discursive view of online media platforms, I have attempted to take a similarly nuanced stance and avoid binarisms that over- or underdetermine the role of agency in hip hop's digital diffusion.

---

[1] H. S. Alim, A. Ibrahim, and A. Pennycook, eds., *Global Linguistic Flows: Hip Hop Cultures, Youth Identities, and the Politics of Language* (New York and London: Routledge, 2009).

[2] J. Griffith Rollefson, 'Hip Hop Interpellation: Rethinking Autochthony and Appropriation in Irish Rap', in *Made in Ireland: Studies in Popular Music*, ed. Áine Mangaoang, John O'Flynn, and Lonán Ó Briain (New York and London: Routledge, 2021), 230.

Digital Flows. Steven Gamble, Oxford University Press. © Oxford University Press 2024.
DOI: 10.1093/oso/9780197656389.003.0008

182 Digital Flows

Instead, I would suggest that the internet—like the turntable, car stereo, and smartphone—is another technology transformed by Black creative innovation, in a long history of such practices.[3] This is the argument André Brock has recently made concerning Black technoculture, an idea I have advanced specifically with regard to hip hop's subversive ethos.[4] Tricia Rose identified this in action far earlier in the lifespan of hip hop, writing that hip hop music producers reject 'dominant conceptions of the value of new technology [and] actively and aggressively deploy strategies that revise and manipulate musical technologies so that they will articulate black cultural priorities.[5] As I have shown, such processes remain active across online platforms today.

Through studies of different manifestations of hip hop on the internet, I have demonstrated that lively debates continue to inform the breadth and boundaries of hip hop: who participates in the culture, and on whose terms. The generational divides invoked by internet rap create tensions, as do the exploitative stances adopted by pop superstars attuned to online culture, magnifying debates around appropriation, accountability, and equity. Communal conventions developed on publicly visible platforms are subject to commercial pressures, while the complex values associated with the consumption of Blackness and womanhood demonstrate the ongoing importance of hip hop feminism. Intrusions by other forms of media—not only video games but also livestreaming and video-sharing apps—challenge the ability of hip hop to retain its core emphases in a period of cultural platformization, polarization, and privatization. Though hip hop is certainly prevalent online, what S. Craig Watkins called 'the struggle for the soul' of the culture rages on in the internet era.[6]

---

[3] Alexander G. Weheliye, *Phonographies: Grooves in Sonic Afro-Modernity* (Durham, NC: Duke University Press, 2005), 87–92; Rayvon Fouché, 'Say It Loud, I'm Black and I'm Proud: African Americans, American Artifactual Culture, and Black Vernacular Technological Creativity', *American Quarterly* 58, no. 3 (2006): 639–661; David Z. Morris, 'Cars with the Boom: Identity and Territory in American Postwar Automobile Sound', *Technology and Culture* 55, no. 2 (2014): 326–353; Steven Gamble and Justin Williams, 'Analyzing Hip-Hop Hacktivism and Automobility in Injury Reserve's (2019) "Jailbreak the Tesla" (Feat. Aminé)', in *Analyzing Recorded Music*, ed. William Moylan, Lori Burns, and Mike Alleyne (London and New York: Routledge, 2022), 38–55.

[4] André Brock, *Distributed Blackness: African American Cybercultures* (New York: New York University Press, 2020).

[5] Tricia Rose, *Black Noise: Rap Music and Black Culture in Contemporary America* (Middletown, CT: Wesleyan University Press, 1994), 96–97.

[6] S. Craig Watkins, *Hip Hop Matters: Politics, Pop Culture, and the Struggle for the Soul of a Movement* (Boston, MA: Beacon Press, 2005).

It's Where You're @   **183**

Opportunities for Further Research

I outlined in the introduction that though hip hop is a conspicuously global form, my focus is on Anglophone expressions of the culture. This has been a useful constraint to stop the scope of my study from becoming unmanageably broad, but it has meant overlooking many striking instances of hip hop online. It has therefore been my privilege to edit (with Raquel Campos Valverde) a special issue of the journal *Global Hip Hop Studies* focused on hip hop and the internet. We worked with authors studying important sites of online hip hop outside the Anglosphere in places such as Palestine, South Africa, and India.[7] Simultaneously, the multitude of emerging researchers working on music and the internet (judging by a succession of innovative conferences) indicates that a more global view of online hip hop will be the subject of many more studies in the coming years.

While I have attempted to demonstrate a range of intersections between hip hop and the internet—on alternative music streaming platforms, in communal forms on YouTube, in rap music videos, in mainstream popular music culture, and in video game concerts—this scope is far from exhaustive. I would encourage interested readers to look at existing work on hip hop's relationships to dance challenges,[8] memes,[9] sex work,[10] internet talent shows,[11] and more, and urge scholars to contribute to this growing body of research.

Because internet technologies are always so rapidly in flux, I have tried to emphasize underlying logics and principles rather than the idiosyncrasies of specific platforms. Recent developments (despite proving my points about the effects of privatization and platform power on cultural practices) concerning Twitter/X somewhat scuppered my attempts. Indeed, many texts about contemporary cultures risk quickly becoming outdated. While snapshots of what the internet looks like at a particular moment in time are worthwhile, attending to developments in terms of relations of power, value, and

---

[7] Steven Gamble and Raquel Campos Valverde, 'Editorial', in 'It's Where You're @: Hip Hop and the Internet', special issue *Global Hip Hop Studies* 2 (November 2021): 153–158.

[8] Cienna Davis, 'Digital Blackface and the Troubling Intimacies of TikTok Dance Challenges', in *TikTok Cultures in the United States*, ed. Trevor Boffone (London and New York: Routledge, 2022), 28–38.

[9] Michael Waugh, '"Every Time I Dress Myself, It Go Motherfuckin" Viral': Post-Verbal Flows and Memetic Hype in Young Thug's Mumble Rap', *Popular Music* 39, no. 2 (May 2020): 208–232.

[10] Jabari Evans, 'Link in Bio: Exploring the Emotional and Relational Labour of Black Women Rappers in Sexual Dance Economies on OnlyFans', in 'It's Where You're @: Hip Hop and the Internet', special issue, *Global Hip Hop Studies* 2 (November 2021): 179–198.

[11] Jingsi Christina Wu, 'Can China Have Its Hip Hop?: Negotiating the Boundaries between Mainstream and Underground Youth Cultural Spaces on the Internet Talent Show Rap of China', in *China's Youth Cultures and Collective Spaces: Creativity, Sociality, Identity and Resistance*, ed. Vanessa Frangville and Gwennaël Gaffric (London and New: Routledge, 2019).

184 Digital Flows

knowledge should help the work presented here remain relevant for longer. My situated case studies on current leading sites and apps like YouTube, Spotify, and TikTok should nonetheless contribute to wider scholarship on these (and other) internet platforms.

Aside from developing research on hip hop and platforms, there may be further opportunities to apply the methodology I used to other internet-mediated cultural forms. Other kinds of popular music would be a straightforward and rewarding application of my approach, as would other participatory arts, fandoms, and communities. The combination of cultural analysis and data science methods allows the potential for contrasting—even contradictory—findings. I suggest that this outcome is worth embracing, for the cultural interactions under study may themselves be marked by discursive and structural contradictions. Hip hop could hardly be a clearer model.

The Future of Online Hip Hop

The history of the internet can be characterized by poor predictions, exaggerations, and simplifications. Writing in 2023, the online technology making waves is in the field of generative artificial intelligence, specifically consumer-facing language, image, and audio models. The recent technological innovations mostly relate to machine learning and deep learning, but AI has become the popular catch-all term. As I have come to expect with new technology, hip hop has been at the forefront of public debates over user-driven and AI-generated media content. In August 2022, a minor scandal emerged about the Capitol-signed virtual rapper FN Meka, which political journalist Akin Olla suggested is 'a strange new form of blackface'.[12] For a time, FN Meka made music, posted images on Instagram, and tweeted like any other rapper with a social media presence. The catch is that FN Meka was a 3D animated character. His social media posts, playing on racialized stereotypes of criminality and lyrics full of African American Vernacular English, bore authorship solely traceable to Meka's non-Black creators at the company Factory New.[13] Though the extent of AI generation involved in FN Meka's music and images have been called into question,[14] its popularity demonstrates the buzz

---

[12] Akin Olla, 'Are AI-Powered "Virtual Rappers" Just a Strange New Form of Blackface?', *The Guardian*, 1 September 2022, https://www.theguardian.com/commentisfree/2022/sep/01/are-ai-powered-virtual-rappers-just-a-strange-new-form-of-blackface.

[13] Industry Blackout (@industryblackout), 'Have You Lost Your FN Minds? @capitolrecords', Instagram post, 23 August 2022, https://www.instagram.com/p/ChnJGi2potN/.

[14] Rapper Kyle the Hooligan publicly claimed to be the voice of FN Meka, at least initially.

It's Where You're @ **185**

around hip hop and artificial intelligence, not to mention an intensification of online hip hop's cultural appropriation discourse (beyond that discussed in Chapter 6).

Kendrick Lamar was one of the earliest artists to embrace the potential of newly affordable—and aesthetically convincing—technology based on machine learning techniques. In May 2022, the music video for his Grammy-winning 'The Heart Part 5' deployed video manipulations known popularly as deepfakes, with the rapper's facial appearance seeming to morph into those of other Black male celebrities including Kanye West, Will Smith, and Nipsey Hussle. This video was made by a professional team under Kendrick Lamar's creative direction, but it is quickly becoming clear that tech-savvy users—particularly the produsers and new amateurs discussed in Chapter 3[15]—can generate impressive audiovisual media without artists' consent.

In April 2023, a new viral trap song by Drake and the Weeknd, 'Heart on My Sleeve', was removed from streaming services by Universal Music Group, the reason being that Drake and the Weeknd had nothing to do with it. In fact, it was developed by a pseudonymous but self-described rap ghostwriter with the aid of AI-generated vocals. There are online communities rapidly forming around AI voice generation, deploying audio models such as SoVitsSvc to insert new guest verses to existing tracks and flesh out artists' unreleased material. The use of machine-learning technology—now good enough to convincingly pass as well-known rappers—evidently reiterates earlier ideas in remix and mashup cultures,[16] and chimes with hip hop production communities centred around leaks.[17] There was outrage about sampling and even interpolation at the dawn of recorded hip hop—as in Chic's 'Good Times' as the basis for 'Rapper's Delight'—just as there will be outrage about accelerating processes of technological appropriation.[18]

---

[15] Nick Prior, 'The Rise of the New Amateurs: Popular Music, Digital Technology and the Fate of Cultural Production', in *Handbook of Cultural Sociology*, ed. J. R. Hall, L. Grindstaff, and M. Lo (London and New York: Routledge, 2010), 398–407; Axel Bruns, 'Prosumption, Produsage', in *The International Encyclopedia of Communication Theory and Philosophy* , ed. Klaus Bruhn Jensen and Robert T. Craig (Chichester and Noboken, NJ: Wiley-Blackwell and the International Communication Association, 2016).

[16] Samantha Bennett, 'The Listener as Remixer: Mix Stems in Online Fan Community and Competition Contexts', in *The Oxford Handbook of Music and Virtuality*, ed. Sheila Whiteley and Shara Rambarran (Oxford: Oxford University Press, 2016), 355–376; Margie Borschke, *This Is Not a Remix: Piracy, Authenticity and Popular Music* (New York and London: Bloomsbury Publishing, 2017); Ragnhild Brøvig-Hanssen and Ellis Jones, 'Remix's Retreat? Content Moderation, Copyright Law and Mashup Music', *New Media & Society* 25, no. 6 (June 2021).

[17] Jamie Ryder, 'Chopped and Screwed? How Studio Leaks Are Creating a New DIY Rap Music', *The Guardian*, 3 January 2020, https://www.theguardian.com/music/2020/jan/03/chopped-and-screwed-how-studio-leaks-are-creating-a-new-diy-rap-music.

[18] Joanna Demers, *Steal This Music: How Intellectual Property Law Affects Musical Creativity* (Athens and London: University of Georgia Press, 2006), 4–10.

186   Digital Flows

The rate of these recent developments appears rapid indeed, echoing Moore's law about the speed, processing power, and reducing cost of computer technology. ChatGPT, the user-facing chat interface developed by OpenAI,[19] broke records to become the fastest-growing consumer technology of all time, gaining 100 million active monthly users in about two months.[20] For comparison, TikTok took nine months, whereas Instagram took two and a half years. Large language models generating informative conversation and human-like text may challenge the stranglehold traditional search engines have sustained on the internet as a filter for information.[21] Fears abound concerning the replacement of human jobs, environmental costs, and the current state of AI safety.[22] The use of AI-driven artwork for purposes of imitation raises important questions about the production of harmful content, the role of computers in creativity, and artists' rights and revenues. Moreover, it shines new light on network effects concerning the monopolistic concentration of mass audiences by mega-celebrity artists.[23] Though it may simply be a short-lived gimmick, there is currently tangible excitement among fan communities reproducing the voices of popular rappers. The hip hop conscience in me wonders why they aren't as excited about discovering emerging rappers, whether in their locality or online, or even getting on the mic themselves.

Hip hop and the internet maintain complex, changing relationships but, as this book shows, ever since their first meeting, they always have. The culture has influenced mainstream online culture just as the web has shaped the way people understand hip hop in the contemporary era. Hip hop is an innovator: from forum to blog to platform, it has resisted drives towards

[19] Despite its user-facing nature and non-profit origins, OpenAI does not produce open-source software and resembles an extension of—rather than a disruptive new challenge to—Big Tech. It is a San Francisco start-up backed by Microsoft, Amazon, and (initially) Elon Musk, and its technologies have sparked an AI arms race among the leading corporations.

[20] Cindy Gordon, 'ChatGPT Is the Fastest Growing App in the History of Web Applications', *Forbes*, 2 February 2023, https://www.forbes.com/sites/cindygordon/2023/02/02/chatgpt-is-the-fastest-growing-ap-in-the-history-of-web-applications/. By mid-2023, this rate seemed to be slowing, with competition increasing and novelty wearing off. See Krystal Hu, 'ChatGPT's Explosive Growth Shows First Decline in Traffic since Launch', *Reuters*, 5 July 2023, https://www.reuters.com/technology/booming-traffic-openais-chatgpt-posts-first-ever-monthly-dip-june-similarweb-2023-07-05/.

[21] More likely, their functionalities will be merged, as demonstrated by Microsoft's Bing Chat, which implements OpenAI's GPT-4 model within the browser Edge's search engine.

[22] Future of Life Institute, *Policymaking in the Pause: What Can Policymakers Do Now to Combat Risks from Advanced AI Systems?* (Future of Life Institute, 2023), https://futureoflife.org/wp-content/uploads/2023/04/FLI_Policymaking_In_The_Pause.pdf; Pengfei Li et al., 'Making AI Less "Thirsty": Uncovering and Addressing the Secret Water Footprint of AI Models', arXiv preprint, arXiv.2304.03271 (2023).

[23] Leslie M. Meier, 'Popular Music, Streaming, and Promotional Media: Enduring and Emerging Industrial Logics', in *Making Media: Production, Practices, and Professions*, ed. Mark Deuze and Mirjam Prenger (Amsterdam University Press, 2019), 321–334.

privatization, reactionary hatred, and appropriation. It is memes and streams, virtual cyphers and dance crazes. It seems inevitable that hip hop will continue to innovate within online contexts as a technologically subversive, popular, and participatory culture. As LL Cool J put it: from the Bronx, to TikTok, to whatever's next.

References

100 *Gecs @ Lavapalooza 2020*. YouTube, 23 December 2020. https://www.youtube.com/watch?v=ICrlKdHc7cU.

Abdalla, Amira, Natasha D'Souza, Ria Gill, Raisa Jadavji, and Claudia Meneguzzi. 'Social Media as a Stage: A Behind the Scenes Analysis of Performative Activism, "Cancel Culture," and Effective Allyship'. *McMaster Undergraduate Journal of Social Psychology* 3, no. 1 (October 2022): 83–122.

Abidin, Crystal. 'Communicative ❤ Intimacies: Influencers and Perceived Interconnectedness'. *Ada: A Journal of Gender, New Media, and Technology*, no. 8: Gender, Globalization and the Digital (November 2015): 1–16.

Abidin, Crystal. 'From "Networked Publics" to "Refracted Publics": A Companion Framework for Researching "Below the Radar" Studies'. *Social Media + Society* 7, no. 1 (January 2021). https://doi.org/10.1177/2056305120984458.

Abidin, Crystal. 'Visibility Labour: Engaging with Influencers' Fashion Brands and #OOTD Advertorial Campaigns on Instagram'. *Media International Australia* 161, no. 1 (November 2016): 86–100. https://doi.org/10.1177/1329878X16665177.

Abidin, Crystal, and Megan Lindsay Brown, eds. *Microcelebrity Around the Globe*. Bingley: Emerald, 2019.

Adams, Mahina. 'The Feminine Musique: Cardi, Megan, and Black Feminism'. *afterglow*, 6 December 2021. https://www.afterglowatx.com/blog/2021/12/6/the-feminine-musique-cardi-megan-and-black-feminism.

Aguiar, Vinícius de. 'Musical Playlisting and Curation on YouTube: What Do Algorithms Know about Music?' In *YouTube and Music: Online Culture and Everyday Life*, edited by Holly Rogers, Joana Freitas, and João Francisco Porfírio, 196–208. London: Bloomsbury Academic, 2023.

Ahmed, Sara. *Living a Feminist Life*. Durham, NC: Duke University Press, 2017.

Ahlgrim, Callie, and Courteney Larocca. 'Ariana Grande Finishes First on Her New Album "Positions"'. *Insider*, 30 October 2020. https://www.insider.com/ariana-grande-positions-review-tracklist-breakdown-2020-10.

Aigrain, Philippe. *Sharing: Culture and the Economy in the Internet Age*. Amsterdam: Amsterdam University Press, 2012.

Alemoru, Kemi. 'Inside YouTube's Calming "Lofi Hip Hop Radio to Relax/Study to" Community'. *Dazed*, 14 June 2018. https://www.dazeddigital.com/music/article/40366/1/youtube-lo-fi-hip-hop-study-relax-24-7-livestream-scene.

Alexander, Julia. 'Lo-Fi Beats to Quarantine to Are Booming on YouTube'. *The Verge*, 20 April 2020. https://www.theverge.com/2020/4/20/21222294/lofi-chillhop-youtube-productivity-community-views-subscribers.

Alim, H. Samy. *Roc the Mic Right: The Language of Hip Hop Culture*. New York and London: Routledge, 2006.

Alim, H. Samy. 'Straight Outta Compton, Straight Aus München: Global Linguistic Flows, Identities, and the Politics of Language in a Global Hip Hop Nation'. In *Global Linguistic Flows: Hip Hop Cultures, Youth Identities, and the Politics of Language*, edited by H. Samy Alim, Awad Ibrahim, and Alastair Pennycook, 1–22. New York and London: Routledge, 2009.

190 References

Alim, H. S., A. Ibrahim, and A. Pennycook, eds. *Global Linguistic Flows: Hip Hop Cultures, Youth Identities, and the Politics of Language*. New York and London: Routledge, 2009.

Allington, Daniel, Byron Dueck, and Anna Jordanous. 'Networks of Value in Electronic Music: SoundCloud, London, and the Importance of Place'. *Cultural Trends* 24, no. 3 (July 2015): 211–222. https://doi.org/10.1080/09548963.2015.1066073.

Anderson, Benedict. *Imagined Communities: Reflections on the Origin and Spread of Nationalism*. Rev. ed. London and New York: Verso, 2006.

Anderson, Crystal S. 'Hybrid Hallyu: The African American Music Tradition in K-Pop'. In *Global Asian American Popular Cultures*, edited by Shilpa Davé, LeiLani Nishime, and Tasha Oren, 290–303. New York: New York University Press, 2016.

Ankerson, Megan Sapnar. *Dot-Com Design: The Rise of a Usable, Social, Commercial Web*. New York: New York University Press, 2018.

Appel, Gil, Lauren Grewal, Rhonda Hadi, and Andrew T. Stephen. 'The Future of Social Media in Marketing'. *Journal of the Academy of Marketing Science* 48, no. 1 (January 2020): 79–95. https://doi.org/10.1007/s11747-019-00695-1.

Appiah, Kwame Anthony. 'The Case for Capitalizing the "B" in Black'. *The Atlantic*, 18 June 2020. https://www.theatlantic.com/ideas/archive/2020/06/time-to-capitalize-blackand-white/613159/.

Arditi, David. *Itake-Over: The Recording Industry in the Streaming Era*. 2nd ed. London: Lexington Books, 2020.

Arditi, David. *Streaming Culture: Subscription Platforms and the Unending Consumption of Culture*. Bingley: Emerald, 2021.

Arriagada, Arturo, and Francisco Ibáñez. '"You Need at Least One Picture Daily, if not, You're Dead": Content Creators and Platform Evolution in the Social Media Ecology'. *Social Media + Society* 6, no. 3 (July 2020). https://doi.org/10.1177/2056305120944624.

Arrieta, Alexandria. 'Splice and the Platformization of Hip Hop Production: Navigating the Online Music Platform for Royalty-Free Samples'. In 'It's Where You're @: Hip Hop and the Internet'. Special issue, *Global Hip Hop Studies* 2 (November 2021): 219–236. https://doi.org/10.1386/ghhs_00045_1.

Aswad, Jem. 'Is the Weeknd Pop, R&B or Hip-Hop? Why the Distinction Matters at the Grammys'. *Variety* (blog), 1 October 2020. https://variety.com/2020/music/news/weeknd-grammys-pop-hip-hop-category-1234789560/.

Atkinson, Sophie. 'The "24/7 Lo-Fi Hip Hop Beats" Girl Is Our Social Distancing Role Model'. *Dazed*, 23 March 2020. https://www.dazeddigital.com/music/article/48486/1/the-24-7-lo-fi-hip-hop-beats-girl-is-our-social-distancing-role-model.

Attali, Jacques. *Noise: The Political Economy of Music*. Translated by Brian Massumi. Minneapolis: University of Minnesota Press, 1985.

Auslander, Philip. *Liveness: Performance in a Mediatized Culture*. 2nd ed. London: Routledge, 2008.

Avdeeff, Melissa. 'Lil Nas X, TikTok, and the Evolution of Music Engagement on Social Networking Sites'. In *Virtual Identities and Digital Culture*, edited by Victoria Kannen and Aaron Langille, 221–230. New York: Routledge, 2023.

Avdeeff, Melissa K. 'TikTok, Twitter, and Platform-Specific Technocultural Discourse in Response to Taylor Swift's LGBTQ+ Allyship in "You Need to Calm Down"'. *Contemporary Music Review* 40, no. 1 (January 2021): 78–98. https://doi.org/10.1080/07494467.2021.1945225.

Averill, Gage. *Four Parts, No Waiting: A Social History of American Barbershop Harmony*. New York: Oxford University Press, 2003.

Aziz, Adam. 'The Coming Battle over Rap Album Lengths'. *Andscape* (blog), 1 October 2021. https://andscape.com/features/the-coming-battle-over-rap-album-lengths/.

Bailey, Moya. *Misogynoir Transformed: Black Women's Digital Resistance*. New York: New York University Press, 2021.

Ball, James. *The System: Who Owns the Internet, and How It Owns Us*. London: Bloomsbury, 2020.

References 191

Ball, Jared A. *I Mix What I Like!: A Mixtape Manifesto*. Oakland, CA: AK Press, 2011.

Banaji, Shakuntala, and Ramnath Bhat. *Social Media and Hate*. Abingdon: Routledge, 2021.

Banet-Weiser, Sarah. *Authentic™: The Politics of Ambivalence in a Brand Culture*. New York: New York University Press, 2012.

Banet-Weiser, Sarah, and Kate M. Miltner. '#MasculinitySoFragile: Culture, Structure, and Networked Misogyny'. *Feminist Media Studies* 16, no. 1 (January 2016): 171–174. https://doi.org/10.1080/14680777.2016.1120490.

Bannister, Matthew. 'Funny Girls and Nowhere Boys: Reversing the Gaze in the Popular Music Biopic'. In *Rethinking Difference in Gender, Sexuality, and Popular Music*, edited by Gavin Lee, 111–128. New York: Routledge, 2018.

Battan, Carrie. 'The Messy Story of How SoundCloud Rap Took Over Everything'. *GQ*, 31 January 2019. https://www.gq.com/story/soundcloud-rap-boom-times.

Baym, Nancy K. 'Data Not Seen: The Uses and Shortcomings of Social Media Metrics'. *First Monday* 18, no. 10 (2013). https://doi.org/10.5210/fm.v18i10.4873.

Baym, Nancy K. *Playing to the Crowd: Musicians, Audiences, and the Intimate Work of Connection*. New York: New York University Press, 2018.

Behr, Adam. 'The Album at 70: A Format in Decline?' *The Conversation*, 11 July 2018. http://theconversation.com/the-album-at-70-a-format-in-decline-99581.

Benkler, Yochai. *The Wealth of Networks*. New Haven, CT: Yale University Press, 2006.

Bennett, Samantha. 'The Listener as Remixer: Mix Stems in Online Fan Community and Competition Contexts'. In *The Oxford Handbook of Music and Virtuality*, edited by Sheila Whiteley and Shara Rambarran, 355–376. Oxford: Oxford University Press, 2016.

Berry, Peter A. '13 Rappers Talking on the Money Phone'. *XXL*, May 2015. http://www.xxlmag.com/news/2015/05/rappers-money-phone-pose/.

Besseny, Amelia. 'Lost in Spotify: Folksonomy and Wayfinding Functions in Spotify's Interface and Companion Apps'. *Popular Communication* 18, no. 1 (January 2020): 1–17. https://doi.org/10.1080/15405702.2019.1701674.

Bhopal, Kalwant. *White Privilege: The Myth of a Post-Racial Society*. Bristol: Policy Press, 2018.

Blackman, Lisa. *Haunted Data: Affect, Transmedia, Weird Science*. London and New York: Bloomsbury Publishing, 2019.

Blair, Ann. *Too Much to Know: Managing Scholarly Information Before the Modern Age*. New Haven, CT: Yale University Press, 2010.

Boellstorff, Tom. *Coming of Age in Second Life. Coming of Age in Second Life*. Princeton and Oxford: Princeton University Press, 2015.

Boise, Sam de. 'Music and Misogyny: A Content Analysis of Misogynistic, Antifeminist Forums'. *Popular Music* 39, no. 3–4 (December 2020): 459–481. https://doi.org/10.1017/S0261143020000410.

Bonilla-Silva, Eduardo. *Racism Without Racists: Color-Blind Racism and the Persistence of Racial Inequality in America*. 6th ed. Lanham, MD: Rowman & Littlefield, 2021.

Bonini, Tiziano, and Alessandro Gandini. '"First Week Is Editorial, Second Week Is Algorithmic": Platform Gatekeepers and the Platformization of Music Curation'. *Social Media + Society* 5, no. 4 (October 2019). https://doi.org/10.1177/2056305119880006.

Bonnette-Bailey, Lakeyta M., Lestina Dongo, Kierra Lawrence, and Noah Nelson. 'The Bigger Picture: Hip-Hop, Black Lives, and Social Justice'. In *Black Popular Culture and Social Justice*, edited by Lakeyta M. Bonnette-Bailey and Jonathan I. Gayles, 109–124. London and New York: Routledge, 2023.

Born, Georgina, and Christopher Haworth. 'From Microsound to Vaporwave: Internet-Mediated Musics, Online Methods, and Genre'. *Music and Letters* 98, no. 4 (2017): 601–647. https://doi.org/10.1093/ml/gcx095.

Borschke, Margie. *This Is Not a Remix: Piracy, Authenticity and Popular Music*. New York and London: Bloomsbury Publishing, 2017.

192 References

Bory, Paolo. *The Internet Myth: From the Internet Imaginary to Network Ideologies.* London: University of Westminster Press, 2020.

Boulton, Clint. 'Is 2023 the Year of AI Transformation?' *Forbes*, 8 February 2023. https://www.forbes.com/sites/delltechnologies/2023/02/08/is-2023-the-year-of-ai-transformation/.

Boutros, Alexandra. 'The Impossibility of Being Drake: Or, What It Means to Be a Successful (Black) Canadian Rapper'. *Global Hip Hop Studies* 1, no. 1 (June 2020): 95–114. https://doi.org/10.1386/ghhs_00006_1.

boyd, danah. *It's Complicated: The Social Lives of Networked Teens.* New Haven, CT: Yale University Press, 2014.

boyd, danah. 'Social Network Sites as Networked Publics: Affordances, Dynamics, and Implications'. In *A Networked Self*, edited by Zizi Papacharissi, 47–66. New York and London: Routledge, 2011.

Boyd, Todd. *The New H.N.I.C.: The Death of Civil Rights and the Reign of Hip Hop.* New York and London: New York University Press, 2002.

Boyd, Todd. *Young, Black, Rich, and Famous: The Rise of the NBA, the Hip Hop Invasion, and the Transformation of American Culture.* Lincoln, NE and London: University of Nebraska Press, 2008.

Brackett, David. *Categorizing Sound: Genre and Twentieth-Century Popular Music.* Berkeley and Los Angeles: University of California Press, 2016.

Bradley, Regina N. *Chronicling Stankonia: The Rise of the Hip-Hop South.* Chapel Hill: University of North Carolina Press, 2021.

Bradley, Regina N. 'Awkwardly Hysterical: Theorizing Black Girl Awkwardness and Humor in Social Media'. *Comedy Studies* 6, no. 2 (July 2015): 148–153. https://doi.org/10.1080/2040610X.2015.1084176.

Bramwell, Richard. *UK Hip-Hop, Grime and the City: The Aesthetics and Ethics of London's Rap Scenes.* New York and London: Routledge, 2015.

Bramwell, Richard, and James Butterworth. 'Beyond the Street: The Institutional Life of Rap'. *Popular Music* 39, no. 2 (May 2020): 169–186. https://doi.org/10.1017/S0261143020000355.

Breihan, Tom. *The Number Ones: Twenty Chart-Topping Hits That Reveal the History of Pop Music.* New York: Hachette, 2022.

Brock, André. 'Beyond the Pale: The Blackbird Web Browser's Critical Reception'. *New Media & Society* 13, no. 7 (2011): 1085–1103.

Brock, André. *Distributed Blackness: African American Cybercultures.* New York: New York University Press, 2020.

Brock, André. 'From the Blackhand Side: Twitter as a Cultural Conversation'. *Journal of Broadcasting & Electronic Media* 56, no. 4 (October 2012): 529–549. https://doi.org/10.1080/08838151.2012.732147.

Brøvig-Hanssen, R., and A. Danielsen. *Digital Signatures: The Impact of Digitization on Popular Music Sound.* Cambridge, MA: MIT Press, 2016.

Brøvig-Hanssen, R., and Ellis Jones. 'Remix's Retreat? Content Moderation, Copyright Law and Mashup Music'. *New Media & Society* 25, no. 6 (June 2021). https://doi.org/10.1177/14614448211026059.

Bruns, Axel. 'Prosumption, Produsage'. In *The International Encyclopedia of Communication Theory and Philosophy*, edited by Klaus Bruhn Jensen and Robert T. Craig, 1–5. Chichester and Noboken, NJ: Wiley-Blackwell and the International Communication Association, 2016.

Brusila, Johannes, Martin Cloonan, and Kim Ramstedt. 'Music, Digitalization, and Democracy'. *Popular Music and Society* 45, no. 1 (October 2021): 1–12. https://doi.org/10.1080/03007766.2021.1984018.

Burgess, Jean, and Nancy K. Baym. *Twitter: A Biography.* New York: New York University Press, 2022.

References   193

Burnard, Pamela, Pete Dale, Simon Glenister, Jim Reiss, Raphael Travis, Elliot Gann, and Alinka Greasley. 'Pursuing Diversity and Inclusivity through Hip-Hop Music Genres: Insights for Mainstream Music Curricula'. In *The Routledge Companion to Creativities in Music Education*, edited by Clint Randles and Pamela Burnard, 241–259. New York: Routledge, 2022.

Burrows, Cedric D. *Rhetorical Crossover: The Black Presence in White Culture*. Pittsburgh, PA: University of Pittsburgh Press, 2020.

Burton, Justin D. *Posthuman Rap*. New York: Oxford University Press, 2017.

Butler, Bethonie. 'Yes, Those Kim Kardashian Photos Are about Race'. *Washington Post* (blog), 21 November 2014. https://www.washingtonpost.com/blogs/she-the-people/wp/2014/11/21/yes-those-kim-kardashian-photos-are-about-race/.

Byrd, Ayana D., and Lori L. Tharps. *Hair Story: Untangling the Roots of Black Hair in America*. Rev. ed. New York: St Martin's Griffin, 2014.

Cabvno. 'F e e l i n g s'. YouTube video, 8 August 2017. https://www.youtube.com/watch?v=0cKzCUdtRh8.

Calhoun, Kendra. Review of *tumblr*, by Katrin Tiidenberg, Natalie Ann Hendry, and Crystal Abidin. *Visual Communication* (July 2022). https://doi.org/10.1177/14703572221109898.

Callender, Brandon. 'Popstar Benny Wants to Make Your Favorite Artist Get Weird'. *The FADER*, 20 December 2021. https://www.thefader.com/2021/12/20/popstar-benny-interview.

Campelo, Isabel. 'The "Virtual" Producer in the Recording Studio: Media Networks in Long-Distance Peripheral Performances'. In *The Art of Record Production*, ed. Simon Zagorski-Thomas, Katia Isakoff, Sophie Stévance, and Serge Lacasse. Vol. 2, 112–126. *Creative Practice in the Studio*. London: Routledge, 2019.

Canceling | ContraPoints. YouTube video, 2 January 2020. https://www.youtube.com/watch?v=OjMPJVmXxV8.

Caramanica, Jon. 'Juice WRLD and the Tragic End of the SoundCloud Rap Era'. *New York Times*, 9 December 2019. https://archive.is/W9SpT.

Caramanica, Jon. 'The Rowdy World of Rap's New Underground'. *New York Times*, 22 June 2017. https://archive.is/b6MX4.

Carter, Daniel, and Tyler Welsh. '"Everybody Wants to Work with Me": Collaborative Labor in Hip Hop'. *Popular Music and Society* 42, no. 3 (2019): 267–283. https://doi.org/10.1080/03007766.2018.1441639.

Castells, Manuel. *Communication Power*. Oxford: Oxford University Press, 2009.

Castells, Manuel. 'The Internet and the Network Society'. In *The Internet in Everyday Life*, edited by Barry Wellman and Caroline Haythornthwaite, xxix–xxxi. Malden, MA: Blackwell, 2002.

Chamberlain, Elizabeth F. '"Our World Is Worth Fighting for": Gas Mask Agency, Copypasta Sit-Ins, and the Material-Discursive Practices of the Blitzchung Controversy'. *Computers and Composition* 65 (September 2022): 102725. https://doi.org/10.1016/j.compcom.2022.102725.

Chang, Jeff. *Can't Stop Won't Stop: A History of the Hip-Hop Generation*. London: Ebury Press, 2005.

Chang, Winnie. 'The Monstrous-Feminine in the Incel Imagination: Investigating the Representation of Women as "Femoids" on /r/Braincels'. *Feminist Media Studies* 22, no. 2 (February 2022): 254–270. https://doi.org/10.1080/14680777.2020.1804976.

Charnas, Dan. *Dilla Time: The Life and Afterlife of J Dilla, the Hip-Hop Producer Who Reinvented Rhythm*. New York: Farrar, Straus and Giroux, 2022.

Cheng, William, ed. *Loving Music Till It Hurts*. New York: Oxford University Press, 2019.

Cherid, Maha Ikram. '"Ain't Got Enough Money to Pay Me Respect": Blackfishing, Cultural Appropriation, and the Commodification of Blackness'. *Cultural Studies ↔ Critical Methodologies* 21, no. 5 (July 2021): 359–364. https://doi.org/10.1177/15327086211029357.

194 References

Cherjovsky, Natalia. 'Virtual Hood: Exploring The Hip-Hop Culture Experience In A British Online Community'. PhD diss., University of Central Florida, 2010. https://stars.library.ucf.edu/etd/4199.

Christgau, Robert. 'Xgau Sez'. *Robert Christgau*, 18 June 2019. https://robertchristgau.com/xgausez.php?d=2019-06-18.

Cinelli, Matteo, Walter Quattrociocchi, Alessandro Galeazzi, Carlo Michele Valensise, Emanuele Brugnoli, Ana Lucia Schmidt, Paola Zola, Fabiana Zollo, and Antonio Scala. 'The COVID-19 Social Media Infodemic'. *Scientific Reports* 10, no. 1 (October 2020): 16598. https://doi.org/10.1038/s41598-020-73510-5.

Cirisano, Tatiana. 'Game On: What Travis Scott Is Teaching Music Stars About the World's Biggest New (Virtual) Stage'. *Billboard*, 24 July 2020. https://www.billboard.com/articles/business/9422287/travis-scott-fortnite-billboard-cover-story-interview-2020.

Citton, Yves. *The Ecology of Attention*. Translated by Barnaby Norman. Cambridge: Polity Press, 2017.

Clark, Trent. 'Review: Migos' "Culture II" Is an Unfocused, Unworthy Sequel to the Original'. *HipHopDX*, 2 February 2018. https://hiphopdx.com/reviews/id.3085/title.review-migos-culture-ii-is-an-unfocused-unworthy-sequel-to-the-original.

Clauhs, Matthew. 'Songwriting with Digital Audio Workstations in an Online Community'. *Journal of Popular Music Education* 4, no. 2 (July 2020): 237–252. https://doi.org/10.1386/jpme_00027_1.

Cobb, William Jelani. *To the Break of Dawn: A Freestyle on the Hip Hop Aesthetic*. New York: New York University Press, 2007.

Coddington, Amy. ' "Check Out the Hook While My DJ Revolves It": How the Music Industry Made Rap into Pop in the Late 1980s'. In *The Oxford Handbook of Hip Hop Music*, edited by Justin D. Burton and Jason Lee Oakes. Oxford: Oxford University Press, 2018.

Coddington, Amy. *How Hip Hop Became Hit Pop: Radio, Rap, and Race*. Berkeley and Los Angeles: University of California Press, 2023.

Code Pioneers. 'Coding in Chicago | 🎧 LoFi Jazz Hip-Hop [Code - Relax - Study]'. YouTube livestream, 24 November 2020. https://www.youtube.com/watch?v=esX7SFtEjHg.

Cohen, Sara. 'Ethnography and Popular Music Studies'. *Popular Music* 12, no. 2 (May 1993): 123–138. https://doi.org/10.1017/S0261143000005511.

Collie, Natalie, and Caroline Wilson-Barnao. 'Playing with TikTok: Algorithmic Culture and the Future of Creative Work'. In *The Future of Creative Work*, edited by Greg Hearn, 172–188. Cheltenham: Edward Elgar, 2020.

Collins, Karen. *Playing with Sound: A Theory of Interacting with Sound and Music in Video Games*. Cambridge, MA: MIT Press, 2013.

Collins, Steve, and Pat O'Grady. 'Off the Charts: The Implications of Incorporating Streaming Data into the Charts'. In *Networked Music Cultures: Contemporary Approaches, Emerging Issues*, edited by Raphaël Nowak and Andrew Whelan, 151–169. London: Palgrave Macmillan, 2016.

Common Sense Media. 'Fortnite Frenzy: New Survey of Parents and Teens Reveals Concerns and Attitudes About the Video Game Everyone Seems to Be Playing'. *Common Sense Media*, 6 December 2018. https://www.commonsensemedia.org/about-us/news/press-releases/fortnite-frenzy-new-survey-of-parents-and-teens-reveals-concerns-and.

Condry, I. *Hip Hop Japan: Rap and the Paths of Cultural Globalization*. Durham, NC: Duke University Press, 2006.

Conner, Thomas. 'Hatsune Miku, 2.0Pac, and Beyond: Rewinding and Fast-Forwarding the Virtual Pop Star'. In *The Oxford Handbook of Music and Virtuality*, edited by Sheila Whiteley and Shara Rambarran, 129–147. New York: Oxford University Press, 2016.

Conservatives. 'lo fi boriswave beats to relax/get brexit done to'. YouTube video, 25 November 2019. https://www.youtube.com/watch?v=cre0in5n-1E.

References   195

Constine, Josh. 'Facebook Changes Mission Statement to "Bring the World Closer Together"'. *TechCrunch* (blog), 22 June 2017. https://techcrunch.com/2017/06/22/bring-the-world-clo ser-together/.

Cook-Wilson, Winston. 'Review: It's Worth Listening to the Rest of Migos' Culture, Too'. *SPIN*, 27 January 2017. https://www.spin.com/2017/01/review-migos-culture-a-story-of-perse verance-tests-the-if-it-aint-broke-dont-fix-it-thesis/.

Cooper, Brittney C., Susana M. Morris, and Robin M. Boylorn. 'Hip Hop Generation Feminism: A Manifesto'. In *The Crunk Feminist Collection*, edited by Brittney C. Cooper, Susana M. Morris, and Robin M. Boylorn, xix–xxii. New York: The Feminist Press at CUNY, 2016.

Cormier, Jacque-Corey. 'I Stank I Can, I Know I Can, I Will: Songwriting Self-Efficacy as an Expression of Identity Orchestration'. In *Identity Orchestration: Black Lives, Balance, and the Psychology of Self Stories*, edited by David Wall Rice, 29–48. Lanham, MD: Lexington Books, 2022.

Corneliussen, Hilde G., and Jill Walker Rettberg, eds. *Digital Culture, Play, and Identity: A World of Warcraft Reader*. Cambridge, MA: MIT Press, 2008.

Crary, Jonathan. *24/7: Late Capitalism and the Ends of Sleep*. London: Verso Books, 2014.

Crary, Jonathan. *Suspensions of Perception: Attention, Spectacle, and Modern Culture*. Cambridge, MA: MIT Press, 2001.

Cristofari, Cécile, and Matthieu J. Guitton. 'Aca-Fans and Fan Communities: An Operative Framework'. *Journal of Consumer Culture* 17, no. 3 (November 2017): 713–731. https://doi. org/10.1177/1469540515623608.

Dandridge-Lemco, Ben. 'The Internet Loves This Picture Of 21 Savage as a Batman Supervillain'. *The FADER*, 9 March 2017. https://www.thefader.com/2017/03/09/21-savage-batman-got ham-supervillian-meme.

Danielsen, Anne. 'The Sound of Crossover: Micro-Rhythm and Sonic Pleasure in Michael Jackson's "Don't Stop 'Til You Get Enough"'. *Popular Music and Society* 35, no. 2 (May 2012): 151–168. https://doi.org/10.1080/03007766.2011.616298.

Dattatreyan, Ethiraj Gabriel. *The Globally Familiar: Digital Hip Hop, Masculinity, and Urban Space in Delhi*. Durham, NC: Duke University Press, 2020.

David, Matthew. *Peer to Peer and the Music Industry: The Criminalization of Sharing*. London: SAGE, 2010.

Davis, Cienna. 'Digital Blackface and the Troubling Intimacies of TikTok Dance Challenges'. In *TikTok Cultures in the United States*, edited by Trevor Boffone, 28–38. London and New York: Routledge, 2022.

Davison, Patrick. 'The Language of Internet Memes'. In *The Social Media Reader*, edited by Michael Mandiberg, 120–134. New York: New York University Press, 2012.

De Zeeuw, Daniël. 'Impersonal Identity: Enacting the Online Self Beyond Networked Individualism'. In *The Aesthetics and Politics of the Online Self*, edited by Donatella Della Ratta, Geert Lovink, Teresa Numerico, and Peter Sarram, 309–330. Cham: Springer International Publishing, 2021.

DeFrantz, Thomas F. 'Hip-Hop in Hollywood: Encounter, Community, Resistance'. In *The Oxford Handbook of Dance and the Popular Screen*, edited by Melissa Blanco Borelli, 113–131. New York: Oxford University Press, 2014.

Demers, Joanna. *Steal This Music: How Intellectual Property Law Affects Musical Creativity*. Athens: University of Georgia Press, 2006.

Denisova, Anastasia. *Internet Memes and Society: Social, Cultural, and Political Contexts*. New York: Routledge, 2019.

Denisova, Anastasia, and Aliaksandr Herasimenka. 'How Russian Rap on YouTube Advances Alternative Political Deliberation: Hegemony, Counter-Hegemony, and Emerging Resistant

196 References

Publics'. *Social Media + Society* 5, no. 2 (April 2019). https://doi.org/10.1177/205630511 9835200.

DENZEL CURRY x MONTREALITY ⋀ *Interview*. YouTube video, 24 January 2018. https://www.youtube.com/watch?v=jiNLTGt4A4M.

Devine, Kyle. *Decomposed: The Political Ecology of Music*. Cambridge, MA: MIT Press, 2019.

Diallo, David. *Collective Participation and Audience Engagement in Rap Music*. Cham: Springer International Publishing, 2019.

D'Ignazio, Catherine, and Lauren F. Klein. *Data Feminism*. Cambridge, MA: MIT Press, 2020.

Dijck, Jose van. *The Culture of Connectivity: A Critical History of Social Media*. The Culture of Connectivity. Oxford: Oxford University Press, 2013.

Dijck, José van, Thomas Poell, and Martijn de Waal. *The Platform Society: Public Values in a Collective World*. New York: Oxford University Press, 2018.

Dimitriadis, G. *Performing Identity/Performing Culture: Hip Hop as Text, Pedagogy, and Lived Practice*. New York: Peter Lang, 2001.

Dobson, Amy Shields. *Postfeminist Digital Cultures*. New York: Palgrave Macmillan, 2015.

Dredge, Stuart. 'Spotify CEO Talks Covid-19, Artist Incomes and Podcasting (Interview)'. *Music Ally*, 30 July 2020. https://musically.com/2020/07/30/spotify-ceo-talks-covid-19-art ist-incomes-and-podcasting-interview/.

Drott, Eric. 'Why the Next Song Matters: Streaming, Recommendation, Scarcity'. *Twentieth-Century Music* 15, no. 3 (October 2018): 325–357. https://doi.org/10.1017/S147857221 8000245.

Dryden, Richard 'Treats'. 'Greg Burke's 10 Favorite Rap Album Covers of the '90s'. *Complex*, 29 January 2014. https://www.complex.com/style/2014/01/greg-burkes-favorite-rap-album-covers-of-the-90s/.

Du Bois, W.E.B. *The Souls of Black Folk*. Edited by B. H. Edwards. New York: Oxford University Press, 2007.

Duffy, Brooke Erin. *(Not) Getting Paid to Do What You Love: Gender, Social Media, and Aspirational Work*. New Haven, CT: Yale University Press, 2017.

Duinker, Ben. 'Good Things Come in Threes: Triplet Flow in Recent Hip-Hop Music'. *Popular Music* 38, no. 3 (October 2019): 423–456. https://doi.org/10.1017/S026114301 900028X.

Duinker, Ben, and Denis Martin. 'In Search of the Golden Age Hip-Hop Sound (1986–1996)'. *Empirical Musicology Review* 12, no. 1–2 (September 2017): 80–100. https://doi.org/ 10.18061/emr.v12i1-2.5410.

Dunham, Ian. 'SoundCloud Rap: An Investigation of Community and Consumption Models of Internet Practices'. *Critical Studies in Media Communication* 39, no. 2 (March 2022): 107–126. https://doi.org/10.1080/15295036.2021.2015537.

Durham, Aisha. 'Class Formation: Beyoncé in Music Video Production'. *Black Camera* 9, no. 1 (2017): 197–204.

Dutton, William H., ed. *The Oxford Handbook of Internet Studies*. Oxford: Oxford University Press, 2013.

eastasiasoft. 'Lofi Ping Pong Trailer (Nintendo Switch)'. YouTube video, 1 April 2021. https://www.youtube.com/watch?v=nLZ8CcAXTAQ.

Eberhardt, Maeve, and Kara Freeman. '"First Things First, I'm the Realest": Linguistic Appropriation, White Privilege, and the Hip-Hop Persona of Iggy Azalea'. *Journal of Sociolinguistics* 19, no. 3 (2015): 303–327. https://doi.org/10.1111/josl.12128.

Eddo-Lodge, Reni. *Why I'm No Longer Talking to White People about Race*. London: Bloomsbury, 2018.

Edgar, Amanda Nell. 'Blackvoice and Adele's Racialized Musical Performance: Blackness, Whiteness, and Discursive Authenticity'. *Critical Studies in Media Communication* 31, no. 3 (May 2014): 167–181. https://doi.org/10.1080/15295036.2013.863427.

References   197

Edwards, Erica B, and Jennifer Esposito. 'Reading the Black Woman's Body Via Instagram Fame'. *Communication, Culture and Critique* 11, no. 3 (September 2018): 341–358. https://doi.org/10.1093/ccc/tcy011.

Eidsheim, Nina Sun. 'Marian Anderson and "Sonic Blackness" in American Opera'. *American Quarterly* 63, no. 3 (2011): 641–671. https://doi.org/10.1353/aq.2011.0045.

Elliott, Richard. '"The Most Annoying Noise of All Time"'. *Australian Humanities Review*, no. 70 (2022): 58–66.

Entertainment Software Association. *2020 Essential Facts About the Video Game Industry* Entertainment Software Association, 2020. https://www.theesa.com/wp-content/uploads/2021/03/Final-Edited-2020-ESA_Essential_facts.pdf.

Epic Games. 'Fortnite and Travis Scott Present: Astronomical'. Fortnite, April 2020. https://www.epicgames.com/fortnite/en-US/news/astronomical.

Eriksson, Maria, Rasmus Fleischer, Anna Johansson, Pelle Snickars, and Patrick Vonderau. *Spotify Teardown: Inside the Black Box of Streaming Music*. Cambridge, MA: MIT Press, 2019.

Erlewine, Stephen Thomas. 'Ariana Grande – Thank u, Next', February 2019. https://www.allmusic.com/album/thank-u-next-mw0003246119.

Esteves, Victoria, and Graham Meikle. '"Look @ This Fukken Doge": Internet Memes and Remix Cultures'. In *The Routledge Companion to Alternative and Community Media*, edited by Chris Atton, 561–570. Abingdon and New York: Routledge, 2015.

Evans, Jabari. 'Link in Bio: Exploring the Emotional and Relational Labour of Black Women Rappers in Sexual Dance Economies on OnlyFans'. In 'It's Where You're @: Hip Hop and the Internet'. Special issue, *Global Hip Hop Studies* 2 (November 2021): 179–198. https://doi.org/10.1386/ghhs_00043_1.

Evans, Jabari. 'Old Hits Verzuz New Technology: How a Pandemic Ushered Legacy Artists into Monetizing the Clout Economy'. In *Sustaining Black Music and Culture during COVID-19: #Verzuz and Club Quarantine*, edited by Niya Pickett Miller, 79–94. Lanham, MD: Lexington Books, 2021.

Evans, Jabari M., and Nancy K. Baym. 'The Audacity of Clout (Chasing): Digital Strategies of Black Youth in Chicago DIY Hip-Hop'. *International Journal of Communication* 16 (May 2022): 19.

Exarchos, Michail. 'Boom Bap Ex Machina'. In *Producing Music*, edited by Russ Hepworth-Sawyer, Jay Hodgson, and Mark Marrington, 32–51. New York: Routledge, 2019.

Fariello, Gabriele, Dariusz Jemielniak, and Adam Sulkowski. 'Does Godwin's Law (Rule of Nazi Analogies) Apply in Observable Reality? An Empirical Study of Selected Words in 199 Million Reddit Posts'. *New Media & Society* 26, no. 1 (December 2021). https://doi.org/10.1177/14614448211062070.

Ferley, Andrew. 'The Semantic Derogation of Female'. Masters thesis, York University, 2022. https://yorkspace.library.yorku.ca/xmlui/bitstream/handle/10315/39771/Ferley%20A%20-%20MRP.pdf?sequence=1&isAllowed=y.

Fitts, Mako. '"Drop It Like It's Hot": Culture Industry Laborers and Their Perspectives on Rap Music Video Production'. *Meridians* 8, no. 1 (September 2008): 211–235. https://doi.org/10.2979/MER.2008.8.1.211.

Fleischer, Rasmus. 'Universal Spotification? The Shifting Meanings of "Spotify" as a Model for the Media Industries'. *Popular Communication* 19, no. 1 (January 2021): 14–25. https://doi.org/10.1080/15405702.2020.1744607.

Fleming, Peter. *The Mythology of Work: How Capitalism Persists Despite Itself*. London: Pluto Press, 2015.

Florini, Sarah. *Beyond Hashtags: Racial Politics and Black Digital Networks*. New York: New York University Press, 2019.

Florini, Sarah. 'Tweets, Tweeps, and Signifyin': Communication and Cultural Performance on "Black Twitter"'. *Television & New Media* 15, no. 3 (March 2014): 223–237. https://doi.org/10.1177/1527476413480247.

198 References

Fogarty, Mary. 'Breaking Expectations: Imagined Affinities in Mediated Youth Cultures'. *Continuum* 26, no. 3 (June 2012): 449–462. https://doi.org/10.1080/10304312.2012.665845.

Fogarty, Mary. 'Sharing Hip-Hop Dance: Rethinking Taste in Cross-Cultural Exchanges of Music'. In *Situating Popular Musics: IASPM 16th International Conference Proceedings*, edited by Ed Montana and Carlo Nardi, 127–131. Umeå, Sweden: IASPM, 2011.

Forman, Murray. *The 'hood Comes First: Race, Space, and Place in Rap and Hip-Hop*. Middletown, CT: Wesleyan University Press, 2002.

Forman, Murray. '"Things Done Changed": Recalibrating the Real in Hip-Hop'. *Popular Music and Society* 44, no. 4 (August 2021): 451–477. https://doi.org/10.1080/03007766.2020.1814628.

Forster, Riva Tukachinsky. *Parasocial Romantic Relationships: Falling in Love with Media Figures*. Lanham, MD: Rowman & Littlefield, 2021.

Fortnite (@FortniteGame). 'Thank You to Everyone Who Attended and Created Content around the Travis Scott Event! Over 27.7 Million Unique Players in-Game Participated Live 45.8 Million Times across the Five Events'. Twitter. 27 April 2020. https://twitter.com/FortniteGame/status/1254817584676929537.

Fouché, Rayvon. 'Say It Loud, I'm Black and I'm Proud: African Americans, American Artifactual Culture, and Black Vernacular Technological Creativity'. *American Quarterly* 58, no. 3 (2006): 639–661.

Freitas, Joana. '"Only People with Good Imaginations Usually Listen to This Kind of Music": On the Convergence of Musical Tags, Video Games and YouTube in the Epic Genre'. In *Remediating Sound: Repeatable Culture, YouTube and Music*, edited by Holly Rogers, Joana Freitas, and João Francisco Porfírio, 145–164. London: Bloomsbury Academic, 2023.

Freitas, Joana, and João Francisco Porfírio. 'Foreword'. In *YouTube and Music: Online Culture and Everyday Life*, edited by Holly Rogers, Joana Freitas, and João Francisco Porfírio, xiii–xxi. London: Bloomsbury Academic, 2023.

Frisby, Cynthia M., and Jennifer Stevens Aubrey. 'Race and Genre in the Use of Sexual Objectification in Female Artists' Music Videos'. *Howard Journal of Communications* 23, no. 1 (January 2012): 66–87. https://doi.org/10.1080/10646175.2012.641880.

Frith, S. *Performing Rites: On the Value of Popular Music*. Oxford: Oxford University Press, 1996.

Frost, Friederike. 'Breaking the Limits? Exploring the Breaking Scene in Havana, Cuba and Belonging in a Global (Imagined) Breaking Community'. *Global Hip Hop Studies* 2, no. 1 (June 2021): 15–36. https://doi.org/10.1386/ghhs_00031_1.

Fuchs, Christian. *Media, Communication and Society*. Vol. 3, *Digital Capitalism*. London and New York: Routledge, 2022.

Fuchs, Christian. *Media, Communication and Society*. Vol. 6, *Digital Democracy and the Digital Public Sphere*. London and New York: Routledge, 2023.

Fuchs, Christian. *Internet and Society: Social Theory in the Information Age*. New York: Routledge, 2008.

Future of Life Institute. *Policymaking in the Pause: What Can Policymakers Do Now to Combat Risks from Advanced AI Systems?* Future of Life Institute, 2023. https://futureoflife.org/wp-content/uploads/2023/04/FLI_Policymaking_In_The_Pause.pdf.

Galuszka, Patryk. 'Music Aggregators and Intermediation of the Digital Music Market'. *International Journal of Communication* 9 (January 2015): 20.

Gamble, Steven. 'Breaking down the Breakdown in Twenty-First-Century Metal'. *Metal Music Studies* 5, no. 3 (September 2019): 337–354. https://doi.org/10.1386/mms.5.3.337_1.

Gamble, Steven. *How Music Empowers: Listening to Modern Rap and Metal*. London: Routledge, 2021.

Gamble, Steven. 'Towards an Ethical Model of Data Analysis for Research on Online Music Cultures'. In *Music and the Internet: Methodological, Epistemological, and Ethical*

Orientations, edited by Christopher Haworth, Danielle S. Sofer, and Edward Katrak Spencer. Abingdon: Routledge, forthcoming.

Gamble, Steven, and Lewis Kennedy. 'From the Studio to the Bedroom (and Back Again?): Distributed Production Practices in 21st Century Metal Music'. In *The Routledge Handbook to Metal Music Composition: Evolution of Structure, Expression, and Production*, edited by Lori Burns and Ciro Scotto. New York: Routledge, forthcoming.

Gamble, Steven, and Raquel Campos Valverde. 'Editorial'. In 'It's Where You're @: Hip Hop and the Internet'. Special issue, *Global Hip Hop Studies* 2 (November 2021): 153–158. https://doi.org/10.1386/ghhs_00041_2.

Gamble, Steven, and Justin Williams. 'Analyzing Hip-Hop Hacktivism and Automobility in Injury Reserve's (2019) "Jailbreak the Tesla" (Feat. Aminé)'. In *Analyzing Recorded Music*, edited by William Moylan, Lori Burns, and Mike Alleyne, 38–55. London and New York: Routledge, 2022.

Garofalo, Reebee. 'Crossing Over: From Black Rhythm & Blues to White Rock "n" Roll'. In *R&B (Rhythm & Business): The Political Economy of Black Music*, edited by Norman Kelley, 112–137. New York: Akashic Books, 2002.

Garofalo, Reebee. 'Industrializing African American Popular Music'. In *Issues in African American Music*, edited by Portia K. Maultsby and Mellonee Burnim, 90–109. New York: Routledge, 2016.

Garrelts, Nate, ed. *Understanding Minecraft: Essays on Play, Community and Possibilities*. Jefferson, NC: McFarland & Company, Inc., 2014.

Garvey, Meaghan. 'Migos: Culture II'. *Pitchfork*, 30 January 2018. https://pitchfork.com/reviews/albums/migos-culture-ii/.

Garza, Joyhanna Yoo. '"Where All My Bad Girls at?": Cosmopolitan Femininity through Racialised Appropriations in K-Pop'. *Gender and Language* 15, no. 1 (March 2021): 11–41. https://doi.org/10.1558/genl.18565.

Gates, Jr., Henry L. *The Signifying Monkey: A Theory of African-American Literary Criticism*. New York: Oxford University Press, 1988.

Gaunt, Kyra D. 'The Disclosure, Disconnect, and Digital Sexploitation of Tween Girls' Aspirational YouTube Videos'. *Journal of Black Sexuality and Relationships* 5, no. 1 (2018): 91–132. https://doi.org/10.1353/bsr.2018.0017.

Gaunt, Kyra. *The Games Black Girls Play: Learning the Ropes from Double-Dutch to Hip-Hop*. New York: New York University Press, 2006.

GEMN Chill Out & Lofi Music. 'Chill Lo-Fi Hip-Hop Beats FREE | Lofi Hip Hop Chillhop Music Mix | GEMN'. YouTube video, 2 May 2020. https://web.archive.org/web/20201220171946/https://www.youtube.com/watch?v=qvUWA45GOMg.

Gerken, Tom. 'Minecraft Becomes First Video Game to Hit 300m Sales'. *BBC News*, 16 October 2023. https://www.bbc.com/news/technology-67105983.

Gill, Rosalind. 'Post-Postfeminism?: New Feminist Visibilities in Postfeminist Times'. *Feminist Media Studies* 16, no. 4 (2016): 610–630. https://doi.org/10.1080/14680777.2016.1193293.

Gilroy, Paul. 'Sounds Authentic: Black Music, Ethnicity, and the Challenge of a "Changing" Same'. *Black Music Research Journal* 11, no. 2 (1991): 111–136. https://doi.org/10.2307/779262.

Gittens, Rhana A. 'Atlanta's Pink Trap House: Reimagining the Black Public Sphere as an Aesthetic Community'. *Theory & Event* 24, no. 2 (April 2021): 434–455. https://doi.org/10.1353/tae.2021.0021.

Glenhaber, Mehitabel. 'Tumblr's Xkit Guy, Social Media Modding, and Code as Resistance'. *Transformative Works and Cultures* 36 (September 2021). https://doi.org/10.3983/twc.2021.2021.

Glitsos, Laura. 'Vaporwave, or Music Optimised for Abandoned Malls'. *Popular Music* 37, no. 1 (January 2018): 100–118. https://doi.org/10.1017/S0261143017000599.

200 References

Gonzalez, Oscar. 'Fortnite: Travis Scott Astronomical Experience Seen by Almost 28 Million Players'. *CNET*, 27 April 2020. https://www.cnet.com/news/fortnite-travis-scott-astronomical-experience-seen-by-almost-28-million-players/.

Gordon, Cindy. 'ChatGPT Is the Fastest Growing App in the History of Web Applications'. *Forbes*, 2 February 2023. https://www.forbes.com/sites/cindygordon/2023/02/02/chatgpt-is-the-fastest-growing-ap-in-the-history-of-web-applications/.

Gorski, Paul C, and Noura Erakat. 'Racism, Whiteness, and Burnout in Antiracism Movements: How White Racial Justice Activists Elevate Burnout in Racial Justice Activists of Color in the United States'. *Ethnicities* 19, no. 5 (October 2019): 784–808. https://doi.org/10.1177/1468796819833871.

Gosa, Travis L. 'The Fifth Element: Knowledge'. In *The Cambridge Companion to Hip-Hop*, edited by Justin A. Williams, 56–70. Cambridge: Cambridge University Press, 2015.

Griffiths, Dai. 'From Lyric to Anti-Lyric: Analyzing the Words in Pop Song'. In *Analyzing Popular Music*, edited by A. F. Moore, 39–59. Cambridge: Cambridge University Press, 2003.

Hagen, Anja N, and Marika Lüders. 'Social Streaming? Navigating Music as Personal and Social'. *Convergence: The International Journal of Research into New Media Technologies* 23, no. 6 (December 2017): 643–659. https://doi.org/10.1177/1354856516673298.

Hagen, Anja Nylund. 'The Playlist Experience: Personal Playlists in Music Streaming Services'. *Popular Music and Society* 38, no. 5 (October 2015): 625–645. https://doi.org/10.1080/03007766.2015.1021174.

Hagen, Sal, and Daniël de Zeeuw. 'Based and Confused: Tracing the Political Connotations of a Memetic Phrase across the Web'. *Big Data & Society* 10, no. 1 (2023). https://journals.sagepub.com/doi/10.1177/20539517231163175.

Hall, Perry A. 'African-American Music: Dynamics of Appropriation and Innovation'. In *Borrowed Power: Essays on Cultural Appropriation*, edited by Bruce H. Ziff and Pratima V. Rao, 31–51. New Brunswick, NJ: Rutgers University Press, 1997.

Halliday, Aria S. 'Envisioning Black Girl Futures'. *Departures in Critical Qualitative Research* 6, no. 3 (September 2017): 65–77. https://doi.org/10.1525/dcqr.2017.6.3.65.

Halliday, Aria S. 'Twerk Sumn!: Theorizing Black Girl Epistemology in the Body'. *Cultural Studies* 34, no. 6 (November 2020): 874–891. https://doi.org/10.1080/09502386.2020.1714688.

Halliday, Aria S., and Nadia E. Brown. 'The Power of Black Girl Magic Anthems: Nicki Minaj, Beyoncé, and "Feeling Myself" as Political Empowerment'. *Souls* 20, no. 2 (April 2018): 222–238. https://doi.org/10.1080/10999949.2018.1520067.

Handler, Rachel. 'We Asked a Gyno About "WAP"'. *Vulture*, August 2020. https://www.vulture.com/2020/08/we-asked-a-gyno-about-wap.html.

Hansen, Kai Arne. *Pop Masculinities: The Politics of Gender in Twenty-First Century Popular Music*. Oxford and New York: Oxford University Press, 2021.

Hansen, Kai Arne. '(Re)Reading Pop Personae: A Transmedial Approach to Studying the Multiple Construction of Artist Identities'. *Twentieth-Century Music* 16, no. 3 (October 2019): 501–529. https://doi.org/10.1017/S1478572219000276.

Hansen, Kai Arne, and Steven Gamble. 'Saturation Season: Inclusivity, Queerness, and Aesthetics in the New Media Practices of Brockhampton'. *Popular Music and Society* 45, no. 1 (2021): 13–30. https://doi.org/10.1080/03007766.2021.1984019.

Harkins, Paul, and Nick Prior. '(Dis)Locating Democratization: Music Technologies in Practice'. *Popular Music and Society* 45, no. 1 (January 2022): 84–103. https://doi.org/10.1080/03007766.2021.1984023.

Harlow, Summer, and Anna Benbrook. 'How #Blacklivesmatter: Exploring the Role of Hip-Hop Celebrities in Constructing Racial Identity on Black Twitter'. *Information, Communication & Society* 22, no. 3 (October 2017): 352–368. https://doi.org/10.1080/1369118X.2017.1386705.

Harper, Adam. 'How Internet Music Is Frying Your Brain'. *Popular Music* 36, no. 1 (January 2017): 86–97. https://doi.org/10.1017/S0261143016000696.

References   201

Harper, Adam. 'Lo-Fi Aesthetics in Popular Music Discourse'. DPhil diss., University of Oxford, 2014.

Harper, Adam. 'What Is Lo-Fi? A Genealogy of a Recurrent Term in the Aesthetics of Popular Music Production'. Research Seminar, City University London, December 2020.

Harper, Paula. 'BEYONCÉ: Viral Techniques and the Visual Album'. *Popular Music and Society* 42, no. 1 (January 2019): 61–81. https://doi.org/10.1080/03007766.2019.1555895.

Harper, Paula Clare. 'Unmute This: Circulation, Sociality, and Sound in Viral Media'. PhD diss., Columbia University, 2019. https://doi.org/10.7916/d8-6rte-j311.

Harris, Malcolm. *Kids These Days: Human Capital and the Making of Millennials.* New York: Little, Brown and Company, 2017.

Harrison, Anthony Kwame. '"Cheaper than a CD, Plus We Really Mean It": Bay Area Underground Hip Hop Tapes as Subcultural Artefacts'. *Popular Music* 25, no. 2 (May 2006): 283–301. https://doi.org/10.1017/S0261143006000833.

Harrison, Anthony Kwame, and Craig E. Arthur. 'Hip-Hop Ethos'. *Humanities* 8, no. 1 (March 2019): 39. https://doi.org/10.3390/h8010039.

Harvey, Mark. 'Politics and Power in the Record Industry: The Beatles, the Beach Boys, and the Album as Art Form'. *Musicology Australia* 38, no. 2 (July 2016): 153–171. https://doi.org/10.1080/08145857.2016.1244876.

Haupt, Adam. *Stealing Empire: P2P, Intellectual Property and Hip-Hop Subversion.* Cape Town: HSRC Press, 2008.

Haworth, Christopher, and Georgina Born. 'Music and Intermediality after the Internet: Aesthetics, Materialities and Social Forms'. In *Music and Digital Media: A Planetary Anthropology,* edited by Georgina Born, 378–438. London: UCL Press, 2022.

Hawtin, Steve. 'MusicID Revenue: Music Charts 2000–2021, Data Version 0.3.0063'. *MusicID,* July 2021. http://revenue.musicid.academicrightspress.com/about.htm.

Haynes, Jo, and Lee Marshall. 'Reluctant Entrepreneurs: Musicians and Entrepreneurship in the "New" Music Industry'. *The British Journal of Sociology* 69, no. 2 (2018): 459–482. https://doi.org/10.1111/1468-4446.12286.

Henderson, April K. 'Dancing Between Islands: Hip Hop and the Samoan Diaspora'. In *The Vinyl Ain't Final: Hip Hop and the Globalization of Black Popular Culture,* edited by Dipannita Basu and Sidney J. Lemelle, 180–199. London: Pluto Press, 2006.

Hernandez, Patricia. 'Fortnite's Travis Scott Event Is Incredible, but It Feels Wrong to Call It a Concert'. *Polygon* (blog), 24 April 2020. https://www.polygon.com/2020/4/24/21234398/fortnite-travis-scott-concert-schedule-epic-games-astronomical.

Hesmondhalgh, David. 'Have Digital Communication Technologies Democratized the Media Industries?' In *Media and Society,* edited by James Curran and David Hesmondhalgh, 6th ed., 101–120. New York: Bloomsbury Academic, 2019.

Hesmondhalgh, David. 'Is Music Streaming Bad for Musicians? Problems of Evidence and Argument'. *New Media & Society* 23, no. 12 (December 2021): 3593–3615. https://doi.org/10.1177/1461444820953541.

Hesmondhalgh, David. 'Streaming's Effects on Music Culture: Old Anxieties and New Simplifications'. *Cultural Sociology* 16, no. 1 (June 2021). https://doi.org/10.1177/17499755211019974.

Hesmondhalgh, David, Ellis Jones, and Andreas Rauh. 'SoundCloud and Bandcamp as Alternative Music Platforms'. *Social Media + Society* 5, no. 4 (October 2019). https://doi.org/10.1177/2056305119883429.

Hesmondhalgh, David, Raquel Campos Valverde, D. Bondy Valdovinos Kaye, and Zhongwei Li. *The Impact of Algorithmically Driven Recommendation Systems on Music Consumption and Production: A Literature Review.* Department for Digital, Culture, Media & Sport, 2023. https://www.gov.uk/government/publications/research-into-the-impact-of-stream

202 References

ing-services-algorithms-on-music-consumption/the-impact-of-algorithmically-driven-rec ommendation-systems-on-music-consumption-and-production-a-literature-review.

Hess, Mickey, ed. *Icons of Hip Hop: An Encyclopedia of the Movement, Music, and Culture.* Westport, CT and London: Greenwood Press, 2007.

Hessler, Jennifer. 'Peoplemeter Technologies and the Biometric Turn in Audience Measurement'. *Television & New Media* 22, no. 4 (May 2021): 400–419. https://doi.org/10.1177/1527476419879415.

Higgins, Christina. 'From Da Bomb to Bomba: Global Hip Hop Nation Language in Tanzania'. In *Global Linguistic Flows: Hip Hop Cultures, Youth Identities, and the Politics of Language,* edited by H. Samy Alim, Awad Ibrahim, and Alastair Pennycook, 95–112. New York and London: Routledge, 2009.

Hill, Marc Lamont. *Beats, Rhymes, and Classroom Life: Hip-Hop Pedagogy and the Politics of Identity.* New York: Teachers College Press, 2009.

Hill Collins, Patricia. *Black Feminist Thought: Knowledge, Consciousness, and the Politics of Empowerment.* 2nd ed. New York: Routledge, 2000.

Hill Collins, Patricia. *Black Sexual Politics: African Americans, Gender, and the New Racism.* New York and London: Routledge, 2004.

Hintz, Elizabeth Ann, and Jonathan Troy Baker. 'A Performative Face Theory Analysis of Online Facework by the Formerly Involuntarily Celibate'. *International Journal of Communication* 15, no. 2021 (2021): 3047–3066.

Hochberg, Bill. 'Chill Hop, Jazz Hop, LoFi, Whatever You Call It, It's Catching on with Gen-Z'. *Forbes,* 8 September 2020. https://www.forbes.com/sites/williamhochberg/2020/09/08/chill-hop-jazz-hop-lofi-whatever-you-call-it-its-driving-gen-z-mild/.

Hodgson, Thomas. 'Spotify and the Democratisation of Music'. *Popular Music* 40, no. 1 (February 2021): 1–17. https://doi.org/10.1017/S0261143021000064.

Homework Radio. 'Lo-Fi for Ghosts (Only)'. YouTube video, 6 August 2019. https://www.yout ube.com/watch?v=2GjPQfdQfMY.

Homework Radio. 'Lo-Fi for Witches Only) [Lofi / Calm / Chill Beats]'. YouTube video, 27 March 2020. https://www.youtube.com/watch?v=4Hg1Kudd_x4.

hooks, bell. *Ain't I A Woman: Black Women and Feminism.* Boston, MA: South End Press, 1982.

hooks, bell. *Black Looks: Race and Representation.* New York: Routledge, 2015.

Hosking, Taylor. 'Rappers Like Megan Thee Stallion Are Writing a New Feminist Canon'. *Vice* (blog), 20 August 2019. https://www.vice.com/en/article/evjnnk/rappers-like-megan-thee-stall ion-are-writing-a-new-feminist-canon-cardi-b-city-girls-princess-nokia-rico-nasty-saweetie.

Hu, Cherie. 'The Economics of 24/7 Lo-Fi Hip-Hop YouTube Livestreams'. *Hot Pod News,* January 2020. https://web.archive.org/web/20230531122716/https://hotpodnews.com/the-economics-of-24-7-lo-fi-hip-hop-youtube-livestreams/.

Hu, Krystal. 'ChatGPT's Explosive Growth Shows First Decline in Traffic since Launch'. *Reuters,* 5 July 2023. https://www.reuters.com/technology/booming-traffic-openais-chatgpt-posts-first-ever-monthly-dip-june-similarweb-2023-07-05/.

Hunter, Margaret, and Alhelí Cuenca. 'Nicki Minaj and the Changing Politics of Hip-Hop: Real Blackness, Real Bodies, Real Feminism?' *Feminist Formations* 29, no. 2 (2017): 26–46. https://doi.org/10.1353/ff.2017.0015.

Hwang, Tzung-Jeng, Kiran Rabheru, Carmelle Peisah, William Reichman, and Manabu Ikeda. 'Loneliness and Social Isolation during the COVID-19 Pandemic'. *International Psychogeriatrics* 32, no. 10 (October 2020): 1217–1220. https://doi.org/10.1017/S1041610220000988.

Hyman, Dan. 'Little Simz Has Flow, But Don't Call Her a "Female Rapper"'. *Shondaland,* 1 March 2019. https://www.shondaland.com/inspire/a26541464/little-simz-grey-area-dont-call-her-female-rapper/.

Iandoli, Kathy. *God Save the Queens: The Essential History of Women in Hip-Hop.* New York: HarperCollins, 2019.

References 203

IFPI. *Global Music Report 2023: State of the Industry.* IFPI, 2023.

IFPI. *Music Listening 2019: A Look at How Recorded Music Is Enjoyed around the World.* IFPI, 2019. https://www.ifpi.org/wp-content/uploads/2020/07/Music-Listening-2019-1.pdf.

Ihaza, Jeff. 'A New Podcast Shows How the Rise of Blogs Changed Hip-Hop Forever'. *Rolling Stone* (blog), 19 April 2023. https://www.rollingstone.com/music/music-features/blog-era-rap-podcast-interview-1234719834/.

Industry Blackout (@industryblackout). 'Have You Lost Your FN Minds? @capitolrecords'. Instagram post, 23 August 2022. https://www.instagram.com/p/ChnJGi2potN/.

Internet Rap Fans Go Outside For First Time. YouTube video, 18 June 2023. https://www.yout ube.com/watch?v=jiFcOcXsmRc.

Jackson, Lauren Michele. *White Negroes: When Cornrows Were in Vogue . . . and Other Thoughts on Cultural Appropriation.* Boston, MA: Beacon Press, 2019.

James, Malcolm. *Sonic Intimacy: Reggae Sound Systems, Jungle Pirate Radio and Grime YouTube Music Videos.* New York: Bloomsbury Publishing Inc, 2021.

James, Robin. 'Chill Pop & Feminine Excess: A "Sign of the Times"'. *It's Her Factory* (blog), 5 May 2017. https://www.its-her-factory.com/2017/05/chill-pop-feminine-excess-a-sign-of-the-times/.

James, Robin. 'Toned Down for What? How "Chill" Turned Toxic'. *The Guardian*, 2 July 2018. http://www.theguardian.com/music/2018/jul/02/toned-down-for-what-how-chill-tur ned-toxic.

Jamieson, Lynn. 'Personal Relationships, Intimacy and the Self in a Mediated and Global Digital Age'. In *Digital Sociology: Critical Perspectives*, edited by Kate Orton-Johnson and Nick Prior, 13–33. London: Palgrave Macmillan, 2013.

jamila, shani. 'Can I Get a Witness? Testimony from a Hip-Hop Feminist'. In *Colonize This!: Young Women of Color on Today's Feminism*, edited by Daisy Hernández and Bushra Rehman, 382–394. New York: Seal Press, 2002.

Jane, Emma. *Misogyny Online: A Short (and Brutish) History.* London: SAGE, 2017.

Janssens, Jenny, and Lotte Spreeuwenberg. 'The Moral Implications of Cancel Culture'. *Ethical Perspectives* 29, no. 1 (2022): 89–114.

Jeffries, Michael P. *Thug Life: Race, Gender, and The Meaning of Hip-Hop.* Chicago: University of Chicago Press, 2011.

Jenkins, Henry, Sam Ford, and Joshua Green. *Spreadable Media: Creating Value and Meaning in a Networked Culture.* New York: New York University Press, 2013.

Jennings, Kyesha. 'City Girls, Hot Girls and the Re-Imagining of Black Women in Hip Hop and Digital Spaces'. *Global Hip Hop Studies* 1, no. 1 (June 2020): 47–70. https://doi.org/10.1386/ghhs_00004_1.

John, Nicholas A. *The Age of Sharing.* Cambridge and Malden, MA: Polity, 2017.

Johnson, Adeerya. 'Dirty South Feminism: The Girlies Got Somethin' to Say Too! Southern Hip-Hop Women, Fighting Respectability, Talking Mess, and Twerking Up the Dirty South'. *Religions* 12, no. 11 (November 2021): 1030. https://doi.org/10.3390/rel12111030.

Johnson, Adeerya. 'Hella Bars: The Cultural Inclusion of Black Women's Rap in Insecure'. *Open Cultural Studies* 6, no. 1 (January 2022): 76–87. https://doi.org/10.1515/culture-2022-0144.

Johnson, Amber. 'Confessions of a Video Vixen: My Autocritography of Sexuality, Desire, and Memory'. *Text and Performance Quarterly* 34, no. 2 (April 2014): 182–200. https://doi.org/10.1080/10462937.2013.879991.

Johnson, E. Patrick. *Appropriating Blackness: Performance and the Politics of Authenticity.* Durham, NC: Duke University Press, 2003.

Johnson, Imani Kai. 'Black Culture without Black People: Hip-Hop Dance beyond Appropriation Discourse'. In *Are You Entertained?*, edited by Simone C. Drake and Dwan K. Henderson, 191–206. Durham, NC: Duke University Press, 2020.

204 References

Johnson, Imani Kai. 'Critical Hiphopography in Streetdance Communities (Hard Love Part 2)'. In *The Oxford Handbook of Hip Hop Dance Studies*, edited by Mary Fogarty and Imani Kai Johnson, 217–240. New York: Oxford University Press, 2022.

Johnson, Tom. 'Chance the Rapper, Spotify, and Musical Categorization in the 2010s'. *American Music* 38, no. 2 (2020): 176–196.

Jonsson, Terese. 'The Narrative Reproduction of White Feminist Racism'. *Feminist Review* 113, no. 1 (July 2016): 50–67. https://doi.org/10.1057/fr.2016.2.

Juice WRLD Breaks Down Tupac & Eminem's Influence on His Music. YouTube video, 23 July 2018. https://www.youtube.com/watch?v=fsaolirWIKQ.

Kajikawa, Loren. 'Hip Hop History in the Age of Colorblindness'. *Journal of Music History Pedagogy* 5, no. 1 (2014): 117–123.

Kajikawa, Loren. *Sounding Race in Rap Songs*. Berkeley and Los Angeles: University of California Press, 2015.

Katz, Mark. *Build: The Power of Hip Hop Diplomacy in a Divided World*. Oxford and New York: Oxford University Press, 2019.

Katz, Mark. *Groove Music: The Art and Culture of the Hip-Hop DJ*. New York: Oxford University Press, 2012.

Kaye, D. Bondy Valdovinos, Jing Zeng, and Patrik Wikstrom. *TikTok: Creativity and Culture in Short Video*. Cambridge: Wiley, 2022.

Kearse, Stephen. 'Playboi Carti, Rap Iconoclast'. *The Nation*, 2 March 2021. https://www.thenation.com/article/culture/playboi-carti-whole-lotta-red/.

Kehrer, L. 'Genius (Formerly Rap Genius). Genius Media Group, Inc. Genius.Com'. *Journal of the Society for American Music* 10, no. 4 (November 2016): 518–520.

Keidl, Philipp Dominik, Laliv Melamed, Vinzenz Hediger, and Antonio Somaini. *Pandemic Media: Preliminary Notes Toward an Inventory*. Lüneburg: meson press, 2020.

Kennedy, Lewis. '"I Grew up in Streatham": Rap, Reactions, Comments, and Capital on YouTube'. *London Calling*, 19 May 2020. https://london-calling-iaspm2020.com/lewis-kennedy-independent-scholar-uk/.

Kennedy, Helen. *Post, Mine, Repeat: Social Media Data Mining Becomes Ordinary*. London: Palgrave Macmillan, 2016.

Keyes, C. L. *Rap Music and Street Consciousness*. Urbana and Chicago: University of Illinois Press, 2002.

Khan, Alicia. 'What Ethnicity Is Ariana Grande? Whichever One Makes Her the Most Money'. *Femestella* (blog), 7 December 2021. https://www.femestella.com/ariana-grande-ethnicity-cultural-appropriation-blackfishing-asianfishing/.

Khong, Diana. '"Yeah, I'm in My Bag, but I'm in His Too": How Scamming Aesthetics Utilized by Black Women Rappers Undermine Existing Institutions of Gender'. *Journal of Hip Hop Studies* 7, no. 1 (July 2020). https://scholarscompass.vcu.edu/jhhs/vol7/iss1/8.

Killeen, Gerry F., and Samson S. Kiware. 'Why Lockdown? Why National Unity? Why Global Solidarity? Simplified Arithmetic Tools for Decision-Makers, Health Professionals, Journalists and the General Public to Explore Containment Options for the 2019 Novel Coronavirus'. *Infectious Disease Modelling* 5 (January 2020): 442–458. https://doi.org/10.1016/j.idm.2020.06.006.

Kim, Yeran. 'Globalization of the Privatized Self-Image: The Reaction Video and Its Attention Economy on YouTube'. In *Routledge Handbook of New Media in Asia*, edited by Larissa Hjorth and Olivia Khoo, 333–342. London and New York: Routledge, 2016.

Kirby, Justin, and Paul Marsden, eds. *Connected Marketing: The Viral, Buzz and Word of Mouth Revolution*. Oxford and Burlington, MA: Butterworth-Heinemann, 2007.

Kitwana, B. *Why White Kids Love Hip Hop: Wankstas, Wiggers, Wannabes, and the New Reality of Race in America*. New York: Basic Civitas Books, 2005.

References 205

Know Your Meme. 'Aesthetic'. *Know Your Meme*, January 2015. Accessed 12 August 2021. https://knowyourmeme.com/memes/aesthetic.

Know Your Meme. 'Drakeposting: Image Gallery'. *Know Your Meme*. Accessed 6 July 2023. https://knowyourmeme.com/memes/drakeposting/photos.

Koh, Jing Xuan, and Tau Ming Liew. 'How Loneliness Is Talked about in Social Media during COVID-19 Pandemic: Text Mining of 4,492 Twitter Feeds'. *Journal of Psychiatric Research* 145 (2022): 317–324. https://doi.org/10.1016/j.jpsychires.2020.11.015.

Kreling, Rebekka, Adrian Meier, and Leonard Reinecke. 'Feeling Authentic on Social Media: Subjective Authenticity Across Instagram Stories and Posts'. *Social Media + Society* 8, no. 1 (January 2022). https://doi.org/10.1177/20563051221086235.

Krogh, Mads. 'Rampant Abstraction as a Strategy of Singularization: Genre on Spotify'. *Cultural Sociology*, online preprint (May 2023). https://doi.org/10.1177/17499755231172828.

Kuo, Rachel. 'Animating Feminist Anger: Economies of Race and Gender in Reaction GIFs'. In *Gender Hate Online: Understanding the New Anti-Feminism*, edited by Debbie Ging and Eugenia Siapera, 173–193. Cham: Springer International Publishing, 2019.

Kurtin, Kate Szer, Nina F. O'Brien, Deya Roy, and Linda Dam. 'Parasocial Relationships with Musicians'. *The Journal of Social Media in Society* 8, no. 2 (December 2019): 30–50.

Lacey, Alex de. 'Live and Direct? Censorship and Racialised Public Morality in Grime and Drill Music'. *Popular Music* 41, no. 4 (December 2022): 495–510. https://doi.org/10.1017/S02611 43022000551.

Lambert, Molly. 'Nicki Minaj Reclaims the Twerk in the "Anaconda" Music Video'. *Grantland* (blog), 20 August 2014. https://grantland.com/hollywood-prospectus/nicki-minaj-recla ims-the-twerk-in-the-anaconda-music-video/.

Lang, Ruth. 'Livestreaming Sets'. *Frame*, no. 138 (January 2021): 102–109. https://ualresearc honline.arts.ac.uk/id/eprint/16386/1/F138_NewTypology.pdf.

Lavengood, Megan. 'Timbre, Genre, and Polystylism in Sonic the Hedgehog 3'. In *On Popular Music and Its Unruly Entanglements*, edited by Nick Braae and Kai Arne Hansen, 209–234. Cham: Springer International Publishing, 2019.

LaVoulle, Crystal, and Tisha Lewis Ellison. 'The Bad Bitch Barbie Craze and Beyoncé: African American Women's Bodies as Commodities in Hip-Hop Culture, Images, and Media'. *Taboo: The Journal of Culture and Education* 16, no. 2 (April 2018): 65–84. https://doi.org/ 10.31390/taboo.16.2.07.

Lewis, Hilary. 'Nicki Minaj's "Anaconda" Video Breaks Vevo Record'. *Billboard* (blog), 22 August 2014. https://www.billboard.com/music/music-news/nicki-minaj-anaconda-vevo-record-6229110/.

Li, Pengfei, Jianyi Yang, Mohammad A. Islam, and Shaolei Ren. 'Making AI Less "Thirsty": Uncovering and Addressing the Secret Water Footprint of AI Models'. arXiv preprint, arXiv.2304.03271 (2023). https://doi.org/10.48550/arXiv.2304.03271.

Light, Alan. 'About a Salary or Reality? Rap's Recurrent Conflict'. In *That's The Joint!: The Hip-Hop Studies Reader*, edited by Murray Forman and Mark Anthony Neal, 173–183. New York and London: Routledge, 2004.

Lil Dicky. 'Hannibal Interlude', featuring Hannibal Buress'. *Professional Rapper*, track 7. Commission Records, 2015. https://open.spotify.com/track/3xlxccjYAuqTFORC3sh OSm?si=a0bc6932289b48d6.

Lil Uzi Vert Talks Hating Interviews, Starting To Rap For Attention + Drops Bars!. YouTube video, 24 February 2016. https://www.youtube.com/watch?v=Bq6IsU390E0.

Lindh, Maria. 'As a Utility: Metaphors of Information Technologies'. *Human IT: Journal for Information Technology Studies as a Human Science* 13, no. 2 (May 2016): 47–80.

Lingel, Jessa. *Digital Countercultures and the Struggle for Community*. Cambridge, MA: MIT Press, 2017.

206   References

Lofi Girl. '1 A.M Study Session 📖 [Lofi Hip Hop/Chill Beats]'. YouTube video, 8 December 2019. https://www.youtube.com/watch?v=lTRiuFIWV54.

Lofi Girl. 'Lofi Hip Hop Radio - Beats to Relax/Study To'. YouTube livestream, 22 February 2020. https://www.youtube.com/watch?v=5qap5aO4i9A.

Loignon, Guillaume, and Philippe Messier. 'Vaporwave Pedagogy: Multimodal Learning with an Internet Music Microgenre'. *Liminalities* 16, no. 3 (2020): 1–23.

Lomborg, Stine. 'The Internet in My Pocket'. In *The Ubiquitous Internet: User and Industry Perspectives*, edited by Anja Bechmann and Stine Lomborg, 35–53. New York and London: Routledge, 2015.

Lorenz, Taylor. *Extremely Online: The Untold Story of Fame, Influence, and Power on the Internet*. New York: Simon & Schuster, 2023.

Love, Bettina L. 'A Ratchet Lens: Black Queer Youth, Agency, Hip Hop, and the Black Ratchet Imagination'. *Educational Researcher* 46, no. 9 (December 2017): 539–547. https://doi.org/10.3102/0013189X17736520.

Love, Bettina L. 'Complex Personhood of Hip Hop & the Sensibilities of the Culture That Fosters Knowledge of Self & Self-Determination'. *Equity & Excellence in Education* 49, no. 4 (October 2016): 414–427. https://doi.org/10.1080/10665684.2016.1227223.

Love, Bettina L. *Hip Hop's Li'l Sistas Speak; Negotiating Hip Hop Identities and Politics in the New South*. New edition. New York: Peter Lang, 2012.

Lovink, Geert. *Social Media Abyss: Critical Internet Cultures and the Force of Negation*. Cambridge and Malden, MA: Polity Press, 2016.

Lu, Jessica H., and Catherine Knight Steele. '"Joy Is Resistance": Cross-Platform Resilience and (Re)Invention of Black Oral Culture Online'. *Information, Communication & Society* 22, no. 6 (May 2019): 823–837. https://doi.org/10.1080/1369118X.2019.1575449.

Lund, Emily M., and Kara B. Ayers. 'Ever-Changing but Always Constant: "Waves" of Disability Discrimination during the COVID-19 Pandemic in the United States'. *Disability and Health Journal* 15, no. 4 (October 2022). https://doi.org/10.1016/j.dhjo.2022.101374.

MacDonald, Michael B. *Remix and Life Hack in Hip Hop: Towards a Critical Pedagogy of Music*. Rotterdam: Sense Publishers, 2016.

Mack, Kristen, and John Palfrey. 'Capitalizing Black and White: Grammatical Justice and Equity'. *MacArthur Foundation*, 26 August 2020. https://www.macfound.org/press/perspectives/capitalizing-black-and-white-grammatical-justice-and-equity.

Madden, Sidney. '21 Savage Super Villain Memes Take Over the Internet'. *XXL Magazine*, 10 March 2017. https://www.xxlmag.com/21-savage-meme-taking-over-internet/.

Mahdawi, Arwa. 'The WAP Uproar Shows Conservatives Are Fine with Female Sexuality – as Long as Men Control It'. *The Guardian*, 15 August 2020. https://www.theguardian.com/commentisfree/2020/aug/15/cardi-b-megan-thee-stalion-wap-conservatives-female-sexuality.

Makuch, die. 'Fortnite Sets New Records with Travis Scott Event'. *GameSpot* (blog), 26 April 2020. https://www.gamespot.com/articles/fortnite-sets-new-records-with-travis-scott-event/1100-6476508/.

Mamo, Heran. 'Ben Shapiro Reads the Censored Lyrics to Cardi B and Megan Thee Stallion's "WAP" & He Can't Handle It'. *Billboard* (blog), 10 August 2020. https://www.billboard.com/music/rb-hip-hop/ben-shapiro-reads-censored-wap-lyrics-cardi-b-megan-thee-stallion-9432034/.

Mandiberg, Michael. 'Introduction'. In *The Social Media Reader*, edited by Michael Mandiberg, 1–10. New York: New York University Press, 2012.

Marshall, Lee. '"Let's Keep Music Special. F—Spotify": On-Demand Streaming and the Controversy over Artist Royalties'. *Creative Industries Journal* 8, no. 2 (July 2015): 177–189. https://doi.org/10.1080/17510694.2015.1096618.

References   207

Marshall, Wayne. 'Social Dance in the Age of (Anti-)Social Media'. *Journal of Popular Music Studies* 31, no. 4 (December 2019): 3–15. https://doi.org/10.1525/jpms.2019.31.4.3.

Marwick, Alice E., and danah boyd. 'I Tweet Honestly, I Tweet Passionately: Twitter Users, Context Collapse, and the Imagined Audience'. *New Media & Society* 13, no. 1 (February 2011): 114–133. https://doi.org/10.1177/1461444810365313.

Massanari, Adrienne. '#Gamergate and The Fappening: How Reddit's Algorithm, Governance, and Culture Support Toxic Technocultures'. *New Media & Society* 19, no. 3 (March 2017): 329–346. https://doi.org/10.1177/1461444815608807.

Massanari, Adrienne L., and Shira Chess. 'Attack of the 50-Foot Social Justice Warrior: The Discursive Construction of SJW Memes as the Monstrous Feminine'. *Feminist Media Studies* 18, no. 4 (July 2018): 525–542. https://doi.org/10.1080/14680777.2018.1447333.

McCarthy, Jesse. 'Notes on Trap'. *N+1*, no. 32 (2018). https://www.nplusonemag.com/issue-32/essays/notes-on-trap/.

McCarthy, Lauren. 'Inside #WitchTok, Where Witches of TikTok Go Viral'. *Nylon*, 6 July 2020. https://www.nylon.com/life/witchtok-witches-of-tiktok.

McCracken, Allison, Alexander Cho, Louisa Stein, and Indira N. Hoch, eds. *A Tumblr Book: Platform and Cultures*. Ann Arbor: University of Michigan Press, 2020.

McEachern, Montinique Denice. 'Respect My Ratchet: The Liberatory Consciousness of Ratchetness'. *Departures in Critical Qualitative Research* 6, no. 3 (September 2017): 78–89. https://doi.org/10.1525/dcqr.2017.6.3.78.

McGuire, M.R. 'Crime, Control and the Ambiguous Gifts of Digital Technology'. In *The SAGE Handbook of Digital Society*, edited by William Housley, Adam Edwards, Roser Beneito-Montagut, and Richard Fitzgerald, 35–54. London: SAGE, 2023.

McKelvey, Fenwick, Scott DeJong, and Janna Frenzel. 'Memes, Scenes and #ELXN2019s: How Partisans Make Memes during Elections'. *New Media & Society* 25, no. 7 (July 2023): 1626–1647. https://doi.org/10.1177/14614448211020690.

McNally, James. 'Hip-Hop into the Video Age: New York Teenhood, Malcolm McLaren and the British Eye'. *Visual Culture in Britain* 20, no. 1 (January 2019): 40–63. https://doi.org/10.1080/14714787.2019.1574602.

Medina, Eden. *Cybernetic Revolutionaries: Technology and Politics in Allende's Chile*. Cambridge, MA: MIT Press, 2011.

Meehan, Orla. 'A Profile of the Battle Royale Player and How They Compare to Other Gamers'. *Newzoo* (blog), 22 May 2018. https://newzoo.com/insights/articles/a-profile-of-the-battle-royale-player-and-how-they-compare-to-other-gamers/.

Megan Thee Stallion - Thot Shit Song Breakdown. YouTube video, 13 July 2021. https://www.youtube.com/watch?v=aJSkbTC-4I8.

Meier, Leslie M. *Popular Music as Promotion: Music and Branding in the Digital Age*. Cambridge and Malden, MA: Polity, 2016.

Meier, Leslie M. 'Popular Music, Streaming, and Promotional Media: Enduring and Emerging Industrial Logics'. In *Making Media: Production, Practices, and Professions*, edited by Mark Deuze and Mirjam Prenger, 321–334. Amsterdam University Press, 2019.

Meikle, Graham. *Social Media: Communication, Sharing and Visibility*. New York and London: Routledge, 2016.

Miles, Corey. 'Black Rural Feminist Trap: Stylized and Gendered Performativity in Trap Music'. *Journal of Hip Hop Studies* 7, no. 1 (July 2020): 44–70. https://scholarscompass.vcu.edu/jhhs/vol7/iss1/6.

Miller, Kiri. *Playable Bodies: Dance Games and Intimate Media*. New York: Oxford University Press, 2017.

Miller-Young, Mireille. *A Taste for Brown Sugar: Black Women in Pornography*. Durham, NC: Duke University Press, 2014.

208 References

Milligan, Ian. *History in the Age of Abundance?: How the Web Is Transforming Historical Research*. Montreal: McGill-Queen's University Press, 2019.

Milner, Ryan M. *The World Made Meme: Public Conversations and Participatory Media*. Cambridge, MA: MIT Press, 2016.

Miniwatts Marketing Group. 'Internet World Users by Language: Top 10 Languages'. *Internet World Stats*, 31 March 2020. https://www.internetworldstats.com/stats7.htm.

Miniwatts Marketing Group. 'World Internet Users Statistics and 2023 World Population Stats'. *Internet World Stats*, 21 March 2023. https://www.internetworldstats.com/stats.htm.

Monahan, Sean. 'Video Games Have Replaced Music as the Most Important Aspect of Youth Culture'. *The Guardian*, 11 January 2021. http://www.theguardian.com/commentisfree/2021/jan/11/video-games-music-youth-culture.

Monteyne, Kimberly. *Hip Hop on Film: Performance Culture, Urban Space, and Genre Transformation in the 1980s*. Jackson: University Press of Mississippi, 2013.

Moore, Allan F. 'Categorical Conventions in Music Discourse: Style and Genre'. *Music & Letters* 82, no. 3 (January 2001): 432–442.

Morgan, Joan. *When Chickenheads Come Home to Roost: A Hip Hop Feminist Breaks It Down*. New York: Simon & Schuster, 1999.

Morgan, M. H. *The Real Hiphop: Battling for Knowledge, Power, and Respect in the LA Underground*. Durham, NC: Duke University Press, 2009.

Morris, David Z. 'Cars with the Boom: Identity and Territory in American Postwar Automobile Sound'. *Technology and Culture* 55, no. 2 (2014): 326–353.

Morris, Jeremy Wade. 'Hearing the Past: The Sonic Web from MIDI to Music Streaming'. In *The SAGE Handbook of Web History*, by Niels Brügger and Ian Milligan, 491–504. London: SAGE Publications Ltd, 2019.

Morris, Jeremy Wade. 'Music Platforms and the Optimization of Culture'. *Social Media + Society* 6, no. 3 (July 2020). https://doi.org/10.1177/2056305120940690.

Morris, Jeremy Wade. *Selling Digital Music, Formatting Culture*. Berkeley and Los Angeles: University of California Press, 2015.

Morris, Jeremy Wade, and Devon Powers. 'Control, Curation and Musical Experience in Streaming Music Services'. *Creative Industries Journal* 8, no. 2 (July 2015): 106–122. https://doi.org/10.1080/17510694.2015.1090222.

Morris, Jeremy Wade, Robert Prey, and David B. Nieborg. 'Engineering Culture: Logics of Optimization in Music, Games, and Apps'. *Review of Communication* 21, no. 2 (April 2021): 161–175. https://doi.org/10.1080/15358593.2021.1934522.

Morrison, Matthew D. 'Blacksound'. In *The Oxford Handbook of Western Music and Philosophy*, edited by Tomás McAuley, Nanette Nielsen, Jerrold Levinson, and Ariana Phillips-Hutton, 554–577. New York: Oxford University Press, 2021.

Mosley, Della V., Roberto L. Abreu, Ashley Ruderman, and Candice Crowell. 'Hashtags and Hip-Hop: Exploring the Online Performances of Hip-Hop Identified Youth Using Instagram'. *Feminist Media Studies* 17, no. 2 (March 2017): 135–152. https://doi.org/10.1080/14680777.2016.1197293.

Nagle, Angela. *Kill All Normies: Online Culture Wars from 4Chan and Tumblr to Trump and the Alt-Right*. Winchester: Zero Books, 2017.

Nahon, Karine, and Jeff Hemsley. *Going Viral*. Cambridge: Polity, 2013.

Nakamura, Lisa. '"I WILL DO EVERYthing That Am Asked": Scambaiting, Digital Show-Space, and the Racial Violence of Social Media'. *Journal of Visual Culture* 13, no. 3 (December 2014): 257–274. https://doi.org/10.1177/1470412914546845.

Nakamura, Lisa. 'The Unwanted Labour of Social Media: Women of Colour Call Out Culture As Venture Community Management'. *New Formations* 86, no. 86 (December 2015): 106–112. https://doi.org/10.3898/NEWF.86.06.2015.

References 209

Neal, Adam Scott. 'Lo-Fi Today'. *Organised Sound* 27, no. 1 (April 2022): 32–40. https://doi.org/10.1017/S1355771822000188.

Neal, M. A. *What the Music Said: Black Popular Music and Black Public Culture.* New York and London: Routledge, 1999.

Neal, Mark Anthony. 'Up From Hustling: Power, Plantations, and the Hip-hop Mogul'. *Socialism and Democracy* 18, no. 2 (July 2004): 157–182. https://doi.org/10.1080/08854300408428405.

Negus, Keith. 'From Creator to Data: The Post-Record Music Industry and the Digital Conglomerates'. *Media, Culture & Society* 41, no. 3 (April 2019): 367–384. https://doi.org/10.1177/0163443718799395.

NEOTIC. 'N O S T A L G I C'. YouTube video, 14 February 2017. https://www.youtube.com/watch?v=hQyzEyIf7P0.

Newman, Kelley. 'The End of an Era: The Death of the Album and Its Unintended Effects'. *Gnovis Blog* (blog), 28 February 2014. https://gnovisjournal.georgetown.edu/the-gnovis-blog/the-end-of-an-era-the-death-of-the-album-and-its-unintended-effects/.

Ng, Jason. 'Connecting Asia-Pacific Hip-Hop: The Role of the Cross-Cultural Intermediary'. PhD diss., Monash University, 2019. https://doi.org/10.26180/5d4805f266eeb.

Ng, Jason, and Steven Gamble. 'Hip-Hop Producer-Hosts, Beat Battles, and Online Music Production Communities on Twitch'. *First Monday* 27, no. 6 (June 2022). https://doi.org/10.5210/fm.v27i6.12338.

Nieborg, David B, and Thomas Poell. 'The Platformization of Cultural Production: Theorizing the Contingent Cultural Commodity'. *New Media & Society* 20, no. 11 (November 2018): 4275–4292. https://doi.org/10.1177/1461444818769694.

Nielsen Music. *2014 Nielsen Music Report.* The Nielsen Company, 2014. https://www.nielsen.com/wp-content/uploads/sites/3/2019/04/nielsen-2014-year-end-music-report-us-1.pdf.

Nielsen Music. *Mid-Year Report U.S. 2017.* The Nielsen Company, 2017. https://training.nielsen.com/wp-content/uploads/sites/3/2019/04/music-us-mid-year-report-2017.pdf.

Nielsen Music. *Mid-Year Report U.S. 2018.* The Nielsen Company, 2018. https://www.nielsen.com/wp-content/uploads/sites/3/2019/04/us-midyear-music-report-2018.pdf.

Nilsson, Bo, and Kerstin Edin. ' "It Has Seldom Been So Difficult to Try to Dress Up a Sound Experience in Words": Technology and the Rhetoric of Sound and Music Reproduction in Hi-Fi Magazines'. *PULS: Musik- Och Dansetnologisk Tidskrift* 7 (2022): 121–140.

Noble, Denise, and Lisa Amanda Palmer. 'Misogynoir: Anti-Blackness, Patriarchy, and Refusing the Wrongness of Black Women'. In *The Palgrave Handbook of Critical Race and Gender*, edited by Shirley Anne Tate and Encarnación Gutiérrez Rodríguez, 227–245. Cham: Springer International Publishing, 2022.

Noble, Safiya Umoja. *Algorithms of Oppression: How Search Engines Reinforce Racism.* New York: New York University Press, 2018.

Nooney, Laine, and Laura Portwood-Stacer. 'One Does Not Simply: An Introduction to the Special Issue on Internet Memes'. *Journal of Visual Culture* 13, no. 3 (December 2014): 248–252. https://doi.org/10.1177/1470412914551351.

Nowak, Raphaël, and Andrew Whelan. ' "Vaporwave Is (Not) a Critique of Capitalism": Genre Work in An Online Music Scene'. *Open Cultural Studies* 2, no. 1 (November 2018): 451–462. https://doi.org/10.1515/culture-2018-0041.

Nyabola, Nanjala. *Digital Democracy, Analogue Politics: How the Internet Era Is Transforming Politics in Kenya.* London: Bloomsbury, 2018.

Office for National Statistics. *Internet Users, UK: 2020*, 6 April 2021. https://www.ons.gov.uk/businessindustryandtrade/itandinternetindustry/bulletins/internetusers/2020.

Oh, Chuyun. 'Performing Post-Racial Asianness: K-Pop's Appropriation of Hip-Hop Culture'. *Congress on Research in Dance Conference Proceedings* 2014 (October 2014): 121–125. https://doi.org/10.1017/cor.2014.17.

210 References

Ohlendorf, Kristopher R. K. '"No Friends in the Industry": The Dominance of Tech Companies on Digital Music'. In *Virtual Identities and Digital Culture*, edited by Victoria Kannen and Aaron Langille, 231–239. New York: Routledge, 2023.

Ohriner, Mitchell. *Flow: The Rhythmic Voice in Rap Music*. New York: Oxford University Press, 2019.

Olla, Akin. 'Are AI-Powered "Virtual Rappers" Just a Strange New Form of Blackface?' *The Guardian*, 1 September 2022. https://www.theguardian.com/commentisfree/2022/sep/01/are-ai-powered-virtual-rappers-just-a-strange-new-form-of-blackface.

Oloman, Jordan. 'How Fortnite and Minecraft Virtual Concerts Kept Music Alive While We Weren't Allowed Outside'. *Edge Magazine*, 7 July 2021. https://www.gamesradar.com/how-fortnite-and-minecraft-virtual-concerts-kept-music-alive-while-we-werent-allowed-outside/.

Open Pit LAVAPALOOZA Day 1. YouTube video, 22 April 2022. https://www.youtube.com/watch?v=rmV-TGRLBa4.

Open Space: Tekashi69 (6ix9ine). YouTube. 11 May 2017. https://www.youtube.com/watch?v=12f9v1_9K_E.

Orejuela, Fernando. 'Introduction'. In *Black Lives Matter and Music: Protest, Intervention, Reflection*, edited by Stephanie Shonekan and Fernando Orejuela, 1–13. Bloomington: Indiana University Press, 2018.

Orosz, Jeremy. '"Straight Outta Nashville": Allusions to Hip Hop in Contemporary Country Music'. *Popular Music and Society* 44, no. 1 (January 2021): 49–59. https://doi.org/10.1080/03007766.2019.1652794.

Ortner, Christina, Philip Sinner, and Tanja Jadin. 'The History of Online Social Media'. In *The SAGE Handbook of Web History*, edited by Niels Brügger and Ian Milligan, 372–384. London: SAGE, 2019.

Osborn, Brad. 'Resistance Gazes in Recent Music Videos'. *Music and the Moving Image* 14, no. 2 (2021): 51–67.

Painter, Nell Irvin. 'Why "White" Should Be Capitalized, Too'. *Washington Post*, 22 July 2020. https://www.washingtonpost.com/opinions/2020/07/22/why-white-should-be-capitalized/.

Palgi, Yuval, Amit Shrira, Lia Ring, Ehud Bodner, Sharon Avidor, Yoav Bergman, Sara Cohen-Fridel, Shoshi Keisari, and Yaakov Hoffman. 'The Loneliness Pandemic: Loneliness and Other Concomitants of Depression, Anxiety and Their Comorbidity during the COVID-19 Outbreak'. *Journal of Affective Disorders* 275 (October 2020): 109–111. https://doi.org/10.1016/j.jad.2020.06.036.

Paor-Evans, Adam de. 'Mumble Rap: Cultural Laziness or a True Reflection of Contemporary Times?' *The Conversation*, 18 October 2017. http://theconversation.com/mumble-rap-cultural-laziness-or-a-true-reflection-of-contemporary-times-85550.

Paor-Evans, Adam de. *Provincial Headz: British Hip Hop and Critical Regionalism*. South Yorkshire: Equinox, 2020.

Pareles, Jon. 'Low-Fi Rockers'. *The New York Times*, 11 April 1993.

Parham, Marisa. 'Sample | Signal | Strobe: Haunting, Social Media, and Black Digitality'. In *Debates in the Digital Humanities 2019*, edited by Matthew K. Gold and Lauren F. Klein, 101–122. Minneapolis and London: University of Minnesota Press, 2019.

Pariser, Eli. *The Filter Bubble: How the New Personalized Web Is Changing What We Read and How We Think*. New York: Penguin, 2011.

Pearce, Sheldon. 'A Guide to Meme Rappers'. *Pitchfork*, 9 October 2017. https://pitchfork.com/thepitch/a-guide-to-meme-rappers/.

Pelly, Liz. 'Streambait Pop'. *The Baffler*, 11 December 2018. https://thebaffler.com/latest/streambait-pop-pelly.

References 211

Penney, Joel. *Pop Culture, Politics, and the News: Entertainment Journalism in the Polarized Media Landscape*. New York: Oxford University Press, 2022.

Peoples, Whitney A. '"Under Construction": Identifying Foundations of Hip-Hop Feminism and Exploring Bridges between Black Second-Wave and Hip-Hop Feminisms'. *Meridians* 8, no. 1 (September 2008): 19–52. https://doi.org/10.2979/MER.2008.8.1.19.

Perkins, W. E. 'The Rap Attack: An Introduction'. In *Droppin' Science: Critical Essays on Rap Music and Hip Hop Culture*, edited by W. E. Perkins, 1–45. Philadelphia, PA: Temple University Press, 1996.

Perry, Adam L. 'From the McCarthy Era to "Gangsta Rap": The Rhetoric of Popular Music and Moral Panic in America'. PhD diss., Pennsylvania State University, 2013. https://etda.librar ies.psu.edu/catalog/19541.

Perry, I. *Prophets of the Hood: Politics and Poetics in Hip Hop*. Durham, NC: Duke University Press, 2004.

Peters, Benjamin. *How Not to Network a Nation: The Uneasy History of the Soviet Internet*. Cambridge, MA: MIT Press, 2016.

Petridis, Alexis. 'Ariana Grande: Positions Review – All-Night Romps but No Climax'. *The Guardian*, 30 October 2020. https://www.theguardian.com/music/2020/oct/30/ariana-gra nde-positions-review.

Petridis, Alexis. 'Kendrick Lamar: Mr Morale & the Big Steppers Review'. *The Guardian*, 13 May 2022. https://www.theguardian.com/music/2022/may/13/kendrick-lamar-mr-morale-the-big-steppers-review.

Petrusich, Amanda. 'Against Chill: Apathetic Music to Make Spreadsheets To'. *The New Yorker*, 10 April 2019. https://www.newyorker.com/culture/cultural-comment/against-chill-apathe tic-music-to-make-spreadsheets-to.

Pettis, Ben T. 'Know Your Meme and the Homogenization of Web History'. *Internet Histories* 6, no. 3 (August 2021): 1–17. https://doi.org/10.1080/24701475.2021.1968657.

Pew Research Center. 'Internet/Broadband Fact Sheet'. *Pew Research Center: Internet, Science & Tech* (blog), 31 January 2024. https://www.pewresearch.org/internet/fact-sheet/internet-broadband/.

Pfaffenberger, Bryan. '"If I Want It, It's OK": Usenet and the (Outer) Limits of Free Speech'. *The Information Society* 12, no. 4 (November 1996): 365–386. https://doi.org/10.1080/01972249 6129350.

Phelan, Sean. 'Neoliberalism, the Far Right, and the Disparaging of "Social Justice Warriors"'. *Communication, Culture and Critique* 12, no. 4 (December 2019): 455–475. https://doi.org/ 10.1093/ccc/tcz040.

Phillips, Matthew T. 'Soundcloud Rap and Alien Creativity: Transforming Rap and Popular Music through Mumble Rap'. *Journal of Popular Music Studies* 33, no. 3 (September 2021): 125–144. https://doi.org/10.1525/jpms.2021.33.3.125.

Phillips, Whitney. *This Is Why We Can't Have Nice Things: Mapping the Relationship Between Online Trolling and Mainstream Culture*. Cambridge, MA: MIT Press, 2015.

Phillips, Whitney, and Ryan M. Milner. *The Ambivalent Internet: Mischief, Oddity, and Antagonism Online*. Cambridge and Malden, MA: Polity Press, 2017.

Phillips, Yoh. 'Migos "Culture II" 1 Listen Album Review'. *DJBooth*, 12 February 2018. https:// djbooth.net/features/2018-01-26-migos-culture-ii-album-review.

Pierre, Alphonse. 'How Rap's SoundCloud Generation Changed the Music Business Forever'. *Pitchfork*, 27 February 2019. https://pitchfork.com/thepitch/how-raps-soundcloud-generat ion-changed-the-music-business-forever/.

Poell, Thomas, David B. Nieborg, and Brooke Erin Duffy. *Platforms and Cultural Production*. Medford: Polity, 2021.

Polfuß, Jonas. 'Hip-Hop: A Marketplace Icon'. *Consumption Markets & Culture* 25, no. 3 (May 2022): 272–286. https://doi.org/10.1080/10253866.2021.1990050.

212 References

Porfírio, João Francisco. 'YouTube and the Sonification of Domestic Everyday Life'. In *YouTube and Music: Online Culture and Everyday Life*, edited by Holly Rogers, Joana Freitas, and João Francisco Porfírio, 209–229. London: Bloomsbury Academic, 2023.

Pough, Gwendolyn D. *Check It While I Wreck It: Black Womanhood, Hip-Hop Culture, and the Public Sphere*. Lebanon, NH: Northeastern University Press, 2004.

Pough, Gwendolyn D., Elaine Richardson, Aisha Durham, and Rachel Raimist, eds. *Home Girls Makes Some Noise: Hip Hop Feminism Anthology*. Mira Loma, CA: Parker Publishing, 2007.

Powell, Catherine. 'Can You Hear Me? Speech and Power in the Global Digital Town Square'. *Proceedings of the ASIL Annual Meeting* 116 (January 2022): 117–119. https://doi.org/10.1017/amp.2023.5.

Press-Reynolds, Kieran. '6 Years Ago a College Student Made a Fan Video for His Favorite Rapper. Now He's at the Forefront of the YouTube Hip-Hop Scene, Helping Boost Artists into Internet Stardom'. *Insider*, 7 May 2022. https://www.insider.com/dotcomnirvan-interview-youtube-yeat-trippie-redd-plugg-soundcloud-rap-2022-5.

Prey, Robert. 'Locating Power in Platformization: Music Streaming Playlists and Curatorial Power'. *Social Media + Society* 6, no. 2 (April 2020). https://doi.org/10.1177/2056305120933291.

Prey, Robert, Marc Esteve Del Valle, and Leslie Zwerwer. 'Platform Pop: Disentangling Spotify's Intermediary Role in the Music Industry'. *Information, Communication & Society* 25, no. 1 (January 2022): 74–92. https://doi.org/10.1080/1369118X.2020.1761859.

Prior, Nick. *Popular Music, Digital Technology and Society*. Los Angeles: SAGE, 2018.

Prior, Nick. 'The Rise of the New Amateurs: Popular Music, Digital Technology and the Fate of Cultural Production'. In *Handbook of Cultural Sociology*, edited by J. R. Hall, L. Grindstaff, and M. Lo, 398–407. London and New York: Routledge, 2010.

Qiu, Jack Linchuan, and Hongzhe Wang. 'Radical Praxis of Computing in the PRC: Forgotten Stories from the Maoist to Post-Mao Era'. *Internet Histories* 5, nos. 3–4 (October 2021): 214–229. https://doi.org/10.1080/24701475.2021.1949817.

Quinn, Ben. 'David Starkey Claims "the Whites Have Become Black"'. *The Guardian*, 13 August 2011. https://www.theguardian.com/uk/2011/aug/13/david-starkey-claims-whites-black.

Rabaka, Reiland. *Hip Hop's Amnesia: From Blues and the Black Women's Club Movement to Rap and the Hip Hop Movement*. Lanham, MD: Lexington Books, 2012.

Rabaka, Reiland. *Hip Hop's Inheritance: From the Harlem Renaissance to the Hip Hop Feminist Movement*. Lanham, MD: Lexington Books, 2011.

Railton, Diane, and Paul Watson. *Music Video and the Politics of Representation*. Edinburgh: Edinburgh University Press, 2011.

Rainie, Lee, and Barry Wellman. *Networked: The New Social Operating System*. Cambridge, MA: MIT Press, 2012.

Raley, Rita. 'Dataveillance and Countervailance'. In *'Raw Data' Is an Oxymoron*, edited by Lisa Gitelman, 121–145. Cambridge, MA: MIT Press, 2013.

Rambarran, Shara. *Virtual Music: Sound, Music, and Image in the Digital Era*. New York: Bloomsbury Academic, 2021.

Rantakallio, Inka. 'New Spirituality, Atheism, and Authenticity in Finnish Underground Rap'. PhD diss., University of Turku, 2019.

Rap Roundtable - SNL. YouTube video, 13 December 2020. https://www.youtube.com/watch?v=3sxRAeh8f7w.

r/blackfishing. 'Blackfishing'. Reddit, 2023. https://www.reddit.com/r/blackfishing/.

Rebollo-Gil, Guillermo, and Amanda Moras. 'Black Women and Black Men in Hip Hop Music: Misogyny, Violence and the Negotiation of (White-Owned) Space'. *The Journal of Popular Culture* 45, no. 1 (February 2012): 118–132. https://doi.org/10.1111/j.1540-5931.2011.00898.x.

References 213

Redmond, Shana L. 'This Safer Space: Janelle Monáe's "Cold War"'. *Journal of Popular Music Studies* 23, no. 4 (2011): 393–411. https://doi.org/10.1111/j.1533-1598.2011.01303.x.

Reed, Davy. 'Migos: "Culture II" Review'. *Crack Magazine* (blog), 31 January 2018. https://crackmagazine.net/article/album-reviews/migos-culture-ii/.

Reiss, Jonathan. *Look at Me!: The XXXTENTACION Story*. New York: Hachette Books, 2020.

Rendell, James. 'Staying in, Rocking out: Online Live Music Portal Shows during the Coronavirus Pandemic'. *Convergence* 27, no. 4 (December 2020). https://doi.org/10.1177/1354856520976451.

Rettberg, Jill Walker. *Blogging*. 2nd ed. Cambridge: Polity, 2014.

Reuter, Anders. 'Who Let the DAWs Out? The Digital in a New Generation of the Digital Audio Workstation'. *Popular Music and Society* 45, no. 2 (March 2022): 113–128. https://doi.org/10.1080/03007766.2021.1972701.

Richardson, Elaine, and Alice Ragland. '#StayWoke: The Language and Literacies of the #BlackLivesMatter Movement'. *Community Literacy Journal* 12, no. 2 (2018): 27–56.

Ritschel, Chelsea. 'Ariana Grande Apologises on Instagram for Misunderstanding Comment about "7 Rings"'. *The Independent*, 22 January 2019. https://www.independent.co.uk/arts-entertainment/music/ariana-grande-apology-ig-7-rings-instagram-weave-a8740651.html.

R L I F E. 'H o m e w o r k & S t u d y（ミュージック）'. YouTube video, 5 April 2018. https://www.youtube.com/watch?v=mUeZDu9rBH8.

Robards, Brady, Sian Lincoln, Benjamin C. Pinkard, and Jane Harris. 'Remembering Through Facebook: Mediated Memory and Intimate Digital Traces'. In *Digital Intimate Publics and Social Media*, edited by Amy Shields Dobson, Brady Robards, and Nicholas Carah, 75–91. Cham: Springer International Publishing, 2018.

Roblox. 'Explosive Lil Nas X Concert Paves the Way for Bold New Roblox Experiences'. *Roblox Blog*, December 2020. https://web.archive.org/web/20220826072739/https://blog.roblox.com/2020/12/explosive-lil-nas-x-concert-paves-way-bold-new-roblox-experiences/.

Rogers, Holly. '"Welcome to Your World": YouTube and the Reconfiguration of Music's Gatekeepers'. In *YouTube and Music: Online Culture and Everyday Life*, edited by Holly Rogers, Joana Freitas, and João Francisco Porfírio, 1–38. London: Bloomsbury Academic, 2023.

Rojek, Chris. *Presumed Intimacy: Para-Social Relationships in Media, Society and Celebrity Culture*. Cambridge: Polity, 2016.

Rollefson, J. Griffith. 'Hip Hop Interpellation: Rethinking Autochthony and Appropriation in Irish Rap'. In *Made in Ireland: Studies in Popular Music*, edited by Áine Mangaoang, John O'Flynn, and Lonán Ó Briain, 224–236. New York and London: Routledge, 2021.

Rollefson, J. Griffith. '"Yo Nací Caminando": Community-Engaged Scholarship, Hip Hop as Postcolonial Studies, and Rico Pabón's Knowledge of Self'. *Journal of World Popular Music* 5, no. 2 (2018): 169–192.

Roper, Adam. 'The Internet Can't Stop LOLing at This 21 Savage Supervillain Meme'. *Gossip On This* (blog), 11 March 2017. https://gossiponthis.com/2017/03/10/21-savage-supervillain-meme-viral-twitter-facebook-social-media-internet-espn-highly-questionable/.

Rose, Tricia. *Black Noise: Rap Music and Black Culture in Contemporary America*. Middletown: CT: Wesleyan University Press, 1994.

Rose, Tricia. *The Hip-Hop Wars: What We Talk about When We Talk about Hip-Hop and Why It Matters*. New York: Basic Books, 2008.

Rosen, Jody. 'The 2013 VMAs Were Dominated by Miley's Minstrel Show'. *Vulture*, 26 August 2013. https://www.vulture.com/2013/08/jody-rosen-miley-cyrus-vmas-minstrel.html.

Ryder, Jamie. 'Chopped and Screwed? How Studio Leaks Are Creating a New DIY Rap Music'. *The Guardian*, 3 January 2020. https://www.theguardian.com/music/2020/jan/03/chopped-and-screwed-how-studio-leaks-are-creating-a-new-diy-rap-music.

214 References

Saint-Louis, Hervé. 'Understanding Cancel Culture: Normative and Unequal Sanctioning'. *First Monday* 26, no. 7 (June 2021). https://doi.org/10.5210/fm.v26i7.10891.

Samuels, David. 'The Rap on Rap: The "Black Music" That Isn't Either'. In *That's the Joint!*, edited by Murray Forman and Mark Anthony Neal, 184–192. New York and London: Routledge, 2004.

Sanden, Paul. *Liveness in Modern Music: Musicians, Technology, and the Perception of Performance*. New York: Routledge, 2012.

Sanneh, Kelefa. *Major Labels: A History of Popular Music in Seven Genres*. New York: Penguin Press, 2021.

Sarkar, Debarun. '"Azadi's Political until You're Pressing Play": Capitalist Realism, Hip-Hop, and Platform Affordances'. *Convergence* 29, no. 6 (2023). https://doi.org/10.1177/135485 65231174598.

Scanlon, Eileen. 'Digital Scholarship: Identity, Interdisciplinarity, and Openness'. *Frontiers in Digital Humanities* 5 (2018). https://www.frontiersin.org/articles/10.3389/fdigh.2018.00003.

Scheinberg, Missy. 'Understanding SoundCloud Rap'. *LNWY*, October 2017. https://web.arch ive.org/web/20191224225722/https://lnwy.co/read/meet-soundcloud-rap-hip-hops-most-punk-moment-yet/.

Schloss, J. G. *Making Beats: The Art of Sample-Based Hip-Hop*. Middletown, CT: Wesleyan University Press, 2004.

Schmieding, Leonard. 'Taking Beat Street to the Streets in Socialist East Germany'. In *Participating Audiences, Imagined Public Spheres: The Cultural Work of Contemporary American(Ized) Narratives*, edited by Sebastian M. Herrmann, Carolin Alice Hofmann, Katja Kanzler, and Frank Usbeck, 43–61. Leipziger Universitätsverlag, 2012.

Schneider, Christopher J. 'Music Videos on YouTube: Exploring Participatory Culture on Social Media'. In *Symbolic Interactionist Takes on Music*, edited by Christopher J. Schneider and Joseph A. Kotarba, 97–117. Bingley: Emerald, 2016.

Scholz, Trebor. 'Infrastructure: Its Transformations and Effect on Digital Activism'. In *Digital Activism Decoded: The New Mechanics of Change*, edited by Mary Joyce, 17–32. New York: International Debate Education Association, 2010.

Schoon, Alette. '"Makhanda Forever?": Pirate Internet Infrastructure and the Ephemeral Hip Hop Archive in South Africa'. In 'It's Where You're @: Hip Hop and the Internet'. Special issue, *Global Hip Hop Studies* 2 (November 2021): 199–218. https://doi.org/10.1386/ ghhs_00044_1.

Schwartz, Alexandra. 'Portrait of a Friendship in the Face of Cancer'. *The New Yorker*, 31 May 2016. http://www.newyorker.com/culture/photo-booth/portrait-of-a-friendship-in-the-face-of-cancer.

Sciullo, Nick J. *Communicating Hip-Hop: How Hip-Hop Culture Shapes Popular Culture*. Santa Barbara, CA: Praeger, 2018.

Shange, Savannah. 'A King Named Nicki: Strategic Queerness and the Black Femmecee'. *Women & Performance: A Journal of Feminist Theory* 24, no. 1 (January 2014): 29–45. https:// doi.org/10.1080/0740770X.2014.901602.

Sharpley-Whiting, T. D. *Pimps Up, Ho's Down: Hip Hop's Hold on Young Black Women*. New York and London: New York University Press, 2007.

Shifman, Limor. *Memes in Digital Culture*. Cambridge, MA: MIT Press, 2014.

Shrine Studio Ltd. AppAdvice, 'Hiatus', January 2021. https://appadvice.com/app/hiatus/149 3350890.

Shuker, Roy. *Popular Music: The Key Concepts*. 4th ed. London and New York: Routledge, 2017.

Sibilla, Gianni. 'Alive & Digital: La performance musicale dal vivo alla piattaforma'. *Fata Morgana Web*, 13 June 2020. https://www.fatamorganaweb.it/la-piattaformizzazione-della-performance-musicale-dal-vivo/.

References 215

Simmons, Nadirah. 'What Are We to Do with the Term "Female Rapper?"' *The Gumbo*, 8 August 2019. https://thegumbo.net/blog/2019/8/8/what-are-we-to-do-with-the-term-female-rapper.

Singh, Manisha. 'GTA V Becomes Second Best-Selling Game of All Time, Claims Publisher'. *The Times of India*, 8 February 2022. https://timesofindia.indiatimes.com/gadgets-news/gta-v-becomes-second-best-selling-game-of-all-time-claims-take-two/articleshow/89434429.cms.

Sirois, André. *Hip Hop DJs and the Evolution of Technology: Cultural Exchange, Innovation, and Democratization*. New York: Peter Lang, 2016.

Sisario, Ben. '"7 Rings" Is a Hit for Ariana Grande, and a Knockout for Rodgers and Hammerstein'. *The New York Times*, 19 March 2019. https://www.nytimes.com/2019/03/19/business/media/ariana-grande-7-rings-rodgers-hammerstein.html.

Smalls, Shanté Paradigm. *Hip Hop Heresies: Queer Aesthetics in New York City*. New York: New York University Press, 2022.

Smialek, E. T. 'Genre and Expression in Extreme Metal Music, ca. 1990–2015'. PhD diss., McGill University, 2015.

Smith, Aaron. 'Technology Trends Among People of Color'. *Pew Research Center: Internet, Science & Tech* (blog), 17 September 2010. https://www.pewresearch.org/internet/2010/09/17/technology-trends-among-people-of-color/.

Smith, Ben J., and Michelle H. Lim. 'How the COVID-19 Pandemic Is Focusing Attention on Loneliness and Social Isolation'. *Public Health Research & Practice* 30, no. 2 (June 2020). https://doi.org/10.17061/phrp3022008.

Smith, S. *Hip-Hop Turntablism, Creativity and Collaboration*. Surrey: Ashgate, 2013.

Smith, Suzanne E. *Dancing in the Street: Motown and the Cultural Politics of Detroit*. Cambridge, MA: Harvard University Press, 2001.

Smith, Will. 'chill beats to quarantine to'. YouTube video, 20 March 2020. https://www.youtube.com/watch?v=rA56B4JyTgI.

Sobande, Francesca. *The Digital Lives of Black Women in Britain*. Cham: Palgrave Macmillan, 2020.

Söderman, Johan. 'The Formation of "Hip-Hop Academicus" – How American Scholars Talk about the Academisation of Hip-Hop'. *British Journal of Music Education* 30, no. 3 (November 2013): 369–381. https://doi.org/10.1017/S0265051713000089.

Sony Corporation. *Supplemental Information of the Consolidated Financial Results for the First Quarter Ended June 30, 2016*. Sony Corporation, 2016. https://www.sony.com/en/SonyInfo/IR/library/presen/er/16q1_supplement.pdf.

Southern, Eileen. 'The Georgia Minstrels: The Early Years'. In *Inside the Minstrel Mask: Readings in Nineteenth-Century Blackface Minstrelsy*, edited by Annemarie Bean, James Vernon Hatch, and Brooks McNamara, 163–178. Hanover, CT: Wesleyan University Press, 1996.

Spencer, Edward Katrak. 'When Donald Trump Dropped the Bass: The Weaponization of Dubstep in Internet Trolling Strategies, 2011–2016'. *Twentieth-Century Music* forthcoming.

Spigel, Lynn. *Make Room for TV: Television and the Family Ideal in Postwar America*. Chicago: University of Chicago Press, 1992.

Spracklen, Karl. *Digital Leisure, the Internet and Popular Culture*. London: Palgrave Macmillan, 2015.

Srnicek, Nick. *Platform Capitalism*. Cambridge: Polity Press, 2017.

St. Jean, Yanick, and Joe R. Feagin. *Double Burden: Black Women and Everyday Racism*. Armonk, NY: M.E. Sharpe, 1998.

Stallings, L. H. 'Hip Hop and the Black Ratchet Imagination'. *Palimpsest: A Journal on Women, Gender, and the Black International* 2, no. 2 (2013): 135–139. https://doi.org/10.1353/pal.2013.0026.

216 References

Stanfill, Mel. 'Can't Nobody Tell Me Nothin': "Old Town Road", Resisting Musical Norms, and Queer Remix Reproduction'. *Popular Music* 40, nos. 3–4 (December 2021): 347–363. https://doi.org/10.1017/S026114302100057X.

Steele, Catherine Knight. 'Black Bloggers and Their Varied Publics: The Everyday Politics of Black Discourse Online'. *Television & New Media* 19, no. 2 (February 2018): 112–127. https://doi.org/10.1177/1527476417709535.

Steele, Catherine Knight. *Digital Black Feminism*. New York: New York University Press, 2021.

Steele, Catherine Knight. 'The Digital Barbershop: Blogs and Online Oral Culture Within the African American Community'. *Social Media + Society* 2, no. 4 (October 2016). https://doi.org/10.1177/2056305116683205.

Steele, Catherine, and Jessica Lu. 'Defying Death: Black Joy as Resistance Online'. In *A Networked Self and Birth, Life, Death*, edited by Zizi Papacharissi, 143–159. New York: Routledge, 2018.

Stephens, Dionne P., and April L. Few. 'Hip Hop Honey or Video Ho: African American Preadolescents' Understanding of Female Sexual Scripts in Hip Hop Culture'. *Sexuality & Culture* 11, no. 4 (December 2007): 48–69. https://doi.org/10.1007/s12119-007-9012-8.

Sterne, Jonathan. *MP3: The Meaning of a Format*. Durham, NC: Duke University Press, 2012.

Stoever, Jennifer Lynn. 'Crate Digging Begins at Home: Black and Latinx Women Collecting and Selecting Records in the 1960s and 1970s Bronx'. In *The Oxford Handbook of Hip Hop Music*, edited by Justin D. Burton and Jason Lee Oakes. Oxford: Oxford University Press, 2018.

Stoever, Jennifer Lynn. *The Sonic Color Line: Race and the Cultural Politics of Listening*. New York: New York University Press, 2016.

Stuart, Forrest. *Ballad of the Bullet*. Princeton, NJ: Princeton University Press, 2020.

Sweeney, Latanya. 'Only You, Your Doctor, and Many Others May Know'. *Technology Science*, 28 September 2015. https://techscience.org/a/2015092903/.

Syvertsen, Trine. *Digital Detox: The Politics of Disconnecting*. Bingley: Emerald Group Publishing, 2020.

Syvertsen, Trine, and Gunn Enli. 'Digital Detox: Media Resistance and the Promise of Authenticity'. *Convergence* 26, nos. 5–6 (December 2020): 1269–1283. https://doi.org/10.1177/1354856519847325.

Tanner, Grafton. *Babbling Corpse: Vaporwave and the Commodification of Ghosts*. Winchester: Zero Books, 2016.

Tatar, Jeremy. 'Injury, Affirmation, and the Disability Masquerade in Ye's "Through the Wire"'. *Music Theory Online* 29, no. 2 (June 2023). https://www.mtosmt.org/issues/mto.23.29.2/mto.23.29.2.tatar.php.

Tate, Greg. *Everything But the Burden: What White People Are Taking from Black Culture*. New York: Broadway Books, 2003.

The AMP Channel. 'Code-Fi / Lofi Beats to Code/Relax To'. YouTube video, 24 April 2020. https://www.youtube.com/watch?v=f02mOEt11OQ.

the bootleg boy. 'B A D F E E L I N G S'. YouTube video, 25 June 2017. https://www.youtube.com/watch?v=_z442kpDbUY.

The Cipher, the Circle & Its Wisdom: Toni Blackman at TEDxUMassAmherst. YouTube video, 14 May 2013. https://www.youtube.com/watch?v=WYdb5snA1Jc.

Thelwall, Mike. 'Can Museums Find Male or Female Audiences Online with YouTube?' *Aslib Journal of Information Management* 70, no. 5 (January 2018): 481–497. https://doi.org/10.1108/AJIM-06-2018-0146.

Thelwall, Mike. 'Gender Differences in Citation Impact for 27 Fields and Six English-Speaking Countries 1996–2014'. *Quantitative Science Studies* 1, no. 2 (June 2020): 599–617. https://doi.org/10.1162/qss_a_00038.

Thelwall, Mike, and Saheeda Thelwall. 'Covid-19 Tweeting in English: Gender Differences'. arXiv preprint, arXiv.2003.11090 (2020). https://doi.org/10.48550/arXiv.2003.11090.

References 217

@TheOkraProject. 'TheOkraProject'. Twitter feed, July 2023. https://twitter.com/TheOkra Project.

Thio, Vibert, and Douglas Eck. 'Lo-Fi Player'. *Magenta*, 1 September 2020. https://magenta.ten sorflow.org/lofi-player.

Thompson, Paul A. 'Migos: Culture'. *Pitchfork*, 31 January 2017. https://pitchfork.com/reviews/albums/22777-culture/.

Thorhauge, Anne Mette, and Rune K. L. Nielsen. 'Epic, Steam, and the Role of Skin-Betting in Game (Platform) Economies'. *Journal of Consumer Culture* 21, no. 1 (February 2021): 52–67. https://doi.org/10.1177/1469540521993929.

Threadcraft, Torry. 'Lo-Fi Hip Hop YouTube Channels Reporting Significant Boost During Quarantine'. *Okayplayer*, 27 April 2020. https://www.okayplayer.com/culture/lo-fi-hip-hop-quarantine.html.

Tiidenberg, Katrin. 'Research Ethics, Vulnerability, and Trust on the Internet'. In *Second International Handbook of Internet Research*, edited by Jeremy Hunsinger, Matthew M. Allen, and Lisbeth Klastrup, 569–583. Dordrecht: Springer Netherlands, 2020.

Tiidenberg, Katrin, Natalie Ann Hendry, and Crystal Abidin. *Tumblr*. Cambridge: Polity, 2021.

TMZ Staff. 'Tekashi 6ix9ine Claims He's Flashing Fake Cash in Videos, Still Owes Robbery Victims'. *TMZ*, 18 April 2022. https://www.tmz.com/2022/04/18/tekashi-6ix9ine-money-owe-lawsuit-rap/.

Trainer, Adam. 'From Hypnagogia to Distroid: Postironic Musical Renderings of Personal Memory'. In *The Oxford Handbook of Music and Virtuality*, edited by Sheila Whiteley and Shara Rambarran, 419–427. Oxford: Oxford University Press, 2016.

Travis, Raphael. *The Healing Power of Hip Hop*. Santa Barbara, CA: Praeger, 2016.

Travis Scott and Fortnite Present: Astronomical (Full Event Video). YouTube video, 26 April 2020. https://www.youtube.com/watch?v=wYeFAlVC8qU.

Tucker, Beth. ' "That's Problematic": Tracing the Birth of Call-Out Culture'. *Critical Reflections: A Student Journal on Contemporary Sociological Issues*, no. 2018 (April 2018): 1–5.

Tyler, The Creator TV/Radio Room Interview | 2020 GRAMMYs. YouTube video, 27 January 2020. https://www.youtube.com/watch?v=j5a42MwoYsw.

Ugwu, Reggie. 'On "The Blog Era," Resurrecting Rap Media History'. *New York Times*, 18 May 2023. https://www.nytimes.com/2023/05/18/arts/blog-era-podcast-drake.html.

United States Securities and Exchange Commission. 'Form S-1 Registration Statement Under The Securities Act of 1933: Roblox Corporation'. SEC Filing, November 2020. https://www.sec.gov/Archives/edgar/data/1315098/000119312520298230/d87104ds1.htm.

Valdovinos Kaye, D. Bondy, Aleesha Rodriguez, Katrin Langton, and Patrik Wikstrom. 'You Made This? I Made This: Practices of Authorship and (Mis)Attribution on TikTok'. *International Journal of Communication* 15 (2021): 3195–3215.

Varis, Piia, and Jan Blommaert. 'Conviviality and Collectives on Social Media: Virality, Memes, and New Social Structures'. *Multilingual Margins: A Journal of Multilingualism from the Periphery* 2, no. 1 (2015): 31–31. https://doi.org/10.14426/mm.v2i1.50.

Vásquez, Camilla, and Erhan Aslan. '"Cats Be Outside, How about Meow": Multimodal Humor and Creativity in an Internet Meme'. *Journal of Pragmatics* 171 (January 2021): 101–117. https://doi.org/10.1016/j.pragma.2020.10.006.

Vaught, Seneca, and Regina N. Bradley. 'Of the Wings of Traplanta: (Re)Historicizing W.E.B. Du Bois' Atlanta in the Hip Hop South'. *Phylon (1960-)* 54, no. 2 (2017): 11–27.

Vernallis, Carol. *The Media Swirl: Politics, Audiovisuality, and Aesthetics*. Durham, NC: Duke University Press, 2023.

Vernallis, Carol. *Unruly Media: Youtube, Music Video, and the New Digital Cinema*. New York: Oxford University Press, 2013.

218   References

Vito, Christopher. 'Shop Talk: The Influence of Hip Hop on Filipino-American Barbers in San Diego'. *Global Hip Hop Studies* 1, no. 1 (June 2020): 13–23. https://doi.org/10.1386/ghhs_00002_1.

Vivendi. *Financial Report and Unaudited Condensed Financial Statements for the Half Year Ended June 30, 2016*. Vivendi, 2016. https://www.vivendi.com/wp-content/uploads/2016/08/20160825_VIV_PDF_Vivendi_Financial_Report_H1_2016.pdf.

W3Techs. 'Usage Statistics of Content Languages for Websites'. *Web Technology Surveys*, 26 June 2023. https://w3techs.com/technologies/overview/content_language.

Waddingham, Anne, ed. *New Hart's Rules: The Oxford Style Guide*. 2nd ed. Oxford: Oxford University Press, 2014.

Waldron, Janice L. 'Online Music Communities and Social Media'. In *The Oxford Handbook of Community Music*, edited by Brydie-Leigh Bartleet and Lee Higgins, 109–130. Oxford: Oxford University Press, 2018.

Walter, Maggie, Tahu Kukutai, Stephanie Russo Carroll, and Desi Rodriguez-Lonebear, eds. *Indigenous Data Sovereignty and Policy*. Abingdon: Taylor & Francis, 2021.

Warner, Michael. *Publics and Counterpublics*. New York: Zone Books, 2005.

Warner Music Group. *Warner Music Group Corp. Reports Results for Fiscal Second Quarter Ended March 31, 2015*. Warner Music Group, 2015. https://www.wmg.com/news/warner-music-group-corp-reports-results-fiscal-second-quarter-ended-march-31-2015-20696.

Watkins, Lee. 'Keeping It Real: amaXhosa Iimbongi Making Mimesis Do Its Thing in the Hip-Hop and Rap Music of the Eastern Cape'. *African Music: Journal of the International Library of African Music* 8, no. 4 (2010): 24–47.

Watkins, S. Craig. *Hip Hop Matters: Politics, Pop Culture, and the Struggle for the Soul of a Movement*. Boston, MA: Beacon Press, 2005.

Watkins, S. Craig. *Representing: Hip-Hop Culture and the Production of Black Cinema*. Chicago and London: The University of Chicago Press, 1998.

Watson, Allan, Joseph B. Watson, and Lou Tompkins. 'Does Social Media Pay for Music Artists? Quantitative Evidence on the Co-Evolution of Social Media, Streaming and Live Music'. *Journal of Cultural Economy* 16, no. 1 (January 2023): 32–46. https://doi.org/10.1080/17530350.2022.2087720.

Waugh, Michael. '"Every Time I Dress Myself, It Go Motherfuckin' Viral": Post-Verbal Flows and Memetic Hype in Young Thug's Mumble Rap'. *Popular Music* 39, no. 2 (May 2020): 208–232. https://doi.org/10.1017/S026114302000015X.

Weatherby, Taylor. 'Ariana Grande & Her Girlfriends Get Their Bling On In Sassy "7 Rings" Video: Watch'. *Billboard* (blog), 18 January 2019. https://www.billboard.com/music/pop/ariana-grande-7-rings-video-8494008/.

Weheliye, Alexander G. *Phonographies: Grooves in Sonic Afro-Modernity*. Durham, NC: Duke University Press, 2005.

Weingarten, Christopher R. 'Review: Migos Up Their Game, Take Thrilling Victory Lap on "Culture"'. *Rolling Stone* (blog), 26 January 2017. https://www.rollingstone.com/music/music-album-reviews/review-migos-up-their-game-take-thrilling-victory-lap-on-culture-126305/.

Weinstein, Deena. 'Playing with Gender in the Key of Metal'. In *Heavy Metal, Gender and Sexuality: Interdisciplinary Approaches*, edited by Florian Heesch and Niall Scott, 11–25. London and New York: Routledge, 2016.

Wellman, Mariah L. 'Black Squares for Black Lives? Performative Allyship as Credibility Maintenance for Social Media Influencers on Instagram'. *Social Media + Society* 8, no. 1 (January 2022). https://doi.org/10.1177/20563051221080473.

Wheatley, Dawn, and Eirik Vatnoey. '"It's Twitter, a Bear Pit, Not a Debating Society": A Qualitative Analysis of Contrasting Attitudes towards Social Media Blocklists'. *New Media & Society* 22, no. 1 (January 2020): 5–25. https://doi.org/10.1177/1461444819858278.

References 219

Whelan, Andrew. ' "Do You Have a Moment to Talk About Vaporwave?" Technology, Memory, and Critique in the Writing on an Online Music Scene'. In *Popular Music, Technology, and the Changing Media Ecosystem*, edited by Tamas Tofalvy and Emília Barna, 185–200. Cham: Springer, 2020.

White, E. J. *A Unified Theory of Cats on the Internet*. Stanford, CA: Stanford Briefs, 2020.

White, Miles. *From Jim Crow to Jay-Z: Race, Rap, and the Performance of Masculinity*. Urbana: University of Illinois Press, 2011.

Whittaker, James, and Ashley Morgan. ' "They Never Felt These Fabrics Before": How SoundCloud Rappers Became the Dandies of Hip Hop through Hybrid Dress'. In 'Black Masculinities: Dress, Fashion and Style as Gendered Racialized Experiences'. Special issue, *Critical Studies in Men's Fashion* 9 (April 2022): 99–118. https://doi.org/10.1386/csmf_00053_1.

Wiggins, Bradley E. *The Discursive Power of Memes in Digital Culture: Ideology, Semiotics, and Intertextuality*. New York: Routledge, 2019.

Wilke, Claus. *Fundamentals of Data Visualization: A Primer on Making Informative and Compelling Figures*. Sebastopol, CA: O'Reilly, 2019.

Wilkinson, Mark D., Michel Dumontier, IJsbrand Jan Aalbersberg, Gabrielle Appleton, Myles Axton, Arie Baak, Niklas Blomberg, et al. 'The FAIR Guiding Principles for Scientific Data Management and Stewardship'. *Scientific Data* 3, no. 1 (March 2016). https://doi.org/10.1038/sdata.2016.18.

Williams, Apryl, and Vanessa Gonlin. 'I Got All My Sisters with Me (on Black Twitter): Second Screening of How to Get Away with Murder as a Discourse on Black Womanhood'. *Information, Communication & Society* 20, no. 7 (July 2017): 984–1004. https://doi.org/10.1080/1369118X.2017.1303077.

Williams, Jenessa. 'Music Fandom in the Age of #MeToo: Morality Crowdsourcing, Racialised Cancellation and Complicated Listening Habits in Online Hip-Hop and Indie-Alternative Communities'. PhD diss., University of Leeds, 2023.

Williams, Justin A. *Brithop: The Politics of UK Rap in the New Century*. Oxford: Oxford University Press, 2021.

Williams, Justin A. 'Introduction: The Interdisciplinary World of Hip-Hop Studies'. In *The Cambridge Companion to Hip-Hop*, edited by Justin A. Williams, 1–10. Cambridge: Cambridge University Press, 2015.

Williams, Justin A. *Rhymin' and Stealin': Musical Borrowing in Hip-Hop*. Ann Arbor: University of Michigan Press, 2013.

Williams, Quentin. *Remix Multilingualism: Hip Hop, Ethnography and Performing Marginalized Voice*. London and New York: Bloomsbury, 2017.

Winfrey, Amy, dir. *BoJack Horseman*. Season 6, episode 11, 'Sunk Cost and All That'. Netflix, 2020. https://www.netflix.com/watch/81026969.

Winkie, Luke. 'How "Lofi Hip Hop Radio to Relax/Study to" Became a YouTube Phenomenon'. *VICE*, 13 July 2018. https://www.vice.com/en/article/594b3z/how-lofi-hip-hop-radio-to-relaxstudy-to-became-a-youtube-phenomenon.

Winston, Emma, and Laurence Saywood. 'Beats to Relax/Study To: Contradiction and Paradox in Lofi Hip Hop'. *IASPM Journal* 9, no. 2 (December 2019): 40–54.

Witt, Stephen. 'Tekashi 69: The Rise and Fall of a Hip-Hop Supervillain'. *Rolling Stone* (blog), 16 January 2019. https://www.rollingstone.com/music/music-features/tekashi-69-rise-and-fall-feature-777971/.

Woodson, Kamilah Marie. *Colorism: Investigating a Global Phenomenon*. Santa Barbara, CA: Fielding University Press, 2020.

Wu, Jingsi Christina. 'Can China Have Its Hip Hop?: Negotiating the Boundaries between Mainstream and Underground Youth Cultural Spaces on the Internet Talent Show Rap of China'. In *China's Youth Cultures and Collective Spaces: Creativity, Sociality, Identity*

220 References

and Resistance, edited by Vanessa Frangville and Gwennaël Gaffric, 55–71. London and New York: Routledge, 2019.

Wu, Michael. 'What Are Lofi Hip Hop Streams, and Why Are They So Popular?' *Study Breaks*, 2 December 2018. https://studybreaks.com/culture/music/lofi-hip-hop-streams-popular/.

Wu, Tim. *The Attention Merchants: The Epic Scramble to Get Inside Our Heads*. New York: Knopf, 2016.

Yallop, Olivia. *Break the Internet: In Pursuit of Influence*. Melbourne and London: Scribe, 2021.

Younger, Briana. 'Black Musicians on Being Boxed in by R&B and Rap Expectations: "We Fit in So Many Things"'. *Pitchfork*, 28 September 2017. https://pitchfork.com/thepitch/black-musicians-on-being-boxed-in-by-randb-and-rap-expectations-we-fit-in-so-many-things/.

Zeng, Jing, and Crystal Abidin. '"#OkBoomer, Time to Meet the Zoomers": Studying the Memefication of Intergenerational Politics on TikTok'. *Information, Communication & Society* 24, no. 16 (December 2021): 2459–2481. https://doi.org/10.1080/13691 18X.2021.1961007.

Zuboff, Shoshana. *The Age of Surveillance Capitalism: The Fight for a Human Future at the New Frontier of Power*. London: Profile, 2019.

Index

For the benefit of digital users, indexed terms that span two pages (e.g., 52–53) may, on occasion, appear on only one of those pages.

Tables and figures are indicated by an italic *t* and *f* following the page number.

6ix9ine, 55n.22, 66–67, 72–75

African American Vernacular English, 146–47, 149–50, 151–52, 168, 184–85
Amazon, 27–28, 178, 186n.19
Ariana Grande, 16, 131, 138–54
attention economy, 15, 35, 46–48, 70–72, 76

Beastie Boys, 22–23, 152
beatmaking, 13, 31–32
Beyoncé 111n.17, 133n.16
Billie Eilish, 154, 162–63
Blackfishing, 131, 138–45
blogs, 10–11, 25–26, 90–91, 138–40
the bootleg boy, 79–80, 95–96, 96*f*

callout/cancel culture, 16, 112–13, 143–45
Campbell, Cindy, 20, 109
Cardi B, 16, 39–40, 58, 111–12, 116–17, 126
Childish Gambino, 58–59
Chillhop Music, 79–81, 91, 103
Chinese media economy, 3–4, 27–28, 47
City Girls, 111–12, 125–26
clout, 14, 51, 71, 74–76. *See also* virality
commercialism, 19, 21–22, 64–65, 104–6, 127, 149, 177–79
COVID-19 pandemic, 13, 81–82, 87, 88–91, 92–94, 101, 161, 163–64
cultural appropriation, 16, 131, 132–55, 181, 182, 184–85
data ethics, 6–8, 89n.37, 108–9, 117
democratization of cultural production, 10, 11–12

Discord, 13, 68, 97–98, 178–79
DJ Kool Herc, 20, 21n.20
Doja Cat, 58, 111–12, 118, 125–26

Drake, 1, 28n.56, 39–40, 46, 57, 168–69, 185

Ed Sheeran, 28n.56, 154
Eminem, 74n.90, 132, 152, 154n.102, 155, 170–71
Epic Games, 158, 165–66, 169–71, 177–78

Facebook, 3–4, 33–34, 71
fans, 2–3, 8, 45, 68n.65, 95, 126–27, 138, 141–42
Flo Milli, 59–60, 111–12
Fortnite, 16–17, 156–57, 158, 164–71, 177, 178, 179–80
forums, 24, 25–26, 125, 186–87

generative artificial intelligence, 17, 184–86
Genius, 24, 52–53
genre, 18–19, 28–29, 44, 76–77, 82–85, 97, 133–38, 165–66. *See also* music style
geography, 4–5, 22, 23–24, 64–65, 181, 186
    as authenticity discourse in hip hop, 2–3, 55–56, 60–61, 74–75
globalization, 4–5, 24–25, 46, 135, 181
GloRilla, 59–60, 111–12
Golden age hip hop, 18, 69–70
Grammy Awards, 63n.48, 80*f*, 145, 181, 185

hip hop feminism, 16, 57–58, 109–13, 114–15, 116–17, 121–22, 125–29

Instagram, 3–4, 40–41, 55–56, 58–59, 71, 186
internet culture, 12, 38, 47–48, 51, 76–77, 100–1, 112, 178–79

J. Cole, 55, 64
Juice Wrld, 68, 76, 154n.102

222 Index

Justin Bieber, 36–37, 154, 165–66

Kanye West, 33–34, 39–40, 58–59, 62–63, 72–73, 185
Kendrick Lamar, 55–56, 64, 185

Lil B, 50–51, 57
Lil Durk, 39–40, 54
Lil Nas X, 46, 76–77, 133, 171–73, 177, 179–80
Lil Uzi Vert, 62–63, 69, 181
Lil Wayne, 23–24n.33, 66–67, 157
Lil Xan, 62, 76n.95
Lil Yachty, 61–62, 76n.95
Little Simz, 64, 111–12
liveness, 13, 16–17, 102, 103, 158, 159–64, 169–71, 172–73, 174–75, 178–80
Lizzo, 111–12, 162–63
LL Cool J, 61–62, 181, 186–87
locality. *See* geography
Lofi Girl, 78–81, 83, 100–1, 103–4
lyrics, 23, 24, 52–70, 73–74, 125–26, 146–48, 149, 162, 167–69, 184–85

masculinity, 23, 67, 109, 113–14, 122, 123–25
Megan Thee Stallion, 16, 46, 58, 111–12, 116–17, 126
memes, 14, 38–41, 50–51, 72, 83, 99–101, 132–33, 139–40
Microsoft, 173–74, 177–78, 186n.19, 186n.21
Migos, 44–45, 69
Minecraft, 16–17, 156–57, 164, 173–76, 178–79
misogynoir, 16, 108–10, 112–16, 119–21, 122, 123–28
mixtapes, 26, 31, 42
Mojang, 173–74, 177–78
Mozdeh, 87, 117
Mumble rap, 50–51, 69, 70
music streaming, 10–11, 27–30, 41–47, 71–72, 76, 134, 135–37
music style, 21, 50–51, 64, 68–70, 82, 84–86, 134–35, 145–46, 154

networked society, 3–4, 11–12, 14
new amateur, 71–72, 185
Nicki Minaj, 111–12, 121, 127, 142
Noname, 60, 112n.18

Open Pit, 173–80

peer-to-peer file-sharing, 13–14, 26–27, 31–33
Pioneer DJ, 175–76, 177–78

platformization of culture, 15, 41–48
platforms
  centralizing processes, 10–12, 70–71, 73, 137, 180
  feudalism, 11–12, 35
  games as a service, 164–65, 172 (*see also* video games)
  ideals, 11–12
  personalization, 12, 14, 78–79, 164
  social media metrics, 54, 58–59, 74–75
  See also music streaming
Playboi Carti, 61n.38, 66, 69
playlists, 19, 41–42, 43, 44–45, 70–71, 79–80, 103–4, 156–57
positionality, 8, 108–9
Post Malone, 28n.56, 59, 154n.102
Princess Nokia, 55, 111–12, 147
produser, 71–72, 103–4, 185

radio, 19, 21, 24–25, 47, 79–80, 102, 156–57
Rapsody, 58–59, 64
Red Bull, 175–76, 177–78
Reddit, 3–4, 33–34, 97–98, 131, 139–40, 141–42, 155
Rico Nasty, 112n.18, 173
Robinson, Sylvia, 21, 109
Roblox, 16–17, 156, 171–73, 177–78, 179
Run-DMC, 18, 22–23

sampling, 13–14, 21, 30–32, 33–34, 84–86, 101n.79, 185
signifyin(g), 14, 142
SoundCloud, 10, 15, 27–28, 49–52, 54, 71–72, 76, 91, 174
Spotify, 27–29, 43–44, 47, 71–72, 137, 154, 170, 183–84

Taylor Swift, 39–40, 121, 154
TikTok, 10, 40–41, 46–47, 76, 93–94, 136–37, 157, 183–84, 186–87
trap music, 29–30, 49–51, 65–66, 67–69, 145–49, 153, 185
Travis Scott, 158, 165–71, 174–75, 177
Tumblr, 3–4, 101, 131, 139–40, 142–45, 155
Twitch, 10, 13, 163–64, 163*t*, 174, 178–79
Twitter (X), 4n.15, 11–12, 60, 112–13, 117n.47, 142, 143–44, 183–84
Tyler, the Creator, 133, 157

Usenet, 24, 25

vaporwave, 82–83, 92–93, 94–95, 97, 106

video games, 16–17, 83, 156–58, 163–80
virality, 12–13, 49, 71, 73–74, 75, 76–77, 125–26. *See also* clout
virtuality, 11–12, 73, 97–98, 158, 159–62, 163–65, 170, 173–76, 178–80, 184–85

The Weeknd, 133n.16, 170–71, 185
white supremacy, 7n.32, 8–9, 108–9, 116, 122, 126, 150
word frequency analysis, 6, 81–82, 87–88, 116–17

Wu-Tang Clan, 24, 36–37

XXXTentacion, 28n.56, 61n.38, 68, 72–73, 76, 154n.102

Young M. A, 56–57, 111–12
Young Thug, 39–40, 69
YouTube, 25–26, 33, 45, 70, 78–81, 82–83, 99n.71, 102, 103–4, 116, 170–71, 173
comments, 15–16, 87, 88–101, 108, 116–17

The manufacturer's authorised representative in the EU for product safety is Oxford
University Press España S.A. of El Parque Empresarial San Fernando de Henares,
Avenida de Castilla, 2 – 28830 Madrid (www.oup.es/en or product.safety@oup.com).
OUP España S.A. also acts as importer into Spain of products made by the manufacturer.

Printed in the USA/Agawam, MA
August 1, 2025

891350.008